REA's READING COMPREHENSION BUILDER

for Admission & Standardized Tests

by the staff of
Research & Education Association

 **Research & Education Association**
61 Ethel Road West • Piscataway, New Jersey 08854

REA's READING COMPREHENSION BUILDER
for Admission & Standardized Tests

1998 PRINTING

Printed in the United States of America

Library of Congress Catalog Card Number 96-67458

International Standard Book Number 0-87891-793-4

Research & Education Association
61 Ethel Road West
Piscataway, New Jersey 08854

ACKNOWLEDGMENTS

*We would like to thank the following people for their contributions
to the Reading Comprehension Builder*

Sandra Morona, M.Ed., for compiling and technically editing the manuscript

Michele DiBenedetto for her editorial contributions to the manuscript

In addition, special recognition is extended to the following persons

Dr. Max Fogiel, President, for his overall guidance which has brought this
publication to completion

Gary J. Albert, Project Editor, for his efforts in bringing this project to
completion

Larry B. Kling, Revisions Editor, for his editorial contributions

Marty Perzan, for typesetting the book

CONTENTS

CHAPTER 1

About the Reading Comprehension Builder

ABOUT RESEARCH AND EDUCATION ASSOCIATION

Research and Education Association (REA) is an organization of educators, scientists, and engineers specializing in various academic fields. Founded in 1959 with the purpose of disseminating the most recently developed scientific information to groups in industry, government, high schools, and universities, REA has since become a successful and highly respected publisher of study aids, test preps, handbooks, and reference works.

REA's Test Preparation series includes study guides for all academic levels in almost all disciplines. Research and Education Association publishes test preps for students who have not yet completed high school, as well as high school students preparing to enter college. Students from countries around the world seeking to attend college in the United States will find the assistance they need in REA's publications. For college students seeking advanced degrees, REA publishes test preps for many major graduate school admission examinations in a wide variety of disciplines, including engineering, law, and medicine. Students at every level, in every field, with every ambition can find what they are looking for among REA's publications.

Unlike most Test Preparation books that present only a few practice tests which bear little resemblance to the actual exams, REA's series presents tests which accurately depict the official exams in both degree of difficulty and types of questions. REA's practice tests are always based upon the most recently administered exams, and include every type of question that can be expected on the actual exams.

REA's publications and educational materials are highly regarded and continually receive an unprecedented amount of praise from professionals, instructors, librarians, parents, and students. Our authors are as diverse as the subjects and fields represented in the books we publish. They are well-known in their respective fields and serve on the faculties of prestigious universities throughout the United States.

ABOUT THIS BOOK

REA's staff of authors and educators has prepared material, exercises, and tests based on each of the major standardized exams, including the Advanced Placement (AP), College-Level Examination Program (CLEP), General Education Development (GED), Graduate Record Examination (GRE), Scholastic Assessment Test (SAT), Professional Assessments for Core Battery Beginning Teachers (PRAXIS) Core Battery, Graduate Management Admission Test (GMAT), Law School Admission Test (LSAT),and the ACT Assessment Test. The types of questions represented on these exams have been analyzed in order to produce the most comprehensive preparatory material possible. You will find review material, helpful strategies, and exercises geared to your level of studying. This book will teach as well as review and refresh your skills of reading comprehension needed to score high on standardized tests.

HOW TO USE THIS BOOK

If you are preparing to take the AP English Literature exam, AP English Composition exam, CLEP, GRE, GED, SAT, Preliminary Scholastic Assessment Test (PSAT), PRAXIS Core Battery, Texas Academic Skills Program (TASP) exam, California Basic Educational Skills Test (CBEST), LSAT, GMAT, ACT, Armed Services Vocational Aptitude Battery Test (ASVAB), or the Pre-Professional Skills Test (PPST), you will be taking a test that requires excellent reading comprehension skills. This book contains comprehensive reading comprehension reviews and drills that can be tailored to your specific test preparation needs.

Locate your test on the chart shown on pages 6 and 7, and then find the corresponding sections recommended for study. REA suggests that you study the indicated material thoroughly as a review for your exam.

This book will help you prepare for your exam because it includes different types of questions and drills that are representative of what might appear on each exam. The book also includes diagnostic tests so that you can determine your strengths and weaknesses within a specific subject. The explanations are clear and comprehensive, explaining why the answer is correct. The Reading Comprehension Builder gives you practice within a wide range of categories and question types, as well as giving you vocabulary lists at the end of every chapter.

Vocabulary Enhancer prepares students for reading comprehension questions on any standardized examination with questions on reading passages. Lists of commonly confused words, words with similar sounds, explanations of connotation and denotation, roots, prefixes, and suffixes are presented.

Basic Reading Comprehension prepares students for reading questions on the CLEP, GMAT, GED, TASP, SAT, PSAT, PRAXIS Core Battery, ACT, PPST, ASVAB, LSAT, AP English Literature and Composition, AP English Language and Composition, GRE, and CBEST exams. The fundamentals of reading the passages and the questions, answering questions, the different types of reading comprehension questions, and the four-step approach to tackling reading comprehension questions are fully covered.

Reading for Content helps students prepare for questions on the SAT, CLEP, GRE, GMAT, PSAT, GED, TASP, ASVAB, ACT, LSAT, CBEST, PPST, and PRAXIS exams. It reviews the skills specific to reading a passage and answering questions based on the content of that passage. Tips for increasing your reading efficiency, deciphering the purpose and content of the passage, and help for slow readers are presented.

Reading for Style prepares students taking the AP English Literature and Composition, AP English Language and Composition, GRE, CLEP, ACT, LSAT, and GED exams. This chapter teaches the techniques needed to answer questions based on writing style and form found within reading passages. Introductions to reading fiction, poetry, drama, and essays are presented as well as definitions of key literary terms.

Reading Short Passages will prepare students for questions on the CBEST, NTE, and ASVAB exams. Short reading passages (less than 200 words) usually represent three types of comprehension: literal, inferential, and critical. This chapter explains each type of passage and presents strategies for answering short reading passages.

Reading Medium Passages reviews the skills needed to score high on the LSAT,

GMAT, SAT, PSAT, ACT, GRE, TASP, GED, and PPST exams. Specific techniques are given for reading passages that are 200 to 700 words in length. Special sections on reading directions, reading speed, and the types of questions found with medium reading passages are presented.

Reading Long Passages will prepare students to answer questions on the ACT, LSAT, and SAT exams. The chapter reviews the techniques for reading passages longer than 700 words. Included are the specific skills needed to read longer passages and answering the related questions.

Critical Reading reviews the unique style and format of the critical reading questions found on the SAT and PSAT. This chapter defines, and provides methods for answering critical reading questions, including an easy, four-step strategy.

Finally, before getting started, here are a few guidelines:

➤ Study full chapters. If you think after a few minutes that the chapter appears easy, continue studying. Many chapters (like the tests themselves) become more difficult as they continue

➤ Use this guide as a supplement to the review materials provided by the test administrators.

➤ Take the diagnostic test before each review chapter, even if you feel confident that you already know the material well enough to skip a particular chapter. Taking the diagnostic test will put your mind at ease: you will discover either that you absolutely know the material or that you need to review. This will eliminate the panic you might otherwise experience during the test upon discovering that you have forgotten how to approach a certain type of question.

As you prepare for a standardized test with reading comprehension questions, you will want to review the various techniques and steps for answering the specific type of reading passages that will appear on the test. The more familiar you are with these techniques, the better you will do on the test. Our reading comprehension reviews represent the numerous types of reading passages and questions that appear on many standardized tests.

Along with the skill to answer the different types of reading comprehension questions, knowing how to answer such questions quickly and accurately will have an effect on your success. All tests have time limits, so the more questions you can answer correctly in the given period of time, the better off you will be. Our suggestion is to practice taking tests under test-like conditions. First, you should take each diagnostic test. Next, you should complete the drills as you review for extra practice. Finally, take the Mini Tests when you feel confident with the material. Pay special attention to both the time it takes you to complete the diagnostic tests and the Mini Tests, and the number of questions you answer correctly.

The vocabulary lists at the end of each chapter will refresh your memory about definitions of rarely-used words and teach you words you have not used before. The spelling of the word, what part of speech it is, and its definition are all clearly presented to aid you in studying vocabulary.

CROSS-REFERENCING CHART

	Vocabulary Enhancer Chapter 2	Basic Reading Comprehension Chapter 3	Reading for Content Chapter 4	Reading for Style Chapter 5	Reading Short Passages Chapter 6	Reading Medium Passages Chapter 7	Reading Long Passages Chapter 8	Critical Reading Passages Chapter 9
AP English Literature and Composition	X	X		X				
AP English Language and Composition	X	X		X				
GRE	X	X	X	X				
GED	X	X	X	X		X		
SAT	X	X	X			X	X	X
PSAT	X	X	X			X		X
PRAXIS Core Battery	X	X	X		X			

	Vocabulary Enhancer Chapter 2	Basic Reading Comprehension Chapter 3	Reading for Content Chapter 4	Reading for Style Chapter 5	Reading Short Passages Chapter 6	Reading Medium Passages Chapter 7	Reading Long Passages Chapter 8	Critical Reading Passages Chapter 9
TASP	X	X	X			X		
CBEST	X	X	X		X			
LSAT	X	X	X	X		X	X	
GMAT	X	X	X			X		
ACT	X	X	X	X		X	X	
ASVAB	X	X	X		X			
PPST	X	X	X			X		
CLEP	X	X	X	X	X			

CHAPTER 2

Vocabulary Enhancer

➤ Diagnostic Test
➤ Vocabulary Enhancer
Review & Drills

VOCABULARY DIAGNOSTIC TEST

1. Ⓐ Ⓑ Ⓒ Ⓓ Ⓔ
2. Ⓐ Ⓑ Ⓒ Ⓓ Ⓔ
3. Ⓐ Ⓑ Ⓒ Ⓓ Ⓔ
4. Ⓐ Ⓑ Ⓒ Ⓓ Ⓔ
5. Ⓐ Ⓑ Ⓒ Ⓓ Ⓔ
6. Ⓐ Ⓑ Ⓒ Ⓓ Ⓔ
7. Ⓐ Ⓑ Ⓒ Ⓓ Ⓔ
8. Ⓐ Ⓑ Ⓒ Ⓓ Ⓔ
9. Ⓐ Ⓑ Ⓒ Ⓓ Ⓔ
10. Ⓐ Ⓑ Ⓒ Ⓓ Ⓔ
11. Ⓐ Ⓑ Ⓒ Ⓓ Ⓔ
12. Ⓐ Ⓑ Ⓒ Ⓓ Ⓔ
13. Ⓐ Ⓑ Ⓒ Ⓓ Ⓔ
14. Ⓐ Ⓑ Ⓒ Ⓓ Ⓔ
15. Ⓐ Ⓑ Ⓒ Ⓓ Ⓔ
16. Ⓐ Ⓑ Ⓒ Ⓓ Ⓔ
17. Ⓐ Ⓑ Ⓒ Ⓓ Ⓔ
18. Ⓐ Ⓑ Ⓒ Ⓓ Ⓔ
19. Ⓐ Ⓑ Ⓒ Ⓓ Ⓔ
20. Ⓐ Ⓑ Ⓒ Ⓓ Ⓔ
21. Ⓐ Ⓑ Ⓒ Ⓓ Ⓔ
22. Ⓐ Ⓑ Ⓒ Ⓓ Ⓔ
23. Ⓐ Ⓑ Ⓒ Ⓓ Ⓔ
24. Ⓐ Ⓑ Ⓒ Ⓓ Ⓔ
25. Ⓐ Ⓑ Ⓒ Ⓓ Ⓔ

26. Ⓐ Ⓑ Ⓒ Ⓓ Ⓔ
27. Ⓐ Ⓑ Ⓒ Ⓓ Ⓔ
28. Ⓐ Ⓑ Ⓒ Ⓓ Ⓔ
29. Ⓐ Ⓑ Ⓒ Ⓓ Ⓔ
30. Ⓐ Ⓑ Ⓒ Ⓓ Ⓔ
31. Ⓐ Ⓑ Ⓒ Ⓓ Ⓔ
32. Ⓐ Ⓑ Ⓒ Ⓓ Ⓔ
33. Ⓐ Ⓑ Ⓒ Ⓓ Ⓔ
34. Ⓐ Ⓑ Ⓒ Ⓓ Ⓔ
35. Ⓐ Ⓑ Ⓒ Ⓓ Ⓔ
36. Ⓐ Ⓑ Ⓒ Ⓓ Ⓔ
37. Ⓐ Ⓑ Ⓒ Ⓓ Ⓔ
38. Ⓐ Ⓑ Ⓒ Ⓓ Ⓔ
39. Ⓐ Ⓑ Ⓒ Ⓓ Ⓔ
40. Ⓐ Ⓑ Ⓒ Ⓓ Ⓔ
41. Ⓐ Ⓑ Ⓒ Ⓓ Ⓔ
42. Ⓐ Ⓑ Ⓒ Ⓓ Ⓔ
43. Ⓐ Ⓑ Ⓒ Ⓓ Ⓔ
44. Ⓐ Ⓑ Ⓒ Ⓓ Ⓔ
45. Ⓐ Ⓑ Ⓒ Ⓓ Ⓔ
46. Ⓐ Ⓑ Ⓒ Ⓓ Ⓔ
47. Ⓐ Ⓑ Ⓒ Ⓓ Ⓔ
48. Ⓐ Ⓑ Ⓒ Ⓓ Ⓔ
49. Ⓐ Ⓑ Ⓒ Ⓓ Ⓔ
50. Ⓐ Ⓑ Ⓒ Ⓓ Ⓔ

VOCABULARY DIAGNOSTIC TEST

This diagnostic test is designed to help you determine your strengths and your weaknesses in reading short passages. Follow the directions for each part and check your answers.

These types of questions are found in the following tests:
ALL TESTS

---

50 Questions

DIRECTIONS: An analogy is a relationship between two things which may be unlike in some respects, but are similar in at least one way. It is this similarity that is the key to the analogy. It is therefore important that you know the definitions of the words to be compared. Vocabulary is the root of all analogies.

In a verbal analogy, a colon separates two words that can be compared. We would read a verbal comparison as: Word A has a relationship to Word B — A : B. A double colon between two such comparisons means that the relationship Word A to Word B is the same as the relationship Word C to Word D — A : B :: C : D.

In this diagnostic test, one word in the analogy has been replaced with four choices. Only one choice accurately completes the relationship. For example:

CASSETTE : AUDITORY :: BOOK : (a. tactile, b. visual, c. olefactory, d. savory)

The answer that best expresses the relationship is (b) visual. A CASSETTE provides an AUDITORY experience, and a BOOK provides a VISUAL experience. Therefore, you should fill in the oval marked (b) on your answer sheet.

1. COW : HEIFER :: FOX : (a. vixen b. gander c. bitch d. ewe)

2. CALF : WHALE :: (a. foal b. fawn c. chick d. cygnet) : SWAN

3. LATITUDE : PARALLELS :: LONGITUDE : (a. line b. equator c. Degree d. meridian)

4. ORNITHOLOGY : BIRDS :: ICHTHYOLOGY : (a. cancer b. currency c. metals d. fish)

5. CHRONOMETER : TIME :: ANEMOMETER : (a. weight b. atmospheric pressure c. wind speed d. distance)

6. SWARM : BEES :: BUSINESS : (a. bears b. eagles c. ferrets d. elks)

7. BAROMETER : ATMOSPHERIC PRESSURE :: (a. anemometer b. bolometer c. galvanometer d. densitometer) : ELECTRICAL CURRENTS

8. SPHYGMOMANOMETER : (a. doctor b. engineer c. photographer d. astronomer) :: COMPASS : NAVIGATOR

9. ENDOCRINOLOGIST : (a. teeth b. eyes c. glands d. intestines) :: DERMATOLOGIST : SKIN

10. CORONATION : INAUGURATION :: (a. cardinal b. monarch c. bishop d. pope) : PRESIDENT

11. SAXOPHONE : (a. brass b. woodwind c. percussion d. horn) :: PIANO : PERCUSSION

12. DEMOCRACY : CITIZENRY :: THEOCRACY : (a. church b. state c. populace d. monarch)

13. CONSTANTINE : CHRISTIANITY :: ASOKA : (a. Taoism b. Jainism c. Hinduism d. Buddhism)

14. CALORIE : (a. pressure b. volume c. heat d. force) :: ACRE : AREA

15. PHILATELIST : STAMPS :: LEPIDOPTERIST : (a. books b. butterflies c. coins d. clocks)

16. RUPEE : INDIA :: LIRA : (a. Egypt b. Greece c. Italy d. Spain)

17. BIBLIOPHILE : (a. bibles b. religion c. books d. music) :: ANGLO-PHILE : ENGLAND

18. GYNOPHOBE : WOMAN :: ANDROPHOBE : (a. man b. homosexuals c. germs d. animals)

19. REFLECT : ABSORB :: CONVEX : (a. bend b. scatter c. converge d. concave)

20. MELODIOUS : CACOPHONOUS :: (a. dry b. petulant c. sweet d. succulent) : ARID

21. AVIARY : BIRDS :: FORMICARY : (a. fish b. reptiles c. insects d. ants)

22. PARTHENON : (a. Greece b. Athens c. Paris d. Dresden) :: SISTINE CHAPEL : ROME

23. AGGRAVATE : EXACERBATE :: MITIGATE : (a. legislate b. assuage c. abrachiate d. dissociate)

24. BARBARIC : (a. civilized b. savage c. content d. enraged) :: DIVINE : SACRED

25. MULTIPLICATION : DIVISION :: INTEGRATION : (a. substitution b. function c. equation d. derivation)

26. TEMPO : SPEED :: BEAT : (a. metronome b. rhythm c. percussion d. meter)

27. NIGHT : NOCTURNAL :: (a. evening b. morning c. day d. noon) : DIURNAL

28. (a. Tyche b. Thanatos c. Nyx d. Athena) : DEATH :: EROS : LOVE

29. (a. anti b. aero c. acro d. arch) : TOP :: ANDRO : MAN

30. ETHNO : RACE :: (a. cardio b. crypto c. chrono d. choreo) : DANCE

31. (a. pronoun b. preposition c. adjective d. article) : NOUN :: ADVERB : VERB

32. LIE : LAY :: LAY : (a. laid b. laying c. lying d. lain)

33. (a. yellow b. red c. green d. indigo) : ORANGE :: BLUE : VIOLET

34. ELECTRON : NEGATIVE :: NEUTRON : (a. positive b. variable c. proton d. none)

35. EAGLE : (a. feline b. equine c. bovine d. aquiline) :: DOG : CANINE

36. BECOME : (a. became b. becoming c. becomes d. become) :: SHRINK : SHRANK

37. AURAL : ORAL :: EAR : (a. eyes b. nose c. mouth d. hand)

38. ACROPHOBIA : (a. blood b. heights c. food d. death) :: HYDRO-PHOBIA : WATER

39. REGICIDE : (a. king b. president c. friend d. child) :: PATRICIDE : FATHER

40. (a. registration b. license c. patent d. statute) : INVENTION :: COPY-RIGHT : NOVEL

41. CHROMOSOME : (a. gene b. RNA c. DNA d. enzyme) :: CELL : NUCLEUS

42. BIO : LIFE :: HEMI : (a. half b. earth c. split d. world)

43. ESTROGEN : OVARIES :: GASTRIN : (a. stomach glands b. adrenal medulla c. thyroid d. pancreas)

44. ULNA : ARM :: (a. tarsals b. humerus c. mandible d. tibia) : LEG

45. ARABIC : ROMAN :: 600 : (a. MD b. CC c. DC d. MX)

46. MACRO : LARGE :: HOMO : (a. small b. same c. male d. similar)

47. CZAR : RUSSIA :: KHAN : (a. Mongolia b. Egypt c. Turkey d. China)

48. BALL : MUSKET :: (a. wire b. nut c. bolt d. wood) : CROSSBOW

49. SITAR : STRING :: DOUMBEK : (a. keys b. pedals c. stick d. skin)

50. FISSION : SPLITTING :: FUSION : (a. cooling b. heating c. combining d. melting)

VOCABULARY
DIAGNOSTIC TEST

ANSWER KEY

1.	(a)	14.	(c)	27.	(c)	40.	(c)
2.	(d)	15.	(b)	28.	(b)	41.	(a)
3.	(d)	16.	(c)	29.	(c)	42.	(a)
4.	(d)	17.	(c)	30.	(d)	43.	(a)
5.	(c)	18.	(a)	31.	(c)	44.	(d)
6.	(c)	19.	(d)	32.	(a)	45.	(c)
7.	(c)	20.	(d)	33.	(b)	46.	(b)
8.	(a)	21.	(d)	34.	(d)	47.	(a)
9.	(c)	22.	(b)	35.	(d)	48.	(c)
10.	(b)	23.	(b)	36.	(a)	49.	(d)
11.	(b)	24.	(b)	37.	(c)	50.	(c)
12.	(a)	25.	(d)	38.	(b)		
13.	(d)	26.	(b)	39.	(a)		

DETAILED EXPLANATIONS
OF ANSWERS

1. **(a)**   (a) is correct because a vixen is a female fox as a heifer is a female bovine. (b) is incorrect because a gander is a male goose. (c) is incorrect because a bitch is a female dog. (d) is incorrect because an ewe is a female sheep.

2. **(d)**   (d) is correct because a cygnet is a baby swan just as a calf is a baby whale. (a) is incorrect because a foal is a baby horse. (b) is incorrect because a fawn is a baby deer. (c) is incorrect because a chick is a baby chicken.

3. **(d)**   (d) is correct because parallels are another name for lines of latitude as meridians are another name for lines of longitude. (a) is incorrect because line is a general term and could apply to either longitude or latitude. (b) is incorrect because equator refers to a specific line of latitude. (c) is incorrect because degrees are a measurement of longitude and latitude.

4. **(d)**   (d) is correct because just as a bird expert is an ornithologist, a fish expert is an ichthyologist. (a) is incorrect because a cancer expert is called an oncologist. (b) is incorrect because a numismatist is a currency expert. (c) is incorrect because a metallurgist is an expert in metals.

5. **(c)**   (c) is correct because as a chronometer measures time, an anemometer measures wind speed. (a) is incorrect because a scale measures weight. (b) is incorrect because a barometer measures atmospheric pressure. (d) is incorrect because an odometer measures distance.

6. **(c)**   (c) is correct because business is a collective term for ferrets as swarm is a collective term for bees. (a) is incorrect because bears gather in sleuths. (b) is incorrect because a group of eagles is called a convocation. (d) is incorrect because a collective term for elks is gang.

7. **(c)**   (c) is the correct response because just as a barometer measures atmospheric pressure, a galvanometer measures electrical currents. (a) is incorrect because an anemometer measures wind speed. (b) is incorrect because a bolometer measures small amounts of radiant energy. (d) is

incorrect because a densitometer measures the thickness or darkness of film.

8. **(a)**   (a) is the correct response because a sphygmomanometer is an instrument used by a doctor (to measure blood pressure) just as a compass is an instrument used by a navigator. (b), (c), and (d) are incorrect because these occupations would have no use for this instrument.

9. **(c)**   (c) is correct because glands are the specialty of an endocrinologist as the skin is the area of specialization for the dermatologist. (a) is incorrect because a specialist dealing with teeth is an orthodontist. (b) is incorrect because a specialist dealing with eyes is an ophthalmologist. (d) is incorrect because a specialist dealing with intestines is a gastroenterologist.

10. **(b)**   (b) is correct because a coronation is the ceremony during which a monarch receives a crown just as an inauguration is the induction ceremony for a president. (a), (c), and (d) are incorrect because all of the induction ceremonies are religiously, not politically based.

11. **(b)**   (b) is correct because a saxophone belongs to the family of instruments known as woodwinds just as the piano belongs to the family of instruments known as percussion instruments. (a) is incorrect because brass instruments do not use a reed, as does the saxophone. (c) is incorrect because percussion instruments, such as drums, are struck to produce sounds. (d) is incorrect because horn is a general term, and not a specific sub-group of instruments.

12. **(a)**   (a) is correct because democracy refers to a political system governed through the citizenry. In a theocracy, the church is the government. (b) is incorrect because state rule is characteristic of a totalitarian government. (c) is incorrect because populace is analogous to citizenry. (d) is incorrect because a monarchy is ruled by a royal family.

13. **(d)**   (d) is the correct answer because Asoka converted to Buddhism allowing it to spread throughout India. (a) is incorrect because Taoism is a philosophy based on the teachings of Lao Tsu. (b) is incorrect because Jainism was founded by Vardhamana Maravira in 600 B.C.E. (c) is incorrect because Hinduism already existed in India at the time of Asoka's conversion.

14. **(c)**   (c) is correct because a calorie is a unit of heat as an acre is a unit of measurement for area. (a) is incorrect because pressure is measured in p.s.i. (pounds per square inch). (b) is incorrect because the volume of an object refers to its internal capacity. (d) is incorrect because force is measured in foot-pounds.

15. **(b)**   (b) is correct because a collector of butterflies is known as a lepidopterist, whereas a collector of stamps is known as a philatelist. (a) is incorrect because a bibliophile collects books (c) is incorrect because a numismatist collects coins and (d) is incorrect because a collector of clocks is called a chronometist.

16. **(c)**   (c) is correct because Italy's basic monetary unit is the lira, as the rupee is the basic monetary unit of India. (a) is incorrect because Egypt's monetary unit is based on the Egyptian pound. (b) is incorrect because the drachma is Greece's basic monetary unit. (d) is incorrect because Spain uses the peseta as its basic monetary unit.

17. **(c)**   (c) is correct because bibliophiles have an interest in books as Anglophiles have an interest in England. (a) is incorrect because a bible is a type of book a bibliophile may collect. (b) is incorrect because a theologian would study or have a love of religion. (d) is incorrect because audiophiles have an interest in music.

18. **(a)**   (a) is correct because men are feared by androphobes as women are feared by gynophobes. (b) is incorrect because homophobia is the fear of homosexuals. (c) is incorrect because spermaphobia is the fear of germs. (d) is incorrect because zoophobia is a fear of animals.

19. **(d)**   (d) is correct because concave and convex are opposite lens shapes, as they curve in and out, respectively. Reflect and absorb are opposite reactions of light on a surface. (a) is incorrect because light that is bent is said to be refracted. (b) is incorrect because scattered refers to a haphazard arrangement of light. (c) is incorrect because converge refers to light rays coming together.

20. **(d)**   (d) is correct because succulent, filled with water, is the opposite of arid, void of water. Melodious is full harmony, whereas cacophonous refers to discordant sound. (a) is incorrect because dry is a synonym for arid. (b) is incorrect because petulant refers to something or someone ill-tempered. (c) is incorrect because sweet refers to having a sugary taste.

21. **(d)**   (d) is the correct response because just as birds are kept in an aviary, another name for an ant farm is a formicary. (a) is incorrect because fish are kept in an aquarium. (b) and (c) are incorrect because insects and reptiles are kept in a terrarium.

22. **(b)**   (b) is correct because the Parthenon is in Athens as the Sistine Chapel is in Rome. All other choices are irrelevant.

23. **(b)**   (b) is the correct response because aggravate and exacerbate are synonyms meaning to worsen, just as assuage is a synonym for mitigate which means to lessen or make milder. (a) is incorrect because legislate means to create laws. An abrachiate (c) is an animal without gills, and dissociate (d) means to separate.

24. **(b)**   (b) is the correct response because barbaric is a synonym for savage just as divine is a synonym for sacred. (a) is not the correct choice because civilized means refined. (c) is incorrect because content means relaxed, and (d) is incorrect because enraged means angry.

25. **(d)**   (d) is the correct response because multiplication is the mathematical opposite of division just as integration is the mathematical opposite of derivation.

26. **(b)**   (b) is correct because tempo is a musical term referring to speed as beat is a musical term referring to rhythm. A metronome (a) is a machine used for keeping rhythm; percussion (c) refers generally to the percussion section of an orchestra; and meter (d) refers to rhythm as it relates to poetry.

27. **(c)**   (c) is the correct response because nocturnal refers to an animal active mainly at night as diurnal refers to an animal active mainly during the day.

28. **(b)**   (b) is the correct choice because Thanatos is the Greek god of death and Eros is the Greek god of love. Tyche (a) is the goddess of fortune, Nyx (c) is the goddess of night, and Athena (d) is the goddess of wisdom.

29. **(c)**   (c) is the correct answer because acro is a prefix meaning top just as andro is a prefix meaning man. Anti (a) is the prefix meaning against, aero (b) means air, and arch (d) means chief.

30. **(d)**   (d) is the correct response because ethno is a prefix referring to race or ethnicity just as choreo is a prefix referring to dance. Cardio (a) means relating to the heart, crypto (b) means hidden, and chrono (c) means time.

31. **(c)**   (c) is the correct answer because an adjective modifies a noun in the same way that an adverb modifies a verb. A pronoun (a) substitutes for a noun, a preposition (b) defines the relationship of a noun to a verb, and an article (d) (a, an, or the) signals the presence of a noun.

32. **(a)**   (a) is the correct response because lay is the past tense of the verb lie in the same way that laid is the past tense of the verb lay. Laying (b) is the present participle of lay, lying (c) is the present participle of lie, and lain (d) is the past participle of lie.

33. **(b)**   (b) is the right choice because red has a longer wavelength than orange just as blue has a longer wavelength than violet. In order from longest to shortest the colors in the visible spectrum are: red, orange, yellow, green, blue, indigo, violet.

34. **(d)**   (d) is the correct choice because an electron is negatively charged in the same way that a neutron has no charge. A proton is positively charged so (a) and (c) are incorrect. Variable (b) is not relevant to this question.

35. **(d)**   (d) is correct because something with eagle-like features is aquiline just as something with dog-like features is canine. Feline (a) refers to cat-like, equine (b) refers to horse-like, and bovine (c) refers to cow-like.

36. **(a)**   (a) is correct because the past tense of the verb become is became just as the past tense of the verb shrink is shrank. All other choices are incorrect.

37. **(c)**   (c) is correct because just as aural relates to the ear, oral relates to the mouth. Optical relates to the eyes (a), nasal refers to the nose (b), and manual refers to the hand (d).

38. **(b)**   (b) is correct because acrophobia is a fear of heights and hydrophobia is a fear of water. Hemophobia is a fear of blood (a), sitophobia is a fear of food (c), and necrophobia is a fear of death (d).

39. **(a)**   (a) is correct because killing a king is called regicide just as killing one's father is called patricide.

40. **(c)**   (c) is the correct response because just as a patent protects an invention, a copyright protects a written work. Registration (a) and license (b) are general terms that are not specific to protection of ownership. A statute (d) refers to a law.

41. **(a)**   (a) is the correct response because a gene is a constituent part of a chromosome as a nucleus is a constituent part of a cell. RNA (b) and DNA (c) are compounds that carry information, and an enzyme (d) is a chemical that performs a specific function, so these are incorrect.

42. **(a)**   (a) is correct because hemi is Greek for half as bio is Greek for life. (b), (c), and (d) are incorrect because they are not the Greek word for half.

43. **(a)**   (a) is correct because gastrin is a hormone produced by the stomach glands as estrogen is a hormone produced by the ovaries. (b) is incorrect because the adrenal medulla produces the hormone adrenalin. (c) is incorrect because the thyroid produces the hormones thyroxin and calcitonin. (d) is incorrect because the pancreas produces the hormone glucagon.

44. **(d)**   (d) is correct because the tibia is a bone in the leg as the ulna is an arm bone. (a) is incorrect because the tarsal bones are in the foot. (b) is incorrect because the humerus is a bone in the arm. (c) is incorrect because the mandible bone is in the head.

45. **(c)**   (c) is correct because Arabic numeral 600 is equivalent to Roman numeral DC. (a) is incorrect because the Arabic value of the Roman numeral MD is 1,500. (b) is incorrect because the Arabic equivalent of CC is 200. (d) is incorrect because MX equals 1,010.

46. **(b)**   (b) is correct because homo is Greek for same as macro is Greek for large. (a) is incorrect because the Greek word for small is micro (c) is incorrect because the Greek word for male is andro. (d) is incorrect because homeo is Greek for similar.

47. **(a)**   (a) is correct because a khan was a ruler in Mongolia as a czar was a ruler in Russia. (b) is incorrect because a pharaoh ruled in Egypt. (c)

is incorrect because a sultan ruled in Turkey. (d) is incorrect because an emperor ruled in China.

48. **(c)**   (c) is correct because a bolt is shot from a crossbow as a ball is shot from a musket. (a), (b), and (d) are incorrect because these objects were not fired from a crossbow.

49. **(d)**   (d) is correct because sound is produced from the skin of the doumbek as it is produced from the string on a sitar. (a) and (b) are incorrect because they refer to a keyboard instrument, such as a piano, or an organ. (c) is incorrect because this is a general term, musically referring to a percussion instrument.

50. **(c)**   (c) is correct because fusion creates energy by combining the nuclei as fission creates energy by splitting a nucleus. (a), (b), and (d) are incorrect because while these terms are used in the creation of nuclear energy, they do not specifically refer to fusion.

VOCABULARY ENHANCER REVIEW

Before students can begin to enrich their reading comprehension skills, they must begin with their vocabulary. The basis of reading is words; and to better enhance reading skills, it is necessary to expand the number of words a reader understands. This is why this book begins with a vocabulary enhancer; it is important to build a strong vocabulary base before attempting to improve reading comprehension skills.

It is important to understand the meanings of all words — not just the ones you are asked to define. A good vocabulary is a strength that can help you perform well on all sections of this test. The following information will build your skills in determining the meanings of words.

SIMILAR FORMS AND SOUNDS

The complex nature of language sometimes makes reading difficult. Words often become confusing when they have similar forms and sounds. Indeed, the author may have a correct meaning in mind, but an incorrect word choice can alter the meaning of the sentence or even make it totally illogical.

NO: Martha was always part of that *cliché*.

YES: Martha was always part of that *clique*.

(A *cliché* is a trite or hackneyed expression; a *clique* is an exclusive group of people.)

NO: The minister spoke of the soul's *immorality*.

YES: The minister spoke of the soul's *immortality*.

(*Immorality* means wickedness; *immortality* means imperishable or unending life.)

NO: Where is the nearest *stationary* store?

YES: Where is the nearest *stationery* store?

(*Stationary* means immovable; *stationery* is paper used for writing.)

Below are groups of words that are often confused because of their similar forms and sounds.

1. accent – *v.* – to stress or emphasize (You must *accent* the last syllable.)

    ascent – *n.* – a climb or rise (John's *ascent* of the mountain was dangerous.)

    assent – *n.* – consent; compliance (We need your *assent* before we can go ahead with the plans.)

2. accept – *v.* – to take something offered (She *accepted* the gift.)

    except – *prep.* – other than; but (Everyone was included in the plans *except* him.)

3. advice – *n.* – opinion given as to what to do or how to handle a situation (Her sister gave her *advice* on what to say at the interview.)

    advise – *v.* – to counsel (John's guidance counselor *advised* him on which colleges to apply to.)

4. affect – *v.* – to influence (Mary's suggestion did not *affect* me.)

    effect – 1. *v.*– to cause to happen (The plan was *effected* with great success.); 2. *n.* – result (The *effect* of the medicine is excellent.)

5. allusion – *n.* – indirect reference (In the poem, there are many Biblical *allusions.*)

    illusion – *n.* – false idea or conception; belief or opinion not in accord with the facts (Greg was under the *illusion* that he could win the race after missing three weeks of practice.)

6. already – *adv.* – previously (I had *already* read that novel.)

    all ready – *adv. + adj.* – prepared (The family was *all ready* to leave on vacation.)

7. altar – *n.* – table or stand used in religious rites (The priest stood at the *altar.*)

    alter – *v.* – to change (Their plans were *altered* during the strike.)

8. capital – 1. *n.* – a city where the government meets (The senators had a meeting in Albany, the *capital* of New York.); 2. money used in business (They had enough *capital* to develop the industry.)

    capitol – *n.* – building in which the legislature meets (Senator Brown gave a speech at the *capitol* in Washington.)

9. choose – *v.* – to select (Which camera did you *choose*?)

    chose – (past tense, *choose*.) (Susan *chose* to stay home.)

10. cite – *v.* – to quote (The student *cited* evidence from the text.)

    site – *n.* – location (They chose the *site* where the house would be built.)

11. clothes – *n.* – garments (Because she got caught in the rain, her *clothes* were wet.)

    cloths – *n.* – pieces of material (The *cloths* were used to wash the windows.)

12. coarse – *adj.* – rough; unrefined (Sandpaper is *coarse*.)

    course – 1. *n.* – path of action (She did not know what *course* would solve the problem.); 2. passage (We took the long *course* to the lake.); 3. series of studies (We both enrolled in the physics *course*.); 4. part of a meal (She served a five *course* meal.)

13. consul – *n.* – a person appointed by the government to live in a foreign city and represent the citizenry and business interests of his native country there (The *consul* was appointed to Naples, Italy.)

    council – *n.* – a group used for discussion, advisement (The *council* decided to accept his letter of resignation.)

    counsel – *v.* – to advise (Tom *counsels* Jerry on tax matters.)

14. decent – *adj.* – proper; respectable (He was very *decent* about the entire matter.)

    descent – 1. *n.* – moving down (In Dante's *Inferno*, the *descent* into Hell was depicted graphically.); 2. ancestry (He is of Irish *descent*.)

15. device – 1. *n.* – plan; scheme (The *device* helped her win the race.); 2. invention (We bought a *device* that opens the garage door automatically.)

    devise – *v.* – to contrive (He *devised* a plan so John could not win.)

16. emigrate – *v.* – to go away from a country (Many Japanese *emigrated* from Japan in the late 1800s.)

    immigrate – *v.* – to come into a country (Her relatives *immigrated* to the United States after World War I.)

17. eminent – *n.* – prominent (He is an *eminent* member of the community.)

    imminent – *adj.* – impending (The decision is *imminent*.)

    immanent – *adj.* – existing within (Maggie believed that religious spirit is *immanent* in human beings.)

18. fair – 1. *adj.* – beautiful (She was a *fair* maiden.); 2. just (She tried to be *fair*.); 3. *n* – festival (There were many games at the *fair*.)

    fare – *n.* – amount of money paid for transportation (The city proposed that the subway *fare* be raised.)

19. forth – *adv.* – onward (The soldiers moved *forth* in the blinding snow.)

    fourth – *n., adj.* – 4th (She was the *fourth* runner-up in the beauty contest.)

20. its – possessive form of *it* (Our town must improve *its* roads.)

    it's – contraction of it is (*It's* time to leave the party.)

21. later – *adj., adv.* – at a subsequent date (We will take a vacation *later* this year.)

    latter – *n.* – second of the two (Susan can visit Monday or Tuesday. The *latter,* however, is preferable.)

22. lead – 1. *n.* – (led) a metal (The handgun was made of *lead*.); 2. *v.* – (leed) to show the way (The camp counselor *leads* the way to the picnic grounds.)

    led – past tense of *lead* (#2 above) (The dog *led* the way.)

23. loose – *adj.* – free; unrestricted (The dog was let *loose* by accident.)

    lose – *v.* – to suffer the loss of (He was afraid he would *lose* the race.)

24. moral – 1. *adj.* – virtuous (She is a *moral* woman with high ethical standards.); 2. *n.* – lesson taught by a story, incident, etc. (Most fables end with a *moral*.)

    morale – *n.* – mental condition (After the team lost the game, their *morale* was low.)

25. of – *prep.* – from (She is *of* French descent.)

    off – *adj.* – away; at a distance (The television fell *off* the table.)

26. passed – *v.* – having satisfied some requirement (He *passed* the test.)

past – 1. *adj.* – gone by or elapsed in time (His *past* deeds got him in trouble.); 2. *n.* – a period of time gone by (His *past* was shady.); 3. *prep.* – beyond (She ran *past* the house.)

27. personal – *adj.* – private (Jack was unwilling to discuss his childhood; it was too *personal.*)

personnel – *n.* – staff (The *personnel* at the department store was made up of young adults.)

28. principal – *n.* – head of a school (The *principal* addressed the graduating class.)

principle – *n.* – the ultimate source, origin, or cause of something; a law, truth (The *principles* of physics were reviewed in class today.)

29. prophecy – *n.* – prediction of the future (His *prophecy* that he would become a doctor came true.)

prophesy – *v.* – to declare or predict (He *prophesied* that we would win the lottery.)

30. quiet – *adj.* – still; calm (At night all is *quiet.*)

quite – *adv.* – really; truly (She is *quite* a good singer.)

quit – *v.* – to free oneself (Peter had little time to spare so he *quit* the chorus.)

31. respectfully – *adv.* – with respect, honor, esteem (He declined the offer *respectfully.*)

respectively – *adv.* – in the order mentioned (Jack, Susan and Jim, who are members of the club, were elected president, vice-president, and secretary *respectively.*)

32. stationary – *adj.* – immovable (The park bench is *stationary.*)

stationery – *n.* – paper used for writing (The invitations were printed on yellow *stationery.*)

33. straight – *adj.* – not curved (The road was *straight.*)

strait – 1. *adj.* – restricted; narrow; confined (The patient was put in a *strait* jacket.); 2. *n.* – narrow waterway (He sailed through the *Straits* of Magellan.)

34. than – *conj.* – used most commonly in comparisons (Maggie is older *than* I.)

then – *adv.* – soon afterward (We lived in Boston, *then* we moved to New York.)

35. their – possessive form of *they* (That is *their* house on Tenafly Drive.)

    they're – contraction of they are (*They're* leaving for California next week.)

    there – *adv.* – at that place (Who is standing *there* under the tree?)

36. to – *prep.* – in the direction of; toward; as (She made a turn *to* the right on Norman Street.)

    too – 1. *adv.* – more than enough (She served *too* much for dinner.); 2. also (He is going to Maine *too.*)

    two – *n.* – 2; one and one (We have *two* pet rabbits).

37. weather – *n.* – the general condition of the atmosphere (The *weather* is expected to be clear on Sunday.)

    whether – *conj.* – if it be a case or fact (We don't know *whether* the trains are late.)

38. who's – contraction of who is or who has (*Who's* willing to volunteer for the night shift?)

    whose – possessive form of *who* (*Whose* book is this?)

39. your – possessive form of *you* (Is this *your* seat?)

    you're – contraction of you and are (I know *you're* going to do well on the test.)

MULTIPLE MEANINGS

In addition to words that sound alike, you must be careful when dealing with words that have multiple meanings. For example:

The boy was thrilled that his mother gave him a piece of chewing *gum.*

Dentists advise people to floss their teeth to help prevent *gum* disease.

As you can see, one word can have different meanings depending on the context in which it is used.

CONNOTATION AND DENOTATION

Language can become even more complicated. Not only can a single word have numerous definitions and subtle meanings, it may also take on added meanings through implication. The **connotation** is the idea suggested by its place near or association with other words or phrases. The **denotation** of a word is the direct explicit meaning.

Connotation

Sometimes, you will be asked to tell the meaning of a word in the context of the paragraph. You may not have seen the word used in this context before, but from your understanding of the writer's intent, you should be able to figure out what it is she or he is after. For example, read the following paragraph:

Paris is a beautiful city, perhaps the most beautiful on earth. Long, broad avenues are lined with seventeenth and eighteenth century apartments, office buildings, and cafes. Flowers give the city a rich and varied look. The bridges and the river lend an air of lightness and grace to the whole urban landscape.

1. In this paragraph, "rich" most nearly means

    (A) wealthy.   (C) colorful.

    (B) polluted.   (D) dull.

To answer this question, you need to understand the difference between *denotation* and *connotation*. Denotation is the literal meaning of a word; connotation is the non-literal meaning of a word.

If you chose "colorful" you would be right. Although "rich" means "wealthy" (that is, "wealthy" is its *denotation*, or literal meaning), here the writer means more than the word's literal meaning, and seems to be highlighting the variety of color that the flowers add to the avenues. That variety is "rich" in a figurative, or *connotative*, sense.

The writer is using a non-literal meaning, or *connotation* that we associate with the word "rich" to show what s/he means. When we think of something "rich," we usually also think of abundance, variety, color, and not merely numbers.

Denotation

Determining the denotation (its literal meaning) of a word in context is different from determining a word's connotation. Read this paragraph:

Many soporifics are on the market to help people sleep. Take a glass of water and two *Sleepeze* and you get the "zzzzz" you need. *Sominall* supposedly helps you get the sleep you need so you can go on working. With

Morpho, your head hits the pillow and you're asleep before the light goes out.

1. From this paragraph, a "soporific" is probably

    (A) a drug that stimulates you to stay awake.

    (B) a kind of sleeping bag.

    (C) a kind of bed.

    (D) a drug that helps you sleep.

What is a soporific? You can figure out what it means by looking at what is said around it. People take these "soporifics" to go to sleep, not to wake up. So it can't be (A). You can't take two beds and a glass of water to go to sleep, either. So, it can't be (C). Anyway, you might be able to identify what a soporific is because you recognize the brand names used as examples. So, it must be some sort of pill that you take to sleep. Well, pills are usually drugs of some kind. Therefore, the answer is (D).

VOCABULARY BUILDER

Although the context in which a word appears can help you determine the meaning of the word, one sure-fire way to know a definition is to learn it. By studying the following lists of words and memorizing their definition(s), you will be better equipped to answer questions that deal with word meanings.

To benefit most from this vocabulary list, study the words and their definitions and use them in context, in speaking, and in writing. Answer all the drill questions making sure to check your answers with the answer key that appears at the end of the review.

Group 1

abstract – *adj.* – not easy to understand; theoretical

acclaim – *n.* – loud approval; applause

acquiesce – *v.* – agree or consent to an opinion

adamant – *adj.* – not yielding; firm

adversary – *n.* – an enemy; foe

advocate – 1. *v.* – to plead in favor of; 2. *n.* – supporter; defender

aesthetic – *adj.* – showing good taste; artistic

alleviate – *v.* – to lessen or make easier

aloof – *adj.* – distant in interest; reserved; cool

altercation – *n.* – controversy; dispute

altruistic – *adj.* – unselfish

amass – *v.* – to collect together; accumulate

ambiguous – *adj.* – not clear; uncertain; vague

ambivalent – *adj.* – undecided

ameliorate – *v.* – to make better; to improve

amiable – *adj.* – friendly

amorphous – *adj.* – having no determinate form

anarchist – *n.* – one who believes that a formal government is unnecessary

antagonism – *n.* – hostility; opposition

apathy – *n.* – lack of emotion or interest

appease – *v.* – to make quiet; to calm

apprehensive – *adj.* – fearful; aware; conscious

arbitrary – *adj.* – based on one's preference or whim

arrogant – *adj.* – acting superior to others; conceited

articulate – 1. *v.* – to speak distinctly; 2. *adj.* – eloquent; fluent; 3. *adj.* – capable of speech; 4. *v* – to hinge; to connect; 5. *v.* – to convey; to express effectively

Drill 1: Group 1

DIRECTIONS: Match each word in the left column with the word in the right column that is most *opposite* in meaning.

Word			Match	
1. ____ articulate	6. ____ abstract		A. hostile	F. disperse
2. ____ apathy	7. ____ acquiesce		B. concrete	G. enthusiasm
3. ____ amiable	8. ____ arbitrary		C. selfish	H. certain
4. ____ altruistic	9. ____ amass		D. reasoned	I. resist
5. ____ ambivalent	10. ____ adversary		E. ally	J. incoherent

DIRECTIONS: Match each word in the left column with the word in the right column that is most *similar* in meaning.

Word		Match	
11. ____ adamant	14. ____ antagonism	A. afraid	D. insistent
12. ____ aesthetic	15. ____ altercation	B. disagreement	E. hostility
13. ____ apprehensive		C. tasteful	

Group 2

assess – *v.* – to estimate the value of

astute – *adj.* – cunning; sly; crafty

atrophy – *v.* – to waste away through lack of nutrition

audacious – *adj.* – fearless; bold

augment – *v.* – to increase or add to; to make larger

austere – *adj.* – harsh; severe; strict

authentic – *adj.* – real; genuine; trustworthy

authoritarian – *adj.* – acting as a dictator; demanding obedience

banal – *adj.* – common; petty; ordinary

belittle – *v.* – to make small; to think lightly of

benefactor – *n.* – one who helps others; a donor

benevolent – *adj.* – kind; generous

benign – *adj.* – mild; harmless

biased – *adj.* – prejudiced; influenced; not neutral

blasphemous – *adj.* – irreligious; away from acceptable standards

blithe – *adj.* – happy; cheery; merry

brevity – *n.* – briefness; shortness

candid – *adj.* – honest; truthful; sincere

capricious – *adj.* – changeable; fickle

caustic – *adj.* – burning; sarcastic; harsh

censor – *v.* – to examine and delete objectionable material

censure – *v.* – to criticize or disapprove of

charlatan – *n.* – an imposter; fake

coalesce – *v.* – to combine; come together

collaborate – *v.* – to work together; cooperate

Drill 2: Group 2

DIRECTIONS: Match each word in the left column with the word in the right column that is most *opposite* in meaning.

	Word			**Match**	
1. ____ augment		6. ____ authentic	A. permit		F. malicious
2. ____ biased		7. ____ candid	B. heroine		G. neutral
3. ____ banal		8. ____ belittle	C. praise		H. mournful
4. ____ benevolent		9. ____ charlatan	D. diminish		I. unusual
5. ____ censor		10. ____ blithe	E. dishonest		J. genuine

DIRECTIONS: Match each word in the left column with the word in the right column that is most *similar* in meaning.

Word   **Match**

11. ____ collaborate   14. ____ censure   A. harmless   D. cooperate

12. ____ benign   15. ____ capricious   B. cunning   E. criticize

13. ____ astute   C. changeable

Group 3

compatible – *adj.* – in agreement; harmonious

complacent – *adj.* – content; self-satisfied; smug

compliant – *adj.* – yielding; obedient

comprehensive – *adj.* – all-inclusive; complete; thorough

compromise – *v.* – to settle by mutual adjustment

concede – 1. *v.* – to acknowledge; admit; 2. to surrender; to abandon one's position

concise – *adj.* – in few words; brief; condensed

condescend – *v.* – to come down from one's position or dignity

condone – *v.* – to overlook; to forgive

conspicuous – *adj.* – easy to see; noticeable

consternation – *n.* – amazement or terror that causes confusion

consummation – *n.* – the completion; finish

contemporary – *adj.* – living or happening at the same time; modern

contempt – *n.* – scorn; disrespect

contrite – *adj.* – regretful; sorrowful

conventional – *adj.* – traditional; common; routine

cower – *v.* – crouch down in fear or shame

defamation – *n.* – any harm to a name or reputation; slander

deference – *n.* – a yielding to the opinion of another

deliberate – 1. *v.* – to consider carefully; weigh in the mind; 2. *adj.* – intentional

denounce – *v.* – to speak out against; condemn

depict – *v.* – to portray in words; present a visual image

deplete – *v.* – to reduce; to empty

depravity – *n.* – moral corruption; badness

deride – *v.* – to ridicule; laugh at with scorn

Drill 3: Group 3

DIRECTIONS: Match each word in the left column with the word in the right column that is most *opposite* in meaning.

Word			Match	
1. ____ deplete	6. ____ condone	A. unintentional	F. support
2. ____ contemporary	7. ____ conspicuous	B. disapprove	G. beginning
3. ____ concise	8. ____ consummation	C. invisible	H. ancient
4. ____ deliberate	9. ____ denounce	D. respect	I. virtue
5. ____ depravity	10. ____ contempt	E. fill	J. verbose

DIRECTIONS: Match each word in the left column with the word in the right column that is most *similar* in meaning.

Word			Match	
11. ____ compatible	14. ____ comprehensive	A. portray	D. thorough
12. ____ depict	15. ____ complacent	B. content	E. common
13. ____ conventional		C. harmonious	

Group 4

desecrate – *v.* – to violate a holy place or sanctuary

detached – *adj.* – separated; not interested; standing alone

deter – *v.* – to prevent; to discourage; hinder

didactic – 1. *adj.* – instructive; 2. dogmatic; preachy

digress – *v.* – stray from the subject; wander from topic

diligence – *n.* – hard work

discerning – *adj.* – distinguishing one thing from another

discord – *n.* – disagreement; lack of harmony

discriminating – 1. *v.* – distinguishing one thing from another;
    2. *v.* – demonstrating bias; 3. *adj.* – able to distinguish

disdain – 1. *n.* – intense dislike; 2. *v.* – look down upon; scorn

disparage – *v.* – to belittle; undervalue

disparity – *n.* – difference in form, character, or degree

dispassionate – *adj.* – lack of feeling; impartial

disperse – *v.* – to scatter; separate

disseminate – *v.* – to circulate; scatter

dissent – *v.* – to disagree; differ in opinion

dissonance – *n.* – harsh contradiction

diverse – *adj.* – different; dissimilar

document – 1. *n.* – official paper containing information; 2. *v.*– to support;
    substantiate; verify

dogmatic – *adj.* – stubborn; biased; opinionated

dubious – *adj.* – doubtful; uncertain; skeptical; suspicious

eccentric – *adj.* – odd; peculiar; strange

efface – *v.* – wipe out; erase

effervescence – 1. *n.* – liveliness; spirit; enthusiasm; 2. bubbliness

egocentric – *adj.* – self-centered

Drill 4: Group 4

DIRECTIONS: Match each word in the left column with the word in the right column that is most *opposite* in meaning.

Word   Match

1. ____ detached   6. ____ dubious   A. agree   F. respect

2. ____ deter   7. ____ diligence   B. certain   G. compliment

3. ____ dissent   8. ____ disdain   C. lethargy   H. sanctify

4. ____ discord   9. ____ desecrate   D. connected   I. harmony

5. ____ efface   10. ____ disparage   E. assist   J. restore

DIRECTIONS: Match each word in the left column with the word in the right column that is most *similar* in meaning.

Word   Match

11. ____ effervescence   14. ____ document   A. violate   D. liveliness

12. ____ efface   15. ____ eccentric   B. distribute   E. odd

13. ____ disseminate   C. substantiate

Group 5

elaboration – *n.* – act of clarifying; adding details

eloquence – *n.* – the ability to speak well

elusive – *adj.* – hard to catch; difficult to understand

emulate – *v.* – to imitate; copy; mimic

endorse – *v.* – support; to approve of; recommend

engender – *v.* – to create; bring about

enhance – *v.* – to improve; compliment; make more attractive

enigma – *n.* – mystery; secret; perplexity

ephemeral – *adj.* – temporary; brief; short-lived

equivocal – *adj.* – doubtful; uncertain

erratic – *adj.* – unpredictable; strange

erroneous – *adj.* – untrue; inaccurate; not correct

esoteric – *adj.* – incomprehensible; obscure

euphony – *n.* – pleasant sound

execute – 1. *v.* – put to death; kill; 2. to carry out; fulfill

exemplary – *adj.* – serving as an example; outstanding

exhaustive – *adj.* – thorough; complete

expedient – *adj.* – helpful; practical; worthwhile

expedite – *v.* – speed up

explicit – *adj.* – specific; definite

extol – *v.* – praise; commend

extraneous – *adj.* – irrelevant; not related; not essential

facilitate – *v.* – make easier; simplify

fallacious – *adj.* – misleading

fanatic – *n.* – enthusiast; extremist

Drill 5: Group 5

DIRECTIONS: Match each word in the left column with the word in the right column that is most *opposite* in meaning.

	Word			Match			
1.	extraneous	6.	erratic	A.	incomplete	F.	eternal
2.	ephemeral	7.	explicit	B.	delay	G.	abridge
3.	exhaustive	8.	euphony	C.	dependable	H.	relevant
4.	expedite	9.	elusive	D.	comprehensible	I.	indefinite
5.	erroneous	10.	elaborate	E.	dissonance	J.	accurate

DIRECTIONS: Match each word in the left column with the word in the right column that is most *similar* in meaning.

Word		Match	
11. ____ endorse	14. ____ fallacious	A. enable	D. worthwhile
12. ____ expedient	15. ____ engender	B. recommend	E. deceptive
13. ____ facilitate		C. create	

Group 6

fastidious – *adj.* – fussy; hard to please

fervor – *n.* – passion; intensity

fickle – *adj.* – changeable; unpredictable

fortuitous – *adj.* – accidental; happening by chance; lucky

frivolity – *n.* – giddiness; lack of seriousness

fundamental – *adj.* – basic; necessary

furtive – *adj.* – secretive; sly

futile – *adj.* – worthless; unprofitable

glutton – *n.* – overeater

grandiose – *adj.* – extravagant; flamboyant

gravity – *n.* – seriousness

guile – *n.* – slyness; deceit

gullible – *adj.* – easily fooled

hackneyed – *adj.* – commonplace; trite

hamper – *v.* – interfere with; hinder

haphazard – *adj.* – disorganized; random

hedonistic – *adj.* – pleasure seeking

heed – *v.* – obey; yield to

heresy – *n.* – opinion contrary to popular belief

hindrance – *n.* – blockage; obstacle

humility – *n.* – lack of pride; modesty

hypocritical – *adj.* – two-faced; deceptive

hypothetical – *adj.* – assumed; uncertain

illuminate – *v.* – make understandable

illusory – *adj.* – unreal; false; deceptive

Drill 6: Group 6

DIRECTIONS: Match each word in the left column with the word in the right column that is most *opposite* in meaning.

Word

			Match	
1. ____ heresy	6. ____ fervent	A. predictable		F. beneficial
2. ____ fickle	7. ____ fundamental	B. dispassionate		G. orthodoxy
3. ____ illusory	8. ____ furtive	C. simple		H. organized
4. ____ frivolity	9. ____ futile	D. extraneous		I. candid
5. ____ grandiose	10. ____ haphazard	E. real		J. seriousness

DIRECTIONS: Match each word in the left column with the word in the right column that is most *similar* in meaning.

Word

			Match	
11. ____ glutton	14. ____ hackneyed	A. hinder		D. overeater
12. ____ heed	15. ____ hindrance	B. obstacle		E. obey
13. ____ hamper		C. trite		

Group 7

immune – *adj.* – protected; unthreatened by

immutable – *adj.* – unchangeable; permanent

impartial – *adj.* – unbiased; fair

impetuous – 1. *adj.* – rash; impulsive; 2. forcible; violent implication – *n.* – suggestion; inference

inadvertent – *adj.* – not on purpose; unintentional

incessant – *adj.* – constant; continual

incidental – *adj.* – extraneous; unexpected

inclined – 1. *adj.* – apt to; likely to; 2. angled

incoherent – *adj.* – illogical; rambling

incompatible – *adj.* – disagreeing; disharmonious

incredulous – *adj.* – unwilling to believe; skeptical

indifferent – *adj.* – unconcerned

indolent – *adj.* – lazy; inactive

indulgent – *adj.* – lenient; patient

inevitable – *adj.* – sure to happen; unavoidable

infamous – *adj.* – having a bad reputation; notorious

infer – *v.* – form an opinion; conclude

initiate – 1. *v.* – begin; admit into a group; 2. *n.* – a person who is in the process of being admitted into a group

innate – *adj.* – natural; inborn

innocuous – *adj.* – harmless; innocent

innovate – *v.* – introduce a change; depart from the old

insipid – *adj.* – uninteresting; bland

instigate – *v.* – start; provoke

intangible – *adj.* – incapable of being touched; immaterial

Drill 7: Group 7

DIRECTIONS: Match each word in the left column with the word in the right column that is most *opposite* in meaning.

Word

1. ___ immutable	6. ___ innate	A. intentional	F. changeable
2. ___ impartial	7. ___ incredulous	B. articulate	G. avoidable
3. ___ inadvertent	8. ___ inevitable	C. gullible	H. harmonious
4. ___ incoherent	9. ___ intangible	D. material	I. learned
5. ___ incompatible	10. ___ indolent	E. biased	J. energetic

Match

DIRECTIONS: Match each word in the left column with the word in the right column that is most *similar* in meaning.

Word

11. ___ impetuous	14. ___ instigate	A. lenient	D. conclude
12. ___ incidental	15. ___ indulgent	B. impulsive	E. extraneous
13. ___ infer		C. provoke	

Match

Group 8

ironic – *adj.* – contradictory; inconsistent; sarcastic

irrational – *adj.* – not logical

jeopardy – *n.* – danger

kindle – *v.* – ignite; arouse

languid – *adj.* – weak; fatigued

laud – *v.* – to praise

lax – *adj.* – careless; irresponsible

lethargic – *adj.* – lazy; passive

levity – *n.* – silliness; lack of seriousness

lucid – 1. *adj.* – shining; 2. easily understood

magnanimous – *adj.* – forgiving; unselfish

malicious – *adj.* – spiteful; vindictive

marred – *adj.* – damaged

meander – *v.* – wind on a course; go aimlessly

melancholy – *n.* – depression; gloom

meticulous – *adj.* – exacting; precise

minute – *adj.* – extremely small; tiny

miser – *n.* – penny pincher; stingy person

mitigate – *v.* – alleviate; lessen; soothe

morose – *adj.* – moody; despondent

negligence – *n.* – carelessness

neutral – *adj.* – impartial; unbiased

nostalgic – *adj.* – longing for the past; filled with bittersweet memories

novel – *adj.* – new

Drill 8: Group 8

DIRECTIONS: Match each word in the left column with the word in the right column that is most *opposite* in meaning.

Word		Match	
1. ____ irrational	6. ____ magnanimous	A. extinguish	F. ridicule
2. ____ kindle	7. ____ levity	B. jovial	G. kindly
3. ____ meticulous	8. ____ minute	C. selfish	H. sloppy
4. ____ malicious	9. ____ laud	D. logical	I. huge
5. ____ morose	10. ____ novel	E. seriousness	J. stale

DIRECTIONS: Match each word in the left column with the word in the right column that is most *similar* in meaning.

Word		Match	
11. ___ ironic	14. ___ jeopardy	A. lessen	D. carelessness
12. ___ marred	15. ___ negligence	B. damaged	E. danger
13. ___ mitigate		C. sarcastic	

Group 9

nullify – *v.* – cancel; invalidate

objective – 1. *adj.* – open-minded; impartial; 2. *n.* – goal

obscure – *adj.* – not easily understood; dark

obsolete – *adj.* – out of date; passe

ominous – *adj.* – threatening

optimist – *n.* – person who hopes for the best; sees the good side

orthodox – *adj.* – traditional; accepted

pagan – 1. *n.* – polytheist; 2. *adj.* – polytheistic

partisan – 1. *n.* – supporter; follower; 2. *adj.* – biased; one sided

perceptive – *adj.* – full of insight; aware

peripheral – *adj.* – marginal; outer

pernicious – *adj.* – dangerous; harmful

pessimism – *n.* – seeing only the gloomy side; hopelessness

phenomenon – 1. *n.* – miracle; 2. occurrence

philanthropy – *n.* – charity; unselfishness

pious – *adj.* – religious; devout; dedicated

placate – *v.* – pacify

plausible – *adj.* – probable; feasible

pragmatic – *adj.* – matter-of-fact; practical

preclude – *v.* – inhibit; make impossible

predecessor – *n.* – one who has occupied an office before another

prodigal – *adj.* – wasteful; lavish

prodigious – *adj.* – exceptional; tremendous

profound – *adj.* – deep; knowledgeable; thorough

profusion – *n.* – great amount; abundance

Drill 9: Group 9

DIRECTIONS: Match each word in the left column with the word in the right column that is most *opposite* in meaning.

Word		Match	
1. ____ objective	6. ____ plausible	A. scanty	F. minute
2. ____ obsolete	7. ____ preclude	B. assist	G. anger
3. ____ placate	8. ____ prodigious	C. superficial	H. pessimism
4. ____ profusion	9. ____ profound	D. biased	I. modern
5. ____ peripheral	10. ____ optimism	E. improbable	J. central

DIRECTIONS: Match each word in the left column with the word in the right column that is most *similar* in meaning.

Word		Match	
11. ____ nullify	14. ____ pernicious	A. invalidate	D. threatening
12. ____ ominous	15. ____ prodigal	B. follower	E. harmful
13. ____ partisan		C. lavish	

Group 10

prosaic – *adj.* – tiresome; ordinary

provincial – *adj.* – regional; unsophisticated

provocative – 1. *adj.* – tempting; 2. irritating

prudent – *adj.* – wise; careful; prepared

qualified – *adj.* – experienced; indefinite

rectify – *v.* – correct

redundant – *adj.* – repetitious; unnecessary

refute – *v.* – challenge; disprove

relegate – *v.* – banish; put to a lower position

relevant – *adj.* – of concern; significant

remorse – *n.* – guilt; sorrow

reprehensible – *adj.* – wicked; disgraceful

repudiate – *v.* – reject; cancel

rescind – *v.* – retract; discard

resignation – 1. *n.* – quitting; 2. submission

resolution – *n.* – proposal; promise; determination

respite – *n.* – recess; rest period

reticent – *adj.* – silent; reserved; shy

reverent – *adj.* – respectful

rhetorical – *adj.* – having to do with verbal communication

rigor – *n.* – severity

sagacious – *adj.* – wise; cunning

sanguine – 1. *adj.* – optimistic; cheerful; 2. red

saturate – *v.* – soak thoroughly; drench

scanty – *adj.* – inadequate; sparse

Drill 10: Group 10

DIRECTIONS: Match each word in the left column with the word in the right column that is most *opposite* in meaning.

Word		Match	
1. ____ provincial	6. ____ remorse	A. inexperienced	F. affirm
2. ____ reticent	7. ____ repudiate	B. joy	G. extraordinary
3. ____ prudent	8. ____ sanguine	C. pessimistic	H. sophisticated
4. ____ qualified	9. ____ relevant	D. unrelated	I. forward
5. ____ relegate	10. ____ prosaic	E. careless	J. promote

DIRECTIONS: Match each word in the left column with the word in the right column that is most *similar* in meaning.

Word		Match	
11. ____ provocative	14. ____ rescind	A. drench	D. severity
12. ____ rigor	15. ____ reprehensible	B. tempting	E. blameworthy
13. ____ saturate		C. retract	

Group 11

scrupulous – *adj.* – honorable; exact

scrutinize – *v.* – examine closely; study

servile – *adj.* – slavish; groveling

skeptic – *n.* – doubter

slander – *v.* – defame; maliciously misrepresent

solemnity – *n.* – seriousness

solicit – *v.* – ask; seek

stagnant – *adj.* – motionless; uncirculating

stanza – *n.* – group of lines in a poem having a definite pattern

static – *adj.* – inactive; changeless

stoic – *adj.* – detached; unruffled; calm

subtlety – 1. *n.* – understatement; 2. propensity for understatement;
    3. sophistication; 4. cunning

superficial – *adj.* – on the surface; narrow-minded; lacking depth

superfluous – *adj.* – unnecessary; extra

surpass – *v.* – go beyond; outdo

sycophant – *n.* – flatterer

symmetry – *n.* – correspondence of parts; harmony

taciturn – *adj.* – reserved; quiet; secretive

tedious – *adj.* – time-consuming; burdensome; uninteresting

temper – *v.* – soften; pacify; compose

tentative – *adj.* – not confirmed; indefinite

thrifty – *adj.* – economical; pennywise

tranquility – *n.* – peace; stillness; harmony

trepidation – *n.* – apprehension; uneasiness

trivial – *adj.* – unimportant; small; worthless

Drill 11: Group 11

DIRECTIONS: Match each word in the left column with the word in the right column that is most *opposite* in meaning.

Word		Match	
1. ____ scrutinize	6. ____ tentative	A. frivolity	F. skim
2. ____ skeptic	7. ____ thrifty	B. enjoyable	G. turbulent
3. ____ solemnity	8. ____ tranquility	C. prodigal	H. active
4. ____ static	9. ____ solicit	D. chaos	I. believer
5. ____ tedious	10. ____ stagnant	E. give	J. confirmed

DIRECTIONS: Match each word in the left column with the word in the right column that is most *similar* in meaning.

Word		Match	
11.____ symmetry	14.____ subtle	A. understated	D. fear
12.____ superfluous	15.____ trepidation	B. unnecessary	E. flatterer
13.____ sycophant		C. balance	

Group 12

tumid – *adj.* – swollen; inflated

undermine – *v.* – weaken; ruin

uniform – *adj.* – consistent; unvaried; unchanging

universal – *adj.* – concerning everyone; existing everywhere

unobtrusive – *adj.* – inconspicuous; reserved

unprecedented – *adj.* – unheard of; exceptional

unpretentious – *adj.* – simple; plain; modest

vacillation – *n.* – fluctuation

valid – *adj.* – acceptable; legal

vehement – *adj.* – intense; excited; enthusiastic

venerate – *v.* – revere

verbose – *adj.* – wordy; talkative

viable – 1. *adj.* – capable of maintaining life; 2. possible; attainable

vigor – *n.* – energy; forcefulness

vilify – *v.* – slander

virtuoso – *n.* – highly skilled artist

virulent – *adj.* – deadly; harmful; malicious

vital – *adj.* – important; spirited

volatile – *adj.* – changeable; undependable

vulnerable – *adj.* – open to attack; unprotected

wane – *v.* – grow gradually smaller

whimsical – *adj.* – fanciful; amusing

wither – *v.* – wilt; shrivel; humiliate; cut down

zealot – *n.* – believer; enthusiast; fan

zenith – *n.* – point directly overhead in the sky

Drill 12: Group 12

DIRECTIONS: Match each word in the left column with the word in the right column that is most *opposite* in meaning.

Word			Match		
1. ____ uniform	6. ____ vigorous	A. amateur	F. support
2. ____ virtuoso	7. ____ volatile	B. trivial	G. constancy
3. ____ vital	8. ____ vacillation	C. visible	H. lethargic
4. ____ wane	9. ____ undermine	D. placid	I. wax
5. ____ unobtrusive	10.____ valid	E. unacceptable	J. varied

DIRECTIONS: Match each word in the left column with the word in the right column that is most *similar* in meaning.

Word			Match	
11.____ wither	14.____ vehement	A. intense	D. possible
12.____ whimsical	15.____ virulent	B. deadly	E. shrivel
13.____ viable		C. amusing	

Additional Vocabulary

The following words comprise additional vocabulary terms which may be found in reading comprehension questions.

abandon – 1. *v.* – to leave behind; 2. *v.* – to give something up; 3. *n.* – freedom; enthusiasm; impetuosity

abase – *v.* – to degrade; humiliate; disgrace

abbreviate – *v.* – to shorten; compress; diminish

aberrant – *adj.* – abnormal

abhor – *v.* – to hate

abominate – *v.* – to loathe; to hate

abridge – 1. *v.* – to shorten; 2. to limit; to take away

absolve – *v.* – to forgive; to acquit

abstinence – *n.* – self-control; abstention; chastity

accede – *v.* – to comply with; to consent to

accomplice – *n.* – co-conspirator; partner; partner-in-crime

accrue – *v.* – collect; build up

acrid – *adj.* – sharp; bitter; foul smelling

adept – *adj.* – skilled; practiced

adverse – *adj.* – negative; hostile; antagonistic; inimical

affable – *adj.* – friendly; amiable; good-natured

aghast – 1. *adj.* – astonished; amazed; 2. horrified; terrified; appalled

alacrity – 1. *n.* – enthusiasm; fervor; 2. liveliness; sprightliness

allocate – *v.* – set aside; designate; assign

allure – 1. *v.* – to attract; entice; 2. *n.* – attraction; temptation; glamour

amiss – 1. *adj.* – wrong; awry; 2. *adv.* – wrongly; mistakenly

analogy – *n.* – similarity; correlation; parallelism; simile; metaphor

anoint – 1. *v.* – to crown; ordain; 2. to smear with oil

anonymous – *adj.* – nameless; unidentified

arduous – *adj.* – difficult; burdensome

awry – 1. *adj., adv.* – crooked(ly); uneven(ly); 2. wrong; askew

baleful – *adj.* – sinister; threatening; evil; deadly

baroque – *adj.* – extravagant; ornate

behoove – *v.* – to be advantageous; to be necessary

berate – *v.* – scold; reprove; reproach; criticize

bereft – *adj.* – hurt by someone's death

biennial – 1. *adj.* – happening every two years; 2. *n.* – a plant which blooms every two years

blatant – 1. *adj.* – obvious; unmistakable; 2. crude; vulgar

bombastic – *adj.* – pompous; wordy; turgid

burly – *adj.* – strong; bulky; stocky

cache – 1. *n.* – stockpile; store; heap; 2. hiding place for goods

calamity – *n.* – disaster

cascade – 1. *n.* – waterfall; 2. *v.* – pour; rush; fall

catalyst – *n.* – anything which creates a situation in which change can occur

chagrin – *n.* – distress; shame

charisma – *n.* – appeal; magnetism; presence

chastise – *v.* – punish; discipline; admonish; rebuke

choleric – *adj.* – cranky; cantankerous

cohesion – *n.* – the act of holding together

colloquial – *adj.* – casual; common; conversational; idiomatic

conglomeration – *n.* – mixture; collection

connoisseur – *n.* – expert; authority (usually refers to a wine or food expert)

consecrate – *v.* – sanctify; make sacred; immortalize

craven – *adj.* – cowardly; fearful

dearth – *n.* – scarcity; shortage

debilitate – *v.* – deprive of strength

deign – *v.* – condescend; stoop

delineate – *v.* – to outline; to describe

demur – 1. *v.* – to object; 2. *n.* – objection; misgiving

derision – *n.* – ridicule; mockery

derogatory – *adj.* – belittling; uncomplimentary

destitute – *adj.* – poor; poverty-stricken

devoid – *adj.* – lacking; empty

dichotomy – *n.* – branching into two parts

disheartened – *adj.* – discouraged; depressed

diverge – *v.* – separate; split

docile – *adj.* – manageable; obedient

duress – *n.* – force; constraint

ebullient – *adj.* – showing excitement

educe – *v.* – draw forth

effervescence – *n.* – bubbliness; enthusiasm; animation

emulate – *v.* – to follow the example of

ennui – *n.* – boredom; apathy

epitome – *n.* – model; typification; representation

errant – *adj.* – wandering

ethnic – *adj.* – native; racial; cultural

evoke – *v.* – call forth; provoke

exotic – *adj.* – unusual; striking

facade – *n.* – front view; false appearance

facsimile – *n.* – copy; reproduction; replica

fathom – *v.* – comprehend; uncover

ferret – *v.* – drive or hunt out of hiding

figment – *n.* – product; creation

finite – *adj.* – measurable; limited; not everlasting

fledgling – *n.* – inexperienced person; beginner

flinch – *v.* – wince; draw back; retreat

fluency – *n.* – smoothness of speech

flux – *n.* – current; continuous change

forbearance – *n.* – patience; self-restraint

foster – *v.* – encourage; nurture; support

frivolity – *n.* – lightness; folly; fun

frugality – *n.* – thrift

garbled – *adj.* – mixed up

generic – *adj.* – common; general; universal

germane – *adj.* – pertinent; related; to the point

gibber – *v.* – speak foolishly

gloat – *v.* – brag; glory over

guile – *n.* – slyness; fraud

haggard – *adj.* – tired looking; fatigued

hiatus – *n.* – interval; break; period of rest

hierarchy – *n.* – body of people, things, or concepts divided into ranks

homage – *n.* – honor; respect

hubris – *n.* – arrogance

ideology – *n.* – set of beliefs; principles

ignoble – *adj.* – shameful; dishonorable

imbue – *v.* – inspire; arouse

impale – *v.* – fix on a stake; stick; pierce

implement – *v.* – begin; enact

impromptu – *adj.* – without preparation

inarticulate – *adj.* – speechless; unable to speak clearly

incessant – *adj.* – uninterrupted

incognito – *adj.* – unidentified; disguised; concealed

indict – *v.* – charge with a crime

inept – *adj.* – incompetent; unskilled

innuendo – *n.* – hint; insinuation

intermittent – *adj.* – periodic; occasional

invoke – *v.* – ask for; call upon

itinerary – *n.* – travel plan; schedule; course

jovial – *adj.* – cheery; jolly; playful

juncture – *n.* – critical point; meeting

juxtapose – *v.* – place side by side

knavery – *n.* – rascality; trickery

knead – *v.* – mix; massage

labyrinth – *n.* – maze

laggard – *n.* – a lazy person; one who lags behind

larceny – *n.* – theft; stealing

lascivious – *adj.* – indecent; immoral

lecherous – *adj.* – impure in thought and act

lethal – *adj.* – deadly

liaison – *n.* – connection; link

limber – *adj.* – flexible; pliant

livid – 1. *adj.* – black-and-blue; discolored; 2. enraged; irate

lucrative – *adj.* – profitable; gainful

lustrous – *adj.* – bright; radiant

malediction – *n.* – curse; evil spell

mandate – *n.* – order; charge

manifest – *adj.* – obvious; clear

mentor – *n.* – teacher

mesmerize – *v.* – hypnotize

metamorphosis – *n.* – change of form

mimicry – *n.* – imitation

molten – *adj.* – melted

motif – *n.* – theme

mundane – *adj.* – ordinary; commonplace

myriad – *adj.* – innumerable; countless

narcissistic – *adj.* – egotistical; self-centered

nautical – *adj.* – of the sea

neophyte – *n.* – beginner; newcomer

nettle – *v.* – annoy; irritate

notorious – *adj.* – infamous; renowned

obdurate – *adj.* – stubborn; inflexible

obligatory – *adj.* – mandatory; necessary

obliterate – *v.* – destroy completely

obsequious – *adj.* – slavishly attentive; servile

obstinate – *adj.* – stubborn

occult – *adj.* – mystical; mysterious

opaque – *adj.* – dull; cloudy; nontransparent

opulence – *n.* – wealth; fortune

ornate – *adj.* – elaborate; lavish; decorated

oust – *v.* – drive out; eject

painstaking – *adj.* – thorough; careful; precise

pallid – *adj.* – sallow; colorless

palpable – *adj.* – tangible; apparent

paradigm – *n.* – model; example

paraphernalia – *n.* – equipment; accessories

parochial – *adj.* – religious; narrow-minded

passive – *adj.* – submissive; unassertive

pedestrian – *adj.* – mediocre; ordinary

pensive – *adj.* – reflective; contemplative

percussion – *n.* – the striking of one object against another

perjury – *n.* – the practice of lying

permeable – *adj.* – porous; allowing to pass through

perpetual – *adj.* – enduring for all time

pertinent – *adj.* – related to the matter at hand

pervade – *v.* – to occupy the whole of

petty – *adj.* – unimportant; of subordinate standing

phlegmatic – *adj.* – without emotion or interest

phobia – *n.* – morbid fear

pittance – *n.* – small allowance

plethora – *n.* – condition of going beyond what is needed; excess; over-abundance

potent – *adj.* – having great power or physical strength

privy – *adj.* – private; confidential

progeny – *n.* – children; offspring

provoke – *v.* – to stir action or feeling; arouse

pungent – *adj.* – sharp; stinging

quaint – *adj.* – old-fashioned; unusual; odd

quandary – *n.* – dilemma

quarantine – *n.* – isolation of a person to prevent spread of disease

quiescent – *adj.* – inactive; at rest

quirk – *n.* – peculiar behavior; startling twist

rabid – *adj.* – furious; with extreme anger

rancid – *adj.* – having a bad odor

rant – *v.* – to speak in a loud, pompous manner; rave

ratify – *v.* – to make valid; confirm

rationalize – *v.* – to offer reasons for; account for

raucous – *adj.* – disagreeable to the sense of hearing; harsh

realm – *n.* – an area; sphere of activity

rebuttal – *n.* – refutation

recession – *n.* – withdrawal; depression

reciprocal – *n.* – mutual; having the same relationship to each other

recluse – *n.* – solitary and shut off from society

refurbish – *v.* – to make new

regal – *adj.* – royal; grand

reiterate – *v.* – repeat; to state again

relinquish – *v.* – to let go; abandon

render – *v.* – deliver; provide; to give up a possession

replica – *n.* – copy; representation

resilient – *adj.* – flexible; capable of withstanding stress

retroaction – *n.* – an action elicited by a stimulus

reverie – *n.* – the condition of being unaware of one's surroundings; trance

rummage – *v.* – search thoroughly

rustic – *adj.* – plain and unsophisticated; homely

saga – *n.* – a legend; story

salient – *adj.* – noticeable; prominent

salvage – *v.* – rescue from loss

sarcasm – *n.* – ironic, bitter humor designed to wound

satire – *n.* – a novel or play that uses humor or irony to expose folly

saunter – *v.* – walk at a leisurely pace; stroll

savor – *v.* – to receive pleasure from; enjoy

seethe – *v.* – to be in a state of emotional turmoil; to become angry

serrated – *adj.* – having a sawtoothed edge

shoddy – *adj.* – of inferior quality; cheap

skulk – *v.* – to move secretly

sojourn – *n.* – temporary stay; visit

solace – *n.* – hope; comfort during a time of grief

soliloquy – *n.* – a talk one has with oneself (esp. on stage)

somber – *adj.* – dark and depressing; gloomy

sordid – *adj.* – filthy; base; vile

sporadic – *adj.* – rarely occurring or appearing; intermittent

stamina – *n.* – endurance

steadfast – *adj.* – loyal

stigma – *n.* – a mark of disgrace

stipend – *n.* – payment for work done

stupor – *n.* – a stunned or bewildered condition

suave – *adj.* – effortlessly gracious

subsidiary – *adj.* – subordinate

succinct – *adj.* – consisting of few words; concise

succumb – *v.* – give in; yield; collapse

sunder – *v.* – break; split in two

suppress – *v.* – to bring to an end; hold back

surmise – *v.* – draw an inference; guess

susceptible – *adj.* – easily imposed; inclined

tacit – *adj.* – not voiced or expressed

tantalize – *v.* – to tempt; to torment

tarry – *v.* – to go or move slowly; delay

taut – *adj.* – stretch tightly

tenacious – *adj.* – persistently holding to something

tepid – *adj.* – lacking warmth, interest, enthusiasm; lukewarm

terse – *adj.* – concise; abrupt

thwart – *v.* – prevent from accomplishing a purpose; frustrate

timorous – *adj.* – fearful

torpid – *adj.* – lacking alertness and activity; lethargic

toxic – *adj.* – poisonous

transpire – *v.* – to take place; come about

traumatic – *adj.* – causing a violent injury

trek – *v.* – to make a journey

tribute – *n.* – expression of admiration

trite – *adj.* – commonplace; overused

truculent – *adj.* – aggressive; eager to fight

turbulence – *n.* – condition of being physically agitated; disturbance

turmoil – *n.* – unrest; agitation

tycoon – *n.* – wealthy leader

tyranny – *n.* – absolute power; autocracy

ubiquitous – *adj.* – ever present in all places; universal

ulterior – *adj.* – buried; concealed

uncanny – *adj.* – of a strange nature; weird

unequivocal – *adj.* – clear; definite

unique – *adj.* – without equal; incomparable

unruly – *adj.* – not submitting to discipline; disobedient

unwonted – *adj.* – not ordinary; unusual

urbane – *adj.* – cultured; suave

usurpation – *n.* – act of taking something for oneself; seizure

usury – *n.* – the act of lending money at illegal rates of interest

utopia – *n.* – imaginary land with perfect social and political systems

vacuous – *adj.* – containing nothing; empty

vagabond – *n.* – wanderer; one without a fixed place

vagrant – 1. *n.* – homeless person; 2. *adj.* – rambling; wandering; transient

valance – *n.* – short drapery hanging over a window frame

valor – *n.* – bravery

vantage – *n.* – position giving an advantage

vaunted – *adj.* – boasted of

velocity – *n.* – speed

vendetta – *n.* – feud

venue – *n.* – location

veracious – *adj.* – conforming to fact; accurate

verbatim – *adj.* – employing the same words as another; literal

versatile – *adj.* – having many uses; multifaceted

vertigo – *n.* – dizziness

vex – *v.* – to trouble the nerves; annoy

vindicate – *v.* – to free from charge; clear

vivacious – *adj.* – animated; gay

vogue – *n.* – modern fashion

voluble – *adj.* – fluent

waft – *v.* – move gently by wind or breeze

waive – *v.* – to give up possession or right

wanton – *adj.* – unruly; excessive

warrant – *v.* – justify; authorize

wheedle – *v.* – try to persuade; coax

whet – *v.* – sharpen

wrath – *n.* – violent or unrestrained anger; fury

wry – *adj.* – mocking; cynical

xenophobia – *n.* – fear of foreigners

yoke – *n.* – harness; collar; bond

yore – *n.* – former period of time

zephyr – *n.* – a gentle wind; breeze

Drill 13: Additional Vocabulary

DIRECTIONS: Each of the following questions provides a given word in capitalized letters followed by five word choices. Choose the word which is *opposite* in meaning to the given word.

1. AUTHENTIC:
   (A) cheap   (B) competitive   (C) false
   (D) biased   (E) irrational

2. MISERLY:
   (A) unhappy   (B) generous   (C) optimistic
   (D) reticent   (E) golden

3. DILIGENT:
   (A) lethargic   (B) morose   (C) silly
   (D) nostalgic   (E) poor

4. PRECLUDE:
   (A) commence   (B) include   (C) produce
   (D) perpetuate (E) enable

5. EXTOL:
   (A) criticize   (B) expedite   (C) pay
   (D) deport   (E) defer

6. DIVERSE:
   (A) solo   (B) furtive   (C) jovial
   (D) wrinkled   (E) similar

7. DISPERSE:
   (A) despair   (B) belittle   (C) renew
   (D) renege   (E) amass

8. ENDURING:

    (A) fallacious   (B) temporal   (C) dismal

    (D) minute   (E) disseminating

9. BREVITY:

    (A) gravity   (B) gluttony   (C) cowardice

    (D) authenticity   (E) verbosity

10. DEMUR:

    (A) assemble   (B) bereave   (C) approve

    (D) add   (E) ascribe

11. UNWONTED:

    (A) perceptive   (B) ordinary   (C) tepid

    (D) desirable   (E) qualified

12. CHASTISE:

    (A) repudiate   (B) immortalize   (C) endorse

    (D) virility   (E) congratulate

13. INFAMOUS:

    (A) revered   (B) resolute   (C) obscure

    (D) contiguous   (E) unknown

14. DISPASSIONATE:

    (A) resigned   (B) profound   (C) fanatical

    (D) torrid   (E) prudent

15. SCANTY:

    (A) redundant   (B) mediocre   (C) calming

    (D) profuse   (E) partisan

16. PROSAIC:

    (A) poetic   (B) unique   (C) rabid

    (D) disdainful   (E) condescending

17. DIDACTIC:

    (A) dubious   (B) dogmatic   (C) punctual

    (D) rhetorical   (E) reverent

18. COLLOQUIAL:

    (A) poetic   (B) separate   (D) formal

    (D) analogical   (E) anonymous

19. COHESIVE:

    (A) adhesive   (B) opposed   (C) smooth

    (D) adverse   (E) fragmented

20. OBLIGATORY:

    (A) promising   (B) permissible   (C) heaven

    (D) optional   (E) responsible

21. OPAQUE:

    (A) permeable   (B) similar   (C) visible

    (D) opulent   (E) translucent

22. SUNDER:

    (A) unite   (B) create noise   (C) oust

    (D) rise above   (E) freeze

23. NARCISSISTIC:

    (A) flowery   (B) detrimental   (C) gentle

    (D) modest   (E) polite

24. FOSTER:

    (A) destroy   (B) relate   (C) parent

    (D) abort   (E) revere

25. LIVID:

    (A) homeless   (B) bright   (C) calm

    (D) elusive   (E) opulent

26. SUPPRESS:

    (A) justify   (B) advocate   (C) free

    (D) level   (E) immunize

27. DESTITUTE:

    (A) organized   (B) ornate   (C) moral

    (D) wealthy   (E) obsequious

28. PAINSTAKING:

    (A) healthful   (B) sordid   (C) careless

    (D) sadistic   (E) lethal

29. PAROCHIAL:

    (A) melancholy   (B) blasphemous   (C) sporting

    (D) irreligious   (E) broad-minded

30. MANDATE:

    (A) emphasis   (B) sophism   (C) pinnacle

    (D) request   (E) meander

31. LUCID:

    (A) obscure   (B) tedious   (C) calm

    (D) frightening   (E) intelligent

32. IGNOBLE:
    - (A) brave
    - (B) honorable
    - (C) royal
    - (D) attentive
    - (E) informal

33. PERTINENT:
    - (A) respectful
    - (B) detailed
    - (C) dreary
    - (D) blatant
    - (E) irrelevant

34. ABSTINENCE:
    - (A) indulgence
    - (B) concurrence
    - (C) hedonism
    - (D) diligence
    - (E) alcoholism

35. FRUGAL:
    - (A) unplanned
    - (B) tempermental
    - (C) regal
    - (D) ethical
    - (E) extravagant

36. FORTUITOUS:
    - (A) lethargic
    - (B) unprotected
    - (C) weak
    - (D) unlucky
    - (E) antagonistic

37. UNEQUIVOCAL:
    - (A) versatile
    - (B) equal
    - (C) noisy
    - (D) unclear
    - (E) truthful

38. CONTEMPT:
    - (A) respect
    - (B) pettiness
    - (C) politeness
    - (D) resistance
    - (E) compliance

39. GRAVITY:
    - (A) antipathy
    - (B) derision
    - (C) buoyancy
    - (D) eloquence
    - (E) effervescence

40. AUSTERE:

    (A) measurable   (B) resilient   (C) ornate

    (D) indirect   (E) destitute

41. PASSIVE:

    (A) thoughtless   (B) supportive   (C) retentive

    (D) contemporary   (E) assertive

42. STAGNANT:

    (A) celibate   (B) active   (C) effluent

    (D) feminine   (E) polluted

43. ADVERSE:

    (A) friendly   (B) quiescent   (C) poetic

    (D) burly   (E) petty

44. CRAVEN:

    (A) difficult   (B) reptilian   (C) pungent

    (D) birdlike   (E) courageous

45. HEED:

    (A) adjust   (B) resist   (C) attend

    (D) encourage   (E) order

46. IMPARTIAL:

    (A) biased   (B) complete   (C) eternal

    (D) articulate   (E) raucous

47. VINDICATE:

    (A) remove   (B) absolve   (C) evoke

    (D) accuse   (E) ferret

48. DERISION:
    (A) elimination   (B) attention   (C) praise
    (D) entrance   (E) recession

49. REPREHENSIBLE:
    (A) released   (B) aghast   (C) awry
    (D) incidental   (E) commendable

50. RELEGATE:
    (A) promote   (B) nullify   (C) include
    (D) obliterate   (E) placate

51. VAIN:
    (A) addicted   (B) modest   (C) unscented
    (D) abasing   (E) choleric

52. LAGGARD:
    (A) haggard   (B) lustrous   (C) haphazard
    (D) advanced   (E) industrious

53. LABYRINTHINE:
    (A) inconsistent   (B) amazing   (C) direct
    (D) incredulous   (E) mythological

54. SLANDER:
    (A) praise   (B) comfort   (C) discipline
    (D) risk   (E) digress

55. PITTANCE:
    (A) mound   (B) plethora   (C) quirk
    (D) grandeur   (E) phlegm

56. SOLACE:

    (A) lunation   (B) turmoil   (C) distress

    (D) valance   (E) spontaneity

57. DEFERENT:

    (A) current   (B) constructive   (C) erratic

    (D) unyielding   (E) applicant

58. FICKLE:

    (A) bland   (B) cascading   (C) caustic

    (D) dubious   (E) faithful

59. EXOTIC:

    (A) ethnic   (B) diverse   (C) realistic

    (D) mundane   (E) enigmatic

60. THWART:

    (A) imprison   (B) mystify   (C) assist

    (D) fluctuate   (E) saturate

KNOWING YOUR WORD PARTS

Memorization and practice are not the only ways to learn the meanings of new words. While taking tests, you will have nothing but your own knowledge and context clues to refer to when you come into contact with unfamiliar words. Even though we have provided you with a comprehensive list of words, there is a very good chance that you will come across words that you still do not know. Therefore, you will need to study our list of prefixes, roots, and suffixes in order to be prepared. Learning the meanings of these prefixes, roots, and suffixes is essential to a strong vocabulary and, therefore, to performing well on the reading comprehension questions.

Prefix

Prefix	Meaning	Example
ab-, a-, abs-	away, from	absent – away, not present abstain – keep from doing, refrain
ad-	to, toward	adjacent – next to address – to direct towards
ante-	before	antecedent – going before in time anterior – occurring before
anti-	against	antidote – remedy to act against an evil antibiotic – substance that fights against bacteria
be-	over, thoroughly	bemoan – to mourn over belabor – to exert much labor upon
bi-	two	bisect – to divide biennial – happening every two years
cata-, cat-, cath-	down	catacombs – underground passageways catalogue – descriptive list
circum-	around	circumscribe – to draw a circle around circumspect – watchful on all sides
com-	with	combine – join together communication – to have dealing with
contra-	against	contrary – opposed contrast – to stand in opposition
de-	down, from	decline – to bend downward decontrol – to release from government control
di-	two	dichotomy – cutting in two diarchy – system of government with two authorities
dis-, di-	apart, away	discern – to distinguish as separate digress – to turn away from the subject of attention

Prefix	Meaning	Example
epi-, ep-, eph-	upon, among	epidemic – happening among many people
		epicycle – circle whose center moves round in the circumference of a greater circle
ex-, e-	from, out	exceed – go beyond the limit
		emit – to send forth
extra-	outside, beyond	extraordinary – beyond or out of the common method
		extrasensory – beyond the senses
hyper-	beyond, over	hyperactive – over the normal activity level
		hypercritic – one who is critical beyond measure
hypo-	beneath, lower	hypodermic – parts beneath the skin
		hypocrisy – to be under a pretense of goodness
in-, il-, im-, ir-	not	inactive – not active
		irreversible – not reversible
in-, il-, im-, ir-	in, on, into	instill – to put in slowly
		impose – to lay on
inter-	among, between	intercom – to exchange conversations between people
		interlude – performance given between parts in a play
intra-	within	intravenous – within a vein
		intramural – within a single college or its students
meta-	beyond, over, along with	metamorphosis – change over in form or nature
		metatarsus – part of foot beyond the flat of the foot
mis-	badly, wrongly	misconstrue – to interpret wrongly
		misappropriate – to use wrongly

Prefix	Meaning	Example
mono-	one	monogamy – to be married to one person at a time monotone – a single, unvaried tone
multi-	many	multiple – of many parts multitude – a great number
non-	no, not	nonsense – lack of sense nonentity – not existing
ob-	against	obscene – offensive to modesty obstruct – to hinder the passage of
para-, par-	beside	parallel – continuously at equal distance apart parenthesis – sentence inserted within a passage
per-	through	persevere – to maintain an effort permeate – to pass through
poly-	many	polygon – a plane figure with many sides or angles polytheism – belief in existence of many gods
post-	after	posterior – coming after postpone – to put off until a future time
pre-	before	premature – ready before the proper time premonition – a previous warning
pro-	in favor of, forward	prolific – bringing forth offspring project – throw or cast forward
re-	back, against	reimburse – pay back retract – to draw back
semi-	half	semicircle – half a circle semiannual – half-yearly
sub-	under	subdue – to bring under one's power submarine – travel under the surface of the sea

Prefix	Meaning	Example
super-	above	supersonic – above the speed of sound superior – higher in place or position
tele-, tel-	across	telecast – transmit across a distance telepathy – communication between mind and mind at a distance
trans-	across	transpose – to change the position of two things transmit – to send from one person to another
ultra-	beyond	ultraviolet – beyond the limit of visibility ultramarine – beyond the sea
un-	not	undeclared – not declared unbelievable – not believable
uni-	one	unity – state of oneness unison – sounding together
with-	away, against	withhold – to hold back withdraw – to take away

Root

Root	Meaning	Example
act, ag	do, act, drive	activate – to make active agile – having quick motion
alt	high	altitude – height alto – highest singing voice
alter, altr	other, change	alternative – choice between two things altruism – living for the good of others
am, ami	love, friend	amiable – worthy of affection amity – friendship
anim	mind, spirit	animated – spirited animosity – violent hatred

Root	Meaning	Example
annu, enni	year	annual – every year centennial – every hundred years
aqua	water	aquarium – tank for water animals and plants aquamarine – semiprecious stone of sea-green color
arch	first, ruler	archenemy – chief enemy archetype – original pattern from which things are copied
aud, audit	hear	audible – capable of being heard audience – assembly of hearers
auto	self	automatic – self-acting autobiography – story about a person who also wrote it
bell	war	belligerent – a party taking part in a war bellicose – war-like
ben, bene	good	benign – kindly disposition beneficial – advantageous
bio	life	biotic – relating to life biology – the science of life
brev	short	abbreviate – make shorter brevity – shortness
cad, cas	fall	cadence – fall in voice casualty – loss caused by death
capit, cap	head	captain – the head or chief decapitate – to cut off the head
cede, ceed, cess	to go, to yield	recede – to move or fall back proceed – to move onward
cent	hundred	century – hundred years centipede – insect with a hundred legs

Root	Meaning	Example
chron	time	chronology – science dealing with historical dates
		chronicle – register of events in order of time
cide, cis	to kill, to cut	homicide – a killing of one human being by another
		incision – a cut
clam, claim	to shout	acclaim – receive with applause
		proclamation – announce publicly
cogn	to know	recognize – to know again
		cognition – awareness
corp	body	incorporate – combine into one body
		corpse – dead body
cred	to trust, to believe	incredible – unbelievable
		credulous – too prone to believe
cur, curr, curs	to run	current – flowing body of air or water
		excursion – short trip
dem	people	democracy – government formed for the people
		epidemic – affecting all people
dic, dict	to say	dictate – to read aloud for another to transcribe
		verdict – decision of a jury
doc, doct	to teach	docile – easily instructed
		indoctrinate – to instruct
domin	to rule	dominate – to rule
		dominion – territory of rule
duc, duct	to lead	conduct – act of guiding
		induce – to overcome by persuasion
eu	well, good	eulogy – speech or writing in praise
		euphony – pleasantness or smoothness of sound

Root	Meaning	Example
fac, fact, fect, fic	to do, to make	factory – location of production fiction – something invented or imagined
fer	to bear, to carry	transfer – to move from one place to another refer – to direct to
fin	end, limit	infinity – unlimited finite – limited in quantity
flect, flex	to bend	flexible – easily bent reflect – to throw back
fort	luck	fortunate – lucky fortuitous – happening by chance
fort	strong	fortify – strengthen fortress – stronghold
frag, fract	break	fragile – easily broken fracture – break
fug	flee	fugitive – fleeing refugee – one who flees to a place of safety
gen	class, race	engender – to breed generic – of a general nature in regard to all members
grad, gress	to go, to step	regress – to go back graduate – to divide into regular steps
gram, graph	writing	telegram – message sent by telegraph autograph – person's handwriting or signature
ject	to throw	projectile – capable of being thrown reject – to throw away
leg	law	legitimate – lawful legal – defined by law

Root	Meaning	Example
leg, lig, lect	to choose, gather, read	illegible – incapable of being read election – the act of choosing
liber	free	liberal – favoring freedom of ideals liberty – freedom from restraint
log	study, speech	archaeology – study of human antiquities prologue – address spoken before a performance
luc, lum	light	translucent – slightly transparent illuminate – to light up
magn	large, great	magnify – to make larger magnificent – great
mal, male	bad, wrong	malfunction – to operate incorrectly malevolent – evil
mar	sea	marine – pertaining to the sea submarine – below the surface of the sea
mater, matr	mother	maternal – motherly matriarchy – government exercised by a mother
mit, miss	to send	transmit – to send from one person or place to another mission – the act of sending
morph	shape	metamorphosis – a changing in shape anthropomorphic – having a human shape
mut	change	mutable – subject to change mutate – to change a vowel
nat	born	innate – inborn native – a person born in a place
neg	deny	negative – expressing denial renege – to deny

Root	Meaning	Example
nom	name	nominate – to put forward a name anonymous – no name given
nov	new	novel – new renovate – to make as good as new
omni	all	omnipotent – all powerful omnipresent – all present
oper	to work	operate – to work on something cooperate – to work with others
pass, path	to feel	pathetic – affecting the tender emotions passionate – moved by strong emotion
pater, patr	father	paternal – fatherly patriarchy – government exercised by a father
ped, pod	foot	pedestrian – one who travels on foot podiatrist – foot doctor
pel, puls	to drive, to push	impel – to drive forward compulsion – irresistible force
phil	love	philharmonic – loving harmony or music philanthropist – one who loves and seeks to do good for others
port	carry	export – to carry out of the country portable – able to be carried
psych	mind	psychology – study of the mind psychiatrist – specialist in mental disorders
quer, ques, quir, quis	to ask	inquiry – to ask about question – that which is asked
rid, ris	to laugh	ridiculous – laughable derision – to mock

Root	Meaning	Example
rupt	to break	interrupt – to break in upon erupt – to break through
sci	to know	science – systematic knowledge of physical or natural phenomena conscious – having inward knowledge
scrib, script	to write	transcribe – to write over again script – text of words
sent, sens	to feel, to think	sentimental – feel great emotion sensitive – easily affected by changes
sequ, secut	to follow	sequence – connected series consecutive – following one another in unbroken order
solv, solu, solut	to loosen	dissolve – to break up absolute – without restraint
spect	to look at	spectator – one who watches inspect – to look at closely
spir	to breathe	inspire – to breathe in respiration – process of breathing
string, strict	to bind	stringent – binding strongly restrict – to restrain within bounds
stru, struct	to build	misconstrue – to interpret wrongly construct – to build
tang, ting, tact, tig	to touch	tangent – touching, but not intersecting contact – touching
ten, tent, tain	to hold	tenure – holding of office contain – to hold
term	to end	terminate – to end terminal – having an end

Root	Meaning	Example
terr	earth	terrain – tract of land
		terrestrial – existing on earth
therm	heat	thermal – pertaining to heat
		thermometer – instrument for measuring temperature
tort, tors	to twist	contortionist – one who twists violently
		torsion – act of turning or twisting
tract	to pull, to draw	attract – draw toward
		distract – to draw away
vac	empty	vacant – empty
		evacuate – to empty out
ven, vent	to come	prevent – to stop from coming
		intervene – to come between
ver	true	verify – to prove to be true
		veracious – truthful
verb	word	verbose – use of excess words
		verbatim – word for word
vid, vis	to see	video – picture phase of television
		vision – act of seeing external objects
vinc, vict, vang	to conquer	invincible – unconquerable
		victory – defeat of enemy
viv, vit	life	vital – necessary to life
		vivacious – lively
voc	to call	provocative – serving to excite or stimulate to action
		vocal – uttered by voice
vol	to wish, to will	involuntary – outside the control of will
		volition – the act of willing or choosing

Suffix

Suffix	Meaning	Example
-able, -ble	capable of	believable – capable of believing legible – capable of being read
-acious, *-icious, -ous*	full of	vivacious – full of life wondrous – full of wonder
-ant, -ent	full of	eloquent – full of eloquence expectant – full of expectation
-ary	connected with	honorary – for the sake of honor disciplinary – enforcing instruction
-ate	to make	ventilate – to make public consecrate – to dedicate
-fy	to make	magnify – to make larger testify – to make witness
-ile	pertaining to, capable of	docile – capable of being managed easily civil – pertaining to a city or state
-ism	belief, ideal	conservationism – ideal of keeping safe sensationalism – matter, language designed to excite
-ist	doer	artist – one who creates art pianist – one who plays the piano
-ose	full of	verbose – full of words grandiose – striking, imposing
-osis	condition	neurosis – nervous condition psychosis – psychological condition
-tude	state	magnitude – state of greatness multitude – state of quantity

VOCABULARY ENHANCER DRILLS

ANSWER KEY

Drill 1 — Group 1

1.	(J)	9.	(F)
2.	(G)	10.	(E)
3.	(A)	11.	(D)
4.	(C)	12.	(C)
5.	(H)	13.	(A)
6.	(B)	14.	(E)
7.	(I)	15.	(B)
8.	(D)		

Drill 2 — Group 2

1.	(D)	9.	(B)
2.	(G)	10.	(H)
3.	(I)	11.	(D)
4.	(F)	12.	(A)
5.	(A)	13.	(B)
6.	(J)	14.	(E)
7.	(E)	15.	(C)
8.	(C)		

Drill 3 — Group 3

1.	(E)	9.	(F)
2.	(H)	10.	(D)
3.	(J)	11.	(C)
4.	(A)	12.	(A)
5.	(I)	13.	(E)
6.	(B)	14.	(D)
7.	(C)	15.	(B)
8.	(G)		

Drill 4 — Group 4

1.	(D)	9.	(H)
2.	(E)	10.	(G)
3.	(A)	11.	(D)
4.	(I)	12.	(A)
5.	(J)	13.	(B)
6.	(B)	14.	(C)
7.	(C)	15.	(E)
8.	(F)		

Drill 5 — Group 5

1.	(H)	9.	(D)
2.	(F)	10.	(G)
3.	(A)	11.	(B)
4.	(B)	12.	(D)
5.	(J)	13.	(A)
6.	(C)	14.	(E)
7.	(I)	15.	(C)
8.	(E)		

Drill 6 — Group 6

1.	(G)	9.	(F)
2.	(A)	10.	(H)
3.	(E)	11.	(D)
4.	(J)	12.	(E)
5.	(C)	13.	(A)
6.	(B)	14.	(C)
7.	(D)	15.	(B)
8.	(I)		

Drill 7 — Group 7

1.	(F)	9.	(D)
2.	(E)	10.	(J)
3.	(A)	11.	(B)
4.	(B)	12.	(E)
5.	(H)	13.	(D)
6.	(I)	14.	(C)
7.	(C)	15.	(A)
8.	(G)		

Drill 8 — Group 8

1.	(D)	9.	(F)
2.	(A)	10.	(J)
3.	(H)	11.	(C)
4.	(G)	12.	(B)
5.	(B)	13.	(A)
6.	(C)	14.	(E)
7.	(E)	15.	(D)
8.	(I)		

Drill 9 — Group 9

1.	(D)	9.	(C)
2.	(I)	10.	(H)
3.	(G)	11.	(A)
4.	(A)	12.	(D)
5.	(J)	13.	(B)
6.	(E)	14.	(E)
7.	(B)	15.	(C)
8.	(F)		

Drill 10 — Group 10

1.	(H)	9.	(D)
2.	(I)	10.	(G)
3.	(E)	11.	(B)
4.	(A)	12.	(D)
5.	(J)	13.	(A)
6.	(B)	14.	(C)
7.	(F)	15.	(E)
8.	(C)		

Drill 11 — Group 11

1.	(F)	9.	(E)
2.	(I)	10.	(G)
3.	(A)	11.	(C)
4.	(H)	12.	(B)
5.	(B)	13.	(E)
6.	(J)	14.	(A)
7.	(C)	15.	(D)
8.	(D)		

Drill 12 — Group 12

1.	(J)	9.	(F)
2.	(A)	10.	(E)
3.	(B)	11.	(E)
4.	(I)	12.	(C)
5.	(C)	13.	(D)
6.	(H)	14.	(A)
7.	(D)	15.	(B)
8.	(G)		

Drill 13 — Additional Vocabulary

1.	(C)	16.	(B)	31.	(A)	46.	(A)
2.	(B)	17.	(B)	32.	(B)	47.	(D)
3.	(A)	18.	(C)	33.	(E)	48.	(C)
4.	(E)	19.	(E)	34.	(A)	49.	(E)
5.	(A)	20.	(D)	35.	(E)	50.	(A)
6.	(E)	21.	(E)	36.	(D)	51.	(B)
7.	(E)	22.	(A)	37.	(D)	52.	(E)
8.	(B)	23.	(D)	38	(A)	53.	(C)
9.	(E)	24.	(A)	39.	(E)	54.	(A)
10.	(C)	25.	(C)	40.	(C)	55.	(B)
11.	(B)	26.	(B)	41.	(E)	56.	(C)
12.	(E)	27.	(D)	42.	(B)	57.	(D)
13.	(A)	28.	(C)	43.	(A)	58.	(E)
14.	(C)	29.	(E)	44.	(E)	59.	(D)
15.	(D)	30.	(D)	45.	(B)	60.	(C)

CHAPTER 3

Basic Reading Comprehension

➤ Diagnostic Test
➤ Basic Reading Comprehension
Review & Drills
➤ Vocabulary List

BASIC READING COMPREHENSION DIAGNOSTIC TEST

1. Ⓐ Ⓑ Ⓒ Ⓓ Ⓔ   26. Ⓐ Ⓑ Ⓒ Ⓓ Ⓔ
2. Ⓐ Ⓑ Ⓒ Ⓓ Ⓔ   27. Ⓐ Ⓑ Ⓒ Ⓓ Ⓔ
3. Ⓐ Ⓑ Ⓒ Ⓓ Ⓔ   28. Ⓐ Ⓑ Ⓒ Ⓓ Ⓔ
4. Ⓐ Ⓑ Ⓒ Ⓓ Ⓔ   29. Ⓐ Ⓑ Ⓒ Ⓓ Ⓔ
5. Ⓐ Ⓑ Ⓒ Ⓓ Ⓔ   30. Ⓐ Ⓑ Ⓒ Ⓓ Ⓔ
6. Ⓐ Ⓑ Ⓒ Ⓓ Ⓔ   31. Ⓐ Ⓑ Ⓒ Ⓓ Ⓔ
7. Ⓐ Ⓑ Ⓒ Ⓓ Ⓔ   32. Ⓐ Ⓑ Ⓒ Ⓓ Ⓔ
8. Ⓐ Ⓑ Ⓒ Ⓓ Ⓔ   33. Ⓐ Ⓑ Ⓒ Ⓓ Ⓔ
9. Ⓐ Ⓑ Ⓒ Ⓓ Ⓔ   34. Ⓐ Ⓑ Ⓒ Ⓓ Ⓔ
10. Ⓐ Ⓑ Ⓒ Ⓓ Ⓔ   35. Ⓐ Ⓑ Ⓒ Ⓓ Ⓔ
11. Ⓐ Ⓑ Ⓒ Ⓓ Ⓔ   36. Ⓐ Ⓑ Ⓒ Ⓓ Ⓔ
12. Ⓐ Ⓑ Ⓒ Ⓓ Ⓔ   37. Ⓐ Ⓑ Ⓒ Ⓓ Ⓔ
13. Ⓐ Ⓑ Ⓒ Ⓓ Ⓔ   38. Ⓐ Ⓑ Ⓒ Ⓓ Ⓔ
14. Ⓐ Ⓑ Ⓒ Ⓓ Ⓔ   39. Ⓐ Ⓑ Ⓒ Ⓓ Ⓔ
15. Ⓐ Ⓑ Ⓒ Ⓓ Ⓔ   40. Ⓐ Ⓑ Ⓒ Ⓓ Ⓔ
16. Ⓐ Ⓑ Ⓒ Ⓓ Ⓔ   41. Ⓐ Ⓑ Ⓒ Ⓓ Ⓔ
17. Ⓐ Ⓑ Ⓒ Ⓓ Ⓔ   42. Ⓐ Ⓑ Ⓒ Ⓓ Ⓔ
18. Ⓐ Ⓑ Ⓒ Ⓓ Ⓔ   43. Ⓐ Ⓑ Ⓒ Ⓓ Ⓔ
19. Ⓐ Ⓑ Ⓒ Ⓓ Ⓔ   44. Ⓐ Ⓑ Ⓒ Ⓓ Ⓔ
20. Ⓐ Ⓑ Ⓒ Ⓓ Ⓔ   45. Ⓐ Ⓑ Ⓒ Ⓓ Ⓔ
21. Ⓐ Ⓑ Ⓒ Ⓓ Ⓔ   46. Ⓐ Ⓑ Ⓒ Ⓓ Ⓔ
22. Ⓐ Ⓑ Ⓒ Ⓓ Ⓔ   47. Ⓐ Ⓑ Ⓒ Ⓓ Ⓔ
23. Ⓐ Ⓑ Ⓒ Ⓓ Ⓔ   48. Ⓐ Ⓑ Ⓒ Ⓓ Ⓔ
24. Ⓐ Ⓑ Ⓒ Ⓓ Ⓔ   49. Ⓐ Ⓑ Ⓒ Ⓓ Ⓔ
25. Ⓐ Ⓑ Ⓒ Ⓓ Ⓔ   50. Ⓐ Ⓑ Ⓒ Ⓓ Ⓔ

BASIC READING COMPREHENSION DIAGNOSTIC TEST

This diagnostic test is designed to help you determine your strengths and your weaknesses in reading comprehension. Follow the directions for each part and check your answers.

These types of questions are found in the following tests: GMAT, GED, TASP, PSAT, SAT, CLEP, PRAXIS Core Battery, ACT, PPST, ASVAB, LSAT, GRE, AP, and CBEST.

---

50 Questions

DIRECTIONS: Each passage is followed by questions based on its content. After reading the passage, choose the best answer to each question. Answer all questions based on what is indicated or implied in that passage.

Questions 1–5 are based on the following passage.

Spa water quality is maintained through a filter to ensure cleanliness and clarity. Wastes such as perspiration, hairspray, and lotions which cannot be removed by the spa filter can be controlled by shock treatment or super chlorination every other week. Although the filter traps most of the solid material to control bacteria and algae and to oxidize any organic material, the addition of disinfectants such as bromine or chlorine is necessary.

As all water solutions have a pH which controls corrosion, proper pH balance is also necessary. A pH measurement determines if the water is acid or alkaline. Based on a 14-point scale, a pH reading of 7.0 is considered neutral while a lower reading is considered acidic, and a higher reading indicates alkalinity or basic. High pH (above 7.6) reduces sanitizer efficiency, clouds water, promotes scale formation on surfaces and equipment, and interferes with filter operation. When pH is high, add a pH decreaser such as sodium bisulphate (e.g., Spa Down). Because the spa water is hot, scale is deposited more rapidly. A weekly dose of a stain and scale fighter also will help to control this problem. Low pH (below 7.2) is equally damaging, causing equipment corrosion, water which is irritating, and rapid sanitizer dissipation. To increase pH add sodium bicarbonate (e.g., Spa Up).

The recommended operating temperature of a spa (98°–104°) is a fertile environment for the growth of bacteria and virus. This growth is prevented when appropriate sanitizer levels are continuously monitored. Bacteria can also be controlled by maintaining a proper bromine level of 3.0 to 5.0 parts per million (ppm) or a chlorine level of 1.0–2.0 ppm. As bromine tablets should not be added directly to the water, a bromine floater will properly dispense the tablets. Should chlorine be the chosen sanitizer, a granular form is recommended, as liquid chlorine or tablets are too harsh for the spa.

1. Although proper chemical and temperature maintenance of spa water is necessary, the most important condition to monitor is

    (A) preventing growth of bacteria and virus.

    (B) preventing equipment corrosion.

    (C) preventing soap build up.

    (D) preventing scale formation.

    (E) preventing cloudy water.

2. Of the chemical and temperature conditions in a spa, the condition most dangerous to one's health is

    (A) spa water temperature above 104°.

    (B) bromine level between 3.0 and 5.0.

    (C) pH level below 7.2.

    (D) spa water temperature between 90° and 104°.

    (E) cloudy and dirty water.

3. The primary purpose of the passage is to

    (A) relate that maintenance of a spa can negate the full enjoyment of the spa experience.

    (B) provide evidence that spas are not a viable alternative to swimming pools.

    (C) convey that the maintenance of a spa is expensive and time consuming.

(D) explain the importance of proper spa maintenance.

(E) detail proper spa maintenance.

4. The spa filter can be relied upon to

(A) control algae and bacteria.

(B) trap most solid material.

(C) oxidize organic material.

(D) assure an adequate level of sanitation.

(E) maintain clear spa water.

5. Which chemical should one avoid when maintaining a spa?

(A) Liquid chlorine   (D) Baking soda

(B) Bromine   (E) All forms of chlorine

(C) Sodium bisulfate

Questions 6–10 refer to the following passage:

The relationship of story elements found in children's generated stories to reading achievement was analyzed. Correlations ranged from .61101 (p=.64) at the beginning of first grade to .83546 (p=.24) at the end of first grade, to .85126 (p=.21) at the end of second grade, and to .82588 (p=.26) for fifth/sixth grades. Overall, the correlation of the story elements to reading achievement appeared to indicate a high positive correlation trend even though it was not statistically significant.

Multiple regression equation analyses dealt with the relative contribution of the story elements to reading achievement. The contribution of certain story elements was substantial. At the beginning of first grade, story conventions added 40 percent to the total variance while the other increments were not significant. At the end of first grade, story plot contributed 44 percent to the total variance, story conventions contributed 20 percent, and story sources contributed 17 percent. At the end of second grade, the story elements contributed more equal percentages to the total partial correlation of .8513. Although none of the percentages were substantial, story plot (.2200), clausal connectors (.1858), and T-units (.1590), contributed the most to the total partial correlation. By the fifth and sixth grades three other story elements—T=units (.2241), story characters (.3214), and clausal connectors (.1212)— contributed most to the total partial correlation. None of these percentages were substantial.

6. Which of the following is the most complete and accurate definition of the term **statistically significant** as used in the passage?

    (A) Consists of important numerical data

    (B) Is educationally significant

    (C) Departs greatly from chance expectations

    (D) Permits prediction of reading achievement by knowing the story elements

    (E) Indicates two measures (reading achievement and story elements) give the same information

7. The passage suggests which of the following conclusions about the correlation of story elements to reading achievement?

    (A) That there are other more important story elements that should also be included in the analyses

    (B) That children's inclusion of story elements in their stories causes them to achieve higher levels in reading

    (C) That these story elements are important variables to consider in reading achievement

    (D) That correlations of more than 1.0 are needed for this study to be statistically significant

    (E) That this correlation was not statistically significant because there was little variance between story elements and reading achievement

8. The relative contribution of story conventions and story plot in first grade suggests that

    (A) children may have spontaneously picked up these story elements as a result of their exposure to stories.

    (B) children have been explicitly taught these story elements.

    (C) these story elements were not important because in fifth/sixth grades other story elements contributed more to the total partial correlation.

    (D) other story elements were more substantial.

    (E) children's use of story conventions and plots were not taken from story models.

9. The content of the passage suggests that the passage would most likely appear in which of the following?

(A) *Psychology Today*

(B) *The Creative Writer*

(C) *Educational Leadership*

(D) *Language Arts*

(E) *Reading Research Quarterly*

10. "None of these percentages were substantial" is the last statement in the passage. It refers to

(A) the story elements for fifth/sixth grades.

(B) the story elements for second grade.

(C) the story elements at the end of first grade.

(D) the story elements at the beginning of first grade.

(E) the story elements for all of the grades, i.e., first grade, second grade, and fifth/sixth grade.

Questions 11–15 refer to the following passage:

Mark Twain has been characterized as "an authentic American author" and as "a representative American author." These descriptions seem to suit the man and his writings. He was born Samuel Clemens in 1835, when Missouri and Louisiana were the only states west of the Mississippi River. His birthplace was less than fifty miles from the river. His father, John Clemens, a lawyer and merchant, was rarely far from financial disaster. When Samuel Clemens was four, the family settled in Hannibal, Missouri, and it was there beside the great river that Samuel lived out the adventurous life he describes in his best-loved novels. Samuel traveled extensively and tasted life as no other author had done. He said of his life, "Now then: as the most valuable capital, or culture, or education usable in the building of novels is personal experience, I ought to be well equipped for that trade." He acquired a wealth of personal experiences for his novels. As a boy of twelve he was apprenticed to the printer of his brother's newspaper in Hannibal. Six years later, in 1853, he set out to see the world as a printer in St. Louis, then in Chicago, Philadelphia, Keokuk, and Cincinnati. In 1857 he impulsively apprenticed himself to Horace Bixby, a riverboat pilot, and traveled all 1,200 miles of the Mississippi River. He said of his years on the river, "I got personally and familiarly acquainted with all the different types of human nature that are to be found in fiction, biography, or history."

The Civil War ended his steamboating and he served briefly in a Confederate militia company. Following his stint in the military, he set out with his brother, Orion, by stagecoach over the Rockies. While in the West he tried prospecting and speculating, but found his true calling in journalism. He was greatly influenced by the literary comedians and local colorists of the period, Bret Harte and Artemus Ward. He became more skillful than his teachers in developing his rich characterizations. In 1865 he attained national fame using his pseudonym, Mark Twain, with his story "The Notorious Jumping Frog of Calaveras County." He also discovered a new vocation as a popular lecturer in San Francisco, keeping his audiences convulsed with tales of his adventures. Full public recognition came with the publishing of *Innocents Abroad* (1869) a wild and rollicking account of his invasion of the Old World, much of which would seem quite languid by today's standards. Some of his finest writings were three works filled with lively adventures on the Mississippi River and based on his boyhood, *Tom Sawyer* (1876), *Old Times on the Mississippi* (1883), and *Huckleberry Finn* (1884). Throughout his career Twain preferred to display his flair for journalistic improvisation rather than maintain the artist's concern for form. In his artfully told stories, Mark Twain conveyed his keen powers of observation and perception, his broad understanding of human nature, and his refreshing sense of humor.

11. The author's main purpose in writing this passage is to

    (A) suggest when Samuel Clemens started writing.

    (B) survey the variety of jobs Clemens held in his life.

    (C) explain Clemens' philosophy of writing.

    (D) argue that Clemens is one of the best American authors.

    (E) discuss some of the major events that shaped Clemens' writing.

12. From the passage, the author's point of view regarding Clemens' writing is

    (A) a literary criticism of his local color style.

    (B) primarily one of extolling his writing.

    (C) a defense of Clemens' journalistic style.

    (D) indifferent to Clemens' writing style.

    (E) a comparison of Clemens to other writers of the period.

13. In the sentence about *Innocents Abroad,* "a wild and rollicking account of his travels through the Old World, much of which would seem quite languid by today's standards," languid probably means which of the following?

    (A) Similar to   (D) Impossible

    (B) Difficult   (E) Expensive

    (C) Tame

14. The passage supports which of the following conclusions about Clemens' career as a writer?

    (A) Clemens acquired great personal wealth from his writing.

    (B) Clemens was a better journalist than novelist.

    (C) Clemens' lectures provided material for his writing.

    (D) Clemens' personal experiences shaped his writing.

    (E) Clemens' professional progress was aided by his associations with Bret Hart and Artemus Ward.

15. According to the passage, which of the following best describes Clemens' appeal to his public?

    (A) His use of the humorous side of human nature

    (B) His descriptions of life on the Mississippi River

    (C) His tales of life in the West

    (D) Seeing him as the typical American writer

    (E) Viewing him as the impulsive world traveler

Questions 16–20 are based on the following passage.

In medieval times, an almanac was a chart showing the movements of the stars over a period of several years. Eventually, almanacs were printed in book form and included information which was especially useful to farmers. In the sixteenth century, almanacs began to be issued every year and included predictions of the weather based on previous weather patterns. At about the same time, almanacs included elaborate calendars that listed church feast days. In the seventeenth century, almanacs included jokes and short accounts of humorous incidents. Benjamin Franklin continued this tradition with *Poor Richard's Almanac,* which was published from 1732–1758. In Germany, almanacs of the eighteenth century included sophisticated, contemporary poetry by serious authors. The almanacs printed in the United States from 1835–1856 were called "Davy Crockett" almanacs because they included many frontier tall tales based mainly on oral tradition.

16. When did almanacs begin predicting the weather?

    (A) Almanacs have always predicted the weather.

    (B) In medieval times

    (C) In the sixteenth century

    (D) In the seventeenth century

    (E) In the eighteenth century

17. What was unique about the "Davy Crockett" almanacs?

    (A) They were printed in Germany but sold in the United States.

    (B) They included tall tales.

    (C) They included stories about Davy Crockett.

    (D) They were printed during the U.S. Civil War.

    (E) They predicted the weather.

18. What was the purpose of the first almanacs?

    (A) To list church holidays   (D) To chart the movement of the stars

    (B) To predict the weather   (E) All of the above.

    (C) To print poetry and humorous stories

19. Which of the following statements best describes the author's attitude toward almanacs?

    (A) Almanacs are an example of popular thinking in the sixteenth century.

    (B) Almanacs are archaic.

    (C) Almanacs made Franklin famous.

    (D) Almanacs are the only reliable source of weather predictions.

    (E) The purpose and content of almanacs has changed over time.

20. Which of the following is NOT included in the passage?

    (A) Some almanacs included serious poetry.

    (B) Jokes were included in some almanacs.

    (C) Davy Crockett wrote almanacs in the 1800s.

    (D) Almanacs include calendars and make weather predictions.

    (E) Much of the information included in almanacs is useful to farmers.

Questions 21–26 are based on the following passage.

Six members of the local university basketball team walked off the court during practice last week. They later said they were protesting unfair treatment by the head coach. The day after walking off the court the players held a meeting with the university president to discuss their complaints. They met with the Director of Athletics two days later and expressed their concerns. They also met with the assistant coach. After refusing to practice for four days, the team apologized to the fans, returned to practice, and promised to play the next scheduled game that season. The players also stated that their opinion of the head coach had not changed, but that they thought the assistant coach was fair.

21. What was the basketball players' complaint?

    (A) Unfair treatment by the coach

    (B) Too many practices

    (C) Practice was too long

    (D) No support from fans

    (E) No support from the university president

22. Which of the following did the players not do?

    (A) Walk away from practice

    (B) Apologize to the fans

    (C) Meet with the Director of Athletics

    (D) Meet with the president of the university

    (E) Agree to play for the team next year

23. Which of the following best describes the author's attitude?

    (A) The author believes the players' actions were humorous.

    (B) The author writes objectively about the players' actions.

    (C) The author condemns the players' actions.

    (D) The author believes the players are behaving childishly.

    (E) The author believes the players have damaged the university's reputation.

24. How long did the players protest?

    (A) One day   (D) Four days

    (B) Two days   (E) Seven days

    (C) Three days

25. Who met with the players to discuss their concerns?

    (A) The head coach   (D) The assistant coach

    (B) The university president   (E) (B), (C), and (D) only

    (C) The athletic director

26. Which of the following best describes the team's protest?

    (A) A racial issue

    (B) Unequal player scholarship

    (C) Unequal privileges for some team members

    (D) A misunderstanding with the Director of Athletics

    (E) A conflict with the head coach

Questions 27–31 are based on the following passage.

The issue of adult literacy has finally received recognition as a major social problem. Unfortunately, the issue is usually presented in the media as a "woman's interest issue." Numerous governor's wives and even Barbara Bush have publicly expressed concern about literacy. As well-meaning as the politicians' wives may be, it is more important that the politicians themselves recognize the seriousness of the problem and support increased funding for literacy programs.

Literacy education programs need to be directed at two different groups of people with very different needs. The first group is composed of people who have very limited reading and writing skills. These people are complete illiterates. A second group is composed of people who can read and write but whose skills are not sufficient to meet their needs. This second group is called functionally illiterate. Successful literacy programs must meet the needs of both groups.

Instructors in literacy programs have three main responsibilities. First, the educational needs of the illiterates and functional illiterates must be met. Second, the instructors must approach the participants in the program with empathy, not sympathy. Third, all participants must experience success in the program and must perceive their efforts as worthwhile.

27. What is the difference between illiteracy and functional illiteracy?

    (A) There is no difference.

    (B) A functional illiterate is enrolled in a literacy education program but an illiterate is not.

    (C) An illiterate cannot read or write, a functional illiterate can read and write but not at a very high skill level.

    (D) There are more illiterates than functional illiterates in the United States today.

    (E) Both (B) and (D).

28. What does "woman's interest issue" mean in the passage?

    (A) The issue is only interesting to women.

    (B) Many politicians' wives have expressed concern over the issue.

    (C) Women illiterates outnumber male illiterates.

    (D) Politicians interested in illiteracy often have their wives give speeches on the topic.

    (E) More women need literacy education programs than men.

29. What is the purpose of the passage?

    (A) To discuss the characteristics of successful literacy programs

    (B) To discuss the manner in which literacy programs are viewed by the media

    (C) To discuss some of the reasons for increased attention to literacy as a social issue

    (D) All of the above

    (E) None of the above

30. According to the passage, which of the following is NOT a characteristic of successful literacy programs?

    (A) Participants should receive free transportation.

    (B) Participants should experience success in the program.

    (C) Instructors must have empathy, not sympathy.

    (D) Programs must meet the educational needs of illiterates.

    (E) Programs must meet the educational needs of functional illiterates.

31. What is the author's opinion of the funding for literacy programs?

    (A) Too much

    (B) Too little

    (C) About right

    (D) Too much for illiterates and not enough for functional illiterates

    (E) Directors of literacy programs should be volunteers

Questions 32–36 are based on the following passage.

The price of cleaning up the environment after oil spills is on the increase. After the massive Alaskan spill that created miles of sludge-covered beach, numerous smaller spills have occurred along the Gulf Coast and off the coast of California. Tides and prevailing winds carried much of this oil to shore in a matter of days. Workers tried to contain the oil with weighted, barrel-shaped plastic tubes stretched along the sand near the water. They hoped to minimize the damage. Generally, the barriers were successful, but there remained many miles of oil-covered sand. Cleanup crews shoveled the oil-covered sand into plastic bags for removal.

Coastal states are responding to the problem in several ways. California is considering the formation of a department of oceans to oversee protection programs and future cleanups. Some states have suggested training the National Guard in cleanup procedures. Other states are calling for the creation of an oil spill trust fund large enough to cover the costs of a major spill. Still other states are demanding federal action and funding. Regardless of the specific programs that may be enacted by the various states or the federal government, continued offshore drilling and the shipping of oil in huge tankers creates a constant threat to the nation's shoreline.

32. According to the passage, where have oil spills occurred?

    (A) U. S. Gulf Coast   (D) (A) and (B) only.

    (B) Alaskan coast   (E) (A), (B), and (C).

    (C) California coast

33. What was the purpose of the barrel-shaped plastic tubes?

    (A) To keep sightseers away from the oil

    (B) To keep oil-soaked animals off the beach

    (C) To force the oil to soak into the sand

    (D) To keep the oil from spreading on the beach

    (E) None of the above.

34. Which of the following solutions is NOT discussed in the passage?

    (A) Create an oil cleanup trust fund.

    (B) Increase federal funding for cleanups.

    (C) Reduce oil production.

    (D) Use the National Guard for cleanups.

    (E) Create a department of oceans.

35. According to the passage, which of the following is the largest oil spill?

    (A) Alaskan coastal spill

    (B) Spill off the California coast

    (C) North Sea oil spill

    (D) Spill off the U. S. Gulf Coast

    (E) Spill in the Red Sea

36. What is the author's opinion of the hazards created by oil spills?

   (A) Oil spills must be expected if the present methods of production and shipment continue.

   (B) Oil spills are the result of untrained crews.

   (C) Oil spills would not be a problem if the government was better prepared to cleanup.

   (D) Oil spills are the responsibility of foreign oil producers.

   (E) Oil spills are the result of the consumers demand for oil.

Questions 37–41 are based on the following passage.

It is estimated that over six million Americans suffer from diabetes. This disease, which often runs in families, is the result of insufficient amounts of insulin made by the body to meet its needs. Insulin is produced by the pancreas and is used by the body to take glucose from the blood for use as fuel. A deficiency results in high blood levels and low tissue levels of glucose.

There are two types of diabetes. The first type appears early in life and is the result of abnormal cells in the pancreas so that little or no insulin is made. This is juvenile diabetes. The standard treatment for juvenile diabetes is insulin replacement therapy. The second type of diabetes occurs later in life, usually during a person's fifties or sixties. In this type of diabetes the pancreatic beta cells are normal and produce normal amounts of insulin. However, for some unexplained reason the tissues in the body have become resistant to the action of insulin. This second type of diabetes is more common in obese people than lean people.

Diet is very important in the treatment of both forms of diabetes. High levels of fat in the blood, which interfere with the absorption of insulin, are often associated with diabetes. A person who has either form of diabetes should reduce the total amount of fat to 20–25 percent of the total calories consumed and increase the amount of carbohydrates to approximately 40 percent. Simple sugars should be kept to 10–15 percent of all calories, and protein should not exceed 24 percent.

37. According to the passage, which of the following is true?

   (A) Only adult diabetics need to be concerned with diet.

   (B) Only juvenile diabetics need to be concerned with diet.

   (C) All diabetics need to be concerned with diet.

(D) All diabetics need to count calories very carefully.

(E) None of the above.

38. Diabetes is the result of what condition?

   (A) Abnormal beta cells in the pancreas which do not produce appropriate amounts of insulin

   (B) Body tissues have become resistant to the action of insulin.

   (C) Obesity

   (D) Age, heredity, and obesity

   (E) Both (A) and (B).

39. According to the passage, which of the following is NOT true?

   (A) Adult onset diabetes is more common in lean people than obese people.

   (B) Approximately six million Americans have diabetes.

   (C) Diabetics should consume no more than 15 percent of all calories in the form of simple sugar.

   (D) Juvenile diabetes is usually treated with insulin replacement therapy.

   (E) The tendency to diabetes often runs in families.

40. Which of the following is NOT common about adult onset diabetes?

   (A) Obesity

   (B) Diabetes in other family members

   (C) Usually begins when a person is 50–60 years old

   (D) Normal pancreatic beta cells

   (E) Decreased blood levels of insulin

41. What is the author's purpose in this passage?

   (A) To warn people of the dangers of too much fat in the diet.

   (B) To warn people of the side effect of obesity.

   (C) To inform the reader of the two types of diabetes.

(D) To suggest an appropriate diet for avoiding diabetes.

(E) To discuss the hereditary nature of diabetes.

Questions 42–46 are based on the following passage.

There's no room on the football field for "dumb jocks." Athletes who cannot consistently maintain a 2.0 grade-point average should not be permitted to participate in any sports. Athletes must realize that the purpose of school is to produce scholars, not professional ball players. If, by chance, an athlete is able to acquire a place in the professional ranks of sports, good! But the primary objective of school is the manufacturing and nurturing of productive citizens who can make worthwhile contributions to society. It is irritating to observe star quarterbacks who can't read, to observe star running backs who can't write, to observe star fullbacks who can't speak, and to observe outstanding pitchers who can't add, subtract, or multiply.

42. What is the tone of the author of this passage?

   (A) The author is indifferent, because he doesn't care whether athletes learn or not.

   (B) The author is dismayed.

   (C) The author is surprised that athletes can play sports with less than a 2.0 grade-point average.

   (D) The author is ashamed that athletes can't maintain a 2.0 grade-point average.

   (E) The author displays no certain mood or attitude.

43. What is the main idea of this passage?

   (A) Athletes who cannot make the grades should not be allowed to participate in any sports.

   (B) The purpose of school is not to produce professional athletes.

   (C) Some athletes can't read.

   (D) Some athletes do not possess the required basic skills.

   (E) The purpose of school is to manufacture productive citizens.

44. According to the author of this passage, which of the following is a fact?

    (A) Star quarterbacks can't read.

    (B) Star running backs can't write.

    (C) Star fullbacks can't speak.

    (D) (A), (B), and (C).

    (E) The purpose of school is to manufacture and nurture productive citizens.

45. Which of the following is the best title for this selection?

    (A) "Dumb Jocks"

    (B) "Athletes Lack Basic Skills"

    (C) "Producing Professional Athletes"

    (D) "Grade Requirements for Athletes"

    (E) "Producing Productive Citizens"

46. To what other school organization(s) might the message conveyed in this passage apply?

    (A) The band   (D) Both (A) and (C).

    (B) The cheerleading squad   (E) Both (A) and (B).

    (C) The science club

Questions 47–50 are based on the following passage.

The ocean is constantly in motion—not just in the waves and tides that characterize its surface but in great currents that swirl between continents, moving (among other things) great quantities of heat from one part of the world to another. Beneath these surface currents are others, deeply hidden, that flow as often as not in an entirely different direction from the surface course.

These enormous "rivers"—quite unconstant, sometimes shifting, often branching and eddying in a manner that defies explanation and prediction—occasionally create disastrous results. One example is El Niño, the periodic catastrophe that plagues the west coast of South America. This coast normally is caressed by the cold, rich Humboldt Current. Usually the Humboldt hugs the shore and extends 200 to 300 miles out to sea. It is rich in life. It fosters the largest commercial fishery in the world and is the home of one of the mightiest game fish on record, the black marlin. The droppings of marine birds that feed from its waters are responsible for the fertilizer (guano) exports that undergird the Chilean, Peruvian, and Ecuadorian economies.

Every few years, however, the Humboldt disappears. It moves out from the shore or simply sinks, and a flow of warm, exhausted surface water known as El Niño takes its place. Simultaneously, torrential rains assault the coast. Fishes and birds die by the millions. Commercial fisheries are closed. The beaches reek with death. El Niño is a stark demonstration of man's dependence on the sea and why he must learn more about it.

There are other motions in the restless sea. The water masses are constantly "turning over" in a cycle that may take hundreds of years, yet is essential to bring oxygen down to the creatures of the deeps, and nutrients (fertilizers) up from the sea floor to the surface. Here the floating phytoplankton (the plants of the sea) build through photosynthesis the organic material that will start the nutrient cycle all over again. Enormous tonnages of these tiny sea plants, rather than being rooted in the soil, are separated from solid earth by up to several vertical miles of saltwater. Sometimes, too, there is a more rapid surge of deep water to the surface, a process known as upwelling.

Internal waves, far below the surface, develop between water masses that have different densities and between which there is relative motion. These waves are much like the wind-driven waves on the surface, though much bigger: Internal waves may have heights of 300 feet or more and be six miles or more in length.

47. The primary purpose of the passage is to

   (A) criticize the general scientific community's lack of interest in oceanography.

   (B) explain the phenomenon known as El Niño.

   (C) describe various kinds of ocean movements.

   (D) call attention to the destructive nature of the ocean.

   (E) prove that subsurface ocean currents exist.

48. The passage contains information that answers which of the following questions?

    I.   How does "turning over" contribute to the nutrient cycle?

    II. Why does the Chilean guano industry suffer from the presence of El Niño?

    III. Why are the movements of under-surface "rivers" unpredictable?

    (A) I only

    (B) I and II only

    (C) I and III only

    (D) II and III only

    (E) I, II, and III

49. Which of the following best describes the organization of this passage?

    (A) Paragraphs two through five describe deep, hidden movements mentioned in paragraph one.

    (B) Paragraphs two and three describe harmful ocean movements, while paragraphs four and five describe beneficial ones.

    (C) Paragraphs two through five describe movements that cannot be seen but whose effects are felt.

    (D) Paragraphs two and three describe great surface currents, while paragraphs four and five describe deep, hidden movements.

    (E) Paragraphs two through five describe various kinds of great surface currents.

50. According to the passage, all of the following result from the presence of the Humboldt Current EXCEPT

    (A) abundant marine bird-life.

    (B) commercial fisheries.

    (C) abundant rainfall.

    (D) fertilizer industries.

    (E) game fish.

BASIC READING COMPREHENSION
DIAGNOSTIC TEST

ANSWER KEY

1.	(A)	14.	(D)	27.	(C)	40.	(E)
2.	(A)	15.	(A)	28.	(B)	41.	(C)
3.	(D)	16.	(C)	29.	(D)	42.	(B)
4.	(B)	17.	(B)	30.	(A)	43.	(A)
5.	(A)	18.	(D)	31.	(B)	44.	(E)
6.	(D)	19.	(E)	32.	(E)	45.	(D)
7.	(C)	20.	(C)	33.	(D)	46.	(E)
8.	(A)	21.	(A)	34.	(C)	47.	(C)
9.	(E)	22.	(E)	35.	(A)	48.	(B)
10.	(A)	23.	(B)	36.	(A)	49.	(D)
11.	(E)	24.	(D)	37.	(C)	50.	(C)
12.	(B)	25.	(E)	38.	(E)		
13.	(C)	26.	(E)	39.	(A)		

DETAILED EXPLANATIONS OF ANSWERS

1. **(A)**   Choices (B), (D), and (E) present minor problems in spa maintenance, whereas choice (C) cannot be prevented. As bacteria and virus are controlled by both temperature and chemicals, it becomes a possible source of health problems if ignored.

2. **(A)**   Choices (B), (C), and (D) are correct levels or degrees. Although choice (E) is important, it is not as dangerous as choice (A) where temperatures in excess of 104° can cause dizziness, nausea, fainting, drowsiness, and reduced awareness.

3. **(D)**   Choices (A), (B), and (C) represent an inference that goes beyond the scope of the passage and would indicate biases of the reader. Although the passage explains spa maintenance, choice (E), the information is not adequate to serve as a detailed guide.

4. **(B)**   The other choices (A), (C), and (D) refer to chemical or temperature maintenance. Although choice (E) helps to ensure clarity, choice (B) is explicitly stated in the passage.

5. **(A)**   Choices (B), (C), and (D) are appropriate chemicals. Although chlorine is an alternative to bromine, this passage indicates it should be granular as indicated in choice (A); liquid and tablet chlorines are too harsh for spas, thus all forms are not acceptable as indicated by choice (E).

6. **(D)**   Choices (A) and (B) appear to be acceptable, whereas choice (E) indicates a perfect correlation. Although choice (C) is a definition of statistical significance, choice (D) is correct as the passage is about correlational statistical significance which permits prediction.

7. **(C)**   Choice (A) goes beyond the information provided in the passage. Choice (B) is incorrect as correlation cannot indicate causality, and choice (E) states incorrectly there was no variance. Choice (D) is not statistically possible. The high positive correlation trend indicates that these variables are important to consider for future research, thus choice (C).

8. **(A)** Choices (B), (C), (D), and (E) represent inferences that are based on inadequate information which go beyond the scope of the passage. As these story elements are not taught explicitly in the first grade or prior to entering school, children apparently have picked up these elements from their exposures to stories as indicated by choice (A).

9. **(E)** Although the content might be appropriate for each of the journals, choices (A), (B), (C), and (D), the style of writing suggests that it would be most appropriate for choice (E), *Reading Research Quarterly,* as this passage reports research results.

10. **(A)** The passage provides information for the grade level and mentions if it was significant or substantial. As this statement follows information provided for fifth/sixth grades, it refers to that level, thus choice (A).

11. **(E)** (E) is the correct answer. The passage mentions a variety of occupations Clemens held and travels he made, which provided the substance of many of his characterizations and settings. (A) is irrelevant to the question and choice (B) is a secondary purpose rather than the primary one because it digresses from the topic of Samuel Clemens' career as a writer. Choice (D) suggests the passage is an argument, which is not in keeping with the whole "discussion" tone, and choice (C) is information not given in the passage.

12. **(B)** This choice is supported in the passage with the statement, "He became more skillful than his teachers in developing his rich characterizations." It is also supported in the last sentence of the passage. Choices (A), a literary criticism, (C), a defense of journalistic style, and (E), a comparison, are not suggested by information in the passage. Choice (D) can be eliminated because it contradicts the positive attitude of the passage towards Clemens' writing.

13. **(C)** When test questions involve the meaning of an unfamiliar word, definitions can frequently be determined from the context (surrounding words). Questions of this type are included to assess how well the reader can extract a word's meaning by looking within the passage for clues. Sometimes the opposite of the meaning is given somewhere in the text. The words "wild and rollicking" are being compared to traveling through Europe by today's standards. Choice (A), similar to today's standards, does not make sense when we compare traveling in the 1800s to today's standards. Choices (B), difficult, and (D), impossible, can be eliminated since they are contradictions; traveling is less difficult today, not

impossible. Although choice (E), expensive, is a possible correct answer, the context of the passage should cause the reader to look for the opposite meaning of "wild and rollicking," which would be "tame."

14. **(D)**   Choices (A), (B), and (C) contain information not given in the passage. These can therefore be eliminated as irrelevant. Choice (E) could be considered as a possible answer because Bret Hart and Artemus Ward were mentioned as having an influence on Clemens' writing style. However, it is important not to read into this that they assisted him professionally in the development of his writing career. The discussion that Clemens was a world traveler and experienced a wide variety of occupations which provided background for his writing supports choice (D).

15. **(A)**   Choices (B) and (C) are possible correct answers because these settings provided the background for some of Clemens' most popular works, but these settings did not necessarily appeal to everyone. Choice (D) is not developed in the text as the reason for Clemens' public appeal. Choice (E) is irrelevant. Clemens' use of humor is discussed in relation to his becoming more skillful than the local colorists who influenced him and also in the last sentence of the passage. Choice (A) is the best answer since the passage ends by discussing Clemens' humor and gives examples throughout, and because his humor offered widespread appeal.

16. **(C)**   Choice (C) is correct. The time period when weather predictions were included in almanacs is specifically stated in the passage. Choice (A) is incorrect because early almanacs were charts of the stars and did not include other information.

17. **(B)**   Choice (B) is correct. The only description of features of the Davy Crockett almanacs is in the last sentence of the passage. Choices (B) and (C) are incorrect because there is no mention in the passage of these almanacs being printed in Germany or being written about Davy Crockett. Since the U. S. Civil War was between 1861–1865 and the almanacs were printed between 1835–1856, choice (D) is incorrect. Choice (E) is probably true, but the question asks for a unique feature.

18. **(D)**   According to this passage the purpose of almanacs has changed over time. However, early almanacs were charts of the movements of stars. Therefore, choice (D) is correct. Choices (A), (B) and (C) state items that were included in later almanacs.

19. **(E)**   The entire passage discusses the changing content of almanacs over time, therefore, choice (E) is the best statement of the author's

attitude. Choice (A) is incorrect because it ignores more recent almanacs. Choice (B) is incorrect because "archaic" means out of date, and this does not agree with the author's position. While the author may agree with choice (C), it does not summarize the author's attitude toward almanacs. Choice (D) is incorrect because the author does not discuss the reliability of almanac weather predictions.

20. **(C)**   This question must be answered using the process of elimination. The information stated in (A), (B), (D), and (E) is specifically included in the passage. The passage does not specify who wrote the Davy Crockett almanacs. Therefore, choice (C) is correct.

21. **(A)**   The second sentence of the passage states that the players were protesting unfair treatment, so choice (A) is correct. There is no information in the passage to support any of the other choices.

22. **(E)**   This is another question that requires the process of elimination. Choices (A), (B), (C), and (D) are included in the passage. The players' plans for next year are not discussed, therefore choice (E) is correct.

23. **(B)**   This question requires you to make a judgment concerning the author's attitude based on the information in the passage. There is no evidence to suggest that the author has a humorous attitude, or that the author condemns the players, or believes that they are behaving childishly. The author may agree that the team has damaged the university's reputation, but this is not evident in the passage. Overall, the author writes objectively about the incident, so choice (B) is correct.

24. **(D)**   This question requires you to do some careful reading because several time periods are included in the passage. However, the passage specifically states that the players returned after four days, so choice (D) is correct.

25. **(E)**   (E) is correct because the passage specifically states that the players met with the university president, the assistant coach, and the athletic director. A meeting with the head coach is not discussed.

26. **(E)**   (E) is the best because the passage states that the team's protest concerned unfair treatment by the coach, but it does not specify the nature of the treatment. There is no evidence of a racial issue, so (A) is incorrect. Scholarships and team privileges are not discussed, so choices (B) and (C) are incorrect. The conflict was not with the athletic director, so (D) is incorrect.

27. **(C)**   (C) is correct because this is the definition of illiterate and functional illiterate stated in paragraph two. (A) cannot be correct because the passage clearly distinguishes a difference between illiterates and functional illiterates. (B) is not correct because the definition stated is not related to participation in a program. The relative number of illiterates and functional illiterates is not discussed, so (D) is incorrect. Since choices (B) and (D) are incorrect, (E) is also wrong.

28. **(B)**   (B) is correct because the passage begins by stating that many politicians' wives have expressed interest in literacy. (A) is incorrect because the author of the passage does not suggest that only women are interested. (C) is incorrect because the passage does not discuss the number of male or female illiterates. (D) is incorrect because there is no discussion in the passage of politicians' wives giving speeches. (E) may be correct but there is no information in the passage to indicate that.

29. **(D)**   This passage has several purposes. First, the author presents some complaints concerning the way literacy issues are presented in the media. The author also discusses the attention given literacy issues by politicians' wives. Third, the author discusses many aspects of successful literacy programs. Therefore, (D), which includes all of these purposes, is correct.

30. **(A)**   This question must be answered using the process of elimination. You are asked to select a statement that names a possible program component which is not characteristic of successful literacy programs. (A) is correct because choices (B), (C), (D) and (E) are specifically mentioned in the passage.

31. **(B)**   (B) is correct because the author specifically states that politicians should support increased funding for literacy programs. (A) and (C) are incorrect because the author states that funding should be increased. There is no discussion of funding for different programs so choice (D) is incorrect. (E) is incorrect because the use of volunteers is not discussed.

32. **(E)**   (E) is correct because the passage specifically mentions the California coast, the Alaskan coast, and the U. S. Gulf Coast as sites of oil spills.

33. **(D)**   (D) is correct because workers were trying to keep the oil in the water and away from the beach. (A) is incorrect because sightseers are not discussed in the passage. The problem of oil-soaked animals is not

mentioned in the passage so choice (B) is incorrect. (C) is incorrect because the cleanup crews wanted to remove the oil, not let it soak into the sand.

34. **(C)**   (C) is correct. This question must be answered using the process of elimination. Cleanup trust funds, increased federal spending, using the National Guard, and creating a department of oceans are all discussed in the passage. Therefore, choices (A), (B), (D) and (E) are incorrect. Only choice (C) names a solution not mentioned in the passage.

35. **(A)**   (A) is correct. The passage describes the Alaskan spill as "massive." The spill off the coast of California and the spill off the U.S. Gulf Coast are described as "smaller." Therefore, choices (B) and (D) are incorrect. Spills in the Red Sea and the North Sea are not discussed in the passage, so (C) and (E) are incorrect.

36. **(A)**   (A) is correct. The last sentence of the passage specifically states that spills are a constant threat if offshore drilling and the shipment of oil in tankers continues. (B) is incorrect because the passage does not discuss crews or training programs. While the passage does imply that the government should be better prepared to clean up, the author does not state that oil spills would cease to be a problem if the government was better prepared. Therefore, (C) is incorrect. (D) is incorrect because foreign oil producers are not mentioned. (E) is incorrect because consumers' demand for oil is not discussed in the passage.

37. **(C)**   (C) is correct because the passage specifically states that a person with "either form of diabetes should reduce the total amount of fat...." (A) and (B) are incorrect because both adult and juvenile diabetics need to be concerned about diet. (D) is incorrect because the passage does not discuss the counting of calories, only that the percentage of various foods should be monitored.

38. **(E)**   This question asks for the cause of diabetes. (A) is the cause of juvenile diabetes. (B) is the cause of adult onset diabetes. (C) is only associated with diabetes but is not the cause. (D) lists three factors which are related to diabetes, but these factors are not the cause. Therefore, choice (E) is correct.

39. **(A)**   This question asks you to determine which statement is false. (A) is correct because adult onset diabetes is more common in obese

people than lean people. (B) is incorrect because it is true that approximately six million Americans have diabetes. (C) is a true statement because diabetics should limit the amount of sugar in the diet to 10–15 percent. (C) is, therefore, incorrect. (D) is incorrect because insulin therapy is the standard treatment for juvenile diabetes. (E) is incorrect because diabetes does run in families.

40. **(E)**   (E) is correct. The question asks which statement is not associated with adult onset diabetes. (A) is incorrect, because obesity is common among adult diabetics. (B) is incorrect because all forms of diabetes tend to run in families. (C) is incorrect because 50–60 years is a common time for the onset of diabetes. (D) is incorrect because it is common that adult onset diabetes is characterized by normal pancreatic beta cells. (E) is correct because blood insulin levels increase in diabetes, not decrease.

41. **(C)**   This question asks you to judge the author's overall purpose. (C) is correct because the author has prepared an informative passage concerning the two types of diabetes. (A) is incorrect because although the author mentions the dangers of too much fat in the diet, that is not the major purpose for writing. (B) is incorrect because the author is not suggesting that diabetes is a side effect of obesity. Instead, the author explains that diabetes is common among obese adults, but there is no cause and effect relationship. (D) is incorrect because changes in the diet cannot prevent diabetes, although diet is important in managing diabetes. Although the author discusses the hereditary nature of diabetes, this is not the primary purpose of the passage. Therefore, (E) is incorrect.

42. **(B)**   This question requires you to identify the tone of the author of this passage. Choice (E) is incorrect because the author does display an explicit mood, "irritating." If the situation is irritating, then it can be assumed that the author is dismayed—choice (B). Choice (A) is incorrect because the author is not indifferent. The author actually takes a stand. The adjectives "surprised" and "ashamed" that are used in choices (C) and (D) do not necessarily translate into dismay. Therefore, these two choices are inappropriate.

43. **(A)**   The main idea of this passage is choice (A)—*Athletes who cannot make the grades should not be allowed to participate.* Choices (B), (C), (D) and (E) are supporting details that are too limited to serve as main ideas. There is no support for either of these as the main idea, and the main idea must be supported.

44. **(E)**   According to the author, it is irritating to observe star quarterbacks who can't read. The author is not saying that star quarterbacks, in general, can't read. This is an example of the problem at hand. The same is true of the other statements: star running backs who can't write; star fullbacks who can't speak; and outstanding pitchers who can't add, subtract, or multiply. These are merely examples of the problem detailed by the author. The main idea (E)—*The purpose of school is to manufacture and nurture productive citizens.*

45. **(D)**   Choices (A), (B), (C) and (E) are all supporting details for the main idea. The central idea or thought of this passage is not about dumb jocks, lack of basic skills among athletes, producing professional athletes, or producing productive citizens. The main idea is choice (D)—*Grade Requirements for Athletes.*

46. **(E)**   The message of grade requirements for participation should also apply to the band and the cheerleading squad. Both of these organizations require large amounts of time for participation. Persons with low grades should use their time to study. The correct answer for this question is choice (E). Belonging to the science club does not usually require lots of time, and a person aligned with such a club just might improve his/her grades and/or interest in science.

47. **(C)**   All of the phenomena discussed in the passage are ocean movements. (B) and (D) are true, but secondary. There is no need to prove something not in dispute (E), nor has there been a lack of interest in the subject matter of the passage (A).

48. **(B)**   Paragraph four explains how turning over contributes to the nutrient cycle and paragraphs two and three provide sufficient information to II. The passage makes clear that under-surface rivers are unpredictable, but does not explain why that is so.

49. **(D)**   The passage describes the various kinds of ocean movements, including surface (paragraphs two and three) and under-surface (paragraphs four and five); hence (A), (C), and (E) are incorrect. (B) is incorrect because some movements described in paragraph two (the Humboldt Current, for example) are beneficial, and the passage does not indicate whether internal waves (paragraph six) are harmful or beneficial.

50. **(C)**   The passage indicates that abundant marine bird-life, commercial fisheries, game fish, and fertilizer industries depend on the Humboldt Current. Abundant rainfall may also, but the passage does not indicate that; rather, it indicates that El Niño brings harmful, torrential rains.

BASIC READING COMPREHENSION REVIEW

This review was developed to prepare you for almost any reading comprehension section in almost any standardized test. You will be guided through a step-by-step approach to attacking reading passages and questions. Also included are tips to help you quickly and accurately answer the questions which will appear in reading comprehension sections. By studying our review, you will greatly increase your chances of achieving a passing score on any reading comprehension test.

Remember, the more you know about the skills tested, the better you will perform on the test. In this section, the skills you will be tested on are

- determining what a word or phrase means;
- determining main ideas;
- recognizing supporting details;
- determining purpose;
- determining point of view;
- organizing ideas in the passage; and
- evaluating the validity of the author's argument.

To help you master these skills, we present examples of the types of questions you will encounter and explanations of how to answer them. A drill section is also provided for further practice. Even if you are sure you will perform well on this section, make sure to complete the drills, as they will help sharpen your skills.

THE PASSAGES

The reading passages in this review are specially designed to be on the level of the types of material that you will encounter in college or high school textbooks. They will present you with very diverse subjects. Although you will not be expected to have prior knowledge of the information presented in the passages, you will be expected to know the fundamental reading comprehension techniques presented in this chapter. Only your ability to read and comprehend material will be tested.

THE QUESTIONS

Each passage will be followed by a number of questions. The questions will ask you to make determinations based on what you have read. You will encounter 10 main types of questions in this test. These questions will ask you to

1. determine which of the given answer choices best expresses the main idea of the passage;

2. determine the author's purpose in writing the passage;

3. determine which fact best supports the writer's main idea;

4. know the difference between fact and opinion in a statement;

5. organize the information in the passage;

6. determine which of the answer choices best summarizes the information presented in the passage;

7. recall information from the passage;

8. analyze cause and effect relationships based on information in the passage;

9. determine the definition of a word as it is used in the passage; and

10. answer a question based on information presented in graphic form.

STRATEGIES FOR THE READING COMPREHENSION QUESTIONS

You should follow this plan of attack when answering reading comprehension questions.

Before the test, this is your plan of attack:

➤ Step 1 | Study our review to build your reading skills.

➤ Step 2 | Make sure to study and learn the directions to save yourself time during the actual test. You should simply skim them when beginning the section. The directions will be similar to the following:

DIRECTIONS: You will encounter eight passages in this section of the test, each followed by a number of questions. Only **ONE**

answer to each question is the **best** answer, although more than one answer may appear to be correct. There are between 40 and 50 multiple-choice questions in this section. Choose your answers carefully and mark them on your answer sheet. Make sure that the space you are marking corresponds to the answer you have chosen.

When reading the passage, this is your plan of attack:

➤ Step 1 | Read quickly while keeping in mind that questions will follow.

➤ Step 2 | Uncover the main idea or theme of the passage. Many times it is contained within the first few lines of the passage.

➤ Step 3 | Uncover the main idea of each paragraph. Usually it is contained in either the first or last sentence of the paragraph.

➤ Step 4 | Skim over the detailed points of the passage while circling key words or phrases. These are words or phrases such as *but, on the other hand, although, however, yet,* and *except.*

When answering the questions, this is your plan of attack:

➤ Step 1 | Attack each question one at a time. Read it carefully.

➤ Step 2 | If the question is asking for a general answer, such as the main idea or the purpose of the passage, answer it immediately.

➤ Step 3 | If the question is asking for an answer that can only be found in a specific place in the passage, save it for last since this type of question requires you to go back to the passage and therefore takes more of your time.

➤ Step 4 | For the detail-oriented questions, try to eliminate or narrow down your choices before looking for the answer in the passage.

> ➤ **Step 5** | Go back into the passage, utilizing the key words you circled, to find the answer.

> ➤ **Step 6** | Any time you cannot find the answer, use the process of elimination to the greatest extent and then guess.

Additional Tips

- Look over all the passages first and then attack the passages that seem easiest and most interesting.

- Identify and underline what sentences are the main ideas of each paragraph.

- When a question asks you to draw inferences, your answer should reflect what is implied in the passage, rather than what is directly stated.

- Use the context of the sentence to find the meaning of an unfamiliar word.

- Identify what sentences are example sentences and label them with an "E." Determine whether or not the writer is using facts or opinions.

- Circle key transitions and identify dominant patterns of organization.

- Make your final response and move on. Don't dawdle or get frustrated by the really troubling passages. If you haven't gotten answers after two attempts, answer as best you can and move on.

- If you have time at the end, go back to the passages that were difficult and review them again.

A FOUR-STEP APPROACH

When you take most reading comprehension tests, you will have two tasks:

1. to read the passage and

2. to answer the questions.

Of the two, carefully reading the passage is the most important; answering the questions is based on an understanding of the passage. Here is a four-step approach to reading:

Step 1: preview,

Step 2: read actively,

Step 3: review the passage, and

Step 4: answer the questions.

You should study the following exercises and use these four steps when you complete any reading comprehension test.

STEP 1: Preview

A preview of the reading passage will give you a purpose and a reason for reading; previewing is a good strategy to use in test-taking. Before beginning to read the passage (usually a four-minute activity if you preview and review), you should take about 30 seconds to look over the passage and questions. An effective way to preview the passage is to read quickly the first sentence of each paragraph, the concluding sentence of the passage, and the questions—not all the answers—following the passage. A passage is given below. Practice previewing the passage by reading the first sentence of each paragraph and the last line of the passage.

Passage

That the area of obscenity and pornography is a difficult one for the Supreme Court is well documented. The Court's numerous attempts to define obscenity have proven unworkable and left the decision to the subjective preferences of the justices. Perhaps Justice Stewart put it best when, after refusing to define obscenity, he declared, "But I know it when I see it." Does the Court literally have to see it to know it? Specifically, what role does the fact-pattern, including the materials' medium, play in the Court's decision?

Several recent studies employ fact-pattern analysis in modeling the Court's decision making. These studies examine the fact-pattern or case characteristics, often with ideological and attitudinal factors, as a determinant of the decision reached by the Court. In broad terms, these studies owe their theoretical underpinnings to attitude theory. As the name suggests, attitude theory views the Court's attitudes as an explanation of its decisions.

These attitudes, however, do not operate in a vacuum. As Spaeth explains, "the activation of an attitude involves both an object and the situation in which that object is encountered." The objects to which the court directs its attitudes are litigants. The situation — the subject matter of the case — can be defined in broad or narrow terms. One may define the situation as an entire area of the law (e.g., civil liberties issues). On an even broader scale the situation may be defined as the decision to grant certiorari or whether to defect from a minimum-winning coalition.

Defining the situation with such broad strokes, however, does not allow one to control for case content. In many specific issue areas, the cases present strikingly similar patterns. In examining the Court's search and seizure decisions, Segal found a relatively small number of situational and case characteristic variables explain a high proportion of the Court's decisions.

Despite Segal's success, efforts to verify the applicability of fact-pattern analysis in other issue areas and using broad-based factors have been slow in forthcoming. Renewed interest in obscenity and pornography by federal and state governments, the academic community, and numerous antipornography interest groups indicates the Court's decisions in this area deserve closer examination.

The Court's obscenity and pornography decisions also present an opportunity to study the Court's behavior in an area where the Court has granted significant decision-making authority to the states. In *Miller vs. California* (1973) the Court announced the importance of local community standards in obscenity determinations. The Court's subsequent behavior may suggest how the Court will react in other areas whether it has chosen to defer to the states (e.g., abortion).

Drill 1: Step 1: Preview

DIRECTIONS: Answer the following questions based on the previous passage.

1. The main idea of the passage is best stated in which of the following?

    (A) The Supreme Court has difficulty convicting those who violate obscenity laws.

    (B) The current definitions for obscenity and pornography provided by the Supreme Court are unworkable.

    (C) Fact-pattern analysis is insufficient for determining the attitude of the Court toward the issues of obscenity and pornography.

    (D) Despite the difficulties presented by fact-pattern analysis, Justice Segal found the solution in the patterns of search and seizure decisions.

2. The main purpose of the writer in this passage is to

   (A) convince the reader that the Supreme Court is making decisions about obscenity based on their subjective views only.

   (B) explain to the reader how fact-pattern analysis works with respect to cases of obscenity and pornography.

   (C) define obscenity and pornography for the layperson.

   (D) demonstrate the role fact-pattern analysis plays in determining the Supreme Court's attitude about cases in obscenity and pornography.

3. Of the following, which fact best supports the writer's contention that the Court's decisions in the areas of obscenity and pornography deserve closer scrutiny?

   (A) The fact that a Supreme Court Justice said, "I know it when I see it."

   (B) Recent studies that employ fact-pattern analysis in modeling the Court's decision-making process.

   (C) The fact that attitudes do not operate in a vacuum.

   (D) The fact that federal and state governments, interest groups, and the academic community show renewed interest in the obscenity and pornography decisions by the Supreme Court.

4. Among the following statements, which states an opinion expressed by the writer rather than a fact?

   (A) That the area of obscenity and pornography is a difficult one for the Supreme Court is well documented.

   (B) The objects to which a court directs its attitudes are the litigants.

   (C) In many specific issue areas, the cases present strikingly similar patterns.

   (D) The Court's subsequent behavior may suggest how the Court will react in other legal areas.

5. The list of topics below that best reflects the organization of the topics of the passage is

   (A) I. The difficulties of the Supreme Court

       II. Several recent studies

  III. Spaeth's definition of "attitude"

  IV. The similar patterns of cases

  V. Other issue areas

  VI. The case of *Miller vs. California*

(B) I. The Supreme Court, obscenity, and fact-pattern analysis

  II. Fact-pattern analysis and attitude theory

  III. The definition of "attitude" for the Court

  IV. The definition of "situation"

  V. The breakdown in fact-pattern analysis

  VI. Studying Court behavior

(C) I. Justice Stewart's view of pornography

  II. Theoretical underpinnings

  III. A minimum-winning coalition

  IV. Search and seizure decisions

  V. Renewed interest in obscenity and pornography

  VI. The importance of local community standards

(D) I. The Court's numerous attempts to define obscenity

  II. Case characteristics

  III. The subject matter of cases

  IV. The Court's proportion of decisions

  V. Broad-based factors

  VI. Obscenity determination

6. Which paragraph below is the best summary of the passage?

(A) The Supreme Court's decision-making process with respect to obscenity and pornography has become too subjective. Fact-pattern analyses, used to determine the overall attitude of the Court, reveal only broad-based attitudes on the part of the Court toward the situations of obscenity cases. But these patterns cannot fully account for the Court's attitudes toward case content. Research is not conclusive that fact-pattern analyses work when applied to legal areas. Renewed public and local interest suggests continued study and close examination of how the Court makes decisions. Delegating authority to the states may reflect patterns for Court decisions in other socially sensitive areas.

(B) Though subjective, the Supreme Court decisions are well documented. Fact-pattern analyses reveal the attitude of the Supreme Court toward its decisions in cases. Spaeth explains that an attitude involves both an object and a situation. For the Court, the situation may be defined as the decision to grant certiorari. Cases present strikingly similar patterns, and a small number of variables explain a high proportion of the Court's decisions. Segal has made an effort to verify the applicability of fact-pattern analysis with some success. The Court's decisions on obscenity and pornography suggest weak Court behavior, such as in *Miller vs. California*.

(C) To determine what obscenity and pornography mean to the Supreme Court, we must use fact-pattern analysis. Fact-pattern analysis reveals the ideas that the Court uses to operate in a vacuum. The litigants and the subject matter of cases are defined in broad terms (such as an entire area of law) to reveal the Court's decision-making process. Search and seizure cases reveal strikingly similar patterns, leaving the Court open to grant certiorari effectively. Renewed public interest in the Court's decisions proves how the Court will react in the future.

(D) Supreme Court decisions about pornography and obscenity are under examination and are out of control. The Court has to see the case to know it. Fact-pattern analyses reveal that the Court can only define cases in narrow terms, thus revealing individual egotism on the part of the Justices. As a result of strikingly similar patterns in search and seizure cases, the Court should be studied further for its weakness in delegating authority to state courts, as in the case of *Miller vs. California*.

7. Based on the passage, the rationale for fact-pattern analyses arises out of what theoretical groundwork?

    (A) Subjectivity theory

    (B) The study of cultural norms

    (C) Attitude theory

    (D) Cybernetics

8. Based on data in the passage, what would most likely be the major cause for the difficulty in pinning down the Supreme Court's attitude toward cases of obscenity and pornography?

   (A) The personal opinions of the Court Justices

   (B) The broad nature of the situations of the cases

   (C) The ineffective logistics of certiorari

   (D) The inability of the Court to resolve the variables presented by individual case content

9. In the context of the passage, *subjective* might be most nearly defined as

   (A) personal.

   (B) wrong.

   (C) focussed.

   (D) objective.

By previewing the passage, you should have read the following:

- That the area of obscenity and pornography is a difficult one for the Supreme Court is well documented.

- Several recent studies employ fact-pattern analysis in modeling the Court's decision making.

- These attitudes, however, do not operate in a vacuum.

- Defining the situation with such broad strokes, however, does not allow one to control for case content.

- Despite Segal's success, efforts to verify the applicability of fact-pattern analysis in other issue areas and using broad-based factors have been slow in forthcoming.

- The Court's obscenity and pornography decisions also present an opportunity to study the Court's behavior in an area where the Court has granted significant decision-making authority to the states.

- The Court's subsequent behavior may suggest how the Court will react in other areas where it has chosen to defer to the states (e.g., abortion).

These few sentences tell you much about the entire passage.

As you begin to examine the passage, you should first determine the main idea of the passage and underline it, so that you can easily refer back to it if a question requires you to do so (see question 1). The main idea should be found in the first paragraph of the passage, and may even be the first sentence. From what you have read thus far, you now know that the main idea of this passage is that: the Supreme Court has difficulty in making obscenity and pornography decisions.

In addition, you also know that recent studies have used fact-pattern analysis in modeling the Court's decision. You have learned also that attitudes do not operate independently and that case content is important. The feasibility of using fact-pattern analysis in other areas and broad-based factors have not been quickly verified. To study the behavior of the Court in an area in which they have granted significant decision-making authority to the states, one has only to consider the obscenity and pornography decisions. In summary, the author suggests that the Court's subsequent behavior may suggest how the Court will react in those other areas in which decision-making authority has previously been granted to the states. As you can see, having this information will make the reading of the passage much easier.

You should have looked at the stem of questions, or the part of the question that asks you to answer a question. You do not necessarily need to spend a lot of time reading the answers to each question in your preview. The stem of the question is the most important part to guide you as you read the passage.

The stems of the questions for Passage 1 are:

1. The main idea of the passage is best stated in which of the following?

2. The main purpose of the writer in this passage is to

3. Of the following, which fact best supports the writer's contention that the Court's decisions in the areas of obscenity and pornography deserve closer scrutiny?

4. Among the following statements, which states an opinion expressed by the writer rather than a fact?

5. The list of topics below that best reflects the organization of the topics of the passage is

6. Which paragraph below is the best summary of the passage?

7. Based on the passage, the rationale for fact-pattern analyses arises out of what theoretical groundwork?

8. Based on data in the passage, what would most likely be the major cause for the difficulty in pinning down the Supreme Court's attitude toward cases of obscenity and pornography?

9. In the context of the passage, *subjective* might be most nearly defined as

STEP 2: Read Actively

After you preview, you are now ready ro read actively. This means that as you read, you will be thinking as you note important words, topic sentences, main ideas, and words denoting tone of the passage. If you think underlining can help you save time and help you remember the main ideas, feel free to use your pencil.

Read carefully the first sentence of each paragraph since this often contains the topic of the paragraph. You may wish to underline each topic sentence.

During this stage, you should also determine the writer's purpose in writing the passage (see question 2), as this will help you focus on the main points and the writer's key points in the organization of a passage. You can determine the author's purpose by asking yourself, "Does *the relationship* between the writer's main idea plus evidence the writer uses answer one of four questions?":

- What is the writer's overall primary goal or objective?

- Is the writer trying primarily to persuade you by proving or using facts to make a case for an idea? (P)

- Is the writer trying only primarily to inform and enlighten you about an idea, object, or event? (I)

- Is the writer attempting primarily to amuse you? Keep you fascinated? Laughing? (A)

Read these examples and see if you can decide what the primary purpose of the following statements might be.

(A) Jogging too late in life can cause more health problems than it solves. I will allow that the benefits of jogging are many: lowered blood pressure, increased vitality, better cardiovascular health, and better muscle tone. However, an older person may have a history of injury or chronic ailments that makes jogging counterproductive. For example, the elderly jogger may have hardening of the arteries, emphysema, or undiscovered aneurysms just waiting to burst and cause stroke or death. Chronic arthritis in the joints will only be aggravated by persistent irritation and use. Moreover, for those of us with injuries sustained in our youth—such as torn Achilles' tendons or torn knee cartilage—jogging might just make a painful life more painful, cancelling out the benefits the exercise is intended to produce.

(B) Jogging is a sporting activity that exercises all the main muscle groups of the body. That the arms, legs, buttock, and torso voluntary muscles are engaged goes without question. Running down a path makes you move your upper body as well as your lower body muscles. People do not often take into account, however, how the involuntary muscle system is also put through its paces. The heart, diaphragm, even the eye and face muscles, take part as we hurl our bodies through space at speeds up to five miles per hour over distances as long as twenty-six miles.

(C) It seems to me that jogging styles are as identifying as fingerprints! People seem to be as individual in the way they run as they are in personality. Here comes the Duck, waddling down the track, little wings going twice as fast as the feet in an effort to stay upright. At about the quarter mile mark, I see the Penguin, quite natty in the latest jogging suit, body stiff as a board from neck to ankles and the ankles flexing a mile a minute to cover the yards. And down there at the half-mile post — there comes the Giraffe — a tall fellow in a spotted electric yellow outfit, whose long strides cover about a dozen yards each, and whose neck waves around under some old army camouflage hat that probably served its time in a surplus store in the Bronx rather than in Desert Storm. Once you see the animals in the jogger woods once, you can identify them from miles away just by seeing their gait. And by the way, be careful whose hoof you're stepping on, it may be mine!

In (A) the writer makes a statement that a number of people would debate and which isn't clearly demonstrated in science or common knowledge. In fact, common wisdom usually maintains the opposite thesis. Many would say that jogging improves the health of the aging — even slows down the aging process. As soon as you see a writer point to or identify *an issue open to debate* and standing in need of proof, s/he is setting out to persuade you of one side or the other. You'll notice, too, that the writer in this case takes a stand, here. It's almost as if s/he is saying, "I have concluded that . . ." But a thesis or arguable idea is only a *hypothesis* until evidence is summoned by the writer to prove it. Effective arguments are based on serious, factual, or demonstrable evidence, not opinion.

In (B) the writer is just stating a fact. This is not a matter for debate. From here, the writer's evidence is to *explain* and *describe* what is meant by the fact. S/he proceeds to *analyze* (break down into its elements) the way the different muscle groups come into play or do work when jogging, thus explaining the fact stated as a main point in the opening sentence. That jogging exercises all the muscle groups is not in question or a matter of debate. Besides taking the form of explaining how something works, what parts it is made of (for example, the basic parts of a bicycle are...), writers may show how the idea, object, or event functions. A writer may use this information to prove something. But if s/he doesn't argue to prove a debatable point, then the purpose must be either to inform (as here) or to entertain.

In (C) the writer is taking a stand, but s/he is not attempting to prove anything, merely pointing to a lighthearted observation. Moreover, all of the examples s/he uses to support the statement are either fanciful, funny, odd, or peculiar to the writer's particular vision. Joggers aren't really animals, after all.

Make sure to examine all of the facts that the author uses to support his/her main idea. This will allow you to decide whether or not the writer has made a case, and what sort of purpose s/he supports. Look for supporting details — facts, examples, illustrations, the testimony or research of experts, that are about the topic in question and *show* what the writer *says* is so. In fact, paragraphs and theses consist of *show* and *tell*. The writer *tells* you something is so or not so and then *shows* you facts, illustrations, expert testimony, or experience to back up what s/he says is or is not so. As you determine where the author's supporting details are, you may want to label them with an "S" so that you can refer back to them easily when answering questions (see question 3).

It is also important for you to be able to recognize the difference between the statements of fact presented and statements of the author's opinion. You will be tested on this skill in this section of the test (see question 4). Let's look at the following examples. In each case ask yourself if you are reading a fact or an opinion.

1. Some roses are red.

2. Roses are the most beautiful flower on earth.

3. After humans smell roses, they fall in love.

4. Roses are the worst plants to grow in your backyard.

Number 1 is a fact. All you have to do is go look at the evidence. Go to a florist. You will see that number 1 is true. A fact is anything which can be demonstrated to be true in reality or which has been demonstrated to be true in reality and is documented by others. For example, the moon is in orbit about 250,000 miles from the earth.

Number 2 is an opinion. The writer claims this as truth, but since it is an abstract quality (beauty), it remains to be seen. Others will hold different opinions. This is a matter of taste, not fact.

Number 3 is an opinion. There is probably some time-related coincidence between these two, but there is no verifiable or repeatable and observable evidence that this is always true—at least not the way it is true that if you throw a ball into the air, it will always come back down to earth if left on its own without interference. Opinions have a way of sounding absolute, are held by the writer with confidence, but are not backed up by factual evidence.

Number 4, though perhaps sometimes true, is a matter of opinion. Many variables contribute to the health of a plant in a garden: soil, temperature range, amount of moisture, number, and kinds of bugs. This is a debatable point that the writer would have to prove.

As you read, you should note the structure of the passage. There are several common structures for the passages. Some of these structures are described below.

Main Types of Paragraph Structures

1. The structure is a main idea plus supporting arguments.
2. The structure is a main idea plus examples.
3. The structure includes comparisons or contrasts.
4. There is a pro and a con structure.
5. The structure is chronological.
6. The structure has several different aspects of one idea. For example, a passage on education in the United States in the 1600s and 1700s might first define education, then describe colonial education, then give information about separation of church and state, and then outline the tax opposition and support arguments. Being able to recognize these structures will help you recognize how the author has organized the passage.

Examining the structure of the passage will help you answer questions that ask you to organize (see question 5) the information in the passage, or to summarize (see question 6) the information presented in that passage.

For example, if you see a writer using a transitional pattern that reflects a sequence moving forward in time, such as "In 1982 . . . Then, in the next five years . . . A decade later, in 1997, the xxxx will . . ." chances are the writer is telling a story, history, or the like. Writers often use transitions of classification to analyze an idea, object, or event. They may say something like, "The first part . . . Secondly . . . Thirdly . . . Finally." You may then ask yourself what is this analysis for? To explain or to persuade me of something? These transitional patterns may also help reveal the relationship of one part of a passage to another. For example, a writer may be writing "on the one hand, . . . on the other hand . . ." This should alert you to the fact that the writer is comparing two things or contrasting them. What for? Is one better than the other? Worse?

By understanding the *relationship* among the main point, transitions, and supporting information, you may more readily determine the pattern of organization as well as the writer's purpose in a given piece of writing.

As with the paragraph examples above showing the difference among possible purposes, you must look at the relationship between the facts or information presented (that's the show part) and what the writer is trying to point out to you (that's the tell part) with that data. For example, in the data given in number 6 above, the discussion presented about education in the 1600s might be used

- to prove that it was a failure (a form of argument),

- that it consisted of these elements (an analysis of the status of education during that time), or

- that education during that time was silly.

To understand the author's purpose, the main point and the evidence that supports it must be considered together to be understood. In number 6, no statement appears which controls these disparate areas of information. To be meaningful, a controlling main point is needed. You need to know that that main point is missing. You need to be able to distinguish between the writer showing data and the writer telling or making a point.

In the two paragraphs below, consider the different relationship between the same data above and the controlling statement, and how that controlling statement changes the discussion from explanation to argument:

(A) Colonial education was different than today's and consisted of several elements. Education in those days meant primarily studying the three "r's" (reading, 'riting, and 'rithmetic) and the Bible. The church and state were more closely aligned with one another — education was, after all, for the purpose of serving God better, not to make more money.

(B) Colonial "education" was really just a way to create a captive audience for the Church. Education in those days meant studying the three "r's" in order to learn God's word — the Bible — not commerce. The Church and state were closely aligned with one another, and what was good for the Church was good for the state — or else you were excommunicated, which kept you out of Heaven for sure.

The same information areas are brought up in both cases, but in (A) the writer treats it analytically (. . ."consisted of several elements" . . .), not taking any real debatable stand on the issue. What is, is. However, the controlling statement in (B) puts forth a volatile hypothesis, and then uses the same information to support that hypothesis.

STEP 3: Review the Passage

After you finish reading actively, take 10 or 20 seconds to look over the main idea and the topic sentences that you have underlined, and the key words and phrases you have marked. Now you are ready to enter Step 4 and answer the questions.

STEP 4: Answer the Questions

In Step 2, Read Actively, you gathered enough information from the passage to answer questions dealing with main idea, purpose, support, fact vs. opinion, organization, and summarization. Let's look again at these questions.

Main Idea Questions

Looking back at the questions which follow the passage, you see that question 1 is a "main idea" question:

1. The main idea of the passage is best stated in which of the following?

    (A) The Supreme Court has difficulty convicting those who violate obscenity laws.

    (B) The current definitions for obscenity and pornography provided by the Supreme Court are unworkable.

(C) Fact-pattern analysis is insufficient for determining the attitude of the Court toward the issues of obscenity and pornography.

(D) Despite the difficulties presented by fact-pattern analysis, Justice Segal found the solution in the patterns of search and seizure decisions.

In answering the question, you see that choice (C) is correct. The writer uses the second, third, fourth, and fifth paragraphs to show how fact-pattern analysis is an ineffective determinant of Court attitude toward obscenity and pornography.

(A) is incorrect. Nothing is ever said directly about "convicting" persons accused of obscenity, only that the Court has difficulty defining it.

(B) is also incorrect. Though it is stated as a fact by the writer, it is only used as an effect that leads the writer to examine how fact-pattern analysis does or does not work to reveal the "cause" or attitude of the Court toward obscenity and pornography.

Finally, choice (D) is incorrect. The statement is contrary to what Segal found when he examined search and seizure cases.

Purpose Questions

In examining question 2, you see that you must determine the author's purpose in writing the passage:

2. The main purpose of the writer in this passage is to

(A) convince the reader that the Supreme Court is making decisions about obscenity based on their subjective views only.

(B) explain to the reader how fact-pattern analysis works with respect to cases of obscenity and pornography.

(C) define obscenity and pornography for the layperson.

(D) demonstrate the role fact-pattern analysis plays in determining the Supreme Court's attitude about cases in obscenity and pornography.

Looking at the answer choices, you see that choice (D) is correct. Though the writer never states it directly, s/he summons data consistently to show that fact-pattern analysis only gives us part of the picture, or "broad strokes" about the Court's attitude, but cannot account for the attitude toward individual cases.

Choice (A) is incorrect. The writer doesn't try to convince us of this fact, but merely states it as an opinion resulting from the evidence derived from the "well-documented" background to the problem.

(B) is also incorrect. The writer does more than just explain the role of fact-pattern analysis, but rather shows how it cannot fully apply.

The passage is about the Court's difficulty in defining these terms, not the man or woman in the street. Nowhere do definitions for these terms appear. Therefore, choice (C) is incorrect.

Support Questions

Question 3 requires you to analyze the author's supporting details:

3.   Of the following, which fact best supports the writer's contention that the Court's decisions in the areas of obscenity and pornography deserve closer scrutiny?

   (A) The fact that a Supreme Court Justice said, "I know it when I see it."

   (B) Recent studies that employ fact-pattern analysis in modeling the Court's decision-making process.

   (C) The fact that attitudes do not operate in a vacuum.

   (D) The fact that federal and state governments, interest groups, and the academic community show renewed interest in the obscenity and pornography decisions by the Supreme Court.

To answer this question, let's look at the answer choices. Choice (D) must be correct. In the fifth paragraph, the writer states that the "renewed interest" — a real and observable fact — from these groups "indicates the Court's decisions . . . deserve closer examination," another way of saying scrutiny.

(A) is incorrect. The writer uses this remark to show how the Court cannot effectively define obscenity and pornography, relying on "subjective preferences" to resolve issues.

In addition, choice (B) is incorrect because the writer points to the data in (D), not fact-pattern analyses, to prove this.

(C), too, is incorrect. Although it is true, the writer makes this point to show how fact-pattern analysis doesn't help clear up the real-world "situation" in which the Court must make its decisions.

Fact vs. Opinion Questions

By examining question 4, you can see that you are required to know the difference between fact and opinion:

4. Among the following statements, which states an opinion expressed by the writer rather than a fact?

   (A) That the area of obscenity and pornography is a difficult one for the Supreme Court is well documented.

   (B) The objects to which a court directs its attitudes are the litigants.

   (C) In many specific issue areas, the cases present strikingly similar patterns.

   (D) The Court's subsequent behavior may suggest how the Court will react in other legal areas.

Keeping in mind that an opinion is something that cannot be proven to hold true in all circumstances, you can determine that choice (D) is correct. It is the only statement among the four for which the evidence is yet to be gathered. It is the writer's opinion that this may be a way to predict the Court's attitudes.

(A), (B), and (C) are all taken from data or documentation in existence already in the world, and are, therefore, incorrect.

Organization Questions

Question 5 asks you to organize given topics to reflect the organization of the passage:

5. The list of topics below that best reflects the organization of the topics of the passage is

   (A) I.   The difficulties of the Supreme Court

   II. Several recent studies

   III. Spaeth's definition of "attitude"

   IV. The similar patterns of cases

   V.   Other issue areas

   VI. The case of *Miller vs. California*

   (B) I.   The Supreme Court, obscenity, and fact-pattern analysis

   II. Fact-pattern analysis and attitude theory

    III.   The definition of "attitude" for the Court

    IV.   The definition of "situation"

    V.   The breakdown in fact-pattern analysis

    VI.   Studying Court behavior

(C)   I.   Justice Stewart's view of pornography

    II.   Theoretical underpinnings

    III.   A minimum-winning coalition

    IV.   Search and seizure decisions

    V.   Renewed interest in obscenity and pornography

    VI.   The importance of local community standards

(D)   I.   The Court's numerous attempts to define obscenity

    II.   Case characteristics

    III.   The subject matter of cases

    IV.   The Court's proportion of decisions

    V.   Broad-based factors

    VI.   Obscenity determination

After examining all of the choices, you will determine that choice (B) is the correct response. These topical areas lead directly to the implied thesis that the "role" of fact-pattern analysis is insufficient for determining the attitude of the Supreme Court in the areas of obscenity and pornography. (See question 1.)

(A) is incorrect because the first topic stated in the list is not the topic of the first paragraph. It is too global. The first paragraph is about the difficulties the Court has with defining obscenity and how fact-pattern analysis might be used to determine the Court's attitude and clear up the problem.

(C) is incorrect because each of the items listed in this topic list are supporting evidence or data for the real topic of each paragraph. (See the list in (B) for correct topics.) For example, Justice Stewart's statement about pornography is only cited to indicate the nature of the problem with obscenity for the Court. It is not the focus of the paragraph itself.

Finally, (D) is incorrect. As with choice (C), these are all incidental pieces of information or data used to make broader points.

Summarization Questions

To answer question 6, you must be able to summarize the passage:

6.   Which paragraph below is the best summary of the passage?

(A)   The Supreme Court's decision-making process with respect to obscenity and pornography has become too subjective. Fact-pattern analyses, used to determine the overall attitude of the Court, reveal only broad-based attitudes on the part of the Court toward the situations of obscenity cases. But these patterns cannot fully account for the Court's attitudes toward case content. Research is not conclusive that fact-pattern analyses work when applied to legal areas. Renewed public and local interest suggests continued study and close examination of how the Court makes decisions. Delegating authority to the states may reflect patterns for Court decisions in other socially sensitive areas.

(B)   Though subjective, the Supreme Court decisions are well documented. Fact-pattern analyses reveal the attitude of the Supreme Court toward its decisions in cases. Spaeth explains that an attitude involves both an object and a situation. For the Court, the situation may be defined as the decision to grant certiorari. Cases present strikingly similar patterns, and a small number of variables explain a high proportion of the Court's decisions. Segal has made an effort to verify the applicability of fact-pattern analysis with some success. The Court's decisions on obscenity and pornography suggest weak Court behavior, such as in *Miller vs. California.*

(C)   To determine what obscenity and pornography mean to the Supreme Court, we must use fact-pattern analysis. Fact-pattern analysis reveals the ideas that the Court uses to operate in a vacuum. The litigants and the subject matter of cases is defined in broad terms (such as an entire area of law) to reveal the Court's decision-making process. Search and seizure cases reveal strikingly similar patterns, leaving the Court open to grant certiorari effectively. Renewed public interest in the Court's decisions proves how the Court will react in the future.

(D)   Supreme Court decisions about pornography and obscenity are under examination and are out of control. The Court has to see the case to know it. Fact-pattern analyses reveal that the Court can only define cases in narrow terms, thus revealing individual egotism on the part of the Justices. As a result of strikingly similar patterns in search and seizure cases, the Court should be studied further for its weakness in delegating authority to state courts, as in the case of *Miller vs. California.*

The paragraph that best and most accurately reports what the writer demonstrated based on the implied thesis (see question 1) is answer choice (C) which is correct.

Choice (A) is incorrect. While it reflects some of the evidence presented in the passage, the passage does not imply that all Court decisions are subjective, just the ones about pornography and obscenity. Similarly, the writer does not suggest that delegating authority to the states, as in *Miller vs. California,* is a sign of some weakness, but merely that it is worthy of study as a tool for predicting or identifying the Court attitude.

Response (B) is also incorrect. The writer summons information over and over to show how fact-pattern analysis cannot pin down the Court's attitude toward case content.

(D) is incorrect. Nowhere does the writer say or suggest that the justice system is "out of control" or that the justices are "egotists," only that they are liable to be reduced to being "subjective" rather than based on an identifiable shared standard.

At this point, the four remaining question types must be discussed: recall questions (see question 7), cause/effect questions (see question 8), definition questions (question 9), and questions based on graphs. They are as follows:

Recall Questions

To answer question 7, you must be able to recall information from the passage:

7. Based on the passage, the rationale for fact-pattern analyses arises out of what theoretical groundwork?

   (A) Subjectivity theory

   (B) The study of cultural norms

   (C) Attitude theory

   (D) Cybernetics

The easiest way to answer this question is to refer back to the passage. In the second paragraph, the writer states that recent studies using fact-pattern analyses, "owe their theoretical underpinnings to attitude theory." Therefore, we can conclude that response (C) is correct.

Choices (A), (B), and (D) are incorrect, as they are never discussed or mentioned by the writer.

Cause/Effect Questions

Question 8 requires you to analyze a cause and effect relationship:

8. Based on data in the passage, what would most likely be the major cause for the difficulty in pinning down the Supreme Court's attitude toward cases of obscenity and pornography?

   (A) The personal opinions of the Court Justices

   (B) The broad nature of the situations of the cases

   (C) The ineffective logistics of certiorari

   (D) The inability of the Court to resolve the variables presented by individual case content

Choice (D) is correct, as it is precisely what fact-pattern analyses cannot resolve.

Response (A) is incorrect because no evidence is presented for this, only that they do make personal decisions.

Choice (B) is incorrect because this is one way in which fact-pattern analysis can be helpful.

Finally, (C) is only a statement about certiorari being difficult to administer, and this was never claimed about them by the writer in the first place.

Definition Questions

Returning to question 9, we can now determine an answer:

9. In the context of the passage, *subjective* might be most nearly defined as

   (A) personal.

   (B) wrong.

   (C) focussed.

   (D) objective.

Choice (A) is best. By taking in and noting the example of Justice Stewart provided by the writer, we can see that Justice Stewart's comment is an example not of right or wrong. (He doesn't talk about right or wrong. He uses the verb "know" — whose root points to *know*ledge, understanding, insight, primarily, not ethical considerations.) He probably doesn't mean focussed by this since the focus is provided by the appearance or instance of the case itself. By noting the same word ending and the appearance of the root "object" — meaning an observable thing existing outside of ourselves in time and space, and comparing it with the root of subjective, "subject" — often pointing to something personally studied, we can begin to rule out "objective" as perhaps the opposite of "subjective." Most of the time if we are talking about people's "preferences," they are usually about taste or quality, and they are usually not a result of scientific study or clear reasoning, but arise out of a combination of personal taste and idiosyncratic intuitions. Thus, (A) becomes the most likely choice.

(C) is incorrect because the Court's focus is already in place: on obscenity and pornography.

(B) is incorrect. Nothing is implied or stated about the rightness or wrongness of the decisions themselves. Rather it is the definition of obscenity that seems "unworkable."

(D) is also incorrect. Objective is the direct opposite of subjective. To reason based on the object of study is the opposite of reasoning based upon the beliefs, opinions, or ideas of the one viewing the object, rather than the evidence presented by the object itself independent of the observer.

You may not have been familiar with the word subjective, but from your understanding of the writer's intent, you should have been able to figure out what s/he was after. Surrounding words and phrases almost always offer you some clues in determining the meaning of a word. In addition, any examples that appear in the text may also provide some hints.

INTERPRETATION OF GRAPHIC INFORMATION

Although graphs, charts, and tables will not play a large part on all tests, you should be familiar with them. More than likely, you will encounter at least one passage that is accompanied by some form of graphic information. You will then be required to answer any question(s) based on the interpretation of the information presented in the graph, chart, or table.

Graphs are used to produce visual aids for given sets of information. Often, the impact of numbers and statistics is diminished by an overabundance of tedious numbers. A graph helps a reader visualize rapid or irregular information, as well as trace long periods of decline or increase. The following is a guide to reading the three principal graphic forms which you will encounter when taking many tests.

Line Graphs

Line graphs, like the one that follows, are used to track two elements of one or more subjects. One element is usually a time factor, over whose span the other element increases, decreases, or fluctuates. The lines which compose such a graph are composed of connected points that follow the chart through each integral stage. For example, look at the following graph.

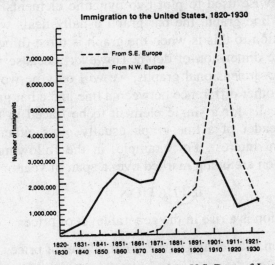

Immigration to the United States, 1820-1930

Source: Immigration and Naturalization Service of the U.S. Dept. of Justice

The average number of immigrants from 1820–1830 is represented at one point; the average number of immigrants from 1831–1840 is represented at the next. The line which connects these points is used only to ease the visual gradation between the points. It is not meant to give an accurate degree for every year between the two decades. If this were so, the line would hardly represent a straight, even progression from year to year. The sharp directness of the lines reveals otherwise. The purpose of the graph is to plot the average increases or decreases from point to point. When dealing with more than one subject, the line graph must use either different color lines (or different types of lines if the graph is black-and-white). In the graph, the dark bold line represents immigration from North-western Europe; the broken line represents immigration from Southeastern Europe.

To read a line graph, find the point of change that interests you. For example, if you want to trace immigration from Northwestern Europe from 1861–1870, you would find the position of the dark line on that point. Next, trace the position to the vertical information on the chart. In this instance, one would discover that approximately 2,000,000 immigrants arrived from Northwestern Europe in the period of time from 1861–1870. If wishing to discover when the number of immigrants reached 4,000,000, you would read across from 4,000,000 on the vertical side of the graph, and see that this number was reached in 1881–1890 from Northwestern Europe, and somewhere over the two decades from 1891–1910 from Southeastern Europe.

Bar Graphs

Bar graphs are likewise used to plot two dynamic elements of a subject. However, unlike a line graph, the bar graph usually deals with only one subject. The exception to this is when the graph is three-dimensional, and the bars take on the dimension of depth. However, because we will only be dealing with two-dimensional graphs, we will only be working with a single subject. The other difference between a line and a bar graph is that a bar graph usually calls for a single element to be traced in terms of another, whereas a reader of a line graph usually plots either of the two elements with equal interest. For example, in the following bar graph, inflation and deflation are being marked over a span of years.

INFLATION

Inflation is a rise in the general level of prices.

Deflation is a decline in the general level of prices.

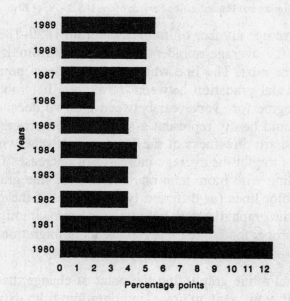

Percentage points are assigned to each year's level of prices and that percentage decreases (deflation) from 1980 to 1981, and from 1981 to 1982. The price level is static from 1982 to 1983. The price level then increases (inflation) from 1983 to 1984. Therefore, it is obvious that the bar graph is read strictly in terms of the changes exhibited over a period of time or against some other element. A line graph, conversely, is used to plot two dynamic elements of equal interest to the reader (e.g., either number of immigrants or the particular decade in question).

To read a bar graph, simply begin at the element at the base of a bar, and trace the bar its full length. Once reaching its length, cross-reference the other element of information which matches the length of the bar.

Pie Charts

Pie charts differ greatly from line or bar graphs. Pie charts are used to help a reader visualize percentages of information with many elements to the subject. An entire "pie" represents 100% of a given quantity of information. The pie is then sliced into measurements that correspond to their respective shares of the 100%. For example, in this pie chart, Myrna's Rent occupies a slice greater than any other in the pie, because no other element equals or exceeds 25% of Myrna's Monthly Budget.

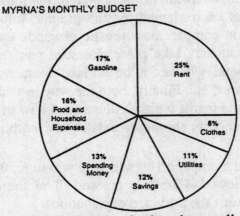

MYRNA'S MONTHLY BUDGET

Another aspect of pie charts is that the smaller percentage elements are moved consecutively to the larger elements. Therefore, the largest element in the chart will necessarily be adjacent to the smallest element in the chart, and the line which separates them is the beginning or endpoint of the chart. From this point the chart fans out to the other elements of the chart, going from the smallest percentages to the largest.

To read a pie chart, choose the element of the subject which interests you, and compare its size to those of the other elements. In cases where the elements are similar in size, do not assume they are equal. The exact percentage of the element will be listed within that slice of the chart. For example, Myrna's Utilities, Savings, and Spending Money are all similar in size, but it is clear when reading the chart that each possesses a different value.

Reading Tables

Tables (see following page) are useful when it is necessary to relate to large bodies of information within a confined area. To read a table, cross-index the headings that run across the top of the table with those that run vertically along the left side. Scanning the table for its content is usually done by reading line by line, just like regular body text, although the reader needs to keep in mind the appropriate headings. In some tables, you will find further subheadings, which help to display more detail on a given subject.

Helpful Hints

You should approach any graphic information you encounter as a key to a larger body of information in abbreviated form. Be sure to use the visual aids of the graphics (e.g., the size of slices on pie charts) as aids only; do not ignore the written information listed on the graph, table, etc. Note especially the title and headings so that you know exactly what it is you are looking at. Also, be aware of the source of the information, where applicable. Know what each element of the graphic information represents; this will help you compare how drastic or subtle any changes are, and over what timespan they take place. Be sure you realize what the actual numbers represent, whether it be dollars, so many thousands of people, millions of shares, etc. Finally, note the way in which the graphic information relates to the text it seeks to illustrate; know in what ways the graphic information supports the arguments of the author of the given passage.

The drills starting on page 148 will help you to reinforce the material you have just reviewed. Carefully answer all of the questions, and check your choices against the provided explanations.

Chemical Disinfectants

Chemical Agent	Action	Examples
Phenolics	Very toxic, disrupt cell membranes and denature proteins	Phenol, cresol, hexachlorophene
Alcohols	Disrupt membranes and denature proteins	Ethanol, methanol isopropanol
Aldehydes (alkylating agents)	Very effective; denature proteins	Formaldehyde, glutaraldehyde
Oxidizing agents	Very toxic to humans, oxidize molecules within cells, generate oxygen gas	Ozone, peroxide
Halogens	Negatively affected by presence of organic matter, oxidize cell components, disrupt membranes	Iodine, chlorine
Heavy metals	Inactivated by organic compounds, combine with sulfhydryl groups, denature proteins	Silver, mercury copper, zinc, selenium, arsenic
Surface-acting agents	Vary in degree, may simply reduce surface tension, allowing organisms to be washed away, or may disrupt membranes and denature proteins	Soaps, detergents (including quaternary ammonium compounds), surfactants
Organic acids	Inhibit fungal metabolism (used as food preservatives)	Benzoic acid, propionic acid, sorbic acid
Gases	Denature proteins	Ethylene oxide (very toxic), vapors from formaldehyde, methyl bromide
Antiseptic dyes	Block cell wall synthesis, interfere with DNA replication	Acriflavine, crystal, violet

The above table is taken from REA's Essentials® of Microbiology. *It provides the reader with a thumbnail summary of chemical disinfectant agents, what they do, and specific examples of agents.*

Drill 2 : A Four-Step Approach

DIRECTIONS: Read the passage and answer the questions that follow.

Water

The most important source of sediment is earth and rock material carried to the sea by rivers and streams; the same materials may also have been transported by glaciers and winds. Other sources are volcanic ash and lava, shells and skeletons of organisms, chemical precipitates formed in seawater, and particles from outer space.

Water is a most unusual substance because it exists on the surface of the earth in its three physical states: ice, water, and water vapor. There are other substances that might exist in a solid and liquid or gaseous state at temperatures normally found at the earth's surface, but there are fewer substances which occur in all three states.

Water is odorless, tasteless, and colorless. It is the only substance known to exist in a natural state as a solid, liquid, or gas on the surface of the earth. It is a universal solvent. Water does not corrode, rust, burn, or separate into its components easily. It is chemically indestructible. It can corrode almost any metal and erode the most solid rock. A unique property of water is that it expands and floats on water when frozen or in the solid state. Water has a freezing point of 0°C and a boiling point of 100°C. Water has the capacity for absorbing great quantities of heat with relatively little increase in temperature. When distilled, water is a poor conductor of electricity, but when salt is added, it is a good conductor of electricity.

Sunlight is the source of energy for temperature change, evaporation, and currents for water movement through the atmosphere. Sunlight controls the rate of photosynthesis for all marine plants, which are directly or indirectly the source of food for all marine animals. Migration, breeding, and other behaviors of marine animals are affected by light.

Water, as the ocean or sea, is blue because of the molecular scattering of the sunlight. Blue light, being of short wavelength, is scattered more effectively than light of longer wavelengths. Variations in color may be caused by particles suspended in the water, water depth, cloud cover, temperature, and other variable factors. Heavy concentrations of dissolved materials cause a yellowish hue, while algae will cause the water to look green. Heavy populations of plant and animal materials will cause the water to look brown.

1. Which of the following lists of topics best organizes the information in the selection?

    (A)   I. Water as vapor

           II. Water as ice

           III. Water as solid

           IV. Water as liquid

    (B)   I. Properties of seawater

           II. Freezing and boiling points of water

           III. Photosynthesis

           IV. Oceans and seas

    (C)   I. Water as substance

           II. Water's corrosion

           III. Water and plants

           IV. Water and algae coloration

    (D)   I. Water's physical states

           II. Properties of water

           III. Effects of the sun on water

           IV. Reasons for color variation in water

2. According to the passage, what is the most unique property of water?

    (A) Water is odorless, tasteless, and colorless.

    (B) Water exists on the surface of the earth in three physical states.

    (C) Water is chemically indestructible.

    (D) Water is a poor conductor of electricity.

3. Which of the following best defines the word distilled as it is used in the last sentence of the third paragraph?

    (A) Free of salt content

    (B) Free of electrical energy

    (C) Dehydrated

    (D) Containing wine

4.   The writer's main purpose in this selection is to

    (A) explain the colors of water.

    (B) examine the effects of the sun on water.

    (C) define the properties of water.

    (D) describe the three physical states of all liquids.

5.   The writer of this selection would most likely agree with which of the following statements?

    (A) The properties of water are found in most other liquids on this planet.

    (B) Water should not be consumed in its most natural state.

    (C) Water might be used to serve many different functions.

    (D) Water is too unpredictable for most scientists.

DIRECTIONS: Read the passage and answer the questions that follow.

The Beginnings of the Submarine

    A submarine was first used as an offensive weapon during the American Revolutionary War. The *Turtle*, a one-man submersible designed by an American inventor named David Bushnell and hand-operated by a screw propeller, attempted to sink a British man-of-war in New York Harbor. The plan was to attach a charge of gunpowder to the ship's bottom with screws and explode it with a time fuse. After repeated failures to force the screws through the copper sheathing of the hull of H.M.S. *Eagle*, the submarine gave up and withdrew, exploding its powder a short distance from the *Eagle*. Although the attack was unsuccessful, it caused the British to move their blockading ships from the harbor to the outer bay.

    On 17 February 1864, a Confederate craft, a hand-propelled submersible, carrying a crew of eight men, sank a Federal corvette that was blockading Charleston Harbor. The hit was accomplished by a torpedo suspended ahead of the Confederate Hunley as she rammed the Union frigate

Housatonic, and is the first recorded instance of a submarine sinking a warship.

The submarine first became a major component in naval warfare during World War I, when Germany demonstrated its full potential. Wholesale sinking of Allied shipping by the German U-boats almost swung the war in favor of the Central Powers. Then, as now, the submarine's greatest advantage was that it could operate beneath the ocean surface where detection was difficult. Sinking a submarine was comparatively easy, once it was found — but finding it before it could attack was another matter.

During the closing months of World War I, the Allied Submarine Devices Investigation Committee was formed to obtain from science and technology more effective underwater detection equipment. The committee developed a reasonably accurate device for locating a submerged submarine. This device was a trainable hydrophone, which was attached to the bottom of the ASW ship, and used to detect screw noises and other sounds that came from a submarine. Although the committee disbanded after World War I, the British made improvements on the locating device during the interval between then and World War II, and named it ASDIC after the committee.

American scientists further improved on the device, calling it SONAR, a name derived from the underlined initials of the words <u>so</u>und <u>na</u>vigation and <u>ra</u>nging.

At the end of World War II, the United States improved the snorkel (a device for bringing air to the crew and engines when operating submerged on diesels) and developed the Guppy (short for greater underwater propulsion power), a conversion of the fleet-type submarine of World War II fame. The superstructure was changed by reducing the surface area, streamlining every protruding object, and enclosing the periscope shears in a streamlined metal fairing. Performance increased greatly with improved electronic equipment, additional battery capacity, and the addition of the snorkel.

6. The passage implies that one of the most pressing modifications needed for the submarine was to

   (A) streamline its shape.

   (B) enlarge the submarine for accommodating more torpedoes and men.

   (C) reduce the noise caused by the submarine.

   (D) add a snorkel.

7. It can be inferred that

   (A) ASDIC was formed to obtain technology for underwater detection.

   (B) ASDIC developed an accurate device for locating submarines.

   (C) the hydrophone was attached to the bottom of the ship.

   (D) ASDIC was formed to develop technology to defend U.S. shipping.

8. SONAR not only picked up the sound of submarines moving through the water but also

   (A) indicated the speed at which the sub was moving.

   (B) gave the location of the submarine.

   (C) indicated the speed of the torpedo.

   (D) placed the submarine within a specified range.

9. According to the passage, the submarine's success was due in part to its ability to

   (A) strike and escape undetected.

   (B) move swifter than other vessels.

   (C) submerge to great depths while being hunted.

   (D) run silently.

10. From the passage, one can infer

   (A) David Bushnell was indirectly responsible for the sinking of the Federal corvette in Charlestown Harbor.

   (B) David Bushnell invented the *Turtle*.

   (C) the *Turtle* was a one-man submarine.

   (D) the *Turtle* sank the *Eagle* on February 17, 1864.

DIRECTIONS: Read the passage and answer the questions that follow.

Immigration

The influx of immigrants that America had been experiencing slowed during the conflicts with France and England, but the flow increased between 1815 and 1837, when an economic downturn sharply reduced their numbers. Thus, the overall rise in population during these years was due more to incoming foreigners than to natural increase. Most of the new-comers were from Britain, Germany, and southern Ireland. The Germans usually fared best, since they brought more money and more skills. Dis-crimination was common in the job market, primarily directed against the Catholics. "Irish Need Not Apply" signs were common. However, the persistent labor shortage prevented the natives from totally excluding the foreign elements. These newcomers huddled in ethnic neighborhoods in the cities, or those who could moved on West to try their hand at farming.

SOURCES OF IMMIGRATION, 1820 – 1840

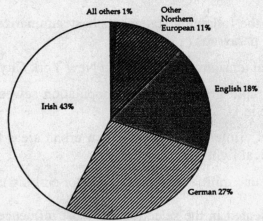

In 1790, 5% of the U.S. population lived in cities of 2,500 or more. By 1860, that figure had risen to 25%. This rapid urbanization created an array of problems.

The rapid growth in urban areas was not matched by the growth of services. Clean water, trash removal, housing, and public transportation all lagged behind, and the wealthy got them first. Bad water and poor sanita-tion produced poor health, and epidemics of typhoid fever, typhus, and cholera were common. Police and fire protection were usually inadequate and the development of professional forces was resisted because of the cost and the potential for political patronage and corruption.

Rapid growth helped to produce a wave of violence in the cities. In New York City in 1834, the Democrats fought the Whigs with such vigor that the state militia had to be called in. New York and Philadelphia witnessed race riots in the mid-1830s, and a New York mob sacked a Catholic convent in 1834. In the 1830s, 115 major incidents of mob vio-lence were recorded. Street crime was common in all the major cities.

11. The author's purpose for writing this essay is

    (A) to bring to light the poor treatment of immigrants.

    (B) to show the violent effects of overpopulation.

    (C) to trace the relation of immigration to the problems of rapid urban growth.

    (D) to dissuade an active life in big cities.

12. Which of the following best defines the word sacked as it is used in the last paragraph?

    (A) Robbed   (C) Trespassed on

    (B) Carried   (D) Vandalized

13. Which of the following statements best summarizes the main idea of the fourth paragraph?

    (A) Racial tensions caused riots in New York City and Philadelphia.

    (B) The rapid growth in urban population sewed the seeds of violence in U.S. cities.

    (C) Street crimes were far worse in urban areas than race riots and political fights.

    (D) The state militia was responsible for curbing urban violence.

14. Ideas presented in the selection are most influenced by which of the following assumptions?

    (A) Urban life was more or less controllable before the flow of immigration in 1820.

    (B) The British had more skills than the Irish.

    (C) Ethnic neighborhoods had always been a part of American society.

    (D) France and England often held conflicts.

15. According to the graph, from 1820–1840

    (A) there were more Irish immigrants than all other nationalities combined.

    (B) the combined number of immigrants from England and Germany exceeded those from Ireland.

    (C) 1% of the immigrants were from Italy.

    (D) there were an equal number of English and German immigrants.

BASIC READING COMPREHENSION DRILLS

ANSWER KEY

Drill 1 — Step 1: Preview

1.	(C)	6.	(C)
2.	(D)	7.	(C)
3.	(D)	8.	(D)
4.	(D)	9.	(A)
5.	(B)		

Drill 2 — A Four-Step Approach

1.	(D)	9.	(A)
2.	(B)	10.	(A)
3.	(A)	11.	(C)
4.	(C)	12.	(D)
5.	(C)	13.	(B)
6.	(A)	14.	(A)
7.	(D)	15.	(B)
8.	(D)		

VOCABULARY LIST

abeyance
   n.- the condition of being temporarily inactive

acerbate
   v.- to irritate or exasperate

allay
   v.- to relieve or to calm

bona fide
   adj.- without fraud or deceit; authentic

broach
   v.- to put forward a topic for discussion

bucolic
   adj.- pastoral; country; rural; rustic

cabal
   n.- a small group joined in a secret scheme; plot

cajole
   v.- to coax with flattery

crux
   n.- a difficult problem; a crucial or essential point

disseminate
   v.- to scatter about; to spread widely

doctrinaire
   adj.- adhering to a doctrine in a dogmatic way

duplicity
   n.- hypocritical cunning or deception

eclectic
   adj.- selecting or selected from various systems, doctrines or sources

edifice
  n.- a building, especially a large imposing one

effusive
  adj.- pouring forth; expressing emotion gushingly; overly demonstrative

facetious
  adj.- lightly joking; jocular

faux pas
  n.- a social blunder

felicitate
  v.- to congratulate, wish happiness to

gallivant
  v.- to go about in search of amusement

germane
  adj.- closely related; relevant

gnostic
  adj.- of or having knowledge

homogeneous
  adj.- the same in structure, quality; composed of similar parts

ignominious
  adj.- shameful, contemptible, humiliating

imbibe
  v.- to drink or drink in; to absorb

imbue
  v.- to saturate; to fill

impasse
  n.- a situation from which there is no escape

infallible
  adj.- incapable of error

insurgent
   adj.- rising up against governmental authority, rebellious

integral
   adj.- necessary for completeness; essential

interpose
   v. - to place or come between; to intervene with

inviolate
   adj. - not violated; kept sacred or unbroken

iridescent
   adj. - having or showing an interplay of rainbow like colors

jocund
   adj. - cheerful; genial

languid
   adj. - without vigor or vitality; weak

latent
   adj. - lying hidden and undeveloped in a person or thing

magnanimous
   adj. - generous in overlooking injury or insult

malign
   v. - to speak evil of; slander

meager
   adj. - thin, lean

mentor
   n. - a wise, loyal advisor

mezzanine
   n. - a low-ceilinged story between two main stories

milieu
   n.- surroundings, environment

misapprehend
   v.- to misunderstand

misnomer
> n.- a name wrongly applied

modicum
> n.- a small amount

rakish
> adj.- having a thin appearance suggesting speed; dashing, jaunty

recompense
> v.- to repay or reward; to compensate

synopsis
> n.- a statement giving a brief, general review or summary

trenchant
> adj.- sharp, keen, incisive; forceful

vilify
> v.- to use abusive language about; defame

wangle
> v.- to get or cause by persuasion, influence, tricks, etc.

CHAPTER 4

Reading for Content

➤ Diagnostic Test
➤ Reading for Content
Review & Drills
➤ Vocabulary List

READING FOR CONTENT DIAGNOSTIC TEST

1. Ⓐ Ⓑ Ⓒ Ⓓ Ⓔ
2. Ⓐ Ⓑ Ⓒ Ⓓ Ⓔ
3. Ⓐ Ⓑ Ⓒ Ⓓ Ⓔ
4. Ⓐ Ⓑ Ⓒ Ⓓ Ⓔ
5. Ⓐ Ⓑ Ⓒ Ⓓ Ⓔ
6. Ⓐ Ⓑ Ⓒ Ⓓ Ⓔ
7. Ⓐ Ⓑ Ⓒ Ⓓ Ⓔ
8. Ⓐ Ⓑ Ⓒ Ⓓ Ⓔ
9. Ⓐ Ⓑ Ⓒ Ⓓ Ⓔ
10. Ⓐ Ⓑ Ⓒ Ⓓ Ⓔ
11. Ⓐ Ⓑ Ⓒ Ⓓ Ⓔ
12. Ⓐ Ⓑ Ⓒ Ⓓ Ⓔ
13. Ⓐ Ⓑ Ⓒ Ⓓ Ⓔ
14. Ⓐ Ⓑ Ⓒ Ⓓ Ⓔ
15. Ⓐ Ⓑ Ⓒ Ⓓ Ⓔ
16. Ⓐ Ⓑ Ⓒ Ⓓ Ⓔ
17. Ⓐ Ⓑ Ⓒ Ⓓ Ⓔ
18. Ⓐ Ⓑ Ⓒ Ⓓ Ⓔ
19. Ⓐ Ⓑ Ⓒ Ⓓ Ⓔ
20. Ⓐ Ⓑ Ⓒ Ⓓ Ⓔ
21. Ⓐ Ⓑ Ⓒ Ⓓ Ⓔ
22. Ⓐ Ⓑ Ⓒ Ⓓ Ⓔ
23. Ⓐ Ⓑ Ⓒ Ⓓ Ⓔ
24. Ⓐ Ⓑ Ⓒ Ⓓ Ⓔ
25. Ⓐ Ⓑ Ⓒ Ⓓ Ⓔ
26. Ⓐ Ⓑ Ⓒ Ⓓ Ⓔ

27. Ⓐ Ⓑ Ⓒ Ⓓ Ⓔ
28. Ⓐ Ⓑ Ⓒ Ⓓ Ⓔ
29. Ⓐ Ⓑ Ⓒ Ⓓ Ⓔ
30. Ⓐ Ⓑ Ⓒ Ⓓ Ⓔ
31. Ⓐ Ⓑ Ⓒ Ⓓ Ⓔ
32. Ⓐ Ⓑ Ⓒ Ⓓ Ⓔ
33. Ⓐ Ⓑ Ⓒ Ⓓ Ⓔ
34. Ⓐ Ⓑ Ⓒ Ⓓ Ⓔ
35. Ⓐ Ⓑ Ⓒ Ⓓ Ⓔ
36. Ⓐ Ⓑ Ⓒ Ⓓ Ⓔ
37. Ⓐ Ⓑ Ⓒ Ⓓ Ⓔ
38. Ⓐ Ⓑ Ⓒ Ⓓ Ⓔ
39. Ⓐ Ⓑ Ⓒ Ⓓ Ⓔ
40. Ⓐ Ⓑ Ⓒ Ⓓ Ⓔ
41. Ⓐ Ⓑ Ⓒ Ⓓ Ⓔ
42. Ⓐ Ⓑ Ⓒ Ⓓ Ⓔ
43. Ⓐ Ⓑ Ⓒ Ⓓ Ⓔ
44. Ⓐ Ⓑ Ⓒ Ⓓ Ⓔ
45. Ⓐ Ⓑ Ⓒ Ⓓ Ⓔ
46. Ⓐ Ⓑ Ⓒ Ⓓ Ⓔ
47. Ⓐ Ⓑ Ⓒ Ⓓ Ⓔ
48. Ⓐ Ⓑ Ⓒ Ⓓ Ⓔ
49. Ⓐ Ⓑ Ⓒ Ⓓ Ⓔ
50. Ⓐ Ⓑ Ⓒ Ⓓ Ⓔ
51. Ⓐ Ⓑ Ⓒ Ⓓ Ⓔ
52. Ⓐ Ⓑ Ⓒ Ⓓ Ⓔ

READING FOR CONTENT
DIAGNOSTIC TEST

This diagnostic test is designed to help you determine your strengths and your weaknesses in reading for content. Follow the directions for each part and check your answers.

**These types of questions are found in the following tests:
GRE, GMAT, CLEP, GED, PSAT, SAT, PRAXIS Core Battery, ACT,
PPST, TASP, ASVAB, LSAT, and CBEST**

---

52 Questions

DIRECTIONS: Each passage is followed by questions based on its content. After reading the passage, choose the best answer to each question. Answer all questions based on what is indicated or implied in that passage.

Questions 1–4 refer to the following passage.

As noted by Favat in 1977, the study of children's stories has been an ongoing concern of linguists, anthropologists, and psychologists. The past decade has witnessed a surge of interest in children's stories from researchers in these and other disciplines. The use of narratives for reading and reading instruction has been commonly accepted by the educational community. The notion that narrative is highly structured and that children's sense of narrative structure is more highly developed than expository structure has been proposed by some researchers.

Early studies of children's stories followed two approaches for story analysis: the analysis of story content or the analysis of story structure. Story content analysis has centered primarily on examining motivational and psychodynamic aspects of story characters as noted in the works of Erikson and Pitcher and Prelinger in 1963 and Ames in 1966. These studies have noted that themes or topics predominate and that themes change with age.

Early research on story structure focused on formal models of structure such as story grammar and story schemata. These models specified basic story elements and formed sets of rules similar to sentence grammar for ordering the elements.

The importance or centrality of narrative in a child's development of communicative ability has been proposed by Halliday (1976) and Hymes (1975). Thus, the importance of narrative for language communicative ability and for reading and reading instruction has been well documented. However, the question still remains about how these literacy abilities interact and lead to conventional reading.

1. This passage is most probably directed at which of the following audiences?

   (A) Reading educators   (D) Reading researchers

   (B) Linguists   (E) Anthropologists

   (C) Psychologists

2. According to the passage, future research should address

   (A) how story structure and story schema interact with comprehension.

   (B) how children's use and understanding of narrative interacts and leads to conventional reading.

   (C) how basal texts and literature texts differ from children's story structure.

   (D) how story content interacts with story comprehension.

   (E) how narrative text structure differs from expository text structure.

3. The major distinction between story content and story structure is that

   (A) story content focuses on motivational aspects whereas story structure focuses on rules similar to sentence grammar.

   (B) story content focuses on psychodynamic aspects whereas story structure focuses on formal structural models.

   (C) story content and story structure essentially refer to the same concepts.

(D) story content focuses on themes and topic whereas story structure focuses on specific basic story elements.

(E) story content focuses primarily on characters whereas story structure focuses on story grammar and schemata.

4. Which of the following is the most complete and accurate definition
of the term surge as used in the following sentence? The past decade
has witnessed a surge of interest in children's stories from researchers
in these and other disciplines.

(A) A heavy swell   (D) A sudden increase

(B) A slight flood   (E) A sudden rush

(C) A sudden rise

Questions 5–8 refer to the following passage.

Seldom has the American school system not been the target of demands for change to meet the social priorities of the times. This theme has
been traced through the following significant occurrences in education:
Benjamin Franklin's advocacy in 1749 for a more useful type of education; Horace Mann's zealous proposals in the 1830s espousing the
tax-supported public school; John Dewey's early twentieth century attack
on traditional schools for not developing the child effectively for his or her
role in society; the post-Sputnik pressure for academic rigor; the prolific
criticism and accountability pressures of the 1970s, and the ensuing disil-
lusionment and continued criticism of schools until this last decade of the
twentieth century. Indeed, the waves of criticism about American education have reflected currents of social dissatisfaction for any given period
of this country's history.

As dynamics for change in the social order result in demands for
change in the American educational system, so in turn insistence has developed for revision of teacher education (witness the more recent Holmes
report (1986). Historically, the education of American teachers has reflected evolving attitudes about public education. With slight modifications, the teacher education pattern established following the demise of the
normal school during the early 1900s has persisted in most teacher preparation programs. The pattern has been one requiring certain academic and
professional (educational) courses often resulting in teachers prone to teach
as they had been taught.

5. The author of this passage would probably agree with which of the following statements?

    (A) Teacher education courses tend to be of no value.

    (B) Social dissatisfaction should drive change in the American school systems.

    (C) Teacher education programs have changed greatly since normal schools were eliminated.

    (D) Critics of American education reflect vested interests.

    (E) Teachers' teaching methods tend to reflect what they have learned in their academic and professional courses.

6. The evolving attitudes about public education are

    (A) stated.   (D) unchanged.

    (B) unstated.   (E) unwarranted.

    (C) alluded.

7. One possible sequence of significant occurrences in education noted in the passage is

    (A) Mann's tax-supported public schools, post-Sputnik pressures for academic rigor, and the Holmes' report.

    (B) Franklin's more useful type of education, Dewey's educating children for their role in society, and Mann's tax-supported public schools.

    (C) Mann's tax-supported public schools, the Holmes' report, and post-Sputnik pressures for academic rigor.

    (D) Franklin's more useful type of education, the Holmes' report, and accountability pressures of the 1970s.

    (E) Mann's tax-supported public schools, accountability pressures of the 1970s, and the post-Sputnik pressures for academic rigor.

8. Which of the following statements most obviously implies dissatisfaction with preparation of teachers in the United States?

    (A) Demands for change in the American education system lead to insistence for revision of teacher education programs.

    (B) The pattern of teacher education requires certain academic and professional education courses.

(C) The education of U.S. teachers has reflected evolving attitudes about public education.

(D) Teachers tend to teach as they were taught.

(E) Teacher education has changed very little since the decline of the normal school.

Questions 9–12 refer to the following passage.

Assignment: Research for a White Paper Proposing U.S. Foreign Policy

Imagine you are in charge (or assigned to) a foreign policy desk in the U.S. Department of State. Select one of the following regions (descriptors are merely suggestions):

Western Europe—A Changing Alliance

Eastern Europe—Out from Behind the Iron Curtain

The U.S.S.R.—Still an Enigma

The Middle East—History and Emotions

Africa—Rising Expectations in the Postwar Continent

South and Southeast Asia—Unrest in Far Away Places

The Far East—Alienation and Alliance

The Western Hemisphere—Neighbors; Pro and Con

Through research, prepare a White Paper for that area which will indicate:

1. a General Policy Statement toward the nations of that region;

2. a statement as to how World War II set the stage for that policy;

3. a summary of the major events since 1945 in that region which have affected U.S. foreign policy;

4. a list of suggested problems and/or possibilities for near-future interactions of that region and the U.S.

9. In order to complete this assignment, research into which of the following disciplines (areas of study) would be most appropriate?

(A) History, Economics, Political Science, and Language

(B) History, Political Science, Education, and Economics

(C) Political Science, Economics, Geography, and Religion

(D) Geography, Education, History, and Political Science

(E) History, Political Science, Economics, and Culture

10. Which of the following is the most complete and accurate definition of the term "enigma" as used in the passage?

(A) Problem   (D) Secret

(B) Riddle   (E) Mystery

(C) Puzzle

11. Which of the following is the most appropriate secondary school audience for the assignment?

(A) Students in a World Geography class

(B) Students in a World History class

(C) Students in a Content Area Reading class

(D) Students in an Economics class

(E) Students in an American Government class

12. "White Paper" as used in the passage is best defined as

(A) a special research-based report which analyzes, summarizes, and/or proposes U.S. Foreign Policy.

(B) a research-based paper which dictates U.S. Foreign Policy.

(C) a paper which white-washes previous U.S. Foreign Policy.

(D) a quasi-official but classified government report.

(E) a research-based paper which includes items 1, 2, 3, and 4 as specified in the passage.

Questions 13–16 refer to the following passage.

The information about the comparison of the technology (duplex versus one-way video and two-way audio) and the comparison of site classes versus regular classes tends to indicate that although there was not much of an apparent difference between classes and technology, student participation and student involvement were viewed as important components in any teaching/learning setting. For the future, perhaps revisiting what learning is might be helpful so that this component of distance learning can be more adequately addressed. The question remains whether or not student participation can be equated with learning. Participation per se does not demonstrate learning. A more rigorous instrument which assesses and determines learning may need to be addressed with future distance learning studies.

13. Duplex, as used in the passage, suggests which of the following when comparing distance learning technology?

   (A) One-way video and two-way audio

   (B) One-way video and one-way audio

   (C) Two-way video and two-way audio

   (D) Two-way video and one-way audio

   (E) Two-way video

14. Which of the following is the most complete and accurate definition of the term *rigorous* as used in the passage?

   (A) Harsh   (D) Dogmatic

   (B) Austere   (E) Precise

   (C) Uncompromising

15. The author of the passage would tend to agree with which of the following statements?

   (A) Learning consists of more than student participation.

   (B) Duplex technology is better than one-way video and two-way audio.

   (C) Student participation and student involvement are not important in learning.

   (D) An instrument which assesses and demonstrates learning is not currently available.

   (E) A review of learning is not important as the topic has been thoroughly researched.

16. The primary purpose of the passage is to

   (A) delineate the issues in distance learning.

   (B) note student participation in distance learning and question this role in learning.

   (C) detail the comparison of site classes versus regular classes.

   (D) share information about duplex technology versus one-way video and two-way audio.

   (E) request an assessment instrument which includes a learning component.

Questions 17–21 refer to the following passage.

Frederick Douglass was born Frederick Augustus Washington Bailey in 1817 to a white father and a slave mother. Frederick was raised by his grandmother on a Maryland plantation until he was eight. It was then that he was sent to Baltimore by his owner to be a servant to the Auld family. Mrs. Auld recognized Frederick's intellectual acumen and defied the law of the state by teaching him to read and write. When Mr. Auld warned that education would make the boy unfit for slavery, Frederick sought to continue his education in the streets. When his master died, Frederick was returned to the plantation to work in the fields at age sixteen. Later, he was hired out to work in the shipyards in Baltimore as a ship caulker. He plotted an escape but was discovered before he could get away. It took five years before he made his way to New York City and then to New Bedford, Massachusetts, eluding slave hunters by changing his name to Douglass.

At an 1841 anti-slavery meeting in Massachusetts, Douglass was invited to give a talk about his experiences under slavery. His impromptu speech was so powerful and so eloquent that it thrust him into a career as an agent for the Massachusetts Anti-Slavery Society.

Douglass wrote his autobiography in 1845 primarily to counter those who doubted his authenticity as a former slave. This work became a classic in American literature and a primary source about slavery from the point of view of a slave. Douglass went on a two-year speaking tour abroad to avoid recapture by his former owner and to win new friends for the abolition movement. He returned with funds to purchase his freedom and to start his own anti-slavery newspaper. He became a consultant to Abraham Lincoln and throughout Reconstruction fought doggedly for full civil rights for freedmen; he also supported the women's rights movement.

17. According to the passage, Douglass's autobiography was motivated by

    (A) the desire to make money for his anti-slavery movement.

    (B) the desire to start a newspaper.

    (C) his interest in authenticating his life as a slave.

    (D) his desire to educate people about slavery.

    (E) his desire to promote the Civil War.

18. The central idea of the passage is that Frederick Douglass

    (A) was influential in changing the laws regarding the education of slaves.

    (B) was one of the most eminent human rights leaders of the century.

    (C) was a personal friend and confidant to a president.

    (D) wrote a classic in American literature.

    (E) supported women's rights.

19. According to the author of this passage, Mrs. Auld taught Frederick to read because

    (A) Frederick wanted to learn like the other boys.

    (B) she recognized his natural ability.

    (C) she wanted to comply with the laws of the state.

    (D) he needed to read to work in the home.

    (E) she obeyed her husband's wishes in the matter.

20. The title that best expresses the ideas of this passage is

    (A) The History of the Anti-Slavery Movement.

    (B) The Dogged Determination of Frederick Douglass.

    (C) Reading: Window to the World.

    (D) Frederick Douglass's Contributions to Freedom.

    (E) The Oratorical and Literary Brilliance of Frederick Douglass.

21. In the context of the passage, "impromptu" is closest in meaning to

    (A) unprepared.

    (D) loud and excited.

    (B) a quiet manner.

    (E) elaborate.

    (C) forceful.

Questions 22–25 refer to the following passage.

A big toxic spill took place on the upper Sacramento River in California on July 13, 1991 about 10 P.M. when a slow moving Southern Pacific train derailed north of the town of Dansmuir. A tank car containing 19,500 gallons of pesticide broke open and spilled into the river. This pesticide is used to kill soil pests. Since the spill, thousands of trout and other fish were poisoned along a 45-mile stretch of river. In addition, 190 people were treated at a local hospital for respiratory and related illnesses. Residents along the river have been warned to stay away from the tainted water. Once this water reaches Lake Shasta, a source of water for millions of Californians, samples will be taken to assess the quality of the water.

22. Which of the following statements conveys the message in the passage?

    (A) Pesticides intended to kill soil pests can be dangerous to all living things.

    (B) Water uncontaminated by pesticides is safe to drink.

    (C) Take every precaution not to come in contact with the pesticide-infected water.

    (D) Pesticides that killed thousands of trout and other fish will not necessarily kill human beings.

    (E) Only residents along the tainted river need worry.

23. The Southern Pacific train that derailed was

    (A) a passenger train.

    (D) a cargo and passenger train.

    (B) a cargo train.

    (E) a special train.

    (C) a commuter train.

24. The most serious problem that can come about as a result of the toxic spill is

    (A) possible movement of residents in Dansmuir to another place of residence.

    (B) reduction in tourism attraction for Dansmuir and other nearby areas.

    (C) the negative effects on those whose livelihood depends on the fishing industry.

    (D) when the tainted water reaches Lake Shasta, which is a source of water supply for millions of Californians.

    (E) the uncertain length of time it will take to make the tainted water safe and healthy again.

25. This unfortunate incident of toxic spill resulting from train derailment implies

    (A) the need for more environmental protection.

    (B) other means for transporting pesticides need to be considered.

    (C) that there should be more precaution for trains running by night-time.

    (D) that there should be an investigation as to the cause of the train derailment and effective measures to prevent its occurrence again should be applied.

    (E) that there should be research on how to expedite making infected water safe and healthy again.

Questions 26–29 refer to the following passage.

Lead poisoning is considered by health authorities to be the most common and devastating environmental disease of young children. According to studies made, it affects 15% to 20% of urban children and from 50% to 75% of inner-city, poor children. As a result of a legal settlement in July 1991, all of California's Medicaid-eligible children, ages one through five, will now be routinely screened annually for lead poisoning. Experts estimate that more than 50,000 cases will be detected in California because of the newly mandated tests. This will halt, at an early stage, a disease that leads to learning disabilities and life-threatening disorders.

26. Lead poisoning among young children, if not detected early, can lead to

    (A) physical disabilities.   (D) heart disease.

    (B) mental disabilities.   (E) death.

    (C) learning disabilities.

27. The new mandate to screen all young children for lead poisoning is required of

    (A) all young children in California.

    (B) all children with learning disabilities.

    (C) all Medicaid-eligible children, ages one through five, in California.

    (D) all minority children in California.

    (E) all school-age children in California.

28. According to findings, more cases of lead poisoning are found among

    (A) urban children.   (D) children in rural areas.

    (B) inner-city poor children.   (E) middle-class children.

    (C) immigrant children.

29. The implication of this new mandate in California regarding lead poisoning is

    (A) non-eligible children will not be screened.

    (B) children older than five years will not be screened.

    (C) middle-class children will not be screened.

    (D) new immigrant children will not be screened.

    (E) thousands of young children in California will remain at risk for lead poisoning.

Questions 30–33 refer to the following passage.

New health research shows that regular vigorous exercise during the middle and late years of life not only keeps the heart healthy, but also may protect against colon cancer, one of the major killers in the U.S. The researchers in the study compared the rate of colon cancer among those who were physically inactive with those who were either active or highly active. Seventeen thousand one hundred forty eight men, ages 30 to 79, were covered in the study. Among men judged to be inactive there were 55 cases of colon cancer; among those moderately active, there were 11; and only 10 cases of colon cancer were found among the very active ones.

30. Which of the following makes an appropriate title for the passage?

    (A) Health Research on Colon Cancer

    (B) Colon Cancer: A Major Killer in the U.S.

    (C) Regular Vigorous Exercise May Prevent Colon Cancer

    (D) Results of Research on Colon Cancer

    (E) A Prescription for Preventing Colon Cancer

31. Based on the result of the research, can one make a generalization regarding colon cancer for men and women?

    (A) Yes   (D) It depends

    (B) No   (E) Not applicable

    (C) Maybe

32. What important message did you get from the passage?

    (A) Regular exercise is good for the health.

    (B) Only middle-aged men get colon cancer.

    (C) Women need not worry about colon cancer.

    (D) Regular exercise is needed only by older people.

    (E) Children are too young to exercise.

33. What is the major limitation of the study?

    (A) It did not explain "vigorous exercise."

    (B) It did not include children.

    (C) It did not include men below 30.

    (D) It did not include women of the same age group.

    (E) None of the above.

Questions 34–37 are based on the following passage.

It is a known fact that for the first time a generation will not outstrip its parents educationally or economically. In fact, this generation of students won't even equal their parents' efforts.

34. What is the main idea of this passage?

    (A) Parents are economically and educationally better off than their children.

    (B) Parents are ahead of their children economically.

    (C) Parents are ahead of their children educationally.

    (D) Parents and their children are about equal educationally.

    (E) Parents and their children are about equal economically.

35. Which of the following is an unstated assumption made by the author?

    (A) This generation of students is lazy.

    (B) This generation of students refuses to study.

    (C) Parents are more industrious than their children.

    (D) Parents are smarter than their children.

    (E) Parents were more interested in school than their children are.

36. Does the author adequately support his/her argument?

    (A) The support is very adequate.

    (B) The support is somewhat adequate.

    (C) Marginally, the author's argument is supported.

    (D) The author's evidence is not appropriate at all.

    (E) The author provides no support for his/her idea presented in the passage.

37. Which of the following is a fact presented in the passage?

    (A) Parents are smarter than their children.

    (B) Parents are more industrious than their children.

(C) Economically, parents are better off than their children.

(D) The author believes that parents are educationally and economically superior to their children.

(E) Educationally, parents are better off than their children.

Questions 38–41 are based on the following passage.

Believe it or not, 45 to 50 percent of the students graduating from high school today do not possess adequate basic skills. On achievement tests, students in the United States rank far below students enrolled in schools of other countries. Because of this, our society is filled with over 23 million Americans who are functionally illiterate. By the year 2000, it is predicted that this number will rise by 100,000. Truly, intellectual mediocrity has invaded our society. This decline in academic excellence is due to a lack of parental involvement. Parents are not actively involved in the education of their children. They do not support the schools, and they continuously make excuses for the mistakes of their children. According to parents, it's always the school's fault, particularly the teachers. Come on parents!!! We need your support.

38. What is the main idea of this passage?

(A) Intellectually, American students are performing poorly.

(B) Parents are not supportive of our schools.

(C) Children are not as smart as they used to be.

(D) Forty-five to fifty percent of our high school graduates lack basic skills.

(E) Over 23 million Americans are functionally illiterate.

39. Which of the following best summarizes this passage?

(A) Parents are not involved in the education of their children.

(B) Intellectually, children are not performing well.

(C) Parents make too many excuses for their children.

(D) Because of a lack of parental involvement, American students are not performing well academically.

(E) Parents and children are responsible for the low academic achievement of American students.

40. Based on the information given, does the author adequately support the main idea of the passage?

    (A) The evidence given adequately supports the main idea.

    (B) The main idea is only marginally supported.

    (C) The evidence given is very limited.

    (D) The author provides an abundance of support for the main idea.

    (E) The main idea is not supported.

41. With reference to the reason for intellectual mediocrity among American students, evaluate the author's argument in terms of strength.

    (A) The author's argument is very strong.

    (B) The author's argument is strong but could have been stronger.

    (C) The argument is too limited.

    (D) The author's argument is too strong.

    (E) There is no argument to support the reason for intellectual mediocrity.

Questions 42–45 are based on the following passage.

Despite what many think, history classes are filled with students who have difficulty reading and understanding their history books. This is called a readability mismatch. Generally, the reading levels of the history books exceed the reading levels of the students who must utilize these books. When this mismatch occurs, students become frustrated and do not perform at levels commensurate with their listening capacity (potential).

In order to alleviate this mismatch, it is recommended that teachers (1) supplement the books with lower level materials that stress the same concepts, (2) rewrite the books, (3) use peer tutoring, (4) tape the books for those students who are experiencing difficulties, or (5) use films and filmstrips to teach different concepts.

42. In this passage, the author states that there is a mismatch between the reading levels of students and the reading levels of the history books they use. Which statement below best supports this idea?

    (A) The author states that students are having difficulty reading their history books.

    (B) The author states that students are having difficulty.

    (C) The author really provides no support for this idea.

    (D) The author states that students become frustrated.

    (E) The author states that students do not perform at levels commensurate with their listening capacity.

43. With reference to the author's idea of a mismatch, which of the statements below adequately evaluates the strength of his argument?

    (A) The argument, even though it is not supported, is very strong.

    (B) The argument is only moderately strong.

    (C) The argument is without substance.

    (D) The argument is weak.

    (E) There is no argument.

44. Of the five suggestions offered by the author, which one is the least appropriate for teachers?

    (A) Supplement the books.   (D) Tape the books.

    (B) Rewrite the books.   (E) Use films and filmstrips.

    (C) Use peer tutoring.

45. One of the author's suggestions is for teachers to tape materials in books that are too difficult. To which of the following subjects would this be *least* applicable?

    (A) Science   (D) Geography

    (B) Economics   (E) Health

    (C) Math

Questions 46–49 are based on the following passage.

    The educational reforms of the 1980s were numerous. Standards were raised, students and teachers were tested and assessed as never before, curriculum revision was at an all-time high, and teacher education programs took on a new look. Sad to say, however, the reformers who have engineered these changes have failed to consider the urban/inner city child—the black child, the Hispanic child, the underachievers, the slow learners, the learning-disabled child. Rather, the reforms of the 1980s have forced schools to return to a system of tracking minority and other less abled students into remedial classes, while their counterparts are enrolled in Greek mythology, Victorian prose, romantic literature, geometry, trigonometry, and calculus. No wonder minority and other less abled students do poorly on standardized entrance examinations!

46. In reference to the educational reforms of the 1980s, which of the following is an opinion, according to this passage?

   (A) These reforms have failed to address the needs of urban/inner city children.

   (B) Standards were raised.

   (C) Students and teachers were tested and assessed as never before.

   (D) Curriculum revision was at an all-time high.

   (E) Teacher training programs have taken on a new look.

47. Which of the following best expresses the topic of this passage?

   (A) Curriculum revision

   (B) Increased standards

   (C) The underserved urban/inner city child

   (D) Revised teacher training programs

   (E) Increased testing of students and teachers

48. Which of the following best expresses the author's reasons for the low performance of urban/inner city children on standardized tests?

   (A) Standards are too high.

   (B) Courses assigned are too difficult.

   (C) Students are tested too frequently.

   (D) Teacher training programs have failed.

   (E) Courses taken do not adequately prepare these children for the tests.

49. What is the author's attitude toward the educational reforms of the 1980s?

    (A) Supportive

    (B) Indifferent

    (C) Critical

    (D) Anger

    (E) Appeasing

Questions 50–52 are based on the following passage.

Teacher negotiation is very beneficial. It leads to an amplification of roles for teachers. This amplification empowers teachers to actively participate in the decision-making process in terms of working conditions and salary improvements.

Other benefits derived from teacher negotiation are not as tangible as the aforementioned ones, but they are equally as important. Research shows that when teachers have input into their professional lives, their self-esteem, morale, and accountability are improved.

Both the tangible and intangible benefits derived from teacher negotiation indicate that teacher negotiation is a worthwhile process.

50. What is the main idea of this passage?

    (A) Through negotiation, teachers' salaries improve.

    (B) Through negotiation, conditions for teachers improve.

    (C) Through negotiation, teachers' self-esteem improves.

    (D) Through negotiation, teachers' morale improves.

    (E) Through negotiation, teachers receive more power.

51. Is the author's argument for teacher negotiation adequately supported by details?

    (A) The argument is fully supported.

    (B) The argument is somewhat supported.

    (C) No argument is made. The passage simply presents facts.

    (D) The argument is too limited.

    (E) The argument is not supported at all.

52. Which of the following best describes the organization of the passage?

(A) A problem is presented and several solutions given.

(B) A major idea is chronologically summarized.

(C) A controversial issue is presented and defended.

(D) Several interrelated ideas are presented to support an implied idea.

(E) A numerical list is delineated to support an idea.

READING FOR CONTENT
DIAGNOSTIC TEST

ANSWER KEY

1.	(D)	14.	(E)	27.	(C)	40.	(A)
2.	(B)	15.	(A)	28.	(B)	41.	(C)
3.	(B)	16.	(B)	29.	(E)	42.	(C)
4.	(D)	17.	(C)	30.	(C)	43.	(A)
5.	(E)	18.	(B)	31.	(E)	44.	(B)
6.	(B)	19.	(B)	32.	(A)	45.	(C)
7.	(A)	20.	(D)	33.	(D)	46.	(A)
8.	(E)	21.	(A)	34.	(A)	47.	(C)
9.	(E)	22.	(C)	35.	(C)	48.	(E)
10.	(C)	23.	(B)	36.	(E)	49.	(C)
11.	(E)	24.	(D)	37.	(D)	50.	(B)
12.	(A)	25.	(D)	38.	(A)	51.	(B)
13.	(C)	26.	(E)	39.	(D)	52.	(C)

DETAILED EXPLANATIONS OF ANSWERS

1. **(D)** As the passage presents information by various researchers on children's stories, the passage ends with an unanswered question that still needs to be addressed by reading researchers as provided in choice (D).

2. **(B)** Although more information may be needed about story content and story structure as indicated in choices (A), (C), (D), and (E), the main question that remains to be answered is choice (B).

3. **(B)** Each choice provides partially correct information about story content and story structure; choice (B) provides the most complete response.

4. **(D)** Each choice is a possible definition. However, choice (D) is most appropriate as there was an increased interest by researchers in these and other areas even though it has been an ongoing concern of some researchers.

5. **(E)** Choices (A) and (C) are not supported by the passage. Choices (B) and (D) go beyond the passage. The last sentence states "The pattern...results in teachers prone to teach as they had been taught"—thus choice (E).

6. **(B)** The other choices (A), (C), (D), and (E) are not supported by the passage. Although the passage mentions that teacher education has reflected evolving attitudes about education, the attitudes are not spelled out—choice (B).

7. **(A)** Only choice (A) has the correct sequence; the other sequences are incorrect.

8. **(E)** Choices (A), (B), (C), and (D) are statements about education, teacher education, and teachers. Choice (E) statement that teacher education has changed very little implies that this lack of change could be a source of dissatisfaction.

9. **(E)** Choices (A), (B), (C), and (D) each contain an area which is

considered a component of culture, such as religion, education, and language. Thus, choice (E) is the most appropriate response.

10. **(C)** Although each definition appears appropriate, choices (B), (D), and (E) assume that a solution is known, or has been known at one time, and could be solved. Although choice (A) suggests difficulty in solving, choice (C) suggests a situation that is intricate enough to perplex the mind. Choice (C) is most appropriate for this passage as a definition of enigma is an inexplicable situation.

11. **(E)** Although choices (A), (B), (C), and (D) may touch on such a topic, the roles and functions of governmental offices and departments are generally addressed in an American Government class, thus choice (E).

12. **(A)** Choices (B), (C), and (D) are incorrect in that a White Paper does not dictate or automatically white-wash U.S. Foreign Policy, nor is it a classified report. Although choice (E) states criteria to include in a report, it may not meet the specifications of a White Paper—thus choice (A).

13. **(C)** The passage compares duplex versus one-way video and two-way audio. The reader must infer that duplex indicates two-way video and two-way audio since duplex refers to two. The other choices (A), (B), (D), and (E) are incorrect.

14. **(E)** Choices (A), (B), (C), and (D) are inappropriate for defining an instrument which assesses learning and demonstrates learning.

15. **(A)** Choices (B), (C), (D), and (E) are not supported by the passage.

16. **(B)** While choices (A), (C), (D), and (E) are mentioned briefly in the passage, the passage focuses on student participation and learning.

17. **(C)** Douglass was interested in raising social consciousness about slavery. The passage stresses his interest in refuting those who doubted his claim to have been a slave.

18. **(B)** Choice (A) is not supported by the text. All other choices, while true, are irrelevant to the question.

19. **(B)** This choice is supported by the statement, "Mrs. Auld recog-

nized Frederick's intellectual acumen." Choices (C) and (E) contradict information in the passage. The passage does not support choices (A) and (D).

20. **(D)**   Choices (A), (B), and (C) are either too broad or too general. Choice (E) is too specific and limited to cover the information in the passage.

21. **(A)**   An "impromptu" speech is one given suddenly without preparation.

22. **(C)**   The question asks for the "message" conveyed in the passage. Choice (C) is the correct answer, as it gives a warning. In choice (A), pesticides cannot necessarily be dangerous to all living things—some are good for the protection of plants, for example; in (B), water can be contaminated by something other than pesticides; the statement in choice (D) may be true, but it is certainly not the best answer.

23. **(B)**   The train is definitely a cargo train, hence, (B) is the correct answer. In (A), if it were a passenger train, hundreds would have been killed; in (C) and (D), according to the clues, the choices here don't apply; and in (E) the choice used "special train" but could have appropriately used "cargo train" instead.

24. **(D)**   The question here asks for the most "serious problem" that can come about; so, of all the choices, (D) provides the most serious problem resulting from the pesticide spill for Californians. Choices (A), (B), (C), and (E) are not life-threatening as is choice (D).

25. **(D)**   Choice (D) is the most logical and straightforward answer. (D) prioritizes which action should be first taken, and is therefore the correct answer. While the choices in (A), (B), (C), and (E) are sound choices, they don't list the most urgent thing to do.

26. **(E)**   All the choices in this question are possible answers, however, since the question asks for what lead poisoning, if not detected early "can lead to," it calls for the ultimate consequence. Hence, (E) is the correct answer inasmuch as the passage states "life-threatening disorders" as among the possible consequences.

27. **(C)**   The correct answer to this question is choice (C)—it gives the complete and precise category. Other choices are incomplete—(A) left out the age group and the medical eligibility; (B) is narrowed down and all

inclusive of "children with learning disabilities," choices (D) and (E) are incorrect.

28. **(B)**   As indicated by figures in the passage, the correct answer is (B). Other choices (A),(C), (D), and (E) are obviously incorrect. This is an example of a question in which the incorrect choices are not possible answers. The correct answer is derived from the figures provided in the passage.

29. **(E)**   The implications provided in choices (A) through (E) are correct. However, each of the implications for (A) through (D) are narrowed down to only one specific category of children—not any one is inclusive of all that needs to be addressed. Hence, (E) is the best and appropriate answer because it addresses the thousands who will not be screened which includes those in the choices to (A) through (D).

30. **(C)**   A title is supposed to synthesize the main idea of a passage. In this passage the best synthesis is (C), hence, the correct answer. Choices (A), (B), (D), and (E) are possible titles but are all incomplete as titles.

31. **(E)**   The question is inappropriate to the passage—it addresses men and women. However, the research addressed in the passage was done on men only. Hence, the correct answer is (E); all the rest of the choices (A), (B), (C), and (D) are incorrect.

32. **(A)**   Choice (A) is sound and is the best and correct answer. Choice (B) is incorrect; choice (C) is an incorrect implication; the same can be said of choices (D) and (E).

33. **(D)**   The study covered only men, hence, a major limitation is the fact that it did not include women of the same age group. The correct answer, therefore, is (D); choice (A) may not be an essential in the study, hence, definitely not a major limitation; choice (B), while a limitation, cannot be considered "major." Besides, "children" could include babies through young adolescents—a rather wide age range; choice (C) is also a limitation, but it does not state the precise age range.

34. **(A)**   This question requires you to identify the main idea of this passage. Choices (B) and (C) are limited because the passage indicates that parents outstrip their children both educationally and economically, choice (A). Choices (D) and (E) are inappropriate because the passage indicates that students will not even equal the educational and economic accomplishments of their parents.

35. **(C)** This question asks you to go beyond the facts that are presented in the passage. Choices (A) and (B) may be true, but the passage neither states nor implies anything that supports them. Also, just because this generation of students will not outstrip or even equal its parents educationally or economically, this does not support the assumptions that parents are smarter than their children, and parents were more interested in school than their children are. It can be assumed, though, that parents are generally more industrious than their children, choice (C).

36. **(E)** A careful rereading of the passage will reveal that the author presents an idea but no support for the idea. No empirical data is presented which clearly shows that parents are educationally and economically superior to their children. For example, in 1945, 85 percent of first-graders entering school graduated. In 1962, only 45 percent of the first-graders entering school graduated. Choice (E) is the correct answer. Choices (A), (B), (C) and (D) are not supported.

37. **(D)** This question requires you to determine which of the statements is a fact. The passage contains no facts. Even though the passage begins with "It is a known fact that ..." no evidence is presented; therefore, choices (A), (B), (C), and (E) are incorrect. However, the author does believe that parents are educationally and economically superior to their children. This is a fact, choice (D).

38. **(A)** The question asks you to identify the main idea, the central thought of this passage. Choices (D) and (E) are supporting details. Neither of them can be supported and therefore cannot be the main idea. Since there is no evidence of how smart children were in the past, no comparison can be made, thus eliminating choice (C). While the passage does state that parents are not supportive of our schools, choice (B) is not the main idea of the passage. It's the main idea of the second paragraph only. Choice (A) is the correct answer.

39. **(D)** The author makes two points in this passage: American students are not performing well academically, and a lack of parental involvement is the reason for this intellectual mediocrity. Choices (A) and (B) only express one of these two points. Choice (C) is true, according to the passage, but it only supports the reason for low academic achievement among American students—a lack of parental involvement. Choice (E) is not appropriate because the author does not hold the children responsible for the problem. The most appropriate answer is choice (D).

40. **(A)**   The author states that 45-50 percent of high school graduates lack basic skills; American students score lower on achievement tests than students in schools of other countries. He also states that over 23 million Americans are functionally illiterate. These three statements more than support the main idea of the passage—inferior academic achievement. To say that the main idea is marginally supported is not true. To say that the evidence is limited or that there is no evidence at all is also untrue. To say that there is an abundance of support is untrue, but the evidence given is adequate to support the main idea, choice (A).

41. **(C)**   Since the author blames only parents for the poor academic performance of American students, the argument has to be judged as being too limited. Certainly, there must be many reasons why American students are not performing well academically. A lack of parental involvement is only one reason—choice (C).

42. **(C)**   The author's idea in this passage is considered an opinion since no empirical data is available to support the idea. Unsupported statements are merely opinions that may be accepted or rejected. The author really provides no support for the idea expressed—choice (C).

43. **(A)**   Even though no concrete evidence is given, the author does make a strong argument that a mismatch does exist. When students have difficulty reading and understanding story books, frustration sets in, and students do not perform at levels commensurate with their listening capacity. Choice (A) is the appropriate answer. One might think that no argument exists, choice (E), but it does. "Despite what many think," sets the stage for the opposing view of the author.

44. **(B)**   This question requires an evaluation. No one, particularly teachers, has the time to rewrite books. The choice is obvious—(B). This is the *least* appropriate strategy for teachers. Be sure to read questions carefully. You may have missed the word *least,* as opposed to *most.*

45. **(C)**   Again, you are asked to make an evaluation with reference to appropriateness. It would be very difficult to tape math formulas and diagrams. Therefore, the most appropriate choice for an answer of least applicability is choice (C)—math.

46. **(A)**   This question requires you to distinguish between facts and opinions. Choices (B), (C), (D) and (E) are facts that need no justification. The general population, especially inservice and preservice teachers, is aware of these striking changes. Whether the reforms mentioned in choices

(B), (C), (D) and (E) have failed to meet the needs of the urban/inner city child is an opinion that cannot be proved as a fact. Everyone will agree that standards were raised, students and teachers were tested and assessed as never before, curriculum revision was at an all-time high, and teacher training programs have taken on new looks. However, not everyone will agree that the needs of the urban/inner city child are not being met—choice (A).

47. **(C)** In order to identify the topic of this passage, you must first identify the main idea—*the reforms of the 1980s have failed to meet the needs of the urban/inner city child.* Choices (A), (B), (D), and (E) are reforms that have taken place. Each is too limited in scope and support to be the main topic. Choice (C), the underserved urban/inner city child, is the main topic.

48. **(E)** This question requires you to engage in analysis. It requires you to identify the stated relationship between the low performance of urban/inner city children on standardized tests and the reasons for such low performance (cause-effect relationship). Choices (A), (B), (C), and (D) are all inappropriate due to inaccurate interpretations of ideas presented in the passage. For example, the passage stated that standards were raised, but it was never indicated that these standards were too high. The most appropriate choice is (E).

49. **(C)** Not much explanation is needed here to explain the author's attitude. His/her attitude is clearly critical because it is established that the reforms have not met the needs of the urban/ inner city child. The appropriate choice is (C).

50. **(B)** This question requires an identification of the main idea of this passage. Nothing in the passage suggests that negotiation gives teachers more power, choice (E). Negotiation is a method of improving conditions (in general) for teachers. Choices (A), (C), and (D) are singularly-improved conditions that are too limited to be the main idea of this passage. The passage speaks to several improved conditions—choice (B).

51. **(B)** The author clearly supports the argument for teacher negotiation, citing research studies for justification. However, since no empirical data is given with sources identified, the argument is not considered fully supported. Therefore, choice (B) is the most appropriate answer.

52. **(C)**   This question requires you to identify the organization of the passage. Choice (A) is inappropriate because no problem is presented. Choices (B) and (E) are inappropriate because no numerical or chronological lists are enumerated. Choice (D) is inappropriate because the main idea is not implied; it's obvious and stated: *Negotiation empowers teachers*....The most appropriate choice is (C). A controversial issue is presented and defended.

READING FOR CONTENT REVIEW

PURPOSE AND CONTENT OF THE READING COMPREHENSION PASSAGES

Basically, the purpose of the reading comprehension passages in most tests is to measure the ability to read with understanding, insight, and discrimination. Reading comprehension passages test the reader's ability to recognize not only what is explicitly stated, but also to recognize underlying assumptions and the implications of statements in the passage.

Reading comprehension passages are usually chosen from four different fields

social sciences; humanities; physical sciences; and life sciences. More than likely, you do not need any specific knowledge or background other than what is presented in the passage in order to answer the questions.

The questions in the reading passages fall into two categories

those where the answer is stated more or less clearly, and those where either the answer is implied or you must reason it out.

Here are some types of reading comprehension questions frequently used. As you read your test, keep these categories in mind. Quoted within each category are common ways in which the question is often phrased.

Main Idea

"The title that best expresses the idea of the passage is...."

"The author's primary purpose is...."

"The passage is primarily concerned with...."

You're certain to get at least one question of this type. To answer it, look for the topic sentence. Read the first and last sentences of each paragraph, especially of the introductory and last paragraphs. Think as you read "What's the author's point? What's he/she up to? What's he/she trying to prove?"

If time is running short, you may be able to answer main idea questions without reading the entire passage. Keep this in mind as a last resort, rather than leaving these questions blank.

Answer Explicitly Stated

"According to the selection...."

"Which of the following is stated...."

In this type of question the answer is specifically stated and can be found by skimming the passage.

Implied Answers or Those Requiring Reasoning and Interpretation

The answers to these questions are not explicit. You must draw conclusions based on your interpretation of the passage. Types of implied answers include the following:

Drawing Inferences

"The author implies...."

"It can be inferred that...."

"Apparently the author believes...."

"The author most probably included _____ in the passage in order to...."

Skimming may help to refresh your memory and to clarify your understanding of the passage, but finding the answer will require you to think carefully about the author's intentions.

Applying the Author's Ideas to Other Situations

"Which of the following most probably provides an appropriate analogy for the distinction made in the passage...?"

"The author would be likely to agree with which of the following...?"

"Which of the following statements would most likely begin the paragraph following the last paragraph quoted here...?"

These questions require that you understand the author's line of reasoning and can apply it to other situations.

The Author's Logic, Reasoning, or Persuasive Techniques

"The author resolves the question of ___ by...."

"The argument of the passage best supports which of the following?"

"The author attempts to...."

Here you must use your reasoning to determine the answer.

Tone or Attitude

"The tone of the passage is chiefly...."

"Which of the following best states the author's attitude...?"

Tone or attitude is implied, rather than stated, so you must interpret. Individual words become very important, especially adjectives and adverbs.

Is the author neutral, supportive, enthusiastic, angry, concerned, skeptical, or sarcastic? The tone and words used will vary according to his/her attitude. The phrase "Jones rightly states" suggests approval, while "Jones's frivolous claim" suggests disapproval.

Compare these two descriptions of a man getting on a horse:

He quickly leaped atop his noble stallion.

He painfully clambered onto his faithful nag.

The first conveys an image of bravery and gallantry, while the second conveys a picture of someone worn out by old age or infirmity.

TO PREPARE FOR THE TEST, INCREASE YOUR READING EFFICIENCY

When your reading efficiency picks up, your comprehension normally picks up also. If you read slowly, there is no time like the present to accelerate your speed. Choose a variety of material—books (including textbooks), magazines (and scholarly journals), newspapers—and practice improving your efficiency. Concentrate on the basic structure of each sentence

subject, verb, object (who did what to whom). Most other words modify or color the SVO (subject, verb, object) in some way. At the beginning you may even find it helpful to underline the SVO to help you focus on the structure of the sentence and thus on its basic meaning.

STRATEGY FOR WHEN YOU TAKE THE TEST

There are several strategies for handling the reading comprehension passages. Practice before the test and decide which you are most comfortable with. Whatever method you choose, be sure to read all of the choices, and, if possible, understand them before making a choice.

1. Save the reading comprehension questions for last. They take longer to answer and are not worth any more points. One possible exception to this rule is if you have a really poor vocabulary, but you have good reading comprehension.

2. If there are two reading comprehension passages (one long and one short) on each verbal section, you may want to take a quick peek at each before you begin answering. If pressed for time, you will want to do the shorter one first. If time is not a determining factor, you may first choose to do a passage selected from a field you are most comfortable with, for example, a biologist may choose the life sciences passage first.

3. Read the selection carefully at a moderate speed. Don't skim, read. But move along at the best speed you can comfortably handle, reading phrases rather than reading a word at a time. When you read at your fastest comfortable speed, concentrate on what is important.

4. Many people find it very helpful to read the questions (but not the answer choices) before reading the passage. This gives purpose to your reading. If you know what you're looking for before you read, you're more likely to find it. For example, had you read the question first you could have answered the following more efficiently

    "the author mentions criticism by X in order to...." Although this is a highly recommended technique, some people find it confusing. Practice it as you do your reading exercises and see if you can become comfortable with it. Be sure to read only the question since the multiple-choice answers will only confuse you if you read them first.

5. Skim both the passage and the questions (but not the answer choices) and then go back and read both the passage and the questions again very carefully. This is effective, but it takes more time.

A NOTE FOR SLOW READERS

If you are a slow reader, skip one of the reading passages in order to leave more time to concentrate on the other areas of the verbal section where you can earn points more quickly. (If time permits, come back to the passage you skipped.) Take a quick peek at each reading passage to see which one is best for you. If you're a physics major, you'll probably prefer a passage that discusses a scientific rather than a historical topic.

TIPS FOR IMPROVING READING COMPREHENSION FOR CONTENT

Read the questions carefully. Make sure you understand what you are being asked before you fill in your answers.

After you have finished the selection and read the questions, if time allows, re-read the passage. This is the time to search for details.

As you read the passage the second time, analyze the author's ideas. Check for his/her attitude. Be sure to draw a distinction between the facts and the author's interpretation of them. Draw a distinction also between the main idea of the passage and any supporting details.

If there are words in the passage that you don't know, substitute a word which seems to be a synonym, based on the context.

True is Not Always Correct

Don't choose an answer simply because it's true. Be sure it answers the question. A choice may often be perfectly true but may not answer the question.

Always is Always Wrong

If an answer contains words like "always" or "never," be very suspicious of it. There are few "no exceptions" absolutes in this world. Mary may love George with all her heart; they may have been married for 50 love-filled years. But surely there have been at least a few moments when she was ready to kick him in the shins.

So, if an answer contains words like **invariably, completely, without exception** (words without any qualifiers), it is (almost) always the wrong answer.

Mark Up the Test Booklet

It is helpful to read with your pencil. Mark up the key words and important ideas. If you've read the questions first, make a mark where you found the answer.

Look for transitional phrases. These signposts give you a road map of the author's thought. Underline them as you read.

A question format that sometimes appears is one in which three or four statements are given, and you must choose from among the following:

(A) I only

(D) II and III only

(B) III only

(E) I, II, and III

(C) I and III only

Questions of this type are perfect for the elimination strategy. If you found that statement I was correct, then the answer must contain I, thus eliminating (B) and (D). If III was definitely incorrect, then you could eliminate any choice containing III, leaving (A) as the correct choice.

Take a Deep Breath

If you get tired or nervous, take a couple of deep breaths, and look up and down (to take your eyes away from the page). Remind yourself that you're a college graduate and an intelligent person. You will be surprised how much this can help. When you look back, the answer may come to you.

Drill 1: Reading for Content

DIRECTIONS: Read the following passage and answer the questions.

Some years ago there arose what has come to be considered an important distinction regarding the purposes of product and programmatic evaluation. It was noted that evaluation serves two different functions. Formative evaluation collects data about products as they are being developed. It helps the developer to form and modify products in order to meet research perceived needs. Occasionally this may result in aborting further development, thus preserving precious resources.

Summative evaluation, on the other hand, determines how worthwhile a fully developed product is, alone or in comparison with other competing products. Rigorous summative evaluations are regularly conducted by such groups as Consumer Reports or Ralph Nader and his associates.

1. The author's main purpose is to

    (A) point out the superiority of summative evaluation over formative.

    (B) point out the essential role of formative evaluation in product development.

(C) explain the differences between formative and summative evaluations.

(D) show the need for product and programmatic evaluation.

(E) show that an important distinction arose 30 years ago.

2. Which of the following is most likely to be true of formative evaluators?

(A) They are dispassionate observers involved in the development of the product.

(B) They enter the process only after the product has been developed.

(C) They are intimately involved in the developmental process.

(D) They compare the value of the completed product with that of other similar products.

(E) They are generally nonprofit.

3. Summative evaluation data would be most useful to

(A) the chief of development for the product involved.

(B) the chief purchasing officer of a corporation.

(C) field researchers.

(D) the chief engineer for the developing company.

(E) all of the above more or less equally.

DIRECTIONS: Read the following passage and answer the questions.

Passive-aggressive personality disorder has as its essential characteristic covert noncompliance to ordinary performance demands made in social and occupational situations. To a greater extent than in other personality disorders, this pattern may be context dependent, appearing only in certain situations.

Aggressive impulses and motives are expressed by passivity. These represent its primary dynamic and may take the form of inaction, inefficiency, procrastination, or obstructionism. It is an interpersonal disorder, the recognition of which depends on the seemingly unjustified frustration and hostility others feel toward such individuals. By the use of verbal expressions indicating compliance or agreement, the passive-aggressive person conceals his actual noncompliance and the secret sadistic satisfaction he derives from the frustration he thereby causes. This dynamic is distinguished from that associated with masochism, in which self-punitive actions are used to control others or to evoke protective responses from them. It is also distinguished from the ambivalence and indecision of obsessive-compulsive persons, who may appear passive and obstructionistic, but are not motivated by a wish to evoke frustration in others.

4. It can be inferred from the passage that a person having passive-aggressive disorder would be most likely to do which of the following?

    (A) Disagree politely with others and act according to his own desires

    (B) Smile in agreement but delay in fulfilling a request

    (C) Evoke masochistic reactions in those with whom he deals

    (D) Provoke aggression from others to satisfy his own masochistic needs

    (E) Feel ambivalent toward his superiors

5. According to the selection . . .

    (A) sexual pleasure is at the root of PA disorder.

    (B) obsessive-compulsive persons do not engage in covert noncompliance.

    (C) the passive-aggressive person's outward expression is in compliance with his inner feelings.

    (D) sadists punish in order to control others.

    (E) passive-aggressive disorder is more likely to appear in some situations than in others.

6. The author implies about passive-aggressive disorder that

    (A) persons with the disorder are nearly always unable to function in normal life.

    (B) the disorder, though common, is often unrecognized.

    (C) persons with PA disorder may present themselves as victims.

(D) persons with PA disorder feel a great need for nurturing and protection.

(E) persons with the disorder act in solitary communion with themselves.

7. Based upon the passage, where would passive-aggressive disorders be most likely to be identified in the largest numbers?

(A) In a primitive and loosely structured society

(B) In the higher levels of a hierarchical society such as the military

(C) In a relatively classless society such as a commune

(D) During the Greco-Roman period of history

(E) In the lower levels of a hierarchical society such as the military

READING FOR CONTENT DRILLS

ANSWER KEY

Drill 1 — Reading for Content

1.	(C)	2.	(C)	3.	(B)
4.	(B)	5.	(E)	6.	(C)
7.	(E)				

VOCABULARY LIST

bastion
   n.- a projection from a fortification; any strong defense

beleaguer
   v.- to besiege by encircling; to surround

circumlocution
   n.- a round about way of expressing something

debase
   v.- to make lower in value, quality, dignity, etc.

elocution
   n.- the art of public speaking

impropriety
   n.- the condition of being improper

injunction
   n.- a command, order

lilliputian
   adj.- tiny, dwarfed

manifold
   adj.- having many forms, parts; of many sorts

maudlin
   adj.- foolishly, often tearfully, sentimental

moribund
   adj.- dying; coming to an end

nebulous
   adj.- of or like a nebula; cloudy, vague

nuance
   n.- a slight variation in tone, color, meaning, expression, etc.

obligate
> v.- to bind by a contract, promise, etc.

obviate
> v.- to do away with or prevent by effective measures; make unnecessary

officiate
> v.- to perform the duties of an office

panacea
> n.- a supposed remedy for all diseases

panegyric
> n.- a formal speech or writing praising a person or event; high praise

parry
> v.- to ward off, as a blow

pedagogue
> n.- a teacher; esp. a pedantic

pellucid
> adj.- transparent, clear; clear and simple

penchant
> n.- a strong liking

perfidy
> n.- betrayal of trust; treachery

perfunctory
> adj.- done merely as a routine; superficial

rancor
> n.- a continuing and bitter hate or ill will

soporific
> adj.- causing sleep; sleepy

spatial
> adj.- of or existing in space

squalid
>adj.- foul; unclean

staid
>adj.- sober, sedate

stalwart
>adj.- strong, sturdy; valiant; firm, resolute

strident
>adj.- harsh sounding; shrill; grating

stultify
>v.- to cause to appear foolish, stupid

taciturn
>adj.- almost always silent

tenet
>n.- a principle, doctrine or opinion maintained as by a school of thought

tensile
>adj.- of, undergoing or exerting tension

timorous
>adj.- full of fear; timid

truncate
>v.- to cut off a part of

tumultuous
>adj.- full of uproar, agitation, etc.

ubiquitous
>adj.- present everywhere at the same time

ulterior
>adj.- lying beyond or on the farther side

umbrage
>n.- resentment and displeasure

undulate
   v.- to move or cause to move in waves

vacuity
   n.- emptiness; an empty void

vehement
   adj.- violent, impetuous; having or showing intense feeling, passionate

veracity
   n.- honesty; accuracy or precision; truth

vernacular
   adj.-of, in or using the native language of a place

vicissitude
   n.- irregular changes in the course of something, esp. change of circumstances in life;

vilify
   v.- to use abusive language about or of; defame

volition
   n.- act or power of willing

voluminous
   adj.- producing or consisting of enough to fill volumes

CHAPTER 5

Reading for Style

➤ Diagnostic Test
➤ Reading for Style Review & Drills
➤ Vocabulary List

READING FOR STYLE DIAGNOSTIC TEST

1. Ⓐ Ⓑ Ⓒ Ⓓ Ⓔ	28. Ⓐ Ⓑ Ⓒ Ⓓ Ⓔ
2. Ⓐ Ⓑ Ⓒ Ⓓ Ⓔ	29. Ⓐ Ⓑ Ⓒ Ⓓ Ⓔ
3. Ⓐ Ⓑ Ⓒ Ⓓ Ⓔ	30. Ⓐ Ⓑ Ⓒ Ⓓ Ⓔ
4. Ⓐ Ⓑ Ⓒ Ⓓ Ⓔ	31. Ⓐ Ⓑ Ⓒ Ⓓ Ⓔ
5. Ⓐ Ⓑ Ⓒ Ⓓ Ⓔ	32. Ⓐ Ⓑ Ⓒ Ⓓ Ⓔ
6. Ⓐ Ⓑ Ⓒ Ⓓ Ⓔ	33. Ⓐ Ⓑ Ⓒ Ⓓ Ⓔ
7. Ⓐ Ⓑ Ⓒ Ⓓ Ⓔ	34. Ⓐ Ⓑ Ⓒ Ⓓ Ⓔ
8. Ⓐ Ⓑ Ⓒ Ⓓ Ⓔ	35. Ⓐ Ⓑ Ⓒ Ⓓ Ⓔ
9. Ⓐ Ⓑ Ⓒ Ⓓ Ⓔ	36. Ⓐ Ⓑ Ⓒ Ⓓ Ⓔ
10. Ⓐ Ⓑ Ⓒ Ⓓ Ⓔ	37. Ⓐ Ⓑ Ⓒ Ⓓ Ⓔ
11. Ⓐ Ⓑ Ⓒ Ⓓ Ⓔ	38. Ⓐ Ⓑ Ⓒ Ⓓ Ⓔ
12. Ⓐ Ⓑ Ⓒ Ⓓ Ⓔ	39. Ⓐ Ⓑ Ⓒ Ⓓ Ⓔ
13. Ⓐ Ⓑ Ⓒ Ⓓ Ⓔ	40. Ⓐ Ⓑ Ⓒ Ⓓ Ⓔ
14. Ⓐ Ⓑ Ⓒ Ⓓ Ⓔ	41. Ⓐ Ⓑ Ⓒ Ⓓ Ⓔ
15. Ⓐ Ⓑ Ⓒ Ⓓ Ⓔ	42. Ⓐ Ⓑ Ⓒ Ⓓ Ⓔ
16. Ⓐ Ⓑ Ⓒ Ⓓ Ⓔ	43. Ⓐ Ⓑ Ⓒ Ⓓ Ⓔ
17. Ⓐ Ⓑ Ⓒ Ⓓ Ⓔ	44. Ⓐ Ⓑ Ⓒ Ⓓ Ⓔ
18. Ⓐ Ⓑ Ⓒ Ⓓ Ⓔ	45. Ⓐ Ⓑ Ⓒ Ⓓ Ⓔ
19. Ⓐ Ⓑ Ⓒ Ⓓ Ⓔ	46. Ⓐ Ⓑ Ⓒ Ⓓ Ⓔ
20. Ⓐ Ⓑ Ⓒ Ⓓ Ⓔ	47. Ⓐ Ⓑ Ⓒ Ⓓ Ⓔ
21. Ⓐ Ⓑ Ⓒ Ⓓ Ⓔ	48. Ⓐ Ⓑ Ⓒ Ⓓ Ⓔ
22. Ⓐ Ⓑ Ⓒ Ⓓ Ⓔ	49. Ⓐ Ⓑ Ⓒ Ⓓ Ⓔ
23. Ⓐ Ⓑ Ⓒ Ⓓ Ⓔ	50. Ⓐ Ⓑ Ⓒ Ⓓ Ⓔ
24. Ⓐ Ⓑ Ⓒ Ⓓ Ⓔ	51. Ⓐ Ⓑ Ⓒ Ⓓ Ⓔ
25. Ⓐ Ⓑ Ⓒ Ⓓ Ⓔ	52. Ⓐ Ⓑ Ⓒ Ⓓ Ⓔ
26. Ⓐ Ⓑ Ⓒ Ⓓ Ⓔ	53. Ⓐ Ⓑ Ⓒ Ⓓ Ⓔ
27. Ⓐ Ⓑ Ⓒ Ⓓ Ⓔ	54. Ⓐ Ⓑ Ⓒ Ⓓ Ⓔ

READING FOR STYLE
DIAGNOSTIC TEST

This diagnostic test is designed to help you determine your strengths and your weaknesses in reading short passages. Follow the directions for each part and check your answers.

**These types of questions are found in the following tests:
AP, GRE, CLEP, LSAT, ACT, and GED.**

---

54 Questions

DIRECTIONS: Each passage is followed by questions based on its content. After reading the passage, choose the best answer to each question. Answer all questions based on what is indicated or implied in that passage.

Questions 1–8 are based on the following passage.

Two paper tendrils, also accordian-pleated, hung down from the clapper of the bell. Miss Faust pulled one. It unfolded stickily and became a long banner with a message written on it. "Here," said Miss Faust, handing the free end to Dr. Breed, "pull it the rest of the way and tack the end to the bulletin board."

Dr. Breed obeyed, stepping back to read the banner's message. "Peace on Earth!" he read out loud heartily.

Miss Faust stepped down from her desk with the other tendril, unfolding it, "Good Will Toward Men!" the other tendril said.

"By golly," chuckled Dr. Breed, "they've dehydrated Christmas! The place looks festive, very festive."

"And I remembered the chocolate bars for the Girl Pool, too," she said. "Aren't you proud of me?"

Dr. Breed touched his forehead, dismayed by his forgetfulness. "Thank God for that! It slipped my mind."

"We musn't ever forget that," said Miss Faust. "It's tradition now—Dr. Breed and his chocolate bars for the Girl Pool at Christmas." She explained to me that the Girl Pool was the typing bureau in the Laboratory's basement. "The girls belong to anybody with access to a dictaphone."

All year long, she said, the girls of the Girl Pool listened to the faceless voices of scientists on dictaphone records—records brought in by the mail girls. Once a year the girls left their cloister of cement block to go a-caroling to get their chocolate bars from Dr. Asa Breed.

"They serve science too," Dr. Breed testified, "even though they may not understand a word of it. God bless them everyone !"

From Cat's Cradle *by Kurt Vonnegut.*

1. "they've dehydrated Christmas" means all of the following EXCEPT

    (A) they've fossilized it.

    (B) they've concentrated it.

    (C) they've decimated it.

    (D) they've dessicated it.

    (E) they've condensed it.

2. Dr. Breed is a nuclear warfare scientist. What is the closest explanation for this name?

    (A) An oxymoron, because of his job

    (B) A pun on his job

    (C) Pathetic fallacy, because he destroys nature

    (D) Ironic, because of his potential for destroying life

    (E) A paradox on what his job entails

3. Miss Faust is his secretary. What is the closest explanation for her name?

    (A) She has overstepped the bounds of learning.

    (B) She dabbles in black magic.

    (C) She serves a Mephistopheles.

    (D) She practices devil worship.

    (E) She is doomed to hell.

4. When Dr. Breed reads the banner's messages, what literary technique is at work?

    (A) Homile

    (B) Irony

    (C) Emblemism

    (D) Symbolism

    (E) Parable

5. What best captures the meaning behind the words: "The girls belong to anybody with access to a dictaphone."

    (A) The girls have sold themselves to the scientists in the way society has prostituted itself to technology.

    (B) The Girl Pool represents the robotised way of modern technology.

    (C) The girls' demeaning and sterile job represents the way women were treated in the work force.

    (D) The girls have become as mechanized as the dictaphones they use.

    (E) The girls must recognize the superior intelligence of the machines and their masters.

6. The use of the words "cloister of cement block" suggests the girls are like

    (A) Nuns trained to work silently in modern surroundings.

    (B) Nuns sequestered in peaceful surroundings.

    (C) Prisoners in a modern efficient facility.

    (D) Prisoners who prefer austere surroundings.

    (E) Nuns immured in modern-day harshness.

7. Miss Faust is talking to

    I.   herself and Dr. Breed.

    II. the Girl Pool and the scientists.

    III. Dr. Breed and the narrator.

    (A) I and II only

    (B) I only

    (C) II and III only

    (D) III only

    (E) II only

8. The parody of Tiny Tim's blessing from Dickens's *Christmas Carol* functions to

   (A) highlight the sterility of this Christmas image as opposed to Dickens's.

   (B) show Dr. Breed's love for the Girl Pool: his chocolate gift.

   (C) show Dr. Breed's Scrooge-like attitude—he forgets the chocolate for the Girl Pool.

   (D) contrast the warmth of this Christmas image as opposed to Dickens's.

   (E) underline the old-fashioned atmosphere of the office at Christmas.

Questions 9–16 are based on the following passage.

Sir Anthony. Madam, a circulating library in a town is as an evergreen tree of diabolical knowledge! It blossoms through the year!—And depend on it. Mrs.—, that they who are so fond of handling the leaves, will long for the fruit at last.

Mrs.— Fie, Fie, Sir Anthony! you surely speak laconically.

Sir Anthony. Why, Mrs.—, in moderation now, what would you have a woman know?

Mrs.— Observe me, Sir Anthony. I would by no means wish a daughter of mine to be a progeny of learning; I don't think so much learning becomes a young woman; for instance, I would never let her meddle with Greek or Hebrew, or algebra, or simony, or fluxions, or paradoxes, or such inflammatory branches of learning—neither would it be necessary for her to handle any of your mathematical, astronomical, diabolical instruments.—But, Sir Anthony, I would send her, at nine years old, to a boarding school, in order to learn a little ingenuity, and artifice. Then, sir, she should have a supercilious knowledge in accounts;—and as she grew up, I would have her instructed in geometry, that she might know something of the contagious countries; but above all, Sir Anthony, she should be mistress of orthodoxy, that she might not mis-spell, and mispronounce words so shamefully as girls usually do; and likewise that she might reprehend the true meaning of what she is saying. This, Sir Anthony, is what I would have a woman know; and I don't think there is a superstitious article in it.

Sir Anthony. Well, well, Mrs.—, I will dispute the point no further with you; though I must confess, that you are a truly moderate and polite arguer, for almost every third word you say is on my side of the question....

From The Rivals, *Act I Sc. ii, by Richard Sheridan.*

9. Mrs.—'s last name gave rise to which of the following dictionary terms?

   (A) Homonym   (D) Synonym

   (B) Altruism   (E) Synecdoche

   (C) Malapropism

10. Which best describes what Mrs.— does to words?

    (A) She changes the meaning to something outrageous.

    (B) She chooses the wrong meaning.

    (C) She gives a word close in meaning that sounds the same.

    (D) She gives a word close in sound that gives a ridiculous meaning.

    (E) She gives a word close in sound but often wrong in meaning.

11. All of the following words Mrs.—uses wrongly EXCEPT

    (A) fluxions.   (D) contagious.

    (B) laconically.   (E) orthodoxy.

    (C) ingenuity.

12. Which of the following best demonstrate the pattern behind Mrs.—'s errors?

    I. Progeny / prodigy

    II. Superstitious / suspicious

    III. Reprehend / apprehend

    (A) I and III only   (D) II and III only

    (B) II only   (E) I, II, and III

    (C) III only

13. What device does Sir Anthony use to describe a circulating library?

    (A) A mixed metaphor   (D) An extended metaphor

    (B) Personification   (E) Pathetic fallacy

    (C) An extended simile

14. What best describes Sir Anthony's meaning behind the notion of the "leaves" and the "fruit"?

    (A) Those who leaf quickly through books will never learn from the tree of knowledge.

    (B) Those who read evil books will become evil.

    (C) Those who read books about exciting adventures will want to experience the same.

    (D) Those who read novels that look exciting will want to read more and more.

    (E) Those who choose a book by its cover will be disappointed at length.

15. All the subjects Mrs.— does *not* want women to know are

    (A) traditionally feminine subjects.

    (B) radically feminine subjects.

    (C) radical university subjects.

    (D) traditionally gentleman subjects.

    (E) traditionally difficult subjects.

16. All the subjects Mrs.— *does* want women to know would equip a woman for the role of

    (A) submissive but knowledgeable homemaker.

    (B) docile but suitably knowledgeable wife.

    (C) docile wife.

    (D) artificial flirt.

    (E) knowledgeable mistress.

Questions 17–23 are based on the following passage.

Oh, to vex me, contraryes meet in one:

Inconstancy unnaturally hath begott

A dangerous habit; that when I would not

I change in vowes, and in devotione.

5   As humourous is my contritione

As my prophane Love, and as soone forgott:

As ridlingly distemper'd, cold and hott,

As praying as mute; as infinite, as none.

I durst not view heaven yesterday; and today

10   In prayers and flattering speaches I court God:

Tomorrow I quake with true feare of his rod.

So my devout fitts come and go away

Like a fantastique Ague: save that here

Those are my best dayes, when I shake with feare.

"19" by John Donne

17. The poem is written as a(n)

    (A) sestina.

    (B) sonnet.

    (C) hymn.

    (D) dramatic monologue.

    (E) aubade.

18. What best explains lines 3–4?

    (A) I want to change my vows and truly love God.

    (B) Just when I want to love God, I change my mind.

    (C) Just when I least want to, I become inconsistent in my love of God.

    (D) I do not want to love God and fight against constancy.

    (E) Just when I want to love God, he changes the vows.

19. Which word best replaces "humorous" in this context?

    (A) Hilarious   (D) Fickle

    (B) Capricious   (E) Ridiculous

    (C) Amusing

20. The word "Love" is capitalized because it

    (A) refers to the poet's mistress.

    (B) refers to the love of the devil.

    (C) personifies any love that is not the love of God.

    (D) personifies the poet's secular love which takes him away from God.

    (E) refers to all the loves the poet has experienced.

21. What best explains the description of the "prophane Love"?

    (A) The poet is laughing at the inconstancy of women.

    (B) The poet is criticizing the fickle nature of women.

    (C) The poet sets up a contrast between the love of women and the love of God.

    (D) The poet sets up a paradox between how he feels about women and how he feels about God.

    (E) The poet sets up a paradigm of how he feels today about women and God.

22. The "Oh" in the first line expresses a cry of

    (A) anger.   (D) ecstasy.

    (B) bewilderment.   (E) misery.

    (C) anguish.

23. All of the following describe the poet's voice EXCEPT

    (A) contrite.   (D) meditative.

    (B) haughty.   (E) perplexed.

    (C) God fearing.

Questions 24–32 are based on the following passage.

1   By the door of the station-keeper's den, outside, was a tin washbasin, on the ground. Near it was a pail and a piece of yellow bar soap, and from the eaves hung a hoary blue woolen shirt, significantly—but this latter was the station-keeper's private towel, and only two persons in all the party
5   might venture to use it—the stage-driver and the conductor. The latter would not, from a sense of decency; the former would not, because he did not choose to encourage the advances of the station-keeper. We had towels—in the valise; they might as well have been in Sodom and Gomorrah. We (and the conductor) used our handkercheifs, and the driver his panta-
10   loons and sleeves. By the door, inside, was fastened a small old-fashioned looking-glass frame, with two little fragments of the original mirror lodged down in one corner of it. This arrangement afforded a pleasant double-barreled portrait of you when you looked into it, with one half of your head set up a couple of inches above the other half. From the glass
15   frame hung the half of a comb by a string—but if I had to describe the patriarch or die, I believe I would order some sample coffins. It had come down from Esau and Samson, and has been accumulating hair ever since— along with certain impurities. . . The table was a greasy board on stilts, and the tablecloth and napkins had not come—and they are not looking for
20   them, either. A battered tin platter, a knife and fork, and a pint tin cup, were at each man's place, and the driver had a queen's-ware saucer that had seen better days. Of course, this duke sat at the head of the table. There was one isolated piece of table furniture that bore about it a touch- ing air of grandeur in misfortune. This was the caster. It was German
25   silver, and crippled and rusty, but it was so preposterously out of place that it was suggestive of a tattered exile king among barbarians, and the majesty of its native position compelled respect even in its degradation. There was only one cruet left, and that was a stopperless, fly-specked, broken-necked thing, with two inches of vinegar in it, and a dozen pre-
30   served flies with their heels up and looking sorry they had invested there.

"Roughing It" *by Mark Twain*

24.   The attitude of the author toward the place he describes is one of

(A) disgust.

(D) deference.

(B) condescension.

(E) sympathy.

(C) amusement.

25. The author expects the members of his audience to be

    (A) bored with the usual recitation of a country they have grown up in.

    (B) shocked but interested in a place they will never visit for themselves.

    (C) amused at the unlikely exaggeration found in the descriptions.

    (D) alarmed by the unsanitary living conditions of people in their own country.

    (E) comfortable in the knowledge that they will never have to live in such a place.

26. The humor of the description of the "towel" in lines 4-7 depends primarily on the fact that

    (A) the shirt had once been blue but has become bleached with time.

    (B) the woolen fabric will not absorb water well enough to make a good towel.

    (C) the shirt is so old that is is probably full of holes.

    (D) the driver and the conductor do not want to soil the only towel available.

    (E) the shirt is probably so filthy that it would get clean hands dirty again.

27. The stage-driver will not use the station-keeper's towel because he is afraid

    (A) the station-keeper will consider it a sign of special friendship, and the driver hates the station-keeper.

    (B) he will have to share his own personal toilet articles with the station-keeper.

    (C) not to follow the good example of the stage conductor.

    (D) the station-keeper will strike him for being so presumptuous as to use that personal an object.

    (E) it will make the station-keeper think he has to offer unusual courtesies to all the travelers.

28. Which of the following does NOT contribute to the description of the age of the comb?

    (A) "the half of a comb" (line 15)

    (B) "patriarch" (line 16)

    (C) "sample coffins" (line 16)

    (D) "Esau and Samson" (line 17)

    (E) "accumulating hair" (line 17)

29. Which of the following creates humor through the greatest contrast of elegant language used to describe something quite disgusting?

    (A) "the driver his pantaloons and sleeves" (lines 9–10)

    (B) "pleasant double-barreled portrait of you" (lines 12–13)

    (C) "along with certain impurities" (line 18)

    (D) "a greasy board on stilts" (line 18)

    (E) "the tablecloth and napkins had not come" (line 19)

30 As it is used in the passage (last line), "invested" can be understood in all of the following senses EXCEPT

    (A) to search into systematically and carefully.

    (B) to spend time or effort with the expectation of receiving pleasure or satisfaction.

    (C) to install in office with ceremony.

    (D) to cover.

    (E) to hem in or besiege.

31. The device the author uses to create humor in such phrases as "in the valise" (line 8), "along with certain impurities" (line 18), and "they were not looking for them, either" (lines 19–20) is

    (A) exaggeration.　　　　(D) imagery.

    (B) afterthought.　　　　(E) anticipation.

    (C) simile.

32. All of the following are elements of contrast in the last 11 lines EXCEPT

  (A) "queen's-ware saucer" (line 21) and "had seen better days" (line 22).

  (B) "this duke" (line 22) and "head of the table" (line 22).

  (C) "grandeur" (line 24) and "misfortune" (line 24).

  (D) "exile king" (line 26) and "among barbarians" (line 26).

  (E) "majesty" (line 27) and "in its degradation" (line 27).

Questions 33–40 are based on the following passage.

Of the Last Verses in the Book

1   When we for age could neither read nor write,

The subject made us able to indite;

The soul, with nobler resolutions decked,

The body stooping, does herself erect.

5 No mortal parts are requisite to raise

Her that, unbodied, can her Maker praise.

    The seas are quiet when the winds give o'er;

So calm are we when passions are no more!

For then we know how vain it was to boast

10 Of fleeting things, so certain to be lost.

Clouds of affection from our younger eyes

Conceal that emptiness which age descries.

    The soul's dark cottage, battered and decayed,

Lets in new light through chinks that time has made;

15 Stronger by weakness, wiser men become,

As they draw near to their eternal home.

Leaving the old, both worlds at once they view,

That stand upon the threshold of the new.

by Edmund Waller.

33. All of the following are elements of opposition in the development of the poem EXCEPT

    (A) "we for age" (line 1) and "nobler resolutions" (line 3).

    (B) "soul" (line 3) and "body" (line 4).

    (C) "mortal parts" (line 5) and "Her" (line 6).

    (D) "calm" (line 8) and "passions" (line 8).

    (E) "dark cottage" (line 13) and "new light" (line 14).

34. The word "Her" (line 6) refers to

    (A) an aged body.

    (B) "subject" (line 2).

    (C) something the author has read or written.

    (D) the soul.

    (E) one of the resolutions mentioned in line 3.

35. What is the literary device used by the author in line 15, "stronger by weakness"?

    (A) Irony

    (B) Allusion

    (C) Comparison

    (D) Paradox

    (E) Metaphor

36. What is the best interpretation of line 15?

    (A) A strong man cannot be wise.

    (B) Young people do not appreciate the advice of older men.

    (C) People become wiser as they grow older and weaker.

    (D) People become weaker as they grow older.

    (E) Physical weakness makes a person appreciate his youth.

37. Which of the following best represents the author's attitude toward old age?

    (A) Resentment at not being able to read and write

    (B) Looking forward to new vistas

(C) Suffering caused by physical infirmities

(D) Confusion about where he is going

(E) Nostalgia for times past

38. According to the context of the poem, what is the best meaning of "indite" (line 2)?

(A) Stand erect.

(B) Give thanks to the Maker.

(C) Write these last verses of this poem.

(D) Look through the chinks of the dark cottage.

(E) Find ourselves after we have been lost.

39. What concept is NOT connected with youth in this poem?

(A) Blowing winds   (D) Clouds

(B) Transience   (E) New beginning

(C) Emptiness

40. According to the context of the poem, what is the probable meaning of "descries" (line 12)?

(A) Resents   (D) Avoids

(B) Sees   (E) Looks forward to

(C) Sings about

Questions 41–48 are based on the following passage.

"What is he, then?"

"Why, I'll tell you what he is," said Mr. Jonas, apart to the young ladies, "he's precious old, for one thing; and I an't best pleased with him for that, for I think my father must have caught it of him. He's a strange old chap, for another," he added in a louder voice, "and don't understand any one hardly, but him!" He pointed to his honoured parent with the carving-fork, in order that they might know whom he meant.

"How very strange!" cried the sisters.

"Why, you see," said Mr. Jonas, "he's been addling his old brains with figures and book-keeping all his life; and twenty years ago or so he went and took a fever. All the time he was out of his head (which was three weeks) he never left off casting up; and he got to so many million at last that I don't believe he's ever been quite right since. We don't do much business now though, and he an't a bad clerk."

"A very good one," said Anthony.

"Well! He an't a dear one at all events," observed Jonas; "and he earns his salt, which is enough for our look-out. I was telling you that he hardly understands any one except my father; he always understands him, though, and wakes up quite wonderful. He's been used to his ways so long, you see! Why, I've seen him play whist, with my father for a partner; and a good rubber too; when he had no more notion what sort of people he was playing against, than you have."

Martin Chuzzlewit by *Charles Dickens.*

41. From this passage it can be inferred that Mr. Jonas is all of the following EXCEPT

   (A) Irritated that the old clerk understands hardly anyone except the father.

   (B) Unconcerned about hurting the old clerk's feelings.

   (C) Worried that the old clerk might make a serious error.

   (D) Intent upon impressing the sisters.

   (E) Terribly rude for saying the things he does about his father and the clerk.

42. If the old clerk is not "quite right" in the head, then why is he kept on as an employee?

   (A) Mr. Jonas will not go against his father's wishes.

   (B) Mr. Jonas does not want to offend the ladies.

   (C) Mr. Jonas reveres peopwle of the older generation.

   (D) Mr. Jonas is somewhat afraid of the "strange old chap."

   (E) Mr. Jonas knows the clerk is the best one in the business.

43. As used in the passage, the word "precious" means

   (A) expensive.

   (B) of high value.

(C) beloved.

(D) very overrefined in behavior.

(E) very great.

44. What has made the old clerk not "quite right" in the head?

(A) Going a bit deaf in his old age

(B) Working with numbers and bookkeeping all his life

(C) Working sums and figures in his fever

(D) Having to put up with Mr. Jonas' abuse

(E) Having too much to do in the business now

45. The sentence "He an't a dear one at all events." can best be interpreted to mean which of the following?

(A) Mr. Jonas does not like the old clerk.

(B) The customers of the business do not like the old clerk.

(C) Sometimes the clerk creates serious problems.

(D) He is only a good clerk with some things in the business.

(E) His wages do not cost the company very much money.

46. All of the following are things Mr. Jonas dislikes about the clerk EXCEPT that he is

(A) old.

(B) a bit strange.

(C) a good whist player.

(D) not always aware of who is around him.

(E) not able to hear well.

47. What is the meaning of "he got to so many million at last"?

(A) He irritated countless customers.

(B) He had trouble keeping up with the high figures.

(C) He became quite advanced in years.

(D) He thought the three weeks was a million days.

(E) He lost the company too much money in revenues.

48. A reasonable description of the old man is that he

   (A) knows what he is doing when it is something he has been accustomed to doing.

   (B) only pretends to be deaf and addled in order to irritate Mr. Jonas.

   (C) can do only the simplest of tasks, although he would like to be able to do more.

   (D) can do anything he wants to do, but only chooses to do what pleases him.

   (E) will only perform such tasks as please Mr. Jonas' father.

Questions 49–54 are based on the following passage.

1   The widow was as complete a contrast to her third bridegroom, in everything but age, as can well be conceived. Compelled to relinquish her first engagement, she had been united to a man of twice her own years, to whom she had become an exemplary wife, and by whose death she was
5 left in possession of a splendid fortune. A southern gentleman, considerably younger than herself, succeeded to her hand, and carried her to Charleston, where, after many uncomfortable years, she found herself again a widow. It would have been singular if any uncommon delicacy of feeling had survived through such a life as Mrs. Dabney's; it could not be crushed
10 and killed by her early disappointment, the cold duty of her first marriage, the dislocation of the heart's principles consequent on a second union, and the unkindness of her southern husband, which had inevitably driven her to connect the idea of his death with that of her comfort. To be brief, she was the wisest, but unloveliest variety of women, a philosopher, bearing
15 troubles of the heart with equanimity, dispensing with all that should have been her happiness, and making the best of what remained. Sage in most matters, the widow was perhaps the more amiable for the one fraility that made her ridiculous. Being childless, she could not remain beautiful by proxy, in the person of a daughter; she therefore refused to grow old and
20 ugly, on any consideration; she struggled with Time, and held fast her roses in spite of him, till the venerable thief appeared to have relinquished the spoil, as not worth the trouble of acquiring it.

by Nathaniel Hawthorne

49. From the first sentence we can assume that Mrs. Dabney is

   (A) much younger than her present groom.

   (B) about the same age as her present groom.

    (C) older than her present groom.

    (D) much older than her present groom.

    (E) impossible to tell for sure.

50. Her first marriage can best be described as

    (A) an exercise in duty but without love.

    (B) the one spot of romantic loveliness in an otherwise lackluster existence.

    (C) an intellectually challenging relationship.

    (D) an experience in poverty made bearable by mutual trust and understanding.

    (E) a relationship marred by disloyalty and unchastity.

51. Her second marriage to the southern gentleman was different from the first in that it was

    (A) based on mutual love and understanding.

    (B) forced upon them by social pressures with which they could not cope.

    (C) the result of her desire for status.

    (D) founded upon greed and lack of tender feelings rather than upon love.

    (E) an illegal arrangement unsanctioned by either civil or religious custom.

52. The "early disappointment" mentioned in line 11 refers to

    (A) her first marriage.

    (B) her second marriage.

    (C) her contemplated third marriage.

    (D) her first serious love.

    (E) a combination of her romantic experiences up to this time.

53. The last part of the paragraph involves the use of an interesting personification. Who is personified?

    (A) The bride   (D) Beauty

    (B) Her third husband   (E) Time

    (C) Marriage

54. How does a woman remain beautiful "by proxy" according to this author?

    (A) She has a beautiful daughter.

    (B) She refuses to grow old.

    (C) She gives way to a ridiculous frailty.

    (D) She avoids remaining single by marrying repeatedly.

    (E) She becomes a philosopher.

READING FOR STYLE DIAGNOSTIC TEST

ANSWER KEY

1. (C)		19. (B)		37. (B)	
2. (D)		20. (D)		38. (C)	
3. (C)		21. (C)		39. (E)	
4. (B)		22. (C)		40. (B)	
5. (B)		23. (B)		41. (C)	
6. (E)		24. (C)		42. (A)	
7. (D)		25. (B)		43. (E)	
8. (A)		26. (E)		44. (C)	
9. (C)		27. (D)		45. (E)	
10. (D)		28. (C)		46. (C)	
11. (A)		29. (C)		47. (B)	
12. (A)		30. (A)		48. (A)	
13. (D)		31. (B)		49. (B)	
14. (C)		32. (B)		50. (A)	
15. (D)		33. (A)		51. (D)	
16. (B)		34. (D)		52. (D)	
17. (B)		35. (D)		53. (E)	
18. (C)		36. (C)		54. (A)	

DETAILED EXPLANATIONS
OF ANSWERS

1. **(C)**   The point of the banner is that it has compressed, preserved the meaning of Christmas into two sides of paper, so all the words that have to do with shrinking or drying are appropriate. Decimated means destroyed in great numbers; this is the odd one out (C).

2. **(D)**   The name is ironic because of the lack of potential for breeding that such a scientist brings to the world (D). To check on the validity of your answer make sure that you know the other terms: oxymoron is usually used in poetry for two paradoxical words in close proximity: "pleasant pain" for example; a pun is a play on words which is what Vonnegut is doing but the answer is not full enough to show how the pun operates; pathetic fallacy is a term used for the empathy often shown for the human race from nature and human characteristics given to nature; paradox is a seemingly self-contradictory phrase which turns out to be true.

3. **(C)**   Faust was of course the learned philosopher and dabbler in "magic" that sold his soul to the devil. Vonnegut plays on the name to suggest that as Breed's secretary doing all his bidding (even remembering the chocolate bars) she is serving the devil in the same way the original Faust did (C).

4. **(B)**   The fact that a nuclear warfare scientist reads out the message of peace and love is irony, because it reverses the truth in an amusing yet sobering way (B). Homile is a simple story used to illustrate a point using folk or country images, similar to a parable which has now taken on more religious connotations. Emblemism was used to give an image a "concrete" reality: a gold-edged love poem for example—whereas symbolism endows the image with greater hidden meanings beyond reality.

5. **(B)**   All the choices have a measure of truth to them, but range from the exaggerated (A) which goes too far, to (C) which is perhaps a feminist approach to the interpretation. The words themselves suggest more of the robotizing of industry where machines "belong" to anyone who can work them (B) rather than any idea of prostitution or demeaning

work, or that the girls are mechanized—it is the "belonging" that is the key idea here.

6. **(E)** The words need to be clearly analyzed to interpret the meaning—"cloister" connotes "nunnery"; "cement block" conjures up the modern prison. You need to know the word "immured" as imprisoned and imagine the harshness of the Girl Pool environment. The answer then is (E).

7. **(D)** In amongst all the banter, the narrator does in fact use the "me" pronoun. The answer is (D). You know that the Girl Pool is not there as they leave their cloisters only once a year. The scientists remain "faceless," certainly they are not there in the office.

8. **(A)** Everyone knows the Tiny Tim blessing; the echo of the words should conjure up for the reader the hope and forgiveness of the Dickens' story at the end. This "Christmas story," in contrast, is harsh and banal so the blessing highlights the sterility (A).

9. **(C)** Mrs. Malaprop is a famous character in English Literature, giving rise to the term "malapropism" (C). First analyze what she does to the language, then, if you are not familiar with the word, analyze the options: homonym—words that sound the same but are spelled differently (there, their, they're); altruism—doing good for the poor; synonym—word that has the same meaning (joyful, glad); synechdoche—part is used for the whole or vice verse (ten sail—ten ships).

10. **(D)** The key here is to find out exactly what Mrs. Malaprop does. It is not just that she uses the wrong word but the one she uses is so close in sound but so ridiculous in meaning (D).

11. **(A)** You need not only to analyze what Mrs. Malaprop is doing to the language but also to appreciate the fact that some words that may sound wrong are in fact in their true use. (A) fluxions here is correct—a mathematical term to do with time. If you do not know the word, work through the others which do tend to stand out in their misuse as long as your vocabulary can substitute the right meaning: (B) ironically; (C) ingenuousness; (D) contiguous; (E) orthography.

12. **(A)** The pattern is interesting in that Mrs. Malaprop is very close in sound but she twists the meaning which makes for humor. Thus in II suspicious almost fits the pattern except the meaning is too close. The answer then is I and III (A).

13. **(D)**   Sir Anthony gives the metaphor of the circulating libraries being "evergreen trees of diabolical knowledge" (with a hint of the biblical tree of Knowledge in the Garden of Eden), not a simile because the words "like" or "as if" are not employed, but then Sir Anthony cannot seem to give the metaphor up and extends it (not mixes it—he still keeps to the tree with blossoms and fruit and leaves). The answer is (D).

14. **(C)**   All of the options have something of truth in them except (E) which plays with another notion of books and their covers. Sir Anthony believes books should be for learned subjects. The books he condemns are the "new" novels full of fantasies and exciting adventures—very tempting to young women who had very little to do in those days. The answer is then (C).

15. **(D)**   The young women of those days learned the art of being ladies in school—drawing, music, deportment. They were not encouraged, in fact often forbidden, to learn the subjects their brothers were learning— math, the classics, astronomy—gentlemanly subjects (D).

16. **(B)**   All young ladies were expected to be good wives—not home-makers because they would have people to run their homes for them. A good wife would be *suitably* knowledgeable in that she would know how to draw, play the piano, sing, and behave in company; she would also be docile to her husband. The answer is (B).

17. **(B)**   A sonnet is easy to recognize because it always has 14 lines— as this does (B). A sestina has six stanzas of six lines each. A hymn extols religious faith; a dramatic monologue gives the impression someone is there giving replies we do not "hear"; an aubade is a poem or song to the dawn.

18. **(C)**   The word "would" here means to like to, or to wish, or desire to; realizing that the negative comes after this verb you should then consider each meaning, sliding the verb sequence into the lines. (C) then reads as the best explanation.

19. **(B)**   The poem deals with the serious subject of a battle of faith: secular love versus religious. Humorous in this context does not have the modern connotation but more that of changing on a whim. The answer then is (B). Fickle is close but holds more the connotation of a deliberate vacillation—here the poet cannot help himself.

20. **(D)** The poet is agonizing over the fact that secular love is not as constant as the love of God. The capital does not suggest one mistress, nor does the word prophane, but a personification of any secular love that takes him away from God (D). Love of the devil is too strong and "all loves" is too general.

21. **(C)** All the terms used for the "prophane Love" could be reversed and there you have the poet's interpretation of the love of God: never capricious, never forgotten, always constant, etc. (C) is the best answer.

22. **(C)** The extremes of emotion can be ruled out here as the poem does not support anger or ecstasy. Misery is also too strong as the poet works his way to the acceptance of the love/fear of God. The choice between bewilderment and anguish depends upon the development of the poem—the poet expresses clearly the state of his predicament. The first cry then is one of sorrow and pain, of anguish (C).

23. **(B)** The word haughty should connote high and mighty, pompous, above it all, on high. These synonyms do not capture the tone of the poem at all. If anything, the poet is humble; a supplicant. The answer then is the odd word out: (B).

24. **(C)** The author is deliberately trying to create a humorous scene. This effect is accomplished through exaggeration of the filth and rusticity of the stagecoach station. Although certain aspects of the place are disgusting—the "private towel," the comb, and the vinegar cruet—the author's tone is gentle. A sly humor is evidenced in such phrases as "sense of decency" (line 6) and "encourage the advances" (line 7), and it is apparent through these that the author has a keen eye in observing human nature. There is no evidence that the author is deferential, condescending, or sympathetic.

25. **(B)** It is unlikely that most people will visit such a place, but the description is certainly interesting. As "local color," a description of something in the West, the audience is probably Easterners who would be a bit shocked but curious. Anyone reading this selection would be uncertain if the descriptions were too exaggerated. "Alarmed" by (D) is too strong a reaction, and (E) would, at best, be only a part of the audience's reaction. People who would live in such an atmosphere would be unlikely to read this description, so (A) can be eliminated.

26. **(E)** The word "hoary" means "white" and "old." Choice (A) might

be a possibility, therefore, but given the conditions in the rest of the station-house, the towel is probably as filthy as everything else. The conductor and the narrator obviously think their handkerchiefs are cleaner than the towel. Choice (B) is illogical. Choice (C) may be true but there is no evidence in the passage to support it, and the shirt's being full of holes would not prevent it from absorbing what little water would be on the men's hands or faces.

27. **(D)** "Advances" in this context is certainly meant to refer to physical violence. This is a rustic location, and it is implied that the only person familiar enough with the station-keeper to use his towel is the conductor. The conductor refuses to use the shirt because of sanitary reasons, so (C) is not correct. There is no sign of friendship or animosity between the station-keeper and the driver. No indication is offered that the station-keeper feels moved to offer special considerations to anyone or expect special sharing from anyone.

28. **(C)** "Sample coffins" is a phrase the narrator uses to refer to his preference for death over describing the comb in more detail. Since the comb is old, it is broken (as the mirror is) and has "accumulated hair" because it has been used much. "Patriarch" indicates an aged object or person, and Esau and Samson are two people who lived during the times of Old Testament history.

29. **(C)** The "certain impurities" are almost certainly lice, among other equally noxious possibilities. As the phrase "certain impurities" is a delicate euphemism for the possibilities, humor is created. The language in (A) is ordinary. Choice (B) does create humor through the contrast of "pleasant" and "double-barreled," but the contrast is not as exaggerated as in choice (C). Ordinary word choice in (D) describes the filthy table, and although choice (E) contains humorous phrasing, there is nothing disgusting about it.

30. **(A)** Choice (A) is the definition for "to investigate." Although the flies obviously did investigate the cruet before they died there, all of the remaining choices are proper definitions of the word "invested." Each of the definitions can be used to describe the flies at various stages of their landing upon and entering the bottle. Choice (C) humorously echoes the pattern of royalty come to a fallen state, and the irony of (B) is particularly effective.

31. **(B)** All of these phrases come at the end of sentences in which the

author has built in an expectation of a surprise or exaggeration at the end. This surprise or exaggeration creates humor by contrast with the rest of the sentence. The anticipation is built into the first part of the sentence, not the phrases in question. Rather than (A), these phrases are more understated than exaggerated.

32. **(B)**   All of the phrases are indicative of the contrast between two extremes. The first quotation in each pair contains wording indicating height of position or royalty, and the second quotation in each pair shows degradation or a "fallen" state. Although "duke" can be considered associated with a high position, "the head of the table" does not show any particular misfortune or change to a low position.

33. **(A)**   Because the author claims people gain "nobler resolutions" as the body ages, choice (A) does not contain opposites. The poet's thesis is that the body is mortal and subject to passions in its youth. The body is metaphorically portrayed as a dark cottage. The soul (portrayed as a female) becomes calmer with the addition of years, and as the body ages new light of resurrection shines throughout the chinks and cracks. Therefore, "soul," "her," "calm," and "new light" are contrasted with "body," "mortal parts," "passions," and "dark cottage."

34. **(D)**   The interrupters in lines 3 and 4 make the passage a bit difficult to read. The sentence, with interrupters deleted, reads, "The soul ... does herself erect." Thus, lines 5 and 6 clearly mean the soul raises herself, without a body, to praise her Maker. "Her" refers to the immortal part of the human, not the aged body (A) or any of the other choices listed.

35. **(D)**   A paradox is a statement that seems contradictory but is nevertheless true. At first glance, it would seem impossible for people to become stronger as they grow weaker, but there is no irony (A) in this passage. People get "stronger" spiritually as they become older (progress in physical "weakness").

36. **(C)**   The author intimates that bodily age engenders wisdom. Old men are no longer swayed by the passions they once had in their youth, so their infirmities and their slower pace make them contemplative and wise. The more time people contemplate the transience of physical life, the more they are made aware of the soul and look forward to eternal life. Choice (D) is, therefore, only partially correct. Rather than age making a person appreciate his youth (E), the aging process makes him look forward to an eternal home. Although the paradox shows a weak and old man becoming

wise, the poem does not deal with the converse (A). There is no evidence of (B) in the poem.

37. **(B)**   The last sestet of the poem deals with the light emanating from the soul's new home. The tone is one of joyous anticipation. Although (C) is probably a logical effect of a body "battered and decayed," suffering is not the main emphasis. There is no indication of resentment of not being able to read and write (A) for age, nor is there (E) nostalgia for times past. The author displays no confusion about where he is going (D), as the soul at the end looks upon "both worlds" and stands "upon the threshold of the new."

38. **(C)**   The word "indite" means "to compose or to write." This meaning can be gleaned from the context of the poem's first two lines. Line 1 can be paraphrased, "Even though we were so old that we could not read or write." Line 2 finishes that thought with the antithesis, "The subject enabled us to write." The title to this poem, "Of the Last Verses in the Book" illuminates the first two lines. The author, inspired by a growing appreciation of the soul's grandeur, is able to write down this poem of praise in the book of his life. Although he is old, and therefore is quite feeble, this advanced age has given the author a glorious insight; the subject has provided the necessary insight for one more poem. The first sestet finishes this thought by stating that the soul does not need the body in order to raise herself to an erect position (A) so that she may praise her Maker (B). Choice (D) is too far away in the poem to be a plausible answer, and (E) is not found in the poem.

39. **(E)**   Usually associated with youth, new beginning in this poem is a sign of extreme old age and imminent death. The last three lines describe men drawing near "to their eternal home," "leaving the old," and standing "upon the threshold of the new." Blowing winds (A) stir up the seas of youth (line 7). A close examination of lines 10 through 12 refutes the remaining answers. When men are calm, they know how vain it is to boast of transient (B), "fleeting things." "Clouds" (D) conceal the "emptiness" (C) of youth.

40. **(B)**   Clues in lines 11 and 12 point to the meaning "sees": when we are young, "clouds" hide or "conceal" something from our young "eyes." The logical conclusion is when we are old, we "see" that which was hidden from us in younger days. Although "sings about" (C) and "looks forward to" (E) seem good choices, they are not as good as (B) when the context of the two lines is considered. Choices (A) and (D) are

illogical since the reward of old age is to be neither resented nor avoided.

41. **(C)** Evidence in the passage indicates the old clerk is still a good records keeper. Mr. Jonas observes that he "an't a bad clerk," to which Anthony adds, "A very good one." Mr. Jonas is obviously unconcerned about hurting the old clerk's feelings (B) as he says terribly rude things (E) in front of his father and the old clerk. Mr. Jonas says the clerk is "old" and he is not "pleased with him for that." Mr. Jonas' irritation with the old man shows through when he points out the clerk's inability (A) to hear no one but Mr. Jonas' father. Perhaps Mr. Jonas is trying to impress the young ladies (D) as he addresses them "apart."

42. **(A)** Mr. Jonas' father is described in the passage as "honored parent." This wording might be taken ironically, and perhaps is humorous given the way he speaks in front of his parent, but Mr. Jonas goes on to say how the two old men are used to each other. As it would probably upset Mr. Jonas' father to do without his longtime companion, (A) is the logical conclusion. Choice (C) is a possible option, but "revere" is too strong a word given the tone Mr. Jonas uses. Choice (E) might be a possibility, but the highest praise the clerk receives is, "very good one." Mr. Jonas is more concerned with impressing than offending the young ladies (B), and there is no evidence to support (D).

43. **(E)** Although "precious" can mean all of the definitions listed as possible choices, "very old" is the best meaning for "precious old" because the rest of the passage details the old clerk's eccentricities brought on by the passing of time. Choice (A) is directly refuted by "He an't a dear one." Choices (B) and (C) may apply to the way Mr. Jonas' father feels about the clerk, but they do not fit Mr. Jonas' feelings. Nowhere in the passage is choice (D) discussed.

44. **(C)** When the old clerk took a fever "twenty years ago or so," he was delirious for three weeks. The entire time he had fever, he "never left off" running figures in his head, and the figures eventually became so high that his brain became addled. Choice (B) may have contributed to the clerk's problem, but it is not the immediate cause. Choice (A) is incorrect as the fever happened many years before he grew deaf. Choice (D) may have contributed, but there is no evidence in the passage to indicate it. Choice (E) is contradicted in the passage.

45. **(E)** During the conversation between Mr. Jonas and Anthony about the clerk's worth as a worker, Mr. Jonas comments, "He an't a dear one" and then explains how he "earns his salt." The idiom "earns his salt"

means he "earns his wages," so "dear" can be taken to mean "expensive" in this context: the old clerk does not have to be paid much but he earns his pay. Although choice (A) may be true, it is not the meaning in this context. There is no evidence to support choices (B), (C), or (D).

46. **(C)**   The clerk's being a good whist player seems to strike a bit of admiration in Mr. Jonas because the old man can play well even when he "had no more notion what sort of people he was playing against, than you have." Even though he seems to be amazed at the old clerk's whist game, Mr. Jonas seems irritated the old man is unaware of anyone else but the "honored parent," choice (D). Mr. Jonas speaks disparagingly of the clerk's age choice (A), strangeness choice (B), and deafness choice (E).

47. **(B)**   During his fever, the old clerk added numbers for three weeks. The numbers mounted steadily into "so many million at last." Choice (D) is a possibility, but evidence in the passage does not indicate this probability. The fever happened before choice (C) became a factor. Choice (E) is refuted by the passage, and choice (A) has no evidence to support it.

48. **(A)**   The old clerk seems sharp enough dealing with accustomed things—clerking, whist, responding to Mr. Jonas' father—but he has difficulties with responding to new people and situations. There is no evidence that (B) is correct, although he could hardly be blamed for getting a little of his own back. Keeping books and playing whist are not "the simplest of tasks," choice (C). What the old clerk "would like" (C) to do or is pleased, choices (D) and (E), to do is not a consideration in this passage. It seems as if the old man's mind is permanently afflicted; Mr. Jonas says of him after the fever, "I don't believe he's ever been quite right since."

49. **(B)**   Since we are told that she is a contrast to him in everything but age, we can assume that Mrs. Dabney and her third bridegroom are about the same age.

50. **(A)**   Mrs. Dabney was during her first marriage an "exemplary" wife to a man twice as old as she was. The marriage was a "cold duty" (line 10) and therefore, it is presumed, was without love.

51. **(D)**   We have to read between the lines for this one. We know he was an unkind husband (lines 7, 8 and 12) and that she had even considered suicide or at least wished for his death during this marriage (line 13). We also know that her first husband had left her well off financially (line 5). From these facts we must assume the nature of the relationship.

52. **(D)**   Line 10 introduces a catalog of Mrs. Dabney's experiences, the first of which is the disappointment spoken of. It can only refer to the first engagement which she was compelled to relinquish (lines 2 and 3).

53. **(E)**   Personification involves giving human qualities to a non-human or abstract object, so the first two answers could not be correct. Of the three abstractions which make up the last three answers, the last, time, is the one being personified. Time is the "venerable thief" (line 21) who at first tries to steal the "rose" of her beauty and finally gives up.

54. **(A)**   Lines 19 and 20 clearly state that it is "in the person of a daughter" that a woman can maintain her beauty.

READING FOR STYLE REVIEW

This review is meant to help you become familiar with the types of reading passages you will find in reading comprehension tests covering prose, poetry, drama, and commentary. Each of these types of writing communicates ideas in a very distinct way. This review will help you understand how each type differs from the others. It will also help you learn how to handle types of writing that may be very unfamiliar to you.

When you begin reading each section in this review, do not become frustrated if some of the vocabulary is new to you. Before long you will understand the new words. You do not have to try to memorize any of the literary terms that may come up, just as long as you understand them while you are reading the review. Relax and consider all the points that the review sections make about the individual types of writing. This will train you to handle these same types of writing when you take an actual reading comprehension test.

INTERPRETING LITERATURE AND THE ARTS TOPICS

The following topics are a sampling of the types of literature you may find on most reading for style tests. You do not have to have an in-depth knowledge of all of these topics, but you should become familiar with the types of literature each topic covers.

Popular Literature

1. Fiction
2. Prose
3. Drama
4. Poetry

Classical Literature

1. Fiction
2. Prose
3. Drama
4. Poetry

Commentary about Literature and the Arts

1. Comments
2. Criticism
3. Reviews

"Popular" literature usually refers to writers of the post-World War II era. This includes everyone from Toni Morrison to William Golding, and Betty Friedan to Ken Kesey.

"Classical" literature usually means writers of the World War II era and preceding. This includes everyone from Edith Wharton to D.H. Lawrence, and Stephen Crane to William Faulkner.

The authors named here are only a very small sample of the authors that could possibly appear on a test. There is no clear dividing line between the two types of literature. The terms "popular" and "classical" are just rough guides to give you an idea of the content breakdown.

The literature on most tests ranges from primarily American authors to a representation of English and Canadian authors, as well as some translations from world literature. These works will include contemporary literature, works from the popular press, fiction, non-fiction, poetry, prose, and criticism, reviews, comments on literature, the fine arts, television, film, and dance.

A casual survey of recent years' exams reveals that the following authors' works are frequently offered for discussion: Edith Wharton, Robert Frost, D.H. Lawrence, Twain, Steinbeck, Emerson, Thoreau, Hemingway, Thomas Wolfe, Tennessee Williams, Stephen Crane, Carl Sandburg, Fitzgerald, Faulkner, Eugene O'Neill, Katherine Ann Porter, G.K. Chesterton, Ralph Ellison, William Golding, Joyce Carol Oates, Mary Gordon, Studs Terkel, James Baldwin, Ken Kesey, Betty Friedan, Gail Godwin, Robert Stone, John Irving, John LeCarré, Toni Morrison, Mary McCarthy, and Maya Angelou. What these authors' works have in common is their significance and relevance to the human condition, as well as their merit as literary works. They have something to say, and they say it well.

Figures of Speech

Figurative language helps to create imaginative and detailed writing. A figure of speech is used in the imaginative rather than the literal sense. It helps the reader to make connections between the writer's thoughts and the external world. Knowing the different types of figures of speech can help you determine the context in which a word is being used and, thereby, help you determine the meaning of that word. The following are some commonly used figures of speech.

Simile

A simile is an explicit comparison between two things. The comparison is made by using *like* and *as*.

Her hair was *like* straw.

The blanket was *as* white as snow.

Metaphor

Like the simile, the metaphor likens two things. However, *like* or *as* are not used in the comparison.

"All the world's a stage." Shakespeare

Grass is nature's blanket.

A common error is the mixed metaphor. This occurs when a writer uses two inconsistent metaphors in a single expression.

The blanket of snow clutched the earth with icy fingers.

Hyperbole

A hyperbole is a deliberate overstatement or exaggeration used to express an idea.

I have told you a thousand times not to play with matches.

Personification

Personification is the attribution of human qualities to an object, animal, or idea.

The wind laughed at their attempts to catch the flying papers.

As you read this review, think about how each of the writing types differs from the rest. Keep in mind the objectives of each of the types (prose, poetry, drama, commentary). Finally, be sure you understand one section before you go on to the next. This understanding will do wonders for you when you take reading for style tests.

READING PROSE

What is prose? Basically, prose is not poetry. Prose is what we write and speak most of the time in our everyday lives: unmetered, unrhymed language. Furthermore, **prose** may be either **fiction** or **nonfiction**. A novel (like a short story) is fiction; an autobiography is nonfiction. While a novel (or short story) may have autobiographical elements, an autobiography is presumed to be entirely factual. Essays are usually described in other terms: expository, argumentative, persuasive, critical, narrative. Essays may have elements of either fiction or nonfiction, but are generally classed as a separate type of prose.

Reading Novels

What is a novel? A good description might be that a novel is a rather long story, filled with many characters and subplots, interlaced with motifs, symbols, and themes, with time and space to develop interrelationships and to present descriptive passages.

Analyzing novels is a bit like asking the journalist's questions "the five W's and an H": who?, what?, when?, where?, why?, and how? The **"what"** is the story, the narrative, the plot, and subplots. Some students may be familiar with Freytag's Pyramid, originally designed to describe the structure of a five-act drama but now widely used to analyze fiction as well. The stages generally specified are **introduction** or **exposition**, **complication**, **rising action**, **climax**, **falling action**, and **denouement** or **conclusion**.

Also important, subplots often parallel or serve as counterpoints to the main plot line, serving to enhance the central story. Minor characters sometimes have essentially the same conflicts and goals as the major characters, but the consequences of the outcome seem less important.

Of course, plots cannot happen in isolation from characters, the "who." Not only are there major and minor characters to consider; we need to note whether the various characters are **static** or **dynamic**. Static characters do not change in significant ways—that is, in ways which relate to the story which is structuring the novel.

Other characters are fully three-dimensional, "rounded," examples of humans in all their virtue, vice, hope, despair, strength, and weakness. This rich variety aids the author in creating characters who are credible and plausible, without being dully predictable or mundane.

We describe major characters or "actors" in novels as **protagonists** or **antagonists**. The *pro*tagonist struggles **toward** or for someone or something; the *an*tagonist struggles **against** someone or something. The possible conflicts are usually cited as man against himself, man against man, man against society, man against nature. Sometimes more than one of these conflicts appears in a story, but usually one is dominant and is the structuring device.

Or a character can be a **stereotype**, without unique characteristics. For instance, a sheriff in a small Southern town; a football player who is all brawn; a librarian clucking over her prized books; the cruel commandant of a POW camp.

Characters often serve as **foils** for other characters, enabling us to see one or both of them better. A classic example is Tom Sawyer, the Romantic foil for Huck Finn's Realism. Or, in Harper Lee's *To Kill a Mockingbird,* Scout is the naive observer of events which her brother Jem, four years older, comes to understand from the perspective of the adult world.

Sometimes characters are **allegorical**, or **symbolic**, standing for qualities or concepts rather than for actual people. For instance, Jim Casey (initials "J. C.") in *The Grapes of Wrath* is often regarded as a Christ figure, pure and self-sacrificing in his aims for the migrant workers.

The interplay of plot and characters determines in large part the **theme** of a work, the "why." First of all, we must distinguish between a mere topic and a genuine theme or thesis; and then between a theme and contributing *motifs.* A **topic** is a phrase, such as "man's inhumanity toward man"; or "the fickle nature of fate." A **theme**, however, turns a phrase into a statement: "Man's inhumanity toward man is barely concealed by 'civilization.'" Or "Man is a helpless pawn, at the mercy of fickle fate." Many writers may deal with the same **topic**, such as the complex nature of true love; but their **themes** may vary widely, from "True love will always win out in the end" to "Not even true love can survive the cruel ironies of fate."

Skilled writers often employ **motifs** to help unify their works. A motif is a detail or element of the story which is repeated throughout, and which may even become symbolic. Television shows are ready examples of the use of motifs. A medical show, with many scenes alternately set in the hospital waiting room and operating room, uses elements such as pacing, anxious parent or loved one, the gradually filling ashtray.

But motifs can become symbolic. The oscilloscope line quits blipping, levels out, and gives off the ominous hum. And the doctor's gloved hand sets down the scalpel and shuts off the oscilloscope. In the waiting room, Dad crushes the empty cigarette pack; Mom quits pacing and sinks into the sofa. The door to the waiting room swings shut silently behind the retreating doctor. All these elements signal "It's over, finished."

Setting is the "where" of the story: interior—what structure; exterior—in what locality; and even the world or realm—this world or another. But setting is also the "when": time of day, time of year, time period or year; it is the dramatic moment, the precise intersection of time and space when this story is being told. Setting is also the atmosphere: positive or negative, calm, chaotic, Gothic, Romantic. The question for the reader to answer is whether the setting is ultimately essential to the plot/theme, or whether it is incidental.

Hopefully, the student will see that the four elements of plot, character, theme, and setting are intertwined and largely interdependent. A work must really be read as a whole, rather than dissected and analyzed in discrete segments.

The final question, "how," relates to an author's style. Style involves language (word choice), syntax (word order, sentence type and length), the balance between narration and dialogue, the choice of narrative voice (first person participant, third person with limited omniscience), use of descriptive passages, and other aspects of the actual words on the page which are basically irrelevant to the first four elements (plot, character, theme, and setting).

Reading Short Stories

The modern short story differs from earlier short fiction, such as the parable, fable, and tale, in its emphasis on character development through scenes rather than summary: through *showing* rather than *telling*. Gaining popularity in the nineteenth century, the short story generally was realistic, presenting detailed accounts of the lives of middle-class people. This tendency toward realism dictates that the plot be grounded in *probability*. There was a good chance that these events could really happen. Furthermore, the characters are human with recognizable human motivations, both social and psychological. Setting—time and place—is realistic rather than fantastic. And, as Poe stipulated, the elements of plot, character, setting, style, point of view, and theme all work toward a single *unified* effect.

Unlike the novel, which has time and space to develop characters and relationships, the short story must rely on flashes of insight and revelation to develop plot and characters. The "slice of life" in a short story is much narrower than that in a novel; the time span is much shorter, the focus much tighter. To attempt anything like the grandness available to the novelist would be to view fireworks through a soda straw: occasionally pretty, but ultimately not very satisfying or enlightening.

The elements of the short story are those of the novel, discussed earlier. However, because of the compression of time and concentration of effect, probably the short story writer's most important decision is **point of view**. A narrator may be *objective,* presenting information without bias or comment. Hemingway frequently uses the objective *third-person* narrator, presenting scenes almost dramatically, i.e., with a great deal of dialogue and very little narrative, none of which directly reveals the thoughts or feelings of the characters. We say that such a narrator is fully or partially *omniscient,* depending on how complete his knowledge is of the characters' psychological and emotional makeup. The least objective narrator is the *first-person* narrator, who presents information from the perspective of a single character who is a participant in the action. Such a narrative choice allows the author to present the discrepancies between the writer's/reader's perceptions and those of the narrator.

Answering questions on short stories is much the same as addressing questions on novels. The student must answer multiple-choice questions which require close reading for such elements as tone, style, atmosphere, and inference. Knowing the story beforehand may help the student, but the ability to analyze is the major component of this type of exam.

Reading Essays

Essays fall into four rough categories: **speculative**, **argumentative**, **narrative**, and **expository**. Depending on the writer's purpose, his essay will fit more or less into one of these groupings.

The **speculative** essay is so named because, as its Latin root suggests, it *looks* at ideas; explores them rather than explains them. While the speculative essay may be said to be *meditative,* it often makes one or more points. But the thesis may not be as obvious or clear-cut as that in an expository or argumentative essay. The writer deals with ideas in an associative manner, playing with ideas in a looser structure than he would in an expository or argumentative essay.

The purposes of the **argumentative** essay, on the other hand, are always clear: to present a point and provide evidence, which may be factual or anecdotal, and to support it. The structure is usually very formal, as in a debate, with counterpositions and counterarguments. Whatever the organizational pattern, the writer's intent in an argumentative essay is to persuade his reader of the validity of some claim, as Francis Bacon does in "Of Love."

Narrative and **expository** essays have elements of both the speculative and argumentative modes. The narrative essay may recount an incident or a series of incidents and is almost always autobiographical, in order to make a point, as in George Orwell's "Shooting an Elephant." The informality of the storytelling makes the narrative essay less insistent than the argumentative essay, but more directed than the speculative essay.

Students are probably most familiar with the **expository** essay, the primary purpose of which is to explain and clarify ideas. While the expository essay may have narrative elements, that aspect is minor and subservient to that of explanation. Furthermore, while nearly all essays have some element of persuasion, argumentation is incidental in the expository essay. In any event, the four categories—speculative, argumentative, narrative, and expository—are neither exhaustive nor mutually exclusive.

As nonfiction, essays have a different set of elements from novels and short stories: **voice**, **style**, **structure**, and **thought**.

Voice in nonfiction is similar to the narrator's tone in fiction; but the major difference is in who is "speaking." In fiction, the author is not the speaker—the **narrator** is the speaker. Students sometimes have difficulty with this distinction, but it is necessary if we are to preserve the integrity of the fictive "story." In an essay, however, the author speaks directly to the reader, even if he is presenting ideas which he may not actually espouse personally. This directness creates the writer's **tone**, his attitude toward his subject.

Style in nonfiction derives from the same elements as style in fiction word choice, syntax, balance between dialogue and narration, voice, use of description—those things specifically related to words on the page. Generally speaking, an argumentative essay will be written in a more formal style than will a narrative essay, and a meditative essay will be less formal than an expository essay. But such generalizations are only descriptive, not prescriptive (rules for writing the essay).

Structure and **thought**, the final elements of essays, are so intertwined as to be inseparable. Just as in our discussion of the interdependence of plot and theme, we must be aware that to change the structure of an essay will alter its meaning. For instance, in White's "The Ring of Time," to abandon the *intercalary* paragraph organization, separating the paragraphs which narrate the scenes with the young circus rider from those which reflect on the nature of time, would alter our understanding of the essay's thesis. Writers signal structural shifts with alterations in focus, as well as with visual clues (spacing), verbal clues (*but, therefore, how-*

ever), or shifts in the kind of information being presented (personal, scientific, etc.).

Thought is perhaps the single element which most distinguishes nonfiction from fiction. The essayist chooses his form not to tell a story but to present an idea. Whether he chooses the speculative, narrative, argumentative, or expository format, the essayist has something on his mind that he wants to convey to his readers. And it is this idea which we are after when we analyze his essay.

Often studied is Orwell's "Shooting an Elephant," a narrative essay recounting (presumably) the writer's experience in Burma as an officer of the British law that ruled the poverty-ridden people of a small town. Orwell begins with two paragraphs which explain that, as a white European authority figure, he was subjected to taunts and abuse by the natives. Ironically, he sympathized with the Burmese and harbored fairly strong anti-British feelings, regarding the imperialists as oppressors rather than saviors. He tells us that he felt caught, trapped between his position of authority, which he himself resented, and the hatred of those he was required to oversee.

The body of the essay—some eleven paragraphs—relates the incident with an otherwise tame elephant gone mad which had brought chaos and destruction to the village. Only occasionally does Orwell interrupt the narrative to reveal his reactions directly, but his descriptions of the Burmese are sympathetically drawn. The language is heavily connotative, revealing the helplessness of the villagers against both the elephant and the miserable circumstances of their lives.

Orwell recounts how, having sent for an elephant gun, he found that he was compelled to shoot the animal, even though its destruction was by now unwarranted and even ill-advised, given the value of the elephant to the village. But the people expected it, demanded it; the white man realized that he did not have dominion over these people of color after all. They were in charge, not he.

To make matters worse, Orwell bungles the "murder" of the beast, which takes half an hour to die in great agony. And in the aftermath of discussions of the rightness or wrongness of his action, Orwell wonders if anyone realizes he killed the elephant only to save face. It is the final sentence of the final paragraph which directly reveals the author's feelings, although he has made numerous indirect references to them throughout the essay. Coupled with the opening paragraphs, this conclusion presents British imperialism of the period in a very negative light: "the unable doing the unnecessary to the ungrateful."

Having discovered Orwell's main idea, we must look at the other elements (voice, style, structure) to see *how* he communicates it to the reader. The voice of the first-person narrative is fairly formal, yet remarkably candid, using connotation to color our perception of the events. Orwell's narrative has many complex sentences, with vivid descriptive phrases in series, drawing our eye along the landscape and through the crowds as he ponders his next move. Structurally, the essay first presents a premise about British imperialism. Next the essay moves to a gripping account of the officer's reluctant shooting of the elephant, and finally ends with an admission of his own guilt as an agent of the institution he detests. Orwell frequently signals shifts between his role as officer and his responses as a humane person by using the word *but* or by using dashes to set off his responses to the events he is recounting.

The exam could conceivably take any work and ask the student to discuss how the writer's attitude toward *time is* revealed; to compare/contrast the attitudes toward time in any pair of essays; to look at the writer's use of language in any essay and discuss the resulting *voice*. The most important thing, as always, is to read and reread the question carefully; the next most important thing is to read and reread the work(s) to be discussed. Try to find the *thought* which the writer means to communicate; then analyze for *voice, style,* and *structure*.

Drill 1: Reading Prose

DIRECTIONS: Read the following passage and answer the questions which follow.

1 And it was at this moment, as I stood there with the rifle in my hands, that I first grasped the hollowness, the futility of the white man's dominion in the East. Here was I, the white man with his gun, standing in front of the unarmed native crowd—seemingly the leading actor of the piece; but in 5 reality I was only an absurd puppet pushed to and fro by the will of those yellow faces behind. I perceived in this moment that when the white man turns tyrant it is his own freedom that he destroys.

George Orwell, "Shooting an Elephant"

1. How is the narrator feeling at this moment?

    (1) Uncomfortable   (2) Joyous

(3) Contented   (4) Arrogant

(5) Resentful

2. What is the setting of the passage?

   (1) England   (4) Australia

   (2) Alaska   (5) Texas

   (3) Asia

3. "Absurd puppet" in line 5 refers to

   (1) the elephant.   (4) the government.

   (2) the native king.   (5) the gun.

   (3) the white man.

READING POETRY

Poetry should be enjoyed; it is definitely "reading for pleasure." This last phrase seems to have developed recently to describe the reading we do other than for information or for study.

Very often the meaning of a poem does not come across immediately and for the modern student this proves to be frustrating. Sometimes it takes years for a poem to take on meaning—the reader simply knows that the poem sounds good and it provokes an emotional response that cannot be explained. With time, more emotional experience, more reading of similar experiences, more life, the reader comes to a meaning of that poem that satisfies. In a few more years that poem may take on a whole new meaning. Think of the way lyrics to certain songs affect you—poetry is no different.

This is all very well for reading for pleasure but you are now called upon, in your present experience, to learn poetry for an important examination. Perhaps the first step in the learning process is to answer the question, "Why do people write poetry?" An easy answer is that they wish to convey an experience, an emotion, an insight, or an observation in a startling or satisfying way, one that remains in the memory for years. Why not just come right out and say it like "normal people" do? An easy answer to these questions is that poetry is not a vehicle for conveying meaning alone. Gerard Manley Hopkins, one of the great innovators of rhythm in poetry, claimed that poetry should be "heard for its own sake and interest even over and above its interest or meaning." Poetry provides intellectual stimulus. Of course, one of the best ways of studying a poem is to consider it a jigsaw puzzle presented to you whole. It can then be taken apart piece by piece (word by word), analyzed scientifically, labelled, and put back together again into a whole. Then, the meaning is complete. But people write poetry to convey more than meaning.

T.S. Eliot maintained that the meaning of the poem existed purely to distract us "while the poem did its work." One interpretation of a poem's "work" is that it changes us in some way. We see the world in a new way because of the way the poet has seen it and told us about it. Maybe one of the reasons people write poetry is to encourage us to see things in the first place. Simple things like daffodils take on a whole new aspect when we read the way Wordsworth saw them in his poem "Daffodils."

If poets enhance our power of sight, they also awaken the other senses as powerfully. We can hear Emily Dickinson's snake in the repeated "s" sound of the lines:

His notice sudden is—
The Grass divides as with a Comb—
A spotted shaft is seen—

and because of the very present sense of sound, we experience the indrawn gasp of breath of fear when the snake appears.

Poets write to awaken the senses. They have crucial ideas, but the words they use are often more important than the meaning. More important still than ideas and sense awakening is the poet's appeal to the emotions. And it is precisely this area that disturbs a number of students. Our modern society tends to block out emotions—we need reviews to tell us if we enjoyed a film, a critic's praise to see if a play or novel is worth our time. We hesitate to laugh at something in case it is not the "in" thing to do. We certainly do not cry—at least in front of others. Poets write to overcome that blocking (very often it is their own blocking of emotion they seek to alleviate), but that is not to say that poetry immediately sets us laughing, crying, loving, hating. The important fact about the emotional release in poetry is that poets help us explore our own emotions, sometimes by shocking us, sometimes by drawing attention to balance and pattern, sometimes by cautioning us to move carefully in this inner world.

Poets tell us nothing really new. They tell us old truths about human emotions that we begin to restructure anew, to reread our experiences in light of theirs, to reevaluate our world view. Whereas a car manual helps us understand the workings of a particular vehicle, a poem helps us understand the inner workings of human beings. Poets frequently write to help their emotional life—the writing then becomes cathartic, purging or cleansing the inner life, feeding that part of us that makes us human.

This last point brings any reader of poetry to ask the next question: Why read poetry? One might contend that a good drama, novel, or short story might provide the same emotional experience. But a poem is much more accessible. Apart from the fact that poems are shorter than other genres, there is a unique directness to them which hinges purely on language. Poets can say in one or two lines what may take novelists and playwrights entire works to express. For example, Keats' lines—

Beauty is truth, truth beauty—that is all

Ye know on earth, and all ye need to know—

On reading a poem the brain works on several different levels: it responds to the sounds; it responds to the words themselves and their connotations; it responds to the emotions; it responds to the insights or learning of the world being revealed. For such a process, poetry is a very good training ground—a boot camp—for learning how to read literature in general. All the other genres have elements of poetry within them. Learn to read poetry well and you will be a more accomplished reader, even of car manuals! Perhaps the best response to reading poetry comes from a poet herself, Emily Dickinson, who claimed that reading a book of poetry made her feel "as if the top of [her] head were taken off!"

Before such a process happens to you, here are some tips for reading poetry before and during the examination.

Before the Exam

1. Make a list of poets and poems you remember; analyze poems you liked, disliked, loved, hated, and were indifferent to. Find the poems. Reread them and for each one analyze your *feelings*, first of all, about the poetry itself. Have your feelings changed? Now what do you like or hate? Then paraphrase the meaning of each poem. Notice how the "magic" goes from the poem, i.e., "Daffodils"; the poet sees many daffodils by the side of a lake and then thinks how the sight of them later comforts him.

2. Choose a poem at random from an anthology or one mentioned in this introduction. Read it a couple of times, preferably aloud, because the speaking voice will automatically grasp the rhythm and that will help the meaning. Do not become bogged down in individual word connotation or the meaning of the poem—let the poetry do its "work" on you; absorb the poem as a whole jigsaw puzzle.

3. Now take the puzzle apart. Look carefully at the title. Sometimes a straightforward title helps you focus. Sometimes a playful title helps you get an angle on the meaning. "Happy Families," of course, is an ironic title because the family playing the card game of that name is not happy.

4. Look carefully at the punctuation. Does the sense of a line carry from one to another? Does a particular mark of punctuation strike you as odd? Ask why that mark was used.

5. Look carefully at the words. Try to find the meaning of words with which you are not familiar within the context. Familiar words may be used differently: ask why that particular use. If you have tapped into your memory bank of vocabulary and find you are still at a loss, go to a dictionary. Once you have the *denotation* of the word, start wondering about the *connotation*. Put yourself in the poet's position and think why that word was used.

6. Look carefully at all the techniques being used. You will gain these as you progress through the test preparation. As soon as you come across a new idea learn the word, see how it applies to poetry, where it is used. Be on the lookout for it in other poetry. Ask yourself questions such as why the poet used alliteration here; why the rhythm changes there; why the poet uses a sonnet form and which sonnet form is in use. Forcing yourself to ask the WHY questions, and answering them, will train the brain to read more perceptively. Poetry is not accidental; poets are deliberate people; they do things for specific reasons. Your task under a learning situation is to discover WHY.

7. Look carefully at the speaker. Is the poet using another persona? Who is that persona? What is revealed about the speaker? Why use that particular voice?

8. Start putting all the pieces of the puzzle together. The rhythm helps the meaning. The word choice helps the imagery. The imagery adds to the meaning. Paraphrase the meaning. Ask yourself simple questions: What is the poet saying? How can I relate to what is being said? What does this poet mean to me? What does this poem contribute to human experience?

9. Write a poem of your own. Choose a particular style; use the sonnet form; parody a famous poem; express yourself in free verse on a crucial, personal aspect of your life. Then analyze your own poetry with the above ideas.

During the Exam

You will have established a routine for reading poetry, but now you are under pressure, you must work quickly and will have no access to a dictionary. You cannot read aloud but you can:

1. Internalize the reading—hear the reading in your head. Read through the poem two or three times following the absorbing procedure.

2. If the title and poet are supplied, analyze the title as before and determine the era of the poetry. Often this pushes you toward the meaning.

3. Look carefully at the questions which should enable you to be able to "tap into" your learning process. Answer the ones that are immediately clear to you: form, technique, language perhaps.

4. Go back for another reading for those questions that challenge you— theme or meaning perhaps—analyze the speaker or the voice at work—paraphrase the meaning—ask the simple question, "What is the poet saying?"

5. If a question asks you about a specific line, metaphor, opening or closing lines, highlight or underline them to force your awareness of each crucial word. Internalize another reading emphasizing the high- lighted area—analyze again the options you have for your answers.

6. Do not waste time on a super-tough question. Move on to another section and let the poetry do its "work." Very often the brain will continue working on the problem on another level of consciousness. When you go back to the difficult question, it may well become clear.

7. If you still are not sure of the answer, choose the option that you feel is the closest to correct.

Go home, relax, and forget about the examination!

Drill 2: Reading Poetry

DIRECTIONS: Read the following poem, then answer the questions which follow.

Why Could She Not Stop for Death?

1   Because I could not stop for Death—
He kindly stopped for me—
The Carriage held but just Ourselves—
And Immortality.

5   We slowly drove—He knew not haste
And I had put away
My labor and my leisure too,
For His Civility—

We passed the School, where Children strove
10   At Recess—in the Ring—
We passed the Fields of Gazing Grain—
We passed the Setting Sun—

Or rather—He passed Us—
The Dews drew quivering and chill—
15   For only Gossamer, my Gown—
My Tippet—only Tulle—

We paused before a House that seemed
A Swelling of the Ground—
The Roof was scarcely visible—
20   The Cornice—in the Ground—

Since then—'tis Centuries—and yet
Feels shorter than the Day
I first surmised the Horses' Heads
Were toward Eternity—

Emily Dickinson, 1863.

1. What is the author's attitude toward dying in the poem?

   (1) She is terrified.
   (4) She is contented.

   (2) She is overjoyed.
   (5) She is frustrated.

   (3) She is angry.

2. Death is personified as

   (1) a horse.
   (4) the devil.

   (2) a king.
   (5) a carriage driver.

   (3) a child.

3. Lines 21–24 signify that

   (1) death is timeless.

   (2) the narrator died yesterday.

   (3) the narrator's horses have died.

   (4) Eternity is a nearby city.

   (5) the horses are lost.

READING DRAMA

The Glass Menagerie by Tennessee Williams begins when one of its four characters, Tom, steps into the downstage light and addresses the audience directly as though he were the chorus from a much earlier play. "I have tricks in my pocket, I have things up my sleeve," says Tom. "But I am the opposite of a stage magician. He gives you illusion that has the appearance of truth. I give you truth in the pleasant disguise of illusion."

These words, the written script separate from the theatrical performance of them, is what we call *drama,* and the words give the spectacle its significance because without them the illusion has neither frame nor content. Truth requires boundaries and substance.

Although drama is literature written to be performed, it closely resembles the other genres. In fact, both poetry and prose also can be performed; but as captivating as these public readings sometimes are, only performed drama best creates the immediate living "illusion as truth" Tom promises. Like fiction and narrative poetry, drama tells a tale—that is, it has plot, characters, and setting—but the author's voice is distant, heard only through the stage directions and perhaps some supplementary notes. With rare exceptions, dialogue dominates the script. Some drama is poetry, such as the works of Shakespeare and Molière, and all plays resemble poems as abstractions because both forms are highly condensed, figurative expressions.

A play contains conflict which can be **enacted** immediately on the stage without any alterations in the written word. **Enacted** means performed by an actor or actors free to use the entire stage and such theatrical devices as sets, costumes, makeup, special lighting, and props for support. This differs from the oral interpretation of prose or poetry. No matter how animated, the public reader is not acting. This is the primary distinction between drama and other literary forms. Their most obvious similarity is that any form of literature is a linguistic expression. There is, however, one other feature shared by all kinds of narratives: the pulsating energy which pushes the action along is generated by human imperfection. We speak of tragic characters as having "flaws," but the same is true about comic characters as well. Indeed, nothing is more boring either on a stage or in a written text than a consistently flawless personality, because such characters can never be the real people of our everyday experiences. The most fundamental human truth is human frailty.

Plot Structure

As with other narrative types, a play's **plot** is its sequence of events, its organized collection of incidents. At one time it was thought that all the actions within a play should be contained within a single 24-hour period. Few lengthy plays have plots which cover only the period of time enacted on the stage. Most plays condense and edit time much as novels do. Decades can be reduced to two hours. Included in the plot is the **exposition**, the revealing of whatever information we need in order to understand the conflict of the play. This exposed material should provide us with a sense of place and time (**setting**), the central participants, important prior incidents, and the play's overall mood. In some plays, such as Shakespeare's, the exposition comes quickly. Notice, for instance, the opening scenes in *Macbeth, Hamlet,* and *Romeo and Juliet:* not one presents us with a central character, yet each—with its witches or king's ghost or street brawl—clearly establishes an essential tension foreshadowing the main conflict to come.

These initial expositions attack the audience immediately and are followed by events in chronological order. The exposition must establish what has come previously, even for an audience familiar with the story, before the plot can advance. Arthur Miller, in his *Death of a Salesman,* continuously interrupts the central action with dislocated expositions from earlier times as though the past were always in the present. He carefully establishes character, place, mood, and conflict throughout the earliest scenes; however, whatever present he places on stage is always caught in a tension between the audience's anticipation of the future and its suspicions of the past.

Fairly soon in a play we must experience some incident that incites the fundamental conflict when placed against some previously presented incident or situation. Potentially, anything can happen in a conflict. The **complication** is whatever presents an element capable of altering the action's direction. Perhaps some new information is discovered or a previously conceived scheme fails, creating a reversal of what had been expected. The plot is not a series of similar events but rather a complication of related events leading to a culmination, a **crisis**. In retrospect, we should be able to accept a drama's progression of actions leading to the crisis as inevitable. After the crisis comes the **resolution** (or denouement), which gives the play its concluding boundary. This does not mean that the play should offer us solutions for whatever human issues it raises. Rather, the playwright's obligation is to make the experience he or she presents to us seem filled within its own boundaries.

Terms such as **exposition**, **complication**, **crisis**, and **resolution**, though helpful in identifying the conflict's currents and directions, at best only artificially define how a plot is molded. If the play provides unity in its revelations, these seams are barely noticeable. Moreover, any successful play clearly shows that the artist accomplished much more than merely plugging components together to create a finished work. There are no rules which all playwrights must follow, except the central precept that the play's unified assortment of actions be complete and contained within itself.

Character

Essential to the plot's success are the characters who participate in it. Midpoint in *Hamlet* when Elsinore Castle is visited by the traveling theater company, the prince joyously welcomes the players, but his mood quickly returns to bitter depression shortly after he asks one actor to recite a dramatic passage in which the speaker recalls the fall of Troy and particularly Queen Hecuba's response to her husband's brutal murder. The player, caught by the speech's emotional power, becomes distraught and cannot finish. Left alone on stage, Hamlet compares the theatrical world created by the player with Hamlet's "real" world and asks: "What's Hecuba to him, or he to Hecuba,/ That he should weep for her!" Even though some characters are more complex and interesting than others, they come in countless types as the playwright's delegates to our imaginations and as the imitations of reality seeking our response.

Types of Plays

When Polonius presents the traveling players to Hamlet, he reads from the theater company's license, which identifies them as

> The best actors in the world, either for tragedy, comedy, history, pastoral, pastoral-comical, historical-pastoral, tragical-historical, tragical-comical-historical-pastoral, scene individable or poem unlimited...

The joke is on those who think all plays somehow can be categorized according to preconceived definitions, as though playwrights follow literary recipes. The notion is not entirely ridiculous, to be sure, since audiences and readers can easily tell a serious play from a humorous one, and a play labeled "tragedy" or "comedy" will generate certain valid expectations from us all, regardless of whether we have read a word by Aristotle or any other literary critic.

We tend to categorize dramatic thought into three clusters: the serious, the comic, and the seriocomic. Thus, in our attempts to interpret life's complexities, it is tempting to place the art forms representing it in precise, fixed designations.

Comedy

The primary aim of comedy is to amuse us with a happy ending, although comedies can vary according to the attitudes they project, which can be broadly identified as either **high** or **low**, terms having nothing to do with an evaluation of the play's merit. Generally, the amusement found in comedy comes from an eventual victory over threats or ill fortune. Much of the dialogue and plot development might be laughable, yet a play need not be funny to be comic. **Farce** is low comedy intended to make us laugh by means of a series of exaggerated, unlikely situations that depend less on plot and character than on gross absurdities, sight gags, and coarse dialogue. The "higher" a comedy goes, the more natural the characters seem and the less boisterous their behavior. The plots become more sustained, and the dialogue shows more weighty thought. As with all dramas, comedies are about things that go wrong. Accordingly, comedies create deviations from accepted normalcy, presenting problems which we might or might not see as harmless. If these problems make us judgmental about the involved characters and events, the play takes on the features of **satire**, a rather high comic form implying that humanity and human institutions are in need of reform. If the action triggers our sympathy for the characters, we feel even less protected from the incongruities as the play tilts more in the direction of **tragi-comedy**.

A more consistent play is Oscar Wilde's *The Importance of Being Earnest,* which opened in 1895. In the following scene, Lady Bracknell questions Jack Worthing, who has just announced that Lady Bracknell's daughter, Gwendolyn, has agreed to marry him. Being satisfied with Jack's answers concerning his income and finding his upper-class idleness and careless ignorance about world affairs an asset, she queries him about his family background. In grave tones, the embarrassed Jack reveals his mysterious lineage. His late guardian, Thomas Cardew—"an old gentleman of a very charitable and kindly disposition"—had found the baby Jack in an abandoned handbag.

LADY BRACKNELL: A hand-bag?

JACK: (very seriously): Yes, Lady Bracknell. I was in a hand-bag—a somewhat large, black leather hand-bag, with handles to it—an ordinary hand-bag in fact.

LADY BRACKNELL: In what locality did this Mr. James, or Thomas, Cardew come across this ordinary hand-bag?

JACK: In the cloak-room at Victoria Station. It was given him in mistake for his own.

LADY BRACKNELL: The cloak-room at Victoria Station?

JACK: Yes. The Brighton line.

LADY BRACKNELL: The line is immaterial, Mr. Worthing. I confess I feel somewhat bewildered by what you have just told me. To be born, or at any rate bred, in a hand-bag, whether it had handles or not, seems to me to display a contempt for the ordinary decencies of family life that reminds one of the worst excesses of the French Revolution. And I presume you know what that unfortunate movement led to? As for the particular locality in which the hand-bag was found, a cloak-room at a railway station might serve to conceal a social indiscretion—has probably, indeed, been used for that purpose before now—but it could hardly be regarded as an assured basis for recognized position in good society.

JACK: May I ask you then what would you advise me to do? I need hardly say I would do anything in the world to ensure Gwendolyn's happiness.

LADY BRACKNELL: I would strongly advise you, Mr. Worthing, to try and acquire some relations as soon as possible, and to make a definite effort to produce at any rate one parent, of either sex, before the season is over.

JACK: Well, I don't see how I could possibly manage to do that. I can produce the hand-bag at any moment. It is in my dressing-room at home. I really think that should satisfy you, Lady Bracknell.

LADY BRACKNELL: Me, sir! What has it to do with me? You can hardly imagine that I and Lord Bracknell would dream of allowing our only daughter—a girl brought up with the utmost care—to marry into a cloakroom, and form an alliance with a parcel. Good morning, Mr. Worthing!

(LADY BRACKNELL sweeps out in majestic indignation.)

This dialogue between Lady Bracknell and Jack is typical of what runs throughout the entire play. It is full of exaggerations, in both the situation being discussed and the manner in which the characters, particularly Lady Bracknell, express their reactions to the situation. Under other circumstances an abandoned baby would not be the focus of a comedy, but we are relieved from any concern for the child since the adult Jack is obviously secure, healthy, and, with one exception, carefree. Moreover, we laugh when Lady Bracknell exaggerates Jack's heritage by comparing it with the excesses of the French Revolution. On the other hand, at the core of their discussion is the deeply ingrained and oppressive notion of English class consciousness, a mentality so flawed it almost begs to be satirized. Could there be more there than light, witty entertainment?

Tragedy

The term "tragedy" when used to define a play has historically meant something very precise, not simply a drama which ends with unfortunate consequences. This definition originated with Aristotle, who insisted that the play be an imitation of complex actions which should arouse an emotional response combining fear and pity. Aristotle believed that only a certain kind of plot could generate such a powerful reaction. Comedy, as we have seen, shows us a progression from adversity to prosperity. Tragedy must show the reverse; moreover, this progression must be experienced by a certain kind of character, says Aristotle, someone whom we can designate as the **tragic hero**. This central figure must be basically good and noble: "good" because we will not be aroused to fear and pity over the misfortunes of a villain, and "noble" both by social position and moral stature because the fall to misfortune would not otherwise be great enough for tragic impact. These virtues do not make the tragic hero perfect, however, for he must also possess **hamartia**—a tragic flaw—the weakness which leads him to make an error in judgment which initiates the reversal in his fortunes, causing his death or the death of others or both. These dire consequences become the hero's catastrophe. The most common tragic flaw is **hubris**, an excessive pride that adversely influences the protagonist's judgment.

Often the catastrophic consequences involve an entire nation because the tragic hero's social rank carries great responsibilities. Witnessing these events produces the emotional reaction Aristotle believed the audience should experience, the **catharsis**. Although tragedy must arouse our pity for the tragic hero as he endures his catastrophe and must frighten us as we witness the consequences of a flawed behavior which anyone could exhibit, there must also be a purgation, "a cleansing," of these emotions which should leave the audience feeling not depressed but relieved and almost elated. The assumption is that while the tragic hero endures a crushing reversal, somehow he is not thoroughly defeated as he gains new stature through suffering and the knowledge that comes with suffering. Classical tragedy insists that the universe is ordered. If truth or universal law is ignored, the results are devastating, causing the audience to react emotionally; simultaneously, the tragic results prove the existence of truth, thereby reassuring our faith that existence is sensible.

Sophocles' plays give us some of the clearest examples of Aristotle's definition of tragedy. Shakespeare's tragedies are more varied and more modern in their complexities. *Othello is* one of Shakespeare's most innovative and troublesome extensions of tragedy's boundaries. The title character commands the Venetian army and soon becomes acting governor of Cypress. He is also a Moor, a dark-skinned African whose secret marriage to the beautiful Desdemona has infuriated her father, a wealthy and influential Venetian, whose anger reveals a racist element in Venice which Othello tries to ignore. Iago hates Othello for granting a promotion to Cassio which Iago believes should rightfully be his. With unrelenting determination and malicious deception, Iago attempts to persuade Othello that Desdemona has committed adultery with Cassio. The following excerpt catches Iago in the early stages of his successful manipulation:

IAGO: In Venice they [wives] do let heaven see pranks
They dare not show their husbands; their best conscience
Is not to leave 't undone, but keep 't unknown.

OTHELLO: Dost thou say so?

IAGO: She did deceive her father, marrying you;

And when she seem'd to shake and fear your looks,
She lov'd them most.

OTHELLO: And so she did.

IAGO: Why, go to, then;
She that so young could give out such a seeming,
To see her father's eyes up close as oak,
He thought 'twas witchcraft; but I am much to blame;
I humbly do beseech you of your pardon
For too much loving you.

OTHELLO: I am bound to thee for ever.

IAGO: I see, this hath a little dash'd your spirits.

OTHELLO: Not a jot, not a jot.

IAGO: I' faith, I fear it has.
I hope you will consider what is spoke
Comes from my love. But I do see you're mov'd;
I am to pray you not to strain my speech
To grosser issues nor to larger reach
Than to suspicion.

OTHELLO: I will not.

IAGO: Should you do so, my lord,
My speech should fall into such vile success
As my thoughts aim not at. Cassio's my worthy friend—
My lord, I see you're mov'd.

OTHELLO: No, not much mov'd:
I do not think but Desdemona's honest.

IAGO: Long live she so! and long live you to think so!

OTHELLO: And yet, how nature erring from itself,—

IAGO: Ay, there's the point: as, to be bold with you,
Not to affect many proposed matches
Of her own clime, complexion, and degree,
Whereto, we see, in all things nature tends;
Foh! one may smell in such, a will most rank,
Foul disproportion, thoughts unnatural.
But pardon me; I do not in position
Distinctly speak of her, though I may fear
Her will, recoiling to her better judgment,

May fall to match you with her country forms

And happily repent.

OTHELLO: Farewell, farewell:
If more thou dost perceive, let me know more;
Set on thy wife to observe. Leave me, Iago.

IAGO: My lord, I take my leave. (Going)

OTHELLO: Why did I marry? This honest creature, doubtless,
Sees and knows more, much more, than he unfolds.

Notice that Iago speaks much more than Othello. This is typical of their conversations, as though Iago were the superior of the two. Dramatically, for Iago's scheme to compel our interests we must perceive in Othello tragic proportions, both in his strengths and weaknesses; otherwise, *Othello* would slip into a mean tale about a rogue and his dupe. Much of the tension in this scene stems from Othello's reluctance either to accept Iago's innuendos immediately or to dismiss them. This confusion places him on the rack of doubt, a torture made more severe because he questions his own desirability as a husband. Consequently, since Iago is not the "honest creature" he appears to be and Othello is unwilling to confront openly his own self-doubts, Iago becomes the dominant personality—a situation which a flawless Othello would never tolerate.

History

The playwright's raw material can spring from any source. A passion play, for instance, is a dramatic adaptation of the Crucifixion as told in the gospels. A history play is a dramatic perspective of some event or series of events identified with recognized historical figures. Television docudramas are the most recent examples.

Ever since the sixteenth century history, plays have seldom risen above the level of patriotic whitewash and political propaganda. Of course there are notable exceptions to this trend: Robert Bolt's *A Man for All Seasons* is one. The title character, Sir Thomas More, is beheaded at the play's conclusion, following his refusal to condone Henry VIII's break from the Roman Catholic Church and the king's establishment of the Church of England with the monarch as its head. Henry wants More to condone these actions because the Pope will not grant Henry a divorce from Queen Catherine so that he can marry Anne Boleyn, who the king believes will bear him the male heir he desperately wants. The central issue for us is not whether More's beliefs are valid but whether any person of conscience can act freely in a world dominated by others far less principled. In Henry's only scene he arrives at Sir Thomas' house hoping his Lord Chancellor will not disappoint him:

[music in background]

HENRY: Son after son she's borne me, Thomas, all dead at birth, or dead within a month; I never saw the hand of God so clear in anything....I have a daughter, she's a good child, a well-set child—But I have no son. (He flares up.) It is my bounden duty to put away the Queen, and all the Popes back to St. Peter shall not come between me and my duty! How is it that you cannot see? Everybody else does.

MORE: (Eagerly) Then why does Your Grace need my poor support?

HENRY: Because you are honest. What's more to the purpose, you're known to be honest....There are those like Norfolk who follow me because I wear the crown, and there are those like Master Cromwell who follow me because they are jackals with sharp teeth and I am their lion, and there is a mass that follow me because it follows anything that moves—and there is you.

MORE: I am sick to think how much I must displease Your Grace.

HENRY: No, Thomas, I respect your sincerity. Respect? Oh, man, it's water in the desert....How did you like our music? That air they played, it had a certain—well, tell me what you thought of it.

MORE: (Relieved at this turn; smiling) Could it have been Your Grace's own?

HENRY: (Smiles back) Discovered! Now I'll never know your true opinion. And that's irksome, Thomas, for we artists, though we love praise, yet we love truth better.

MORE: (Mildly) Then I will tell Your Grace truly what I thought of it.

HENRY: (A little disconcerted) Speak then.

MORE: To me it seemed—delightful.

HENRY: Thomas—I chose the right man for Chancellor.

MORE: I must in fairness add that my taste in music is reputably deplorable.

From A Man for All Seasons *by Robert Bolt*

Bolt's imagination, funneled through the dramatist's obligation to tell an interesting story, presides over the historical data and dictates the play's projections of More, Henry, and the other participants. Thus, we do not have "history"; instead, we have a dramatic perception of history shaped, altered, and adorned by Robert Bolt, writing about sixteenth century figures from a mid-twentieth century vantage point. But as the scene above shows, the characters' personalities are not simple reductions of what historical giants should be. When we read any history play, we should search for similar implications; otherwise, the work can never become more than a theatrical precis with a narrow focus.

Modern Drama

Henrik Ibsen's plays began the modern era with their emphasis on **realism,** a seeking of truth through direct observation using the five senses. As objectively depicted, contemporary life received a closer scrutiny than ever before, showing everyday people in everyday situations. Before Ibsen, theatrical sets were limited, with rare exceptions, to castles and country estates. After Ibsen, the farmhouse and city tenement were suitable for the stage. Ibsen's work influenced many others, and from realism came two main variations. The first, **naturalism**, strove to push realism toward a direct transformation of life on stage, a "slice of life" showing how the scientific principles of heredity and environment have shaped society, especially in depicting the plights of the lower classes. The second variation, **expressionism**, moved in a different direction and actually denied realism's premise that the real world could be objectively perceived; instead—influenced by Sigmund Freud's theories about human behavior's hidden, subconscious motivations and by other modernist trends in the arts, such as James Joyce's fiction and Picasso's paintings—expressionism imitated a disconnected dream-like world filled with psychological images at odds with the tangible world surrounding it. While naturalism attempts to imitate life directly, expressionism is abstract and often relies on symbols.

In a sense, all good drama is modern. No label about a play's origin or form can adequately describe its content. Establishing the people, places, and thought within the play is crucial to our understanding. For the characters to interest us we must perceive the issues that affect their lives, and eventually we will discover why the characters' personalities and backgrounds, together with their social situations, inevitably converge with these issues and create conflicts. *Death of a Salesman* challenges the classical definitions of tragedy by giving us a modern American, Willy Loman, who is indeed a "low man," a person of little social importance and limited moral fiber. His delusionary values have brought him at age 64 to failure and despair, yet more than ever he clings to his dreams and painted memories for solace and hope. Late one night, after Willy has returned from an aborted sales trip, his rambling conversation with his wife, Linda, returns to the topic that haunts him the most, his son Biff.

WILLY: Biff is a lazy bum!

LINDA: They're sleeping. Get something to eat. Go on down.

WILLY: Why did he come home? I would like to know what brought him home.

LINDA: I don't know. I think he's still lost, Willy. I think he's very lost.

WILLY: Biff Loman is lost. In the greatest country in the world a young man with such—personal attractiveness, gets lost. And such a hard worker. There's one thing about Biff—he's not lazy.

LINDA: Never.

WILLY (with pity and resolve): I'll see him in the morning; I'll have a nice talk with him. I'll get him a job selling. He could be big in no time. My God! Remember how they used to follow him around in high school? When he smiled at one of them their faces lit up. When he walked down the street....(He loses himself in reminiscences.)

LINDA (trying to bring him out of it): Willy, dear, I got a new kind of American-type cheese today. It's whipped.

WILLY: Why do you get American cheese when you know I like Swiss?

LINDA: I just thought you'd like a change—

WILLY: I don't want change! I want Swiss cheese. Why am I always being contradicted?

LINDA (with a covering laugh): I just thought it would be a surprise.

WILLY: Why don't you open a window in here, for God's sake?

LINDA (with infinite patience): They're all open dear.

WILLY: The way they boxed us in here. Bricks and windows, windows and bricks.

LINDA: We should have bought the land next door.

WILLY: The street is lined with cars. There's not a breath of fresh air in the neighborhood. The grass don't grow any more, you can't raise a carrot in the backyard. They should've had a law against apartment houses.

Remember those two beautiful elms out there? When I and Biff hung the swing between them?

LINDA: Yeah, like a million miles from the city.

WILLY: They should've arrested the builder for cutting those down. They massacred the neighborhood. (Lost) More and more I think of those days, Linda. This time of year it was lilac and wisteria. And then the peonies would come out, and the daffodils. What fragrance in this room!

LINDA: Well, after all, people had to move somewhere.

WILLY: No, there's more people now.

LINDA: I don't think there's more people. I think—

WILLY: There's more people! That's what's ruining this country! Population is getting out of control. The competition is maddening! Smell the stink from that apartment house! And another on the other side....How can they whip cheese?

In Arthur Miller's stage directions for *Death of a Salesman,* the Loman house is outlined by simple framing with various floors represented by short elevated platforms. Outside the house the towering shapes of the city angle inward presenting the crowded oppressiveness Willy complains about. First performed in 1949, the play continues to make a powerful commentary on modern American life. We see Willy as more desperate than angry about his condition, which he defines in ways as contradictory as his assessments of Biff. In his suffocating world, Willy gropes for peace while hiding from truth; and although his woes are uniquely American, in some ways, they touch broader, more universal human problems as well.

Drill 3: Reading Drama

DIRECTIONS: The following three questions are based on the previous passage. After reading the passage, answer the following questions.

1. Where does the dialogue in the passage take place?

   (1) At a country cottage   (4) At a seaside resort

   (2) At a city residence   (5) At a western ranch

   (3) At a European villa

2. Why is Willy upset that Linda bought American cheese?

   (1) Because Biff likes American cheese

   (2) Because Willy does not like cheese

   (3) Because the whole city stinks like cheese

   (4) Because Willy fears change

   (5) Because American cheese makes Linda sick

3. What would be a good description of Linda?

   (1) She is cruel.   (4) She is selfish.

   (2) She is dishonest.   (5) She is patient.

   (3) She is lazy.

READING COMMENTARY

When you go to see a movie, and it turns out to be a movie that strikes you in many ways, you just cannot wait to talk about it. Right? That discussion after the movie is a commentary. It is a way of expressing your thoughts and impressions about the film you have just seen. If you were to write down your thoughts and impressions, rather than discuss them, you essentially would have an example of the type of commentary that turns up on a test.

Commentary is not just about movies. It also takes as its subject dance, art, sculpture, theater, literature, and music. Commentary is a means of conveying feelings about the arts to an audience. The audience may be a teacher for whom you write a report. It may be a friend who receives a letter in which you talk about a play you have just seen. Most likely, the audience is the reader of a newspaper or magazine since this is where the majority of commentary makes its way to the general public. This type of commentary is the kind you will find in the entertainment section of your newspaper. It is also the kind you will encounter on a test.

What are we looking for when we are presented with a review of something? There are a couple of standard items that we should use as guides when we attempt to understand a review. Here are some important questions to keep in mind as you read such a review:

- What is the author's attitude toward the work? Is the basic opinion favorable to the work or is it disapproving?

- Does the author back up his/her opinion with concrete examples? Are the examples descriptive enough that you understand the critic's point?

You should become able to see how a review works in terms of these points. A critic will *always* have an opinion, and they will *always* cite examples to demonstrate why they feel the way they do. Once you learn to recognize this system, you will be able to follow a reviewer's line of reasoning and understand his interpretations and opinions about a play, poem, or painting. Most tests will not expect you to know the background of any of the artists, literature, or works of art discussed. Instead, it will present to you passages which are descriptive enough to answer all questions without any prior knowledge of the work being discussed.

Here is an example of a typical passage that might appear, with questions that would follow:

Superman, starring Christopher Reeve and Margot Kidder, has the look and feel of a comic book placed on screen. Throughout the movie we are presented with the clear, sharp colors of the original Superman as he was, and is, drawn in Marvel Comics. Not only are the colors clear-cut and bold, but so are the personalities of the characters. There is a simplicity to every character in the movie that lets us clearly know the good guys from the bad guys. In a comic book there just is not the room, nor the inclination, to develop a character in great depth, and so we get characters who are more like cardboard cut-outs than real people. This is what makes comic books so fun. Comic books allow us to escape from the world of real people and give us satisfying conclusions to superheroes' dilemmas. *Superman,* the movie, manages to do the same thing. This is what makes it great entertainment!

In *Superman,* nothing is beyond the hero's control. There is nothing terrible that can happen that Superman cannot fix. His character can bring back a loved one from the dead by turning back time. He is also able to avert nuclear destruction by being faster and more powerful that a ballistic missile. When we, the audience, see the character faced with these situations, we feel as if we are involved in them also. When we see Superman get through these situations and conquer these problems, we feel as if we are also a part of the solution. This gives us the kind power over problems that we do not have in real life. It is that feeling of power that we get by identifying with Superman that allows us a fantasy for just a while. *Superman,* like the comic book that came before it, is guaranteed to entertain with humor, drama, and most importantly, the kind of action that puts you in the sky right alongside the hero himself.

Drill 4: Reading Commentary

DIRECTIONS: The following questions are based on the previous passage. Read each question and choose the correct answer.

1. Which of the following terms would the reviewer most likely use to describe the movie *Superman?*

    (1) Ridiculous   (4) Old-fashioned

    (2) Confusing   (5) Boring

    (3) Satisfying

2. According to the reviewer, the movie *Superman* is most like

    (1) a circus.   (4) a poem.

    (2) an auto race.   (5) a comic book.

    (3) a war.

3. The author believes that *Superman*

    (1) is an accurate portrayal of real life.

    (2) is an entertaining fantasy.

    (3) is a depressing drama.

    (4) is too wordy.

    (5) lacks humor.

You will notice that the commentator expresses a clear opinion about the movie and uses examples to explain why he felt the way he did. Every commentary will work in this way. Remember that the objective of any commentary is to express an opinion or explain an interpretation; learn to recognize this first in any commentary you pick up. After that, learn to pick out the concrete examples that the reviewer uses to back up his opinions. Knowing how to pick up these things will help you greatly on any test. Buy a newspaper and read a review of a local play or current movie. Try to pick it apart. This will be good practice so that by the time you take the actual exam you will understand commentary on all of the arts.

READING FOR STYLE DRILLS

ANSWER KEY

Drill 1 — Reading Prose

1. (1)   2. (3)   3. (3)

Drill 2 — Reading Poetry

1. (4)   2. (5)   3. (1)

Drill 3 — Reading Drama

1. (2)   2. (4)   3. (5)

Drill 4 — Reading Commentary

1. (3)   2. (5)   3. (2)

VOCABULARY LIST

abdicate
> v.- to give up a possession, claim or right

aberration
> n.- abnormality, insanity; deviation from what is normal

abjuration
> n.- retraction of rights, allegiances, etc.

belligerency
> n.- aggression, warlike conflict, fight

capricious
> adj.- following no predictable pattern

catalyst
> n.- an agent that stimulates or precipitates a reaction, development or change

commiserate
> v.- to feel or show pity for

deferential
> adj.- marked by courteous submission or respect

deliberation
> n.- an exchange of views in an attempt to reach a decision

descry
> v.- to catch sight of; to detect

despondent
> adj.- having lost all hope

foible
> n.- a small weakness in character; frailty

forbearance
> n.- self-restraint, patient restraint

fortuitous
> adj.- happening by chance, accidental

impregnable
> adj.- that cannot be overcome or entered by force, invincible

improvident
adj.- reckless esp. in the use of material resources

indoctrinate
v.- to instruct in a body of doctrine or belief

ingratiate
v.- to bring oneself into another's favor

insipid
adj.- lacking the qualities requisite for spiritedness and originality

latent
adj.- existing in a temporarily inactive and hidden form

laud
v.- to honor or to praise

licentious
adj.- morally unrestrained

lymphatic
adj.- languid; sluggish

magnanimous
adj.- generous in overlooking injury or insult; rising above pettiness, noble

malevolence
n.- a desire to harm others or to see others suffer

meliorate
v.- to improve or make better

mercurial
adj.- capricious, quick, changeable, fickle

meretricious
adj.- gaudy, alluring by false showy charms

neophyte
n.- a beginner or novice

obeisance
n.- a gesture of respect such as a bow; homage, deference

obsequious
adj.- excessively willing to serve or obey, servile

obstreperous
adj.- noisy or unruly esp. in resisting

onerous
adj.- burdensome, oppressive

periphery
    n.- an outer border, circumference

pithy
    adj.- precisely meaningful and tersely cogent

querulous
    adj.- ill-tempered; irritable

quixotic
    adj.- full of idealism

rapprochement
    n.- reconciliation

recidivism
    n.- a lapse

sanguine
    adj.- of the color of blood; ruddy; cheerful; confident

schismatic
    n.- a separatist

seditious
    adj.- treasonous

solicitous
    adj.- attentive, eager

sonorous
    adj.- characterized by language that is elevated and sometimes pompous in style

temerity
    n.- foolhardy boldness or disregard of danger

tendentious
    adj.- having a biased view

tenuous
    adj.- having little substance or significance; not solidly based

uncandor
    n.- insincerity

unctuous
    adj.- affectedly and self-servingly earnest

vociferation
    n.- offensively loud and insistent utterances esp. of disapproval

CHAPTER 6

Reading Short Passages

➤ Diagnostic Test
➤ Reading Short Passages
  Review & Drills
➤ Vocabulary List

READING SHORT PASSAGES DIAGNOSTIC TEST

1. Ⓐ Ⓑ Ⓒ Ⓓ Ⓔ		27. Ⓐ Ⓑ Ⓒ Ⓓ Ⓔ
2. Ⓐ Ⓑ Ⓒ Ⓓ Ⓔ		28. Ⓐ Ⓑ Ⓒ Ⓓ Ⓔ
3. Ⓐ Ⓑ Ⓒ Ⓓ Ⓔ		29. Ⓐ Ⓑ Ⓒ Ⓓ Ⓔ
4. Ⓐ Ⓑ Ⓒ Ⓓ Ⓔ		30. Ⓐ Ⓑ Ⓒ Ⓓ Ⓔ
5. Ⓐ Ⓑ Ⓒ Ⓓ Ⓔ		31. Ⓐ Ⓑ Ⓒ Ⓓ Ⓔ
6. Ⓐ Ⓑ Ⓒ Ⓓ Ⓔ		32. Ⓐ Ⓑ Ⓒ Ⓓ Ⓔ
7. Ⓐ Ⓑ Ⓒ Ⓓ Ⓔ		33. Ⓐ Ⓑ Ⓒ Ⓓ Ⓔ
8. Ⓐ Ⓑ Ⓒ Ⓓ Ⓔ		34. Ⓐ Ⓑ Ⓒ Ⓓ Ⓕ
9. Ⓐ Ⓑ Ⓒ Ⓓ Ⓔ		35. Ⓐ Ⓑ Ⓒ Ⓓ Ⓔ
10. Ⓐ Ⓑ Ⓒ Ⓓ Ⓔ		36. Ⓐ Ⓑ Ⓒ Ⓓ Ⓔ
11. Ⓐ Ⓑ Ⓒ Ⓓ Ⓔ		37. Ⓐ Ⓑ Ⓒ Ⓓ Ⓔ
12. Ⓐ Ⓑ Ⓒ Ⓓ Ⓔ		38. Ⓐ Ⓑ Ⓒ Ⓓ Ⓔ
13. Ⓐ Ⓑ Ⓒ Ⓓ Ⓔ		39. Ⓐ Ⓑ Ⓒ Ⓓ Ⓔ
14. Ⓐ Ⓑ Ⓒ Ⓓ Ⓔ		40. Ⓐ Ⓑ Ⓒ Ⓓ Ⓔ
15. Ⓐ Ⓑ Ⓒ Ⓓ Ⓔ		41. Ⓐ Ⓑ Ⓒ Ⓓ Ⓔ
16. Ⓐ Ⓑ Ⓒ Ⓓ Ⓔ		42. Ⓐ Ⓑ Ⓒ Ⓓ Ⓔ
17. Ⓐ Ⓑ Ⓒ Ⓓ Ⓔ		43. Ⓐ Ⓑ Ⓒ Ⓓ Ⓔ
18. Ⓐ Ⓑ Ⓒ Ⓓ Ⓔ		44. Ⓐ Ⓑ Ⓒ Ⓓ Ⓔ
19. Ⓐ Ⓑ Ⓒ Ⓓ Ⓔ		45. Ⓐ Ⓑ Ⓒ Ⓓ Ⓔ
20. Ⓐ Ⓑ Ⓒ Ⓓ Ⓔ		46. Ⓐ Ⓑ Ⓒ Ⓓ Ⓔ
21. Ⓐ Ⓑ Ⓒ Ⓓ Ⓔ		47. Ⓐ Ⓑ Ⓒ Ⓓ Ⓔ
22. Ⓐ Ⓑ Ⓒ Ⓓ Ⓔ		48. Ⓐ Ⓑ Ⓒ Ⓓ Ⓔ
23. Ⓐ Ⓑ Ⓒ Ⓓ Ⓔ		49. Ⓐ Ⓑ Ⓒ Ⓓ Ⓔ
24. Ⓐ Ⓑ Ⓒ Ⓓ Ⓔ		50. Ⓐ Ⓑ Ⓒ Ⓓ Ⓔ
25. Ⓐ Ⓑ Ⓒ Ⓓ Ⓔ		51. Ⓐ Ⓑ Ⓒ Ⓓ Ⓔ
26. Ⓐ Ⓑ Ⓒ Ⓓ Ⓔ		

READING SHORT PASSAGES DIAGNOSTIC TEST

This diagnostic test is designed to help you determine your strengths and your weaknesses in reading short passages. Follow the directions for each part and check your answers.

These types of questions are found in the following tests: CBEST, PRAXIS Core Battery, CLEP, and ASVAB.

---

51 Questions

DIRECTIONS: Each passage is followed by questions based on its content. After reading the passage, choose the best answer to each question. Answer all questions based on what is indicated or implied in that passage.

Questions 1–3 are based on the following passage.

Instructions for Absentee Voting

These instructions describe conditions under which voters may register for or request absentee ballots to vote in the November 5, 1991, election.

(1) If you moved on or prior to October 7, 1991, and did not register to vote at your new address, you are not eligible to vote in this election.

(2) If you move after this date, you may vote via absentee ballot or at your polling place, using your previous address as your address of registration for this election.

(3) You must register at your new address to vote in future elections.

(4) The last day to request an absentee ballot is October 29, 1991.

(5) You must be a registered voter in the county.

(6) You must sign your request in your own handwriting.

(7) You must make a separate request for each election.

(8)   The absentee ballot shall be issued to the requesting voter in person or by mail.

1.   A voter will be able to participate in the November 5, 1991, election as an absentee if he or she

   (A) planned to register for the next election in 1992.

   (B) requested an absentee ballot on November 1, 1991.

   (C) voted absentee in the last election.

   (D) moved as a registered voter on October 13, 1991.

   (E) moved on October 7, 1991.

2.   On October 15, 1991, Mr. Applebee requested an absentee ballot for his daughter, a registered voting college student, to enable her to participate in the election process. Mr. Applebee will most likely need clarification on which of the following instructions?

   (A) 2   (D) 5

   (B) 3   (E) 6

   (C) 4

3.   Which of the following best describes the most important piece of information for potential voters who want to participate in the election process, either in person or by absentee ballot?

   (A) Do not change precincts.

   (B) Do register to vote in the appropriate precinct.

   (C) You may vote at your nearest polling place.

   (D) The last day to register is always October 29.

   (E) Your absentee ballot can be used for any election when you have to be out of town.

Questions 4–6 refer to the following passage.

   One of the many tragedies of the Civil War was the housing and care of prisoners. The Andersonville prison, built by the Confederates in 1864 to accommodate 10,000 Union prisoners, was not completed when prisoners started arriving. Five months later the total number of men incarcerated there had risen to 31,678.

The sounds of death and dying were not diminished by surrender of weapons to a captor. Chances of survival for prisoners in Andersonville were not much better than in the throes of combat. Next to overcrowding, inadequate shelter caused unimaginable suffering. The Confederates were not equipped with the manpower, tools, or supplies necessary to house such a population of captives; prisoners themselves gathered lumber, logs, anything they could find to construct some sort of protection from the elements. Some prisoners dug holes in the ground, risking suffocation from cave-ins, but many hundreds were left exposed to the wind, rain, cold, and heat.

Daily food rations were exhausted by the sheer numbers they had to serve, resulting in severe dietary deficiencies. The overcrowding, meager rations, and deplorable unsanitary conditions resulted in rampant disease and a high mortality rate. The consequences of a small scratch or wound could result in death in Andersonville. During the prison's thirteen-month existence, more than 12,000 prisoners died and were buried in the Andersonville cemetery. Most of the deaths were caused by diarrhea, dysentery, gangrene, and scurvy that could not be treated due to inadequate staff and supplies.

4. What is the central idea of the passage?

   (A) The major problem for the Confederates was finding burial spaces in the cemetery.

   (B) The prison was never fully completed.

   (C) Prison doctors were ill-equipped to handle emergencies.

   (D) Andersonville prison was not adequate to care for three times as many prisoners as it could hold.

   (E) Many prisoners died as a result of shelter cave-ins.

5. From this passage the author's attitude toward the Confederates is one of

   (A) approval.   (D) indifference.

   (B) impartiality.   (E) denial.

   (C) contempt.

6. The first sentence of the second paragraph of this passage can best be described as

    (A) a tribute.   (D) an exposé.

    (B) a digression.   (E) an irony.

    (C) a hypothesis.

Questions 7–9 refer to the following passage.

To the Shakers, perfection was found in the creation of an object that was both useful and simple. Their Society was founded in 1774 by Ann Lee, an Englishwoman from the working classes who brought eight followers to New York with her. "Mother Ann" established her religious community on the belief that worldly interests were evil.

To gain entrance into the Society, believers had to remain celibate, have no private possessions, and avoid contact with outsiders. The order came to be called "Shakers" because of the feverish dance the group performed. Another characteristic of the group was the desire to seek perfection in their work.

Shaker furniture was created to exemplify specific characteristics: simplicity of design, quality of craftsmanship, harmony of proportion, and usefulness. While Shakers did not create any innovations in furniture designs, they were known for fine craftsmanship. The major emphasis was on function, and not on excessive or elaborate decorations that contributed nothing to the product's usefulness.

7. The passage indicates that members of the religious order were called the Shakers because

    (A) they shook hands at their meetings.

    (B) they did a shaking dance at their meetings.

    (C) they took their name from the founder.

    (D) they were named after the township where they originated.

    (E) they developed a shaking disorder.

8. Which of the following is the most appropriate substitute for the use of the term "innovations" in the third paragraph?

    (A) Corrections   (D) Functions

    (B) Colors   (E) Brocades

    (C) Changes

9. The passage suggests which of the following about the Shakers?

   (A) Shaker furniture is well-proportioned and ornate in design.

   (B) Shakers believed in form over function in their designs.

   (C) Shaker furniture has seen a surge in popularity.

   (D) Shakers appeared to believe that form follows function.

   (E) Shaker furniture is noted for the use of brass hardware.

Questions 10–12 refer to the following passage.

Benjamin Franklin began writing his autobiography in 1771, but he set it aside to assist the colonies in gaining independence from England. After a hiatus of 13 years, he returned to chronicle his life, addressing his message to the younger generation. In this significant literary work of the early United States, Franklin portrays himself as benign, kindhearted, practical, and hardworking. He established a list of ethical conduct and recorded his transgressions when he was unsuccessful in overcoming temptation. Franklin wrote that he was unable to arrive at perfection, "yet I was, by the endeavor, a better and happier man than I otherwise should have been if I had not attempted it."

10. Which of the following is the least appropriate substitute for the use of the term ethical near the end of the passage?

   (A) Moral   (D) Honorable

   (B) Depraved   (E) Qualifiable

   (C) Virtuous

11. The passage suggests which of the following about Franklin's autobiography?

   (A) It was representative of early American literature.

   (B) It fell short of being a major work of literary quality.

   (C) It personified Franklin as a major political figure.

   (D) It was a notable work of early American literature.

   (E) It was directed toward his enemies.

12. Which of the following slogans best describes Franklin's assessment of the usefulness of attempting to achieve perfection?

    (A) Cleanliness is next to Godliness.

    (B) Nothing ventured, nothing gained.

    (C) Ambition is its own reward.

    (D) Time is money.

    (E) Humility is everything.

Questions 13–15 refer to the following passage.

The scarlet flamingo is practically a symbol of Florida. Once the West Indian flamingo population wintered in Florida Bay and as far north as St. John's River and Tampa Bay, but the brilliantly colored birds abandoned these grounds around 1885 due to the decimation of their numbers by feather hunters. The flock at Hialeah Race Track is descended from a handful of birds imported from Cuba in the 1930s. It took seven years before the first flamingo was born in captivity, but several thousand have since been hatched.

Flamingo raisers found that the birds require a highly specialized diet of shrimps and mollusks to maintain their attractive coloring. It is speculated that hunters as well as the birds' selective breeding habits perhaps caused the disappearance of these beautiful birds from the wild in North America.

13. The central idea of the passage is that the flamingos of Florida

    (A) are a symbol of Florida.

    (B) are hard to raise in captivity.

    (C) are no longer found in the wild in North America.

    (D) came from Cuba.

    (E) eat shrimps and mollusks.

14. The word decimation is closest in meaning to

    (A) destination.   (D) eradication.

    (B) desecration.   (E) appeasement.

    (C) restoration.

15. According to the passage, which of the following is responsible for the flamingo's brilliant plumage?

    (A) Warm waters off the coast of Florida

    (B) Selective breeding

    (C) Their diet of marine organisms

    (D) Shallow water plants

    (E) Fish and water snakes

Questions 16–18 refer to the following passage.

Teachers should be cognizant of the responsibility they have for the development of children's competencies in basic concepts and principles of free speech. Freedom of speech is not merely the utterance of sounds into the air, rather, it is couched in a set of values and legislative processes that have developed over time. These values and processes are a part of our political conscience as Americans. Teachers must provide ample opportunities for children to express themselves effectively in an environment where their opinions are valued. Children should have ownership in the decision-making process in the classroom and should be engaged in activities where alternative resolutions to problems can be explored. Because teachers have such tremendous power to influence in the classroom, they must be careful to refrain from presenting their own values and biases that could "color" their students' belief systems. If we want children to develop their own voices in a free society, then teachers must support participatory democratic experiences in the daily workings of the classroom.

16. The title that best expresses the ideas in the passage is

    (A) The Nature of the Authoritarian Classroom.

    (B) Concepts and Principles of Free Speech.

    (C) Management Practices that Work.

    (D) Exploring Freedom in American Classrooms.

    (E) Developing Children's Citizenship Competencies.

17. It can be inferred from the passage that instructional strategies that assist children in the development of citizenship competencies include all of the following except

    (A) children participating in rule making.

    (B) fostering self-esteem.

    (C) indoctrination in principles of society.

    (D) consideration of cultural and gender differences.

    (E) conflict management skills taught.

18. It can be inferred from the passage that "color" refers to

    (A) remove.   (D) disintegrate.

    (B) influence.   (E) embellish.

    (C) stipulate.

Questions 19–21 refer to the following passage.

The Indians of California had five varieties of acorn which they used as their principal source of food. This was a noteworthy accomplishment in technology since they first had to make the acorn edible. A process had to be developed for leaching out the poisonous tannic acid. They ground the acorns into a meal and then filtered it many times with water. This had to be done through sand or through tightly woven baskets. Early Indian campsites reveal the evidence of the acorn-processing labor necessary to provide enough food for their subsistence. The women patiently ground acorns into meal with stone pestles. The result, a pinkish flour that was cooked into a mush or thin soup, formed the bulk of their diet.

19. The central idea of the passage is the early Indians of California

    (A) had ample food sources.

    (B) left evidence of their meal processing at ancient campsites.

    (C) differed from other Indians in their use of natural resources.

    (D) contributed distinctive talents and technological expertise in providing food sources.

    (E) produced finely crafted woven baskets.

20. According to the passage, which of the following was a technological innovation developed by the early California Indians in the production of food?

    (A) Irrigation of crops
    (D) Dams
    (B) Grinding meal
    (E) Removal of tannic acid
    (C) Filtration system

21. It can be inferred from the passage that the early Indians faced a major problem in their production of food. What was it?

    (A) They needed many pounds of acorns to produce enough meal.

    (B) Acorns had to be carried a great distance to their campsites for grinding.

    (C) The acorn grinding took many hours of hard labor.

    (D) Acorns were scarce.

    (E) It was difficult to filter the meal without losing it.

Questions 22–24 refer to the following passage.

Representatives of the world's seven richest and most industrialized nations held a three-day economic summit in London on July 14–16, 1991. On the second day of the summit, Mikhail Gorbachev, who appealed for help, was offered support by the seven leaders for his economic reforms and his "new thinking" regarding political reforms. However, because the allies were split on giving a big aid package to Gorbachev, the seven leaders decided to provide help in the form of technical assistance in fields such as banking and energy, rather than in hard cash.

22. Which of the following statements best synthesizes what the passage is about?

    (A) A seven-nation economic summit was held in London in July 1991.

    (B) An economic summit of the world's richest nations was held in London in July.

    (C) Mikhail Gorbachev appealed for help and the seven leaders agreed to support his economic reforms.

(D) At a three-day economic summit held in London in July 1991, leaders of the world's seven richest and most industrialized nations agreed to provide technical assistance to Gorbachev.

(E) Representatives of the world's seven most industrialized nations, at a summit conference in London, were split on giving Gorbachev assistance in the form of hard cash.

23. The passage implies

(A) that, under the leadership of Gorbachev, the Soviet Union is faced with a financial crisis.

(B) that Gorbachev's "new thinking" on democratic reforms needs support from the seven nations meeting in London.

(C) that the seven leaders meeting in London were split on giving Gorbachev economic and political support.

(D) that with only technical assistance from the seven nations that met in London, the Soviet Union under the leadership of Gorbachev is heading for economic disaster.

(E) that with the support of political and economic reforms along with provisions for technical assistance from the seven nations that met in London, the Soviet Union under the leadership of Gorbachev can achieve political and economic stability.

24. The passage suggests that technical assistance will be provided to the Soviet Union

(A) only in the fields of banking and energy.

(B) in the fields of banking and energy and possibly other fields also.

(C) by the U.S. in the fields of banking and energy.

(D) by any of the seven nations that met at a summit in London.

(E) by all seven nations—U.S., Great Britain, France, Germany, Italy, Canada, and Japan.

Questions 25–27 refer to the following passage.

A follow-up survey of the 1990 census showed an estimated undercount of 5.2 million people nationwide. This "undercount" was greatest in California where approximately 1.1 million people were not recorded. This estimated undercount was based on a post-census survey of 171,390 households nationwide. Failure to achieve an accurate count would affect federal funding and political representation. If the higher numbers were used, California would gain eight congressional seats instead of seven and about $1 billion in federal funds. Last July 14, 1991, however, Commerce Secretary Robert Mosbacher decided to stick to the original figures of the 1990 census.

25. Which of the following statements gives the main idea of the passage you just read?

    (A) California will gain an additional congressional seat and more federal money if the 1.1 million people undercounted in the census are included.

    (B) The population in a state is the basis for determining the political representation for that state.

    (C) An undercount in the census, if not considered, will be a disadvantage to any state.

    (D) A post-census survey is necessary in getting to a more accurate population figure for the states.

    (E) California will suffer the most because of the 1.1 million undercount in the 1990 census.

26. If the 1.1 million undercount was considered for California

    (A) it would settle any political dispute arising from the undercount.

    (B) it would give California eight congressional seats and $1 billion in federal funds.

    (C) it would discourage the practice of a post-census survey.

    (D) it would create political unrest for other states.

    (E) it would reverse the decision made by Commerce Secretary Mosbacher.

27. What would it mean for California if the original figures of the 1990 census were to remain the same?

    (A) No additional federal funding will be given.

    (B) There will be no additional political representation.

    (C) The amount of federal funding and number of congressional seats will remain the same.

(D) The census undercount will not make a difference.

(E) The results of the follow-up survey of the 1990 census will be meaningless.

Questions 28–30 refer to the following passage.

Labor Day, a national holiday observed in the United States, is really a day we should remember to give thanks to the labor unions. In the days before the unions became effective, a holiday meant a day off, but the loss of a day's pay to working people. It was not until World War II that unions succeeded, through negotiations with the federal government, in making paid holidays a common practice.

28. The main idea in the passage you just read is

(A) the role labor unions played in employer-employee relations.

(B) Labor Day as a national holiday in the U.S.

(C) the role labor unions played in effecting paid holidays.

(D) the dispute between paid and unpaid holidays.

(E) Labor Day before World War II.

29. The passage implies that before World War II

(A) a holiday gave working people a chance to rest from work.

(B) Labor Day meant losing a day's pay.

(C) a holiday was a day to make up for upon returning to work.

(D) labor unions were ineffective.

(E) taking off from work set a worker one day behind in his or her work.

30. As a national holiday, Labor Day should really be a day to remember and be thankful for

(A) working people.

(B) help from the federal government.

(C) paid holidays.

(D) labor unions.

(E) a free day.

Questions 31–33 refer to the following passage.

Ash from Mt. Pinatubo in the Philippines has been found to contain gold and other precious metals. However, officials warned against any hopes of a new "gold rush." They found gold content of only 20 parts per billion, which is far below commercial levels. Other metals found were chromium, copper, and lithium.

31. The passage indicates

   (A) the possibility of existing gold mines beneath Mt. Pinatubo.

   (B) the need for further exploration of what else lies beneath the volcano.

   (C) that there is a new resource for boosting the economy of the Philippines.

   (D) other active volcanoes might be worth exploring as possible gold resources.

   (E) that the gold content of the ash from Mt. Pinatubo does not warrant a commercial level.

32. Which of the following makes a good title for the passage you just read?

   (A) A New Gold Rush

   (B) Mt. Pinatubo's Gold Mine

   (C) Ash Content from Mt. Pinatubo

   (D) A Philippine Discovery

   (E) Precious Metals

33. What might be a possible research project resulting from the ash content finding of Mt. Pinatubo?

   (A) Research on the ash content from the eruption of Mt. Fujiyama in Japan

   (B) Potential market value of the gold and other metals content in the volcanic ash from Mt. Pinatubo

   (C) Further excavation into possible gold underneath Mt. Pinatubo

   (D) Research on what lies underneath active volcanoes

   (E) Compare volcanic ash content with what lies underneath the same volcano when it is inactive

Questions 34–36 refer to the following passage.

Gary Harris, a farmer from Conrad, Montana, has invented and patented a motorcycle helmet. It provides a brake light which can signal traffic intentions to other drivers behind. In the U.S., all cars sold are now required to carry a third, high-mounted brake light. Harris' helmet will meet this requirement for motorcyclists.

34. The passage tells about

    (A) a new invention for motorcyclists.

    (B) a requirement for all cars in the U.S.

    (C) a brake light for motorcyclists.

    (D) Harris' helmet.

    (E) Gary Harris, inventor.

35. An implication regarding the new invention is

    (A) any farmer can come up with a similar traffic invention.

    (B) the new brake light requirement for cars should likewise apply to motorcycles.

    (C) the new brake light requirement for cars cannot apply to motorcycles.

    (D) if you buy a car from outside of the U.S., you are exempted from the brake light requirement.

    (E) as an inventor, Gary Harris can make more money if he leaves farming.

36. Because of the new brake light requirement for cars

    (A) drivers can readily see the traffic signals of car drivers ahead of them.

    (B) less accidents can happen on the road.

    (C) car prices will go up and will be less affordable to buy.

    (D) more lights on the road can be hazardous.

    (E) more traffic policemen will be needed.

Questions 37–39 refer to the following passage.

The U.S. Postal Service issued a 50-cent stamp in Anchorage, Alaska on October 12, 1991 to commemorate the 500th anniversary of the arrival of the Italian explorer Christopher Columbus in the New World. The stamp depicts how Americans may have appeared to Asians crossing the Bering Strait. The stamp series will show the pre-Columbian voyages of discovery.

37. Which of the following makes an appropriate title for the passage?

    (A) The Discovery of the Americas

    (B) 500th Anniversary of the Discovery of America

    (C) The Significance of the Bering Strait

    (D) A Commemorative New U.S. Postal Stamp

    (E) A Tribute to Asians

38. The passage implies that

    (A) historical facts need to be verified.

    (B) Christopher Columbus was not the first to arrive in the New World.

    (C) Asians discovered America.

    (D) native Americans came from Asia.

    (E) history books need to be rewritten.

39. Which of the following would you consider as the most historically significant?

    (A) Asians crossed over the Bering Strait to the New World before Columbus came.

    (B) It has been 500 years since Christopher Columbus arrived in the New World.

    (C) A tribute to Christopher Columbus was held on October 12, 1991.

    (D) Native Americans are of Asian origin.

    (E) There were other voyages undertaken before Christopher Columbus'.

Questions 40–42 refer to the following passage.

Popular U.S. attractions such as Disneyland, the Golden Gate Bridge, Las Vegas, and the Statue of Liberty have attracted millions of foreign tourists whose spending helped the U.S. post a $31.7 billion service trade surplus in 1990 compared with a $101 billion merchandise trade deficit in the same year. The heavy-spending Japanese tourists accounted for the biggest portion of the tourism trade surplus, spending $5.5 billion more touring the U.S than U.S. tourists spent visiting Japan. Canadians also outspent American tourists to Canada by $2.2 billion.

40. The main idea in the foregoing passage is

    (A) foreign tourists in the U.S. spend more than American tourists spend abroad.

    (B) there are more tourist attractions in the U.S. than any foreign country.

    (C) Japanese tourists are the biggest spenders among tourists to the U.S.

    (D) Canadians rank second to Japan in tourism spending in the U.S.

    (E) tourism is very important to the economy of the U.S.

41. A significant implication of the passage is

    (A) that Japan will have to reduce its tourist spending in U.S.

    (B) that the U.S. should increase its tourist spending in Japan.

    (C) that tourist spending in the U.S. reduces its trade deficit.

    (D) that Canada needs to improve its tourism attractions.

    (E) that Japan has more money on which to spend on tourism than any other country.

42. Based on the passage, which of the following would be an appropriate topic of discussion with students?

    (A) International relations

    (B) Global relations

    (C) Balance in global tourism industry

    (D) Interdependency of nations

    (E) Global competition

Questions 43–45 refer to the following passage.

Results of a study released by the College Board and the Western Interstate Commission for Higher Education show that by 1994, the majority of California's high school graduates will be non-white and that by 1995, one-third of all the nation's students will be from minority groups. It is also predicted that, nationally, the total non-white and Hispanic student population for all grade levels will increase from 10.4 million in 1985–1986 to 13.7 million in 1994–1995. The figures suggest that now, more than ever, equal educational opportunity for all students must be our nation's number one priority.

43. The foregoing passage suggests

   (A) that this nation is, educationally, at risk.

   (B) that something needs to be done to reduce the growing numbers of minority students in the school system.

   (C) that urgent educational reforms are needed to provide equal opportunity for all students.

   (D) that a Spanish bilingual system be endorsed.

   (E) that immigration laws be strictly enforced to balance the numbers of white and non-white student populations.

44. Because of changes in demographics, what reform is needed in California in the area of teacher preparation?

   (A) Recruit more minority teachers

   (B) Increase budget appropriation for schools

   (C) Enforce school desegregation

   (D) Encourage non-Hispanic, white students to enroll in private schools

   (E) Revise teacher preparation programs to reflect appropriate preparation for multicultural classrooms

45. What problem could result from the increasing minority population in the nation?

   (A) Strong resentment from mainstream whites towards the school system

   (B) Increase in enrollment in private and parochial schools

(C) "White flight" to the suburbs where minorities are not yet the majority

(D) School budget crisis

(E) Inappropriate and inadequate school curriculum and teacher preparation to meet the needs in multicultural classrooms

Questions 46–48 refer to the following passage.

The United States' final offer on a lease agreement for the Subic Bay Naval Base in the Philippines was rejected by the Philippine Senate. Hence, for the first time in nearly a century, U.S. military strategy for the Asia-Pacific region will no longer be centered on the Philippines, and the nation's economic survival and development will no longer rely on U.S. dependency. Somehow, this dependency on the U.S. has served as an impediment to the Philippines' ability to join East Asia's economic boom.

46. Which of the following best summarizes what the passage is about?

(A) Philippine-U.S. military relations have come to an end.

(B) The Philippines' economic dependency on the U.S. ended with its Senate's rejection of the U.S. lease offer.

(C) The U.S. lease offer for the Subic Naval Base was rejected by the Philippine Senate, hence the U.S. will no longer have its military base in the Asia-Pacific region.

(D) The Philippines is now on its own in its economic survival and development.

(E) The U.S. military strategy for the Asia-Pacific Region will no longer be on the Philippines following the Philippine Senate's rejection of the U.S. lease offer.

47. The U.S. military's pullout from Subic Bay would mean

(A) less jobs for Filipinos.

(B) less Americans in the Philippines.

(C) a chance for the Philippines to survive on its own.

(D) weakening of U.S.-Philippine relations.

(E) less protection for the Philippines.

48. What could be the reason that the Philippine Senate rejected the U.S. lease offer?

   (A) Filipinos are getting more nationalistic.

   (B) It will be an opportunity for the Philippines to survive and develop on its own economically.

   (C) Less money was offered by the U.S.

   (D) The U.S. would be better off somewhere else.

   (E) To defeat President Aquino's stand on the issue

Questions 49–51 refer to the following passage.

   The Matsushita Electric Industrial Co. in Japan has developed a computer program that can use photographs of faces to predict the aging process and, also, how an unborn child will look. The system can show how a couple will look after 40 years of marriage and how newlyweds' future children will look. The computer analyzes facial characteristics from a photograph based on shading and color differences, and then creates a three-dimensional model in its memory. The system consists of a personal computer with a program and circuit board and will be marketed by the Matsushita Company soon.

49. The main idea in the passage you just read is about

   (A) a computer that shows the aging process.

   (B) a computer that chooses the right mate.

   (C) a computer that predicts the number of children for newlyweds.

   (D) a computer that predicts the looks of future children as well as their parents.

   (E) a computer that analyzes photographs.

50. The new computer program developed in Japan uses

   (A) a three-dimensional face model.

   (B) photographs of faces to predict the aging process and looks of an unborn child.

   (C) shading and color differences in photographs.

   (D) a personal computer and circuit board.

   (E) facial characteristics from a photograph.

51. What might result from this new computer system developed in Japan?

    (A) The U.S. will develop an even more sophisticated computer system.

    (B) Competition among trading partners of Japan will be keener.

    (C) Japan's economy will skyrocket.

    (D) The trade imbalance between Japan and the U.S. will increase.

    (E) The next computer system Japan will develop will be even more refined and sophisticated.

READING SHORT PASSAGES DIAGNOSTIC TEST

ANSWER KEY

1. (D)	14. (D)	27. (C)	40. (A)
2. (E)	15. (C)	28. (C)	41. (C)
3. (B)	16. (E)	29. (B)	42. (C)
4. (D)	17. (C)	30. (D)	43. (C)
5. (B)	18. (B)	31. (E)	44. (E)
6. (E)	19. (D)	32. (C)	45. (E)
7. (B)	20. (C)	33. (B)	46. (E)
8. (C)	21. (E)	34. (A)	47. (C)
9. (D)	22. (D)	35. (B)	48. (B)
10. (B)	23. (E)	36. (A)	49. (D)
11. (D)	24. (B)	37. (D)	50. (B)
12. (B)	25. (A)	38. (B)	51. (E)
13. (C)	26. (B)	39. (A)	

DETAILED EXPLANATIONS OF ANSWERS

1. **(D)** Choice (D) fulfills requirements stated in rules 2 and 4 of the instructions for absentee voting. All other choices do not.

2. **(E)** Mr. Applebee's daughter must sign her own request for an absentee ballot. Since the passage indicates that she is registered, the most important instruction for her is number 6 (E).

3. **(B)** Choices (A), (D), and (E) are not stated in the passage. Choice (C) is not true unless voters have registered, choice (B).

4. **(D)** The passage states that housing of prisoners was "one of many tragedies of the Civil War," and that "overcrowding, meager rations...resulted in high mortality," implying that the prison facility was inadequate for the number of prisoners. All other choices are discussed, but the main issue was overcrowded conditions.

5. **(B)** The author emphasizes a lack of supplies and manpower to care for the prisoners, not a lack of interest in doing so by the Confederates. Hence, choices (C), (D), and (E) are not appropriate. Choice (A) is not suggested by the text.

6. **(E)** An irony is a result that is the opposite of what might be expected or appropriate. The passage implies that being captured was not a guarantee of survival in Andersonville. This choice is supported by the second sentence of the second paragraph.

7. **(B)** This choice is supported by the first paragraph of the passage. All other choices are irrelevant to information in the passage.

8. **(C)** Innovation means to introduce something new or make changes.

9. **(D)** The passage discusses the importance of usefulness as well as simplicity to the Shakers; therefore, the function of the piece of furniture would be more important than the particular form. Choices (A), (B), and (E) are contradictory to the information given, while choice (C) is beyond information given in the text.

10. **(B)** Depraved means corrupted or perverted. All other choices have to do with accepted standards of conduct.

11. **(D)** The author states that Franklin's work was a "significant work of the early United States." Each of the other choices are not supported by the text.

12. **(B)** The final sentence of the paragraph supports this choice. Choice (C) might apply, but choice (B) is closest to the overall mood of the passage. Choices (A), (D), and (E) are not relevant to the question.

13. **(C)** The author's use of the word "decimation" as well as the last sentence in the second paragraph supports this choice. All other choices are secondary to the central idea of the passage.

14. **(D)** To decimate is to eradicate or destroy a large part of something.

15. **(C)** This choice is supported by the first sentence of the second paragraph. All other choices are irrelevant to the discussion of the flamingo's plumage.

16. **(E)** The first and last sentences of the passage support this choice. Choice (A) contradicts information in the passage, and choices (B), (C), and (D) are too broad in nature and go beyond the scope of the passage.

17. **(C)** Reviewing the author's discussion of developing children's citizenship competencies, we may conclude that indoctrination is contradictory to information given in the passage.

18. **(B)** In the context of the passage, to "color" means to influence.

19. **(D)** This choice is supported in the second sentence. All other choices are secondary to the central idea.

20. **(C)** The passage states that this was a "noteworthy accomplishment in technology."

21. **(E)** The passage emphasizes the complicated process of filtering the meal through sand or tightly woven baskets. Choices (A), (B), and (C), while true, are not the most difficult problem. Choice (D) is contradictory to information given in the text.

22. **(D)**   The question asks for the best synthesis of the passage and (D) is the best and most complete answer. Choices (A), (B), (C), and (E) are not as complete. For example, (A) left out the duration of the conference, (B) left out the number of the nations represented at the summit, (C) left out both the duration of the conference and the number of the nations represented at the summit, and (E) left out the number of nations represented and support for Gorbachev's "new thinking."

23. **(E)**   Of the choices provided, (E) gives the most logical and sound implication of the passage. (A) falls short of the capabilities of Gorbachev's leadership, in (B) the "new thinking" referred to already has the support of the seven leaders at the summit, (C) is a rather sweeping, unfair statement; and (D) left out support for economic and political reforms.

24. **(B)**   The mention of banking and energy did not rule out technical assistance in other fields; hence, (B) is the correct answer. Choice (A) limited the assistance to only the fields of banking and energy, in (C) the statement is only partly true—the U.S. is not alone in providing support, in (D) the statement implies that there is no consensus among the seven nations, and in (E) technical assistance can likewise come from other nations outside of the seven.

25. **(A)**   The question asks for the main idea in the passage and (A) gives the best and complete main idea. Choices (B), (C), and (D) are generalizations derived from the passage and (E), while it is true and specific to the passage, is stated in the negative.

26. **(B)**   (B) gives the most specific consequence for California. The other choices, while all plausible or possible answers, do not get to the "root" of the issue specific to California.

27. **(C)**   Based on the passage read, the answer to this question is (C)—two things are mentioned that could affect California and these are federal funding and the number of congressional seats. While (A) and (B) are correct, they are incomplete. Choices (D) and (E) are consequential generalizations which are both correct but lack the preciseness of (C).

28. **(C)**   The correct answer here is (C) because this choice synthesizes the key or main idea in the passage. The other choices, while partly true, don't give the main idea.

29. **(B)**   Since the depression years preceded World War II, one can easily presume that people were more practical or money minded, there-

fore, Labor Day as celebrated then could mean the loss of a day's pay for working people. Therefore, (B) is the correct answer. While choices (A), (C), (D), and (E) are also possible answers they don't get to the "root" of the issue.

30. **(D)**   Explicitly given in the passage is (D), the correct answer. Choices (A), (B), (C), and (E), while they may all be true and correct, are not what is precisely given in the passage.

31. **(E)**   The gold content found in the volcanic ash from Mt. Pinatubo could easily stir or trigger a "gold rush." However, people are warned that the gold content found is not at a "commercial level." Hence, (E) is the correct answer. The other choices provided are all mere speculations.

32. **(C)**   Choice (C) is the most appropriate answer—it also synthesizes the content of the reading passage; hence, it is the correct answer. Choices (A) and (B) are both incorrect. Choices (D) and (E) are somewhat applicable as titles but do not really synthesize the main idea of the passage as does choice (C).

33. **(B)**   If priorities will have to be established, to determine the most immediate research needed on the ash content from Mt. Pinatubo, choice (B) will have to be the most logical choice because there is already some data with which to work. Other research possibilities such as those in choice (A), (D), (C), and (E) will have to come later.

34. **(A)**   The best and correct answer here is (A)—it's the main idea of the passage. Choice (B) is incorrect. Choice (C) is partially correct—if it has to be specific, it should refer to the brake lights on the helmet. Choice (D) is incomplete as a key or main idea of the passage and the same could be said of choice (E).

35. **(B)**   It would follow that the rationale behind the new brake light requirement for cars in California is the same for all other vehicles on the road. Hence, choice (B) is the correct answer. The implication provided in (A) is not necessarily true; (C) is illogical; in (D) any car driven in California, wherever its been bought, cannot be exempted from the requirement; and in (E) Harris can go on inventing while remaining a farmer—he'll make more money doing both.

36. **(A)**   Choice (A) is the most logical and appropriate answer, hence, it is the correct answer. Choice (B) can be, but is not necessarily true; (C) is a logical possibility but will not drastically raise car prices beyond

affordability; (D) may be true, but not as road hazards; and (E), the contrary may also be true.

37. **(D)**   A title is supposed to synthesize the main idea and (D) does. Choice (A) left out the main idea of a commemorative stamp; choice (B) is incorrect because it implies Columbus discovered the Americas; choice (C) is not the main idea of the passage; and choice (E), while it may be implied in the passage, does not synthesize its focus.

38. **(B)**   The underlying fact behind the passage is explicitly implied, therefore, (B) is the correct answer. Choice (A) while true, is a generalized implication, not addressing the specific issue; choice (C) is debatable and so is choice (D); choice (E) like (A) is also a generalized implication.

39. **(A)**   Of the choices given (A) is the most historically significant, and therefore, the correct answer. Choice (B) is significant but left out the fact that Columbus was not the first to arrive in the New World, the main point in the passage; choice (C) is a mere commemoration day; choice (D) remains a debatable assumption; and choice (E) is not specific enough as an historically significant fact.

40. **(A)**   Choice (A) clearly synthesizes the main idea in the passage, hence, it is the correct answer. Choice (B) is more of an implication, hence, the wrong answer; choice (C) is merely stating a fact which does not speak of the main idea; the same can be said of choice (D); and choice (E), while it may be true, is not really the passage's main idea.

41. **(C)**   The most sound and significant implication of the passage is stated in (C), hence, this is the correct answer. Choices (A) and (B) are not sound, they reflect a rather immature reasoning; choice (D) merely states some degree of competitiveness which is not the issue focus; and (E) is a "so what" kind of statement and not a sound implication.

42. **(C)**   The passage is really on global tourism providing comparisons and implying some inter-nation balance in tourism trade, hence, (C) is the appropriate and correct answer. Choices (A), (B), (D), and (E) are stated in general terms, missing out on the specific focus or topic of the passage, hence, not the logical and immediate topics to discuss.

43. **(C)**   The suggestion in (C) is the most sound and logical if equal opportunity for all students is to be our nation's priority, hence, this is the correct answer. Choice (A) is a mere statement of concern and does not

provide a plan for action; choice (B) is illogical—you cannot cut down the number of minority students who are already in the system; choice (D) disregards other languages existing in the school system and in the community at large; and (E) is only secondary to the major issue.

44. **(E)** Since the passage points out the fact that there will soon be more minority students in the classroom, priority should be in providing the appropriate teacher preparation; hence, the correct answer is (E). Choice (A) is a need but secondary to those who are already in the system; choice (B) has always been an issue even before the rapid changes in the demographics; choice (C) is something that has triggered legislation since the 1950s—the natural composition of the classroom today is already desegregated. While the other choices are a need, the one that needs immediate action is (E).

45. **(E)** The answer to this question has to tie in with the foregoing answer, hence, the correct choice should be (E). Choices (A), (B), (C), and (D), while also problems arising from the changes in demographics, are secondary to (E).

46. **(E)** The most complete summary of the passage is stated in (E); hence, this is the correct answer. Choice (A) is not true, therefore, is incorrect; choice (B) is put in rather general terms—the U.S. pullout is not the only issue related to the Philippine economy. The interdependence of nations will remain no matter what, i.e., trade relations will continue; choice (C) is incorrect. The U.S. military strategy will have to be relocated elsewhere in the Asia-Pacific region, the same can be said for choice (D)—the Philippines will not be completely on its own—it continues to maintain its trade relations with the U.S. and other trading partners.

47. **(C)** The passage is quite explicit in stating that the U.S. presence on the Philippines has been an impediment to the nation's capability in joining East Asia's "economic boom"; hence, the correct answer is (C); choices (A), (B), (D), and (E) are all possible consequences but are all quite debatable.

48. **(B)** Again, this question requires an answer that has to be consistent with the answers in the foregoing questions and, therefore, the answer has to be (B). The other choices—(A), (C), (D), and (E) are all possible and acceptable answers but do not directly relate to the key message in the passage.

49. **(D)**   Choice (D) states the most complete main idea in the passage, hence, it is the correct answer. Choice (A) addresses only one part of the correct answer; choices (A) and (C) are incorrect; and choice (E) is an incomplete answer.

50. **(B)**   Of the choices provided, (B) provides the most complete answer—namely, the two things that the computer program does: predicts the aging process and predicts how an unborn child will look. The other choices, (A), (C), (D), and (E) while all true, are incomplete in providing the main capability of the new computer program developed in Japan.

51. **(E)**   A logical answer to this question has got to be (E). With this new computer system it certainly will follow that Japan will do a more refined and sophisticated system next. Choices (A) and (B) are related— the answers are natural outgrowths of the competitive market among nations; and choices (C) and (D) have been an on-going trend anyway.

READING SHORT PASSAGES REVIEW

Short reading comprehension passages measure your ability to understand information given through concise written words as well as charts and graphs. The emphasis is on comprehension of text materials, not your knowledge of different topics. Some of these passages can be as long as 200 words and as short as one or two lines.

The questions usually represent three types of comprehension: literal (facts and figures), inferential (implied ideas), and critical (analysis and interpretation).

LITERAL COMPREHENSION

Questions in this category assess your ability to comprehend information explicitly stated in the text. The questions will be on the main idea in the section. You may have to identify specific facts about persons, places, events, or ideas included in the passage. Sometimes the question is based on a graph or chart.

Literal comprehension questions include:

- identifying the main idea or focus of a passage

- finding details or facts provided within the passage

- recognizing information provided in a graph or chart

INFERENTIAL COMPREHENSION

Questions in this category require you to search for suggested meanings or conclusions that can be appropriately drawn from, though not explicitly stated in, the information provided in the passage. Some questions may ask you to make comparisons, draw conclusions, or apply the information to other examples. You may have to identify statements that are implied or can be inferred from information given in a passage.

Specific inferential comprehension skills include:

- recognizing ideas or situations related to those presented in the passage

- identifying a logical conclusion based on facts or ideas provided in the passage or in illustrations

- applying ideas to problems or situations beyond the passage or charts

- recognizing ideas that are implied in the passage or in the illustrations or charts

- recognizing relationships that exist between ideas provided in the passage or in the illustrations

- making generalizations that can be deduced from facts given in the passage

- comparing information, facts, or ideas given in various parts of the section

CRITICAL COMPREHENSION

The questions in this subsection refer to the organization or style of the selection. You may be asked to identify the author's point of view or reason for writing this piece, or to identify the writing style or tone of a selection. Some questions may require you to identify the implicit assumptions from a single statement or from the entire passage. You may be asked to select the appropriate definition of a word or phrase based upon the sentence or paragraph in which it appears, or to determine the meaning of a figure of speech, or to identify the organization of a passage.

Specific critical comprehension skills include:

- identifying the author's attitude or feelings about the subject of the passage

- identifying the author's primary purpose

- determining the author's tone in a passage

- identifying the organization of the selection

- selecting the best definition of a word or a figure of speech within the passage

- identifying the type of publication in which the passage would most likely appear

- identifying statements that tend to weaken or strengthen the points made in the selection

Following are general strategies for answering reading comprehension questions. These strategies apply to all text questions. Sample passages are given, along with an analysis and strategies for answering each type of reading section.

KEY STRATEGIES FOR ANSWERING THE SHORT READING COMPREHENSION QUESTIONS

1. **Read all directions through carefully**. Preview the questions before reading the passage so that you are acquainted with the subject.

2. **If possible, allocate your time for each question**. Do not spend too much time on any one question. If you can't answer the question easily after reading the passage twice, skip it and move on to the next item.

3. **Skim through the questions before reading each passage;** this will help you locate key words and ideas.

4. **Underline key words or sentences** and make any necessary notes in the margins.

5. **Be certain to mark each passage as you read**. Should you skip an answer to return to later, make a notation so that you do not mark an answer in the wrong place.

6. **If there are unfamiliar words, do not spend too much time attempting to define them until you have read through the entire passage.** Reading the phrase or sentence a couple of times and using the context (surrounding words) is valuable in determining meanings of vocabulary words.

7. **Decide whether the question asked is a literal, inferential, or critical comprehension question.**

8. **Choices of answers that are not relevant, reasonable, or that contradict the information in the passage should be eliminated at the beginning.**

Drill 1: Key Strategies for Answering the Short Reading Comprehension Questions

DIRECTIONS: One or more questions follow each statement or passage in this test. The question(s) are based on the content of the passage. After you have read a statement or passage, select the one best answer to each question from among the five possible choices. Your answers to the questions should be based on the stated (literal) or implied (inferential) information given in the statement or passage. Mark all answers on your answer sheet.

Analysis

You are asked to select the one best answer from the five choices. In certain cases, the "best" answer will not be what you might believe is an ideal answer. Also, note that you must base your choice only on information given in the passage or implied by the information. Frequently, people who perform poorly on this test do so because they attempt to read more into the passage from their own experiences. Going with your first choice of answers is usually the best strategy.

Passage Sample

Experienced lawyers know that most lawsuits are won or lost before they are ever heard in court. Thus, successful lawyers prepare their cases carefully, undertaking exhaustive research and investigation prior to going to court. Interviews and statements taken from all available witnesses ascertain those who are likely to be called as witnesses for the other side. This is the time for strategy planning in the building of the case; decisions to be made about expert witnesses to be called (such as doctors, chemists, or others who have special knowledge of the subject matter); books and articles to be read pertaining to the subject matter of the case; and meetings with witnesses to prepare them for possible questions by the opposing lawyers and to review the case. Finally, in preparing the case, a trial memorandum of law is handed to the judge at the outset of the trial. As a result of this thorough preparation, experienced lawyers know their strong and weak points and can serve their clients well.

Question

1.   The main idea expressed in this passage is to

   (A) describe the function of expert witnesses.

   (B) explain the importance of pretrial preparation by lawyers.

   (C) warn persons who break the law.

   (D) verify the importance of the trial memorandum.

   (E) refute the belief that all lawyers are trial lawyers.

Analysis

   Passages such as this one are typically followed by one or two questions. Usually the main idea of the reading passage is not explicitly stated but becomes apparent as you read. Always ask yourself: What was the most important thing that the author was trying to tell the reader in this passage?

   It is important to read through the entire passage and to mark any key words and phrases that relate to the question. After you have read carefully and thoroughly one time, reread and consider each possible answer. Avoid marking an answer before you have read all of the choices. Frequently, there are two or more options that are very close, but one must be the best answer.

   When considering a question that asks for the main idea, the reader should note the central theme or essential idea being developed in each sentence in the paragraph or paragraphs. It is also important to examine the first word of each of the answers for responses that can be eliminated. In the case of the above passage, choice (C), warn, and choice (E), refute, are not consistent with the rather objective nature of the passage; these two choices can therefore be eliminated. Also, these choices are irrelevant to the information in the passage, since the passage does not address people who break the law or the belief that all lawyers are trial lawyers. The remaining choices can be considered based on how central they are to the main idea or if they are subsidiary to the main idea. Choices (A), expert witnesses, and (D), importance of trial memorandum, are mentioned but are subsidiary to the overall theme of the passage. Choice (B) is the best choice. It discusses the preparation done by the lawyers before the trial begins (pretrial).

Drill 2: Reading Short Passages

DIRECTIONS: Each passage is followed by questions based on its content. After reading the passage, choose the best answer to each question. Answer all questions based on what is indicated or implied in the passage.

Questions 1-3 are based on the following passage.

There is an importance of learning communication and meaning in language. Yet the use of notions such as communication and meaning as the basic criteria for instruction, experiences, and materials in classrooms may misguide a child in several respects. Communication in the classroom is vital. The teacher should use communication to help students develop the capacity to make their private responses become public responses. Otherwise, one's use of language would be in danger of being what the younger generation refers to as mere words, mere thoughts, and mere feelings.

Learning theorists emphasize specific components of learning: behaviorists stress behavior in learning; humanists stress the affective in learning; and cognitivists stress cognition in learning. All three of these components occur simultaneously and cannot be separated from each other in the learning process. In 1957, Festinger referred to dissonance as the lack of harmony between what one does (behavior) and what one believes (attitude). Attempts to separate the components of learning either knowingly or unknowingly create dissonances wherein language, thought, feeling, and behavior become diminished of authenticity. As a result, ideas and concepts lose their content and vitality, and the manipulation and politics of communication assume prominence.

1. Which of the following best describes the author's attitude toward the subject discussed?

    (A) A flippant disregard   (D) A passive resignation

    (B) A mild frustration   (E) An informed concern

    (C) A moral indignation

2. The primary purpose of the passage is to

    (A) explain the criteria for providing authentic communication in classroom learning.

(B) discuss the relationships between learning and communication.

(C) assure teachers that communication and meaning are the basic criteria for learning in classrooms.

(D) stress the importance of providing authentic communication in classroom learning.

(E) address the role of communication and meaning in classrooms.

3. Which of the following is the most complete and accurate definition of the term mere as used in the passage?

(A) Small   (D) Poor

(B) Minor   (E) Insignificant

(C) Little

Questions 4-6 refer to the following passage.

In 1975, Sinclair observed that it had often been supposed that the main factor in learning to talk is being able to imitate. Schlesinger (1975) noted that at certain stages of learning to speak, a child tends to imitate everything an adult says to him or her, and it therefore seems reasonable to accord to such imitation an important role in the acquisition of language.

Moreover, various investigators have attempted to explain the role of imitation in language. In his discussion of the development of imitation and cognition of adult speech sounds, Nakazema (1975) stated that although the parent's talking stimulates and accelerates the infant's articulatory activity, the parent's phoneme system does not influence the child's articulatory mechanisms. Slobin and Welsh (1973) suggested that imitation is the reconstruction of the adult's utterance and that the child does so by employing the grammatical rules that he has developed at a specific time. Schlesinger proposed that by imitating the adult the child practices new grammatical constructions. Brown and Bellugi (1964) noted that a child's imitations resemble spontaneous speech in that they drop inflections, most function words, and sometimes other words. However, the word order of imitated sentences usually was preserved. Brown and Bellugi assumed that imitation is a function of what the child attended to or remembered. Shipley et al. (1969) suggested that repeating an adult's utterance assists the child's comprehension. Ervin (1964) and Braine (1971) found that a child's imitations do not contain more advanced structures than his or her spontaneous utterances; thus, imitation can no longer be regarded as the simple behavioristic act that earlier scholars assumed it to be.

4. The author of the passage would tend to agree with which of the following statements?

    (A) Apparently, children are physiologically unable to imitate a parent's phoneme system.

    (B) Apparently, children require practice with more advanced structures before they are able to imitate.

    (C) Apparently, children only imitate what they already do, using whatever is in their repertoire.

    (D) Apparently, the main factor in learning to talk remains being able to imitate.

    (E) Apparently, children cannot respond meaningfully to a speech situation until they have reached a stage where they can make symbol-orientation responses.

5. The primary purpose of the passage is to

    (A) explain language acquisition.

    (B) explain the role of imitation in language acquisition.

    (C) assure parents of their role in assisting imitation in language acquisition.

    (D) relate the history of imitation in language acquisition.

    (E) discuss relationships between psychological and physiological processes in language acquisition.

6. An inference that parents may make from the passage is that they should

    (A) be concerned when a child imitates their language.

    (B) focus on developing imitation in their child's language.

    (C) realize that their child's imitations may reflect several aspects of language acquisition.

    (D) realize that their talking may over-stimulate their child's articulatory activity.

    (E) not be concerned as imitation is too complex for anyone to understand.

Questions 7 and 8 refer to the following passage.

A major problem with reading/language arts instruction is that practice assignments from workbooks often provide short, segmented activities
that do not really resemble the true act of reading. Perhaps more than any
computer application, word processing is capable of addressing these issues.

7. The author would tend to agree that a major benefit of computers in
    reading/ language arts instruction is

    (A) that the reading act may be more closely resembled.

    (B) that short segmented assignments will be eliminated.

    (C) that the issues in reading/language arts instruction will be ad-
         dressed.

    (D) that computer application will be limited to word processing.

    (E) that reading practice will be eliminated.

8. The appropriate use of a word processor to assist in making practice
    resemble a reading act is

    (A) detailed.   (D) alluded.

    (B) desirable.   (E) costly.

    (C) unstated.

Questions 9-11 refer to the following passage.

In view of the current emphasis on literature-based reading instruction, a greater understanding by teachers of variance in cultural, language,
and story components should assist in narrowing the gap between reader
and text and improve reading comprehension. Classroom teachers should
begin with students' meaning and intentions about stories before moving
students to the commonalities of story meaning based on common background and culture. With teacher guidance students should develop a fuller
understanding of how complex narratives are when they are generating
stories as well as when they are reading stories.

9. Which of the following is the intended audience for the passage?

    (A) Students in a reading class

    (B) Teachers using literature-based curriculum

(C) Professors teaching a literature course

(D) Parents concerned about their child's comprehension of books

(E) Teacher educators teaching reading methods courses

10. Which of the following is the most complete and accurate definition of the term variance as used in the passage?

(A) Change

(B) Fluctuations

(C) Diversity

(D) Deviation

(E) Incongruity

11. The passage supports a concept of meaning primarily residing in

(A) culture, language, and story components.

(B) comprehension.

(C) student's stories only.

(D) students only.

(E) students and narratives.

Questions 12–14 refer to the following passage.

Beginning readers, and those who are experiencing difficulty with reading, benefit from assisted reading. During assisted reading the teacher orally reads a passage with a student or students. The teacher fades in and out of the reading act. For example, the teacher lets his or her voice drop to a whisper when students are reading on their own at an acceptable rate and lets his/her voice rise to say the words clearly when the students are having difficulty.

Students who are threatened by print, read word-by-word, or rely on grapho-phonemic cues, will be helped by assisted reading. These students are stuck on individual language units which can be as small as a single letter or as large as phrases or sentences. As Frank Smith (1977) and other reading educators have noted, speeding up reading, not slowing it down, helps the reader make sense of a passage. This strategy allows students to concentrate on meaning as the short-term memory is not overloaded by focusing on small language units. As the name implies, assisted reading lets the reader move along without being responsible for every language unit; the pressure is taken off the student. Consequently, when the reading act is sped up, it sounds more like language, and students can begin to integrate the cueing systems of semantics and syntax along with grapho-phonemics.

12. As a strategy, assisted reading is best for

   (A) beginning readers who are relying on grapho-phonemic cues.

   (B) learning disabled readers who are experiencing neurological deficits.

   (C) beginning readers who are relying on phono-graphic cues.

   (D) remedial readers who are experiencing difficulty with silent reading.

   (E) beginning readers who are experiencing difficulty with silent reading.

13. Language units as presented in the passage refer to

   (A) individual letters, syllables, or phrases.

   (B) individual letters, syllables, or sentences.

   (C) individual letters, phrases, or paragraphs.

   (D) individual letters, phrases, or sentences.

   (E) individual letters, sentences, or paragraphs.

14. According to the passage, to make sense of a passage a reader must

   (A) focus on small language units.

   (B) overload short-term memory.

   (C) slow down when reading.

   (D) read word-by-word.

   (E) speed up the reading act.

READING SHORT PASSAGES DRILLS

ANSWER KEY

Drill 1 — Key Strategies for Answering the Short Reading Comprehension Questions
1. (B)

Drill 2 — Reading Short Passages
1.	(E)	8.	(C)
2.	(D)	9.	(B)
3.	(E)	10.	(C)
4.	(C)	11.	(E)
5.	(B)	12.	(A)
6.	(C)	13.	(D)
7.	(A)	14.	(E)

VOCABULARY LIST

capitulate
  v.- to succumb on prearranged conditions

chiding
  n.- a rebuke or scolding

cognizance
  n.- an awareness or perception; knowledge

edict
  n.- a public order, announcement, law, ruling

extemporaneous
  adj.- spoken, performed or composed with little or no preparation or forethought

histrionic
  adj.- dramatic; of acting or actors; overacted

hyperbolize
  v.- exaggerate for effect

illusory
  adj.- tending to deceive; of the nature of an illusion

impetus
  n.- stimulus, motivating force

incongruous
  adj.- made up of parts or qualities that are disparate or otherwise lacking in consistency

indemnify
  v.- to compensate; to insure against loss or damage

judicious
  adj.- having sound judgment

licit
adj.- permitted, lawful

limpid
adj.- perfectly clear, transparent

liturgical
adj.- ritualistic

lucent
adj.- bright

mephitic
adj.- poisonous, smelly

mordacious
adj.- biting, sarcastic

myriad
adj.- a large number of persons or things, many

nefarious
adj.- corrupt, evil

negligible
adj.- that can be neglected or disregarded, petty, remote

niggardly
adj.- stingy, miserly

nonpareil
n.- a person or thing so excellent as to have no equal or match

novitiate
n.- the condition or period of being a beginner or novice

obloquy
n.- widespread censure or calumny, disgrace, tirade

odious
adj.- filthy, hateful

parenthetic
adj.- digressive

penitent
adj.- apologetic, remorseful; sorry for having done wrong

perfervid
adj.- passionate

placate
v.- to pacify or appease

plebeian
adj.- lowly, vulgar, coarse or common

polemic
n.- argument; of or involving dispute

posthumous
adj.- occurring or done after death

qualm
n.- a feeling of uncertainty about the fitness or correctness of an action

reciprocate
v.- to give or to take mutually

renitence
n.- resistance

repudiate
v.- to refuse to recognize or acknowledge

sententious
adj.- full of or fond of using maxims, proverbs, etc.

sophism
n.- fallacy; a clever and plausible but fallacious argument

spurious
adj.- artificial, counterfeit, illegitimate

stigmatize
v.- to mark with disgrace or infamy

synchronous
> adj.- happening at the same time; simultaneous

vehemence
> adj.- having or showing intense feeling; violent, impetuous

verboten
> adj.- forbidden

visceral
> adj.- inner, instinctive

wantonness
> n.- reckless abandon

waxen
> adj.- pale, smooth, like wax

weal
> n.- welfare, well-being

wrangle
> v.- to argue, quarrel, esp. noisily

yore
> n.- past, long ago, formerly

CHAPTER 7

Reading Medium Passages

➤ Diagnostic Test
➤ Reading Medium Passages
   Review & Drills
➤ Vocabulary List

READING MEDIUM PASSAGES DIAGNOSTIC TEST

1. Ⓐ Ⓑ Ⓒ Ⓓ Ⓔ		27. Ⓐ Ⓑ Ⓒ Ⓓ Ⓔ
2. Ⓐ Ⓑ Ⓒ Ⓓ Ⓔ		28. Ⓐ Ⓑ Ⓒ Ⓓ Ⓔ
3. Ⓐ Ⓑ Ⓒ Ⓓ Ⓔ		29. Ⓐ Ⓑ Ⓒ Ⓓ Ⓔ
4. Ⓐ Ⓑ Ⓒ Ⓓ Ⓔ		30. Ⓐ Ⓑ Ⓒ Ⓓ Ⓔ
5. Ⓐ Ⓑ Ⓒ Ⓓ Ⓔ		31. Ⓐ Ⓑ Ⓒ Ⓓ Ⓔ
6. Ⓐ Ⓑ Ⓒ Ⓓ Ⓔ		32. Ⓐ Ⓑ Ⓒ Ⓓ Ⓔ
7. Ⓐ Ⓑ Ⓒ Ⓓ Ⓔ		33. Ⓐ Ⓑ Ⓒ Ⓓ Ⓔ
8. Ⓐ Ⓑ Ⓒ Ⓓ Ⓔ		34. Ⓐ Ⓑ Ⓒ Ⓓ Ⓔ
9. Ⓐ Ⓑ Ⓒ Ⓓ Ⓔ		35. Ⓐ Ⓑ Ⓒ Ⓓ Ⓔ
10. Ⓐ Ⓑ Ⓒ Ⓓ Ⓔ		36. Ⓐ Ⓑ Ⓒ Ⓓ Ⓔ
11. Ⓐ Ⓑ Ⓒ Ⓓ Ⓔ		37. Ⓐ Ⓑ Ⓒ Ⓓ Ⓔ
12. Ⓐ Ⓑ Ⓒ Ⓓ Ⓔ		38. Ⓐ Ⓑ Ⓒ Ⓓ Ⓔ
13. Ⓐ Ⓑ Ⓒ Ⓓ Ⓔ		39. Ⓐ Ⓑ Ⓒ Ⓓ Ⓔ
14. Ⓐ Ⓑ Ⓒ Ⓓ Ⓔ		40. Ⓐ Ⓑ Ⓒ Ⓓ Ⓔ
15. Ⓐ Ⓑ Ⓒ Ⓓ Ⓔ		41. Ⓐ Ⓑ Ⓒ Ⓓ Ⓔ
16. Ⓐ Ⓑ Ⓒ Ⓓ Ⓔ		42. Ⓐ Ⓑ Ⓒ Ⓓ Ⓔ
17. Ⓐ Ⓑ Ⓒ Ⓓ Ⓔ		43. Ⓐ Ⓑ Ⓒ Ⓓ Ⓔ
18. Ⓐ Ⓑ Ⓒ Ⓓ Ⓔ		44. Ⓐ Ⓑ Ⓒ Ⓓ Ⓔ
19. Ⓐ Ⓑ Ⓒ Ⓓ Ⓔ		45. Ⓐ Ⓑ Ⓒ Ⓓ Ⓔ
20. Ⓐ Ⓑ Ⓒ Ⓓ Ⓔ		46. Ⓐ Ⓑ Ⓒ Ⓓ Ⓔ
21. Ⓐ Ⓑ Ⓒ Ⓓ Ⓔ		47. Ⓐ Ⓑ Ⓒ Ⓓ Ⓔ
22. Ⓐ Ⓑ Ⓒ Ⓓ Ⓔ		48. Ⓐ Ⓑ Ⓒ Ⓓ Ⓔ
23. Ⓐ Ⓑ Ⓒ Ⓓ Ⓔ		49. Ⓐ Ⓑ Ⓒ Ⓓ Ⓔ
24. Ⓐ Ⓑ Ⓒ Ⓓ Ⓔ		50. Ⓐ Ⓑ Ⓒ Ⓓ Ⓔ
25. Ⓐ Ⓑ Ⓒ Ⓓ Ⓔ		51. Ⓐ Ⓑ Ⓒ Ⓓ Ⓔ
26. Ⓐ Ⓑ Ⓒ Ⓓ Ⓔ		52. Ⓐ Ⓑ Ⓒ Ⓓ Ⓔ

READING MEDIUM PASSAGES DIAGNOSTIC TEST

This diagnostic test is designed to help you determine your strengths and your weaknesses in reading medium passages. Follow the directions for each part and check your answers.

> **These types of questions are found in the following tests: GED, LSAT, GMAT, TASP, PSAT, SAT, GRE, ACT, and PPST.**

52 Questions

DIRECTIONS: Each passage is followed by questions based on its content. After reading the passage, choose the best answer to each question. Answer all questions based on what is indicated or implied in that passage.

Questions 1–5 are based on the following passage.

1   Passion! What better word is there to describe opera? The vital core of opera is passion—sometimes violent, or joyful, loving, hateful, ecstatic, melancholic, vengeful; the gamut of emotions are exposed on the operatic stage and are transformed through the beauty of the music and the human
5 voice. These emotions enter into an exalted state and, like everything else about opera, they are bigger than life. In opera, the ordinary becomes extraordinary.

Not only does passion reign on the operatic stage, but it also elicits as intense a response on the other side of the curtain. Opera audiences are
10 known to erupt into wild outbursts—either giving performers wildly enthusiastic ovations and showering the stage with bouquets of flowers, or loudly hissing and booing and, even worse, throwing tomatoes and other "symbols of displeasure" onto the stage. Passion is returned with passion; indeed, the ardent devotion of some opera fans has stimulated the forma-
15 tion of cult-like groups around certain charismatic performers. It isn't difficult to understand how listeners can be awed by opera's grandeur and transported by the passions unfolding onstage.

Opera stands as one of the great cultural achievements of Western

20 civilization. It represents a glorious fusion of the arts, combining drama, music, dance, and the visual arts. No one art form can be discounted, opera requires each of its components to fulfill its essential role—anything less, and the opera suffers. Perhaps no one understood this better than Richard Wagner, who insisted that he did not compose opera as such but, rather, created *Gesamtkunstwerk* ("Total-artwork"). He meant by this a
25 synthesis of poetry, music, drama, and spectacle, in which each element cooperatively subordinates itself to the total purpose. That total purpose—the music-drama (opera)—is not a mere "entertainment" but a profound and compelling work of art that elevates the listeners and resonates with our humanity.

30 Yet opera is pure artifice. If in the ordinary theater our disbelief must be willingly suspended in order to make the illusion of the play work, in opera that is no longer the question. We simply accept a world in which, among other things, people sing—beautifully—whether of love, of death, or of murder, or whatever. Thus, Samuel Johnson had a valid point in
35 defining opera as "an irrational entertainment." The late Kenneth Clark, the eminent British art historian, once asked, "What on earth has given opera its prestige in Western civilization—a prestige that has outlasted so many different fashions and ways of thought?" He finds the answer in Dr. Johnson's definition: "...because it is irrational. 'What is too silly to be
40 said may be sung'—well, yes; but what is too subtle to be said, or too deeply felt, or too revealing or too mysterious—these things can also be sung and only be sung."

Unusual for a rarefied pleasure (which it is oftentimes considered), opera today enjoys a flourishing and growing popularity. With the advent
45 of modern technology, opera is able to reach millions of people around the world who would otherwise not be exposed to its splendor. The phonograph enabled opera to be brought into people's homes and, later, radio provided opera with a powerful and pervasive forum from which it attracted new listeners. More recently, the cinema and, especially, television
50 have been instrumental in introducing opera to uninitiated audiences and converting many into fans.

1. The primary purpose of the passage is to

   (A) compare the works of Wagner.

   (B) describe the joy of opera.

   (C) report on the resurgence of opera.

   (D) critique the artificiality of opera.

   (E) compare the works of *Gesamtkunstwerk*.

2. By calling opera *pure artifice,* the author in Line 30

    (A) is attacking its value.

    (B) recognizes the importance of *Gesamtkunstwerk.*

    (C) agrees with the comment of Samuel Johnson.

    (D) acknowledges its unrealistic character.

    (E) is criticizing Wagner's operas.

3. From the passage, Clark's explanation for the longevity of opera

    (A) relies precisely on its artificial nature.

    (B) is based on the mutual passion created by audience and artists.

    (C) is that it has adapted to technological change.

    (D) is derived from *Gesamtkunstwerk.*

    (E) denies its irrationality.

4. The author argues wild outbursts of approval or symbols of displea-
    sure by opera fans show

    (A) the inconsistent quality of modern opera.

    (B) the lack of sophistication of most audiences.

    (C) audience indifference.

    (D) the artificial nature of opera.

    (E) the depth and breadth of emotional reactions.

5. Based on the information in the passage, one can conclude

    (A) that a booming video market may put an end to opera atten-
         dance.

    (B) that videos may bring opera to many homes.

    (C) that opera is an art form of the past.

    (D) that opera has never been popular but may become so in the
         future.

    (E) that opera was popular at the time it was first performed but was
         never popular after that time.

Questions 6–10 are based on the following passage.

The promise of finding long-term technological solutions to the problem of world food shortages seems difficult to fulfill. Many innovations that were once heavily supported and publicized, such as fish-protein concentrate and protein from algae grown on petroleum substrates, have since fallen by the wayside. The proposals themselves were technically feasible, but they proved to be economically unviable and to yield food products culturally unacceptable to their consumers. Recent innovations, such as opaque-2 maize, Antarctic krill, and the wheat-rye hybrid triticale, seem more promising, but it is too early to predict their ultimate fate.

One characteristic common to unsuccessful food innovations has been that, even with extensive government support, they often have not been technologically adapted or culturally acceptable to the people for whom they had been developed. A successful new technology, therefore, must fit the entire sociocultural system in which it is to find a place. Security of crop yield, practicality of storage, palatability, and costs are much more significant than had previously been realized by the advocates of new technologies. For example, the better protein quality in tortillas made from opaque-2 maize will be of only limited benefit to a family on the margin of subsistence if the new maize is not culturally acceptable or is more vulnerable to insects.

The adoption of new food technologies depends on more than these technical and cultural considerations; economic factors and governmental policies also strongly influence the ultimate success of any innovation. Economists in the Anglo-American tradition have taken the lead in investigating the economics of technological innovation. Although they exaggerate in claiming that profitability is the key factor guiding technical change—they completely disregard the substantial effects of culture—they are correct in stressing the importance of profits. Most technological innovations in agriculture can be fully used only by large landowners and are only adopted if these profit-oriented business people believe that the innovation will increase their incomes. Thus, innovations that carry high rewards for big agribusiness groups will be adopted even if they harm segments of the population and reduce the availability of food in a country. Further, should a new technology promise to alter substantially the profits and losses associated with any production system, those with economic power will strive to maintain and improve their own positions? Since large segments of the populations of many developing countries are close to the subsistence margin and essentially powerless, they tend to be the losers in this system unless they are aided by a government policy that takes into account the needs of all sectors of the economy. Therefore, although technical advances in food production and processing will perhaps be needed to ensure food availability, meeting food needs will depend much more on equalizing economic power among the various segments of the populations within the developing countries themselves.

6. With which of the following statements would the author most likely agree?

    (A) Agribusiness groups have consistently opposed technological innovations.

    (B) Agribusiness groups act chiefly out of economic self-interest.

    (C) Agribusiness groups have been misunderstood by Anglo–American economists.

    (D) Agribusiness groups nearly always welcome technological innovations.

    (E) The economic success of agribusiness groups in developing countries will automatically improve living conditions for all people in those countries.

7. Which of the following statements best summarizes the author's evaluation of the importance of technological advances in solving the problem of world food shortages?

    (A) They will succeed only if all people are given adequate technological educations.

    (B) They remain the single greatest hope in solving the problem of world food shortages.

    (C) They are ultimately less important than economic reforms in developing nations.

    (D) They will succeed only if the governments of developing countries support them.

    (E) They will succeed only if they receive widespread acceptance among powerful agribusiness groups.

8. According to the passage, some past technological food innovations, such as protein from algae grown on petroleum substrates, have failed because

    (A) they were not technologically feasible.

    (B) they did not receive adequate governmental support.

(C) local producers did not understand the new technology.

(D) they did not produce culturally acceptable food products.

(E) producers were unwilling to alter their production systems.

9. Which of the following constitutes the author's primary criticism of Anglo-American economists' studies of technological innovations?

(A) They do not understand that profit motives have a major influence on technology.

(B) They are biased in favor of technological innovations.

(C) Their focus has been almost exclusively on Western societies and cultures.

(D) They do not understand the role of Third World governments in shaping economic developments.

(E) They underestimate the importance of sociocultural factors in analyzing technological changes.

10. According to the passage one can assume that *triticale* is

(A) a nonliving form.

(B) an animal.

(C) a rock produced by grains of sand subjected to pressure.

(D) a low form of animal life.

(E) a plant.

Questions 11–18 are based on the following passage.

The judicial branch is a coequal part of the United States government, and yet it has escaped the degree of scientific scrutiny given to the executive and legislative branches. This is not to say the judicial branch has lacked all scrutiny, only that it has traditionally been viewed from a perspective different from the other two branches of government. The executive and legislative branches have traditionally been viewed as political entities. Judges and the judicial branch have fostered the idea that they are nonpolitical arbiters of the law. In *Marbury v. Madison,* the landmark United States Supreme Court case which established judicial review under the United States Constitution, Chief Justice John Marshall rhetorically asked who should determine the meaning of the Constitution. He answered himself by pointing to the fact that members of the other two branches were politically motivated, and only judges were qualified to be truly nonpolitical arbiters of the law. These statements by Chief Justice Marshall were certainly not the beginning of what is generally known as the "cult of the robe," but they are a classic example in American jurisprudence.

Following Marshall's reasoning, the study of the judiciary has traditionally used the case analysis method, which concentrates on individual cases. Each case must be decided on the basis of cases which have preceded it. Although it may be acknowledged that each case differs from any other case in many ways, past cases must still be examined to find the general principles which are then applied to the present dispute.

This reliance on precedent, known in legal terms as *stare decisis,* and its accompanying detailed examination of each case has caused legal scholars, to paraphrase Wieland, to not be able to see the forest for the trees. To get a more accurate picture of the workings of the judiciary it is necessary to step back from the cases. One must remain cognizant of the details, but not to such a degree that they inhibit the ability to see the greater whole. This is not to say analysis of individual cases has no place in the scientific study of the judiciary. Indeed, as was pointed out by Joyce Kilmer, there is always a place to appreciate the beauty of a tree, but there are also times when we must consider the tree as a part of the greater forest.

Although judicial scholars by and large do not subscribe to the myth that judges are nonpolitical arbiters of the law, there is substantial interest in judicial biographies, and case studies. Judicial biographies and case studies are certainly useful in interpreting particular judicial decisions, examining the opinions of a particular judge, or discussing specific points of law, but to optimize the results of such efforts, in terms of scientific study, such research must be viewed within the framework of a more comprehensive theory of judicial decision making.

11. The primary purpose of the passage is to

(A) suggest that judges are political decision makers.

(B) complain that no one studies the judiciary.

(C) advocate another way of studying the judiciary.

(D) describe the case analysis method.

(E) attack the doctrine of judicial review.

12. Chief Justice Marshall's argument assumes

    (A) judges are better educated than executives or legislators.

    (B) politically motivated individuals are biased.

    (C) only judges understand the Constitution.

    (D) it is better to study individual cases.

    (E) reliance on precedent is unnecessary.

13. According to the passage, the "cult of the robe" (line 16) can be best described as

    (A) the interpretation of the Constitution.

    (B) the study of prior cases.

    (C) a method of studying the courts.

    (D) the use of individual cases in decision making.

    (E) the belief judges are neutral decision makers.

14. According to the author, the "cult of the robe"

    (A) should be studied more closely.

    (B) should be used instead of *stare decisis.*

    (C) has misled researchers.

    (D) has led to a lack of scientific study of courts.

    (E) has inhibited the study of individual cases.

15. The reference to Wieland in line 26 is intended to

    (A) advocate broader studies of the courts.

    (B) suggest that courts are organic entities.

    (C) argue that judges are political.

    (D) decry the use of precedent.

    (E) support the case analysis method.

16. The reference to Kilmer in lines 31-33 is intended to

    (A) point out the beauty of studying court.

    (B) argue that individual courts are unimportant.

(C) support reliance on precedent.

(D) suggest case analysis has some benefits.

(E) discourage belief in the "cult of the robe."

17. According to the author, the problem with detailed examination of each case is that

(A) every case is different.

(B) it does not recognize the political aspects of courts.

(C) too many details obscure a broader understanding of how courts work.

(D) it relies on the "cult of the robe."

(E) one should ignore the details of cases.

18. The author's attitude toward case studies and judicial biographies can be summarized as being

(A) skeptical.   (D) disdainful.

(B) supportive.   (E) indifferent.

(C) neutral.

Questions 19–25 are based on the following passage.

Duke William the Conqueror's victory at Hastings guaranteed to him and his army a permanent stay in England. Harold, the one Anglo-Saxon leader of great ability, had perished and no man or group of men left behind was equal to organizing successful resistance to the Normans. Thus,
5 despite the fine opportunity that yet remained to inspire the mass of the Anglo-Saxons to heroic and stubborn resistance, there was no leadership to call it forth. It was now but a question of how long it would take the Normans to march around the island suppressing local and ill-organized defenses. Rightfully, some Anglo-Saxon lords and prelates regarded Lon-
10 don as the key to defense and rallied the surviving forces there. They immediately elected as king Edgar the Etheling, the last male descendant of the West Saxon dynasty, to provide a symbol of resistance and unity. But he was a mere youth with no flair for leadership. Within five days of Hastings, William had his army on the march towards London. Dover and
15 Canterbury fell without resistance, but he failed to take London Bridge by assault. Not having the equipment necessary to storm London, William fell to devastating a band of land encircling London, blocking all ap-

proaches. Deprived of reinforcements and obviously impressed by the terrible and methodical thoroughness with which William laid waste the
20 approaches, some of Edgar's followers soon lost heart; the first to offer submission to William was Stigand, the Archbishop of Canterbury. The rest were soon to follow. A meeting was then held between William and the leading Anglo-Saxon lords and Londoners; the latter, realizing the futility of further fighting and the desirability of a strong ruler, agreed to
25 cease resistance and surrender London. On Christmas Day William was crowned king of England in Westminster Abbey and was acknowledged lawful sovereign by the verbal assent of the assembled Anglo-Saxons and Normans. Meanwhile William strengthened his hold upon the new land, starting construction of castles such as the Tower of London, levying taxes
30 to pay for his army, receiving the homage of lords, and confiscating the lands of those who had resisted his invasion. By March of 1067 he was so completely in control that he felt able to return to Normandy, leaving England under the direction of trusted Norman lieutenants.

However much William's presence was required in his duchy, he had
35 to neglect it for England within nine months. His lieutenants ruled a seething land too harshly and caused more discontent than order by their undiplomatic policies. The suppression of an abortive attempt by Kentishmen to make the Norman Eustace of Boulogne king signaled to William the urgency for return. During the next eight years he was to be sporadically
40 occupied in stamping out the last embers of Anglo-Saxon resistance to foreign rule.

19. The primary purpose of the passage is to

   (A) chronicle the exploits of William the Conqueror.

   (B) describe the importance of London in the fall of England.

   (C) show the importance of strong leadership.

   (D) attack William's decision to return to Normandy.

   (E) downplay the importance of Harold's death at Hastings.

20. According to the author, London was the key to England's defense but

   (A) it could not withstand William's assault.

   (B) it could not stand after being cut off.

   (C) it fell due to the treachery of Anglo-Saxon lords.

(D) William conquered England without it.

(E) it did not resist William's advance.

21. Given the importance of a lack of leadership in England's fall, the author probably feels William's decision to return to Normandy to be

(A) unnecessary. (D) ironic.

(B) important. (E) administrative.

(C) of no consequence.

22. If William's lieutenants had ruled less harshly and more diplomatically William would not have been forced to return to England. According to the passage, this statement is

(A) unlikely, given the length of time William needed to stamp out resistance efforts.

(B) quite likely, given the necessity of administrative delegation.

(C) false since William did not leave England.

(D) irrelevant since William was from England originally and would have returned anyway.

(E) unimportant since William would have returned to England in any event.

23. According to the author, the election of Edgar as king (lines 10–12) was to

(A) return a Saxon to the throne after Harold's defeat.

(B) serve as a rallying point for the remaining forces.

(C) prevent William from becoming king.

(D) follow the line of succession from Harold.

(E) abide by the English constitution.

24. According to the author, after Harold's death the fate of England was

(A) in serious doubt.

(B) dependent on the rise of another strong leader.

(C) in the hands of the archbishop of Canterbury.

(D) dependent on a counterattack from Normandy.

(E) clear as to the final result.

25. After his assault on London, William

(A) returned to Normandy.

(B) went to Hastings where he defeated Harold.

(C) marched to Kent to put down a rebellion.

(D) increased his power over England.

(E) defeated Edgar at Saxony.

Questions 26–32 are based on the following passage.

The idea that moral rules are absolute, allowing no exceptions, is implausible in light of such cases as The Case of the Inquiring Murderer, and Kant's arguments for it are unsatisfactory. But are there any convincing arguments against the idea, apart from its being implausible?

5   The principal argument against absolute moral rules has to do with the possibility of conflict cases. Suppose it is held to be absolutely wrong to do A in any circumstances and also wrong to do B in any circumstances. Then what about the case in which a person is faced with the choice between doing A and doing B—when he must do something and 10 there are no other alternatives available? This kind of conflict case seems to show that it is *logically* untenable to hold that moral rules are absolute.

Is there any way that this objection can be met? One way would be for the absolutist to deny that such cases ever actually occur. The British philosopher P. T. Geach takes just this view. Like Kant, Geach argues that 15 moral rules are absolute; but his reasons are very different from Kant's. Geach holds that moral rules must be understood as absolute divine commands, and so he says simply that God will not allow conflict situations to arise. We can describe fictitious cases in which there is no way to avoid violating one of the absolute rules, but, he says, God will not permit such 20 circumstances to exist in the real world.

Do such circumstances ever actually arise? The Case of the Inquiring Murderer is, of course, a fictitious example; but it is not difficult to find real-life examples that make the same point. During the Second World War, Dutch fishermen regularly smuggled Jewish refugees to England in 25 their boats, and the following sort of thing sometimes happened. A Dutch boat, with refugees in the hold, would be stopped by a Nazi patrol boat. The Nazi captain would call out and ask the Dutch captain where he was bound, who was on board, and so forth. The fishermen would lie and be allowed to pass. Now it is clear that the fishermen had only two alterna-

30 tives, to lie or to allow their passengers (and themselves) to be taken and shot.

Now suppose the two rules "It is wrong to lie" and "It is wrong to permit the murder of innocent people" are both taken to be absolute. The Dutch fishermen would have to do one of these things; therefore a moral

35 view that absolutely prohibits both is incoherent. Of course this difficulty could be avoided if one held that only one of these rules is absolute; that would apparently be Kant's way out.

But this dodge cannot work in every such case; so long as there are at least two "absolute rules," whatever they might be, the possibility will

40 always exist that they might come into conflict. And that makes the view of those rules as absolute impossible to maintain.

26. The primary purpose of this passage is to

   (A) discuss the role of Dutch fishermen during the Second World War.

   (B) argue against absolute moral rules.

   (C) show the difference between Kant and Geach.

   (D) point out the inconsistency of moral rules.

   (E) consider hypothetical philosophical problems.

27. According to the author, Geach's position (lines 13–20) is

   (A) the Dutch fishermen were breaking the law so no conflict exists.

   (B) absolute moral rules are an impossibility.

   (C) the same as Kant's position.

   (D) illustrated by The Case of the Inquiring Murderer.

   (E) divine intervention prevents conflicts between absolute moral rules.

28. From the context of the passage, The Case of the Inquiring Murderer is most likely

   (A) a hypothetical one, illustrating potential conflict.

   (B) the name for the situation in which the Dutch fishermen found themselves.

(C) an example Geach used to illustrate his position.

(D) an argument in support of absolute moral rules.

(E) a real example of conflicting moral rules.

29. The author's attitude toward Kant's position is

(A) agreement.   (D) reluctant acceptance.

(B) disbelief.   (E) disdain.

(C) indifference.

30. According to the author, Geach finds cases of hypothetical conflict to be

(A) irrelevant to the real world.

(B) impossible to find.

(C) unlikely to occur.

(D) proof that absolute moral rules do not exist.

(E) an important support for Kant's position.

31. If there are at least two absolute moral rules the author argues

(A) they might not come into conflict.

(B) only hypothetical cases will show potential conflict.

(C) the possibility of conflict detracts from the possibility of both being absolute.

(D) Geach's position is untenable.

(E) then one of them must not be absolute.

32. The author's basic argument is

(A) the impossibility of absolute moral rules.

(B) a denunciation of the writings of Kant.

(C) an illustration of the difference between free will and determinism.

(D) an example of the moral dilemma faced by the Dutch fishermen.

(E) a listing of important moral rules.

Questions 33–39 are based on the following passage.

In earlier years during the Industrial Revolution, personnel practices of business and industry were mostly confined to hiring enough people to do the work, close supervision of employees to see that they did the work, and firing people if they did not abide by management guidelines. Labor had little influence on the system in the private sector. The management system was simple. In contrast, today personnel practices of business and industry have become complex and subject to influence of labor and government. Changes have occurred because society expects leaders in the private and public sectors to be sensitive to a number of social issues and to resolve difficulties that arise in the workplace.

Toward the end of the nineteenth century and early in the twentieth century, social issues were rarely considered part of the decision making process of employers. On occasion, constituents would press state or federal legislators to pass laws which would protect the health and/or morals of employees. Immediately the laws would be challenged in court. For example, a 1923 case dealt with a law that established a board authorized among other things, to determine minimum wages of female and child workers. In that case, the Supreme Court majority stated that "adult women...are legally as capable of contracting for themselves as men." The law was struck, and employer personnel practices continued to discriminate against women and children. If in the late 1880s and early 1900s the Supreme Court felt that the legislature had overstepped constitutional boundaries, those laws were made void, and management continued its harsh management policies, not only toward women and children, but also toward men.

Among the first of several court cases during the hectic years of the Industrial Revolution in America, comparison of policies showed that legislative and judicial branches were rarely unified in legal philosophy, setting national goals, and what could or could not be regulated. In a major case in 1918, the Supreme Court struck a federal law that penalized industry when it failed to abide regulations that specified ages and working hours of child employees. The children continued to work long hours. In 1923, a reporter interviewed the young man who was a child plaintiff in the landmark case. At the time of interview, the respondent was a young man who was married. The toll of working in a cotton mill long hours for many years had affected Reuben Dagenhart's growth and denied him the opportunity to be educated. His mood was somber when he told the reporter: "It would have been a good thing for all the kids in the state if that law they passed had been kept." Had Reuben read the dissenting opinion when his case was reported by the Supreme Court in 1918, he would have found that four justices also felt that the child labor law should have not been struck. They concurred that Congress does indeed have a role in protecting the national welfare and in enforcing policy designed to "benefit...the nation as a whole." In contrast, the majority of the court prevailed with a different interpretation of the Constitution and decried Congress's ulterior motive "to standardize the ages at which children may be employed...."

33. Which statement best illustrates personnel management in American history?

   (A) Since the beginning of the twentieth century, Congress and state legislatures have had wide latitude in correcting social ills in the private sector of business and industry.

   (B) Personnel practices have been fairly stable with little change after 1901.

   (C) During the years of the Industrial Revolution "big business" was highly respected by sociologists for its grave concern for the welfare of children and women employees—especially standardization of working hours.

   (D) Personnel management of business and industry has become increasingly complex as ideas change about social welfare.

   (E) If you read between the lines carefully, you will find that the executive branch played a key role in crumbling resistance to changes in working conditions.

34. Which statement describes some of the problems that have occurred in personnel management?

   (A) The author proposes that health of employees is a private matter and that government should keep out of personal lives of employees.

   (B) The author *applauds* the early twentieth century Supreme Court because it was a staunch advocate of equal rights of children and females by striking laws that provided special protections in the workplace.

   (C) Mood and attitude of ordinary workers toward personnel practices have not changed very much since 1900.

(D) The Supreme Court's legal and social philosophy in two cases cited above were aligned with industry's management theories and social philosophy.

(E) Male workers were exempt from unfair personnel rules in the workplace.

35. What values are reflected in the narrative provided by the author?

(A) The author is apparently a religious person because of his emphasis on moral issues.

(B) The author unfairly criticizes capitalism in the United States and is therefore a socialist.

(C) The author unfairly criticizes justices who write dissenting opinions and therefore leaves law unsettled.

(D) The author's choice of historical facts might lead the reader to consider motives of business and industry—such as profits—that led to hiring small children.

(E) One of the most important underlying premises in this article is a method of keeping children off the streets and out of mischief.

36. How would students of history describe the plight of women in the workplace toward the end of the nineteenth century?

(A) Opportunity to get away from the children

(B) Happy to have freedom to make contracts with their bosses

(C) Competitive for higher positions usually held by men

(D) Repressive

(E) Employment mostly restricted to single women

37. In the early twentieth century, what was the role of government in determining wages of women who worked in factories, hospitals, and other businesses?

(A) The Supreme Court majority felt that government should not set minimum wages for private employers.

(B) The legislature was filled with men whose wives did not work; thus, they were insensitive to needs of working women.

(C) Presidents finally bargained with industrial owners who caved in and established a business board that established minimum wages.

(D) Some legislators tried to protect economic welfare and morals of women by establishing an agency with authority to set minimum wages, but courts abolished the law and the agency.

(E) The judicial branch was more active in protecting women, children, and men than the legislative branch.

38. How would one evaluate the judicial process and its influence on the economic and/or social realm of society?

(A) The Supreme Court became a cohesive group of judges when considering the plight of child labor and the attempt to regulate personnel practices in the private sector.

(B) Within a few years after his case was decided, the child plaintiff realized that his case proved detrimental to the welfare of large numbers of children in his state.

(C) The majority opinion vividly portrayed a conscientious group of judges who were dedicated to the improvement of working conditions in factories and mills.

(D) In the choice of a respondent for interview purposes, the reporter was obviously trying to cast governmental regulation in a poor light.

(E) The judges who disagreed with the majority court opinion felt that legislatures must be restricted from too broad interpretation of the constitution.

39. Which observation is the most appropriate conclusion that can be drawn from the author's text?

(A) Some of the justices on the Supreme Court had difficulty in persuading most of the justices that legislation should be upheld when social welfare of the nation is at stake.

(B) Congressional leaders failed to persuade most of the members of the House and the Senate that legislation should be passed in order to protect the social welfare of the nation.

(C) The passage above is an excellent illustration of how the legislative branch and the judicial branch can lose their identities in the face of strong voter appeal in working class neighborhoods.

(D) Young Reuben's case was first filed in the trial court in 1918 and was not decided until 1923, too late to help the child laborer.

(E) The Supreme Court majority proposed that for the law to stand, Congress must standardize ages of employment.

Questions 40–45 are based on the following passage.

Today the role of business and government in solving social problems remains a controversial topic. Children no longer work in factories. Working hours for both men and women are regulated by government. Some observers feel that New Deal legislation sponsored by President Franklin D. Roosevelt provided the major thrust for governmental regulation of private sector personnel practices that were too long within the exclusive jurisdiction of industry and business management. At first the Supreme Court struck Roosevelt-initiated statutes. But the sentiment of the country and appointment of men politically sensitive to the political goals of the President led to judicial support of laws designed to deal with social ills in the country. In the 1930s and early 1940s, Congress followed the leadership of the top executive who proposed such legislation as Social Security, workers' compensation, and mandatory minimum wages. At that time a desire for change was ripe due to economic chaos caused by the Great Depression. Business and industry managers were suddenly cast into a different role when Congress and the Supreme Court became allies in authorizing governmental intrusion into the private sector's arena. Swift changes led to new professional expertise required for interpretation of law, additional paperwork, and implementation of personnel policies.

By the 1950s, long-standing racial discrimination was challenged. Congress had remained too long aloof and generally ignored problems associated with inequality. The NAACP bypassed the legislative branch and took its case to the judicial branch. By the 1960s, President Lyndon Johnson influenced Congress to take bold steps that eventually called for changes in the workplace. Title VII was passed, and a reduction of inequities was expected. However, NAACP director of labor, Joann Aiggs, said in 1987 that racial discrimination remains, but federal legislation "does provide an avenue people can use to seek redress."

America has often been called a "melting pot" because of the variety of ethnic, cultural, and racial heritages of its citizens. With the exception of the great flow of people from Africa before the early 1800s and the Chinese in the late 1880s, the majority of immigrants came from western Europe. The government set a national quota system. By the 1960s, laws changed and so did the national origin of immigrants, with the majority entering the country from Asia and Latin America. The number of immigrants has grown to around nine million people coming into the country during a 10 year span. When employers hire immigrants, citizens whose ancestors could be traced back to more than one generation feel threatened when jobs are scarce. Competition for jobs is a major issue. Congressional response placed a large paperwork burden on the personnel departments of business and industry. The Immigration Reform and Control Act of 1986 penalizes employers who hire illegal aliens. Today, personnel offices must be accountable to government with regard to the legal status of their employees. Documents must show that non-citizens have acquired authorization to work in this country. Some observers feel that governmental rules may drive illegal aliens from the workplace and that no one else will want to perform the low-level tasks required in some of the jobs.

40. Where was political leadership lodged in the mid-twentieth century?

    (A) It is evident that the author felt that President Roosevelt as chief executive should have stayed out of the legislative process and relied more on the judicial process.

    (B) The author explained how President Roosevelt changed direction of government by showing a stronger social orientation than national leaders of judicial and executive branches in earlier years.

    (C) Although new legislation was passed, the laws more or less left business and industry personnel policies intact by the 1940s.

    (D) At first President Roosevelt had to rely more on the courts than on stubborn legislators in order to pass laws designed to deal with social problems.

    (E) The above paragraphs show that personnel practices of business and industry have little impact on social problems in the country.

41. What kinds of changes occurred due to strong leadership from the Oval Office?

    (A) One can gather that bills sponsored by Roosevelt were successful in Congress because they were supported by the effective lobbying influence of business and industry.

    (B) The reader can assume that when the Roosevelt administration enforced new laws described above, the manufacturing and business labor expenditures increased accordingly.

(C) Organizations representing the interests of business most likely welcomed changes in Supreme Court personnel appointed by Roosevelt.

(D) Roosevelt's keen interest lay in ending racial discrimination through passage of the Special Security Act.

(E) President Roosevelt was elected. He immediately appointed new justices on the Supreme Court. Then he submitted to Congress proposed legislation. The Supreme Court approved the bills, and then Congress passed the laws.

42. Although observers may argue about what really happened during Roosevelt's term of office, interpret the factual information presented by the author by selecting the the best description below.

(A) New Deal legislation received its name from the deals the President made with business and industry for the purpose of pulling the rug out from under Congress, so to speak.

(B) Evolution and transformation of labor policies increased at a rapid pace during the Roosevelt administration.

(C) The author has inferred that historically the name "Great Depression" was a phrase that caught on after the press disclosed Roosevelt's mood when the Supreme Court struck the first three social welfare bills passed by Congress.

(D) Strange alliances are often formed in the political arena. Unorganized labor and their representatives in the legislature were seldom impressed with promises of reforms which would lead to a welfare state.

(E) During Roosevelt's term of office, racial discrimination was addressed vigorously, ending with the passage of the Civil Rights Act of 1964.

43. Below are several statements that deal with discrimination in the workplace. Choose the sentence that conforms to the author's analysis.

(A) The recent immigration act is possibly the best example of affirmative action in recent years.

(B) Illegal aliens are part of the establishment.

(C) When business and industry employers ignored social problems associated with hiring illegal aliens, government eventually stepped into the vacuum created by private sector negligence and mandated constructive activities.

(D) Private sector and public sector policy makers by and large have the same goals when trying to solve social problems of employees.

(E) The author implies that the statement made by Joann Riggs shows how the ruling elite often fails to be responsive to public opinion through institutional mechanisms.

44. What is the major problem that stems from the way problems of non-Caucasians are handled by government?

(A) Conflict among job applicants competing for scarce jobs has heightened friction among citizens whose differences are based on cultural, racial, or ethnic factors.

(B) The term "melting pot" reflects the resolution of problems through direct representation.

(C) The author maintains that political socialization, in the long run, must be the major responsibility of each ethnic and racial group living in the United States.

(D) The author refused to deal with the problem of income distribution for illegal aliens.

(E) One of the most interesting disclosures is the under-the-table wheeling and dealing of President Johnson who sought to undermine the NAACP's goals when he proposed separate-but-equal policies in schools and the factories.

45. How did the federal government respond to evidence of widely practiced discrimination during other presidential administrations that followed the Roosevelt years?

(A) Legislative leadership in eradicating racial discrimination was apparent, especially after special interests effectively pressured individual members of Congress immediately after World War II.

(B) At first the judicial branch was the pathfinder in approving policies for eliminating racial discriminatory practices, but the administrative chief of the federal executive branch eventually prodded the legislative branch to pass major civil rights laws.

(C) During the 10 to 15 years following President Roosevelt's death, the legislative branch moved speedily in the policy-making arena and protected black citizens more than the judicial and executive branches combined.

(D) President Roosevelt, had he lived another 30 years, would have been ashamed of the executive and judicial branches when they overturned strong civil rights laws that he managed to push through Congress.

(E) President Johnson was too busy with domestic and foreign policies to provide leadership in the civil rights movement. Besides, everyone knows that he was from Texas.

Questions 46–52 are based on the following passage.

Universal health coverage for all citizens is a political question staunchly supported by proponents and vigorously opposed by detractors. Both groups are emotionally committed to their idea of what is best for the nation. Today, health care coverage varies from business to business. Employees may or may not be covered by health insurance and/or retirement pension plans provided by employers. Congress has made small steps toward a national health plan through several laws. For instance, the Health Maintenance Organization Act was passed in 1973. Lobbyists have pressed for leaves of absence without fear of job loss when babies are born, children or parents are ill, or a parent experiences serious illness.

The central issue for business and industry is a personnel management problem and labor cost. Who will perform work duties for up to 26 weeks while the employee is on leave without pay?

Not surprisingly, many female employees support leaves of absence for child-rearing purposes. The National Organization for Women has worked actively to support passage of the federal law. Senator Christopher Dodd feels that the bill will address problems of working mothers. He cited statistics to prove his point: "half of all mothers with infants less than a year old work outside home" and "85% of all women working outside the home are likely to become pregnant at some point during their career." Dodd maintained that "we must no longer force parents to choose between their job and caring for a new or sick child." The bill has its critics. The president of the California Merchants and Manufacturers Association projects discrimination against women in hiring practices if the bill is passed. Roberta Cook of the California Chamber of Commerce said, "We're compassionate. We just don't think the issue should be the employer's responsibility. *That's* the issue."

Another social issue yet unresolved is drug use and management/ labor relations. Employers must consider the problem from several vantage points. Accidents, absenteeism, and reduction of productive labor are expensive and wasteful. The constitutional right of privacy is often argued when personnel policies for testing and/or searches are proposed. Courts have given qualified approval to some methods that employers may implement. Employers in the private sector may require drug testing as a precondition for employment. Government personnel directors must be cautious in devising new policies. Based on nothing more than the goal of a drug-free work place in the public sector, large-scale drug testing of employees violates their right of privacy.

When comparing social issues in the late nineteenth and the early twentieth centuries with current social issues that affect personnel policies, the increasing number of complexities of labor/management relations are apparent. Yet the question can be asked: Were the emotional, physical, and economic damages experienced by workers in the early years less important than the emotional, physical, and economic damages experienced today? Reuben Dagenhart, plaintiff in the child labor case, was in his 20s an uneducated man who weighed only about 105 pounds. Today, the "Reubens" do not quit school at a tender age and work long hours at factories, but modern-day mothers are distraught when in some workplaces they face job loss if they take leave to attend to a sick child or parent. In the late twentieth century the legislative branch continues its struggles with competing pressures from labor and management while the judicial branch intercedes from time to time and makes hard decisions based on what the Constitution requires. Again national leaders must structure social policies when legal and social philosophies collide and when economic theories clash in the market place of ideas.

46. Why should people disagree about the health insurance issue described by the author?

    (A) In a truly representative democracy, voters naturally feel that the ultimate decision on health care should be made by Congressmen who are wise and know best.

    (B) Many voters embrace the capitalist system where many decisions should be confined to the private sector without governmental policies which assure all people health care protection.

    (C) In the interest of promoting socialism, leaders of welfare groups fear expanded coverage.

(D) Resistance to significant health care coverage at taxpayers' expense may be due to other factors, such as fear that government will refuse to pay for abortions and AIDS care.

(E) The controversy about health care among groups can be explained in one word—entropy. The term means degradation followed by inert uniformity.

47. Given the difficulty of legislating a universal health care plan, what appears to be the relationship between the business community and Congress?

(A) With Congress under pressure to expand health coverage and yet not wanting to lose the support of business, it has passed a few laws allocating enough programs and funds to meet the immediate need of pleasing constituents who want to increase public health care.

(B) The business world has already developed a universal health plan in which if a man or woman works, he/she has nothing to worry about.

(C) Participative management in factories where workers help choose insurance plans has been sufficient to argue against Congress moving forward on health care issues.

(D) Business has taken advantage of proponents of universal health care who follow the philosophy of Boren's testimony: "When in charge ponder;...When in doubt mumble."

(E) The business community lacks concern for employees and their families.

48. What is the current status of leaves of absence without pay?

(A) Most employees are appalled at the new idea because they do not want to be away from their jobs which would mean loss of income and lowering of the standard of living.

(B) Business's cry that it cannot afford to let people have a month or more off from work because it would drive up the price of products is ridiculous and is nothing more than the little boy crying "wolf."

(C) Business opposes unpaid leaves of absence on the grounds that it will be burdened with training and paying replacement workers.

(D) The policy on leaves seems to place an emotional hardship on families.

(E) Congressmen who listen to supporters of the policy in which laws would protect people from being fired after the leave probably hear these lobbyists repeat time and again: "Caveat emptor" or "Let the buyer beware."

49. What is the social significance of the leaves of absence policy?

(A) Under the proposed policy, bonding of family members will be promoted.

(B) With the prediction of an 85% growth in family units, our nation will naturally face a population explosion if the policy is ratified.

(C) A subsystem will develop in society composed of "working mothers" who only work occasionally between births and between child sickness.

(D) Business is solidifying its opposition against the bill through such spokespersons as Dodd and Cook.

(E) The Chamber of Commerce is compassionate toward working mothers, and therefore is pro-labor.

50. What are the constitutional issues of drug use in the workplace?

(A) The author infers that the right of privacy protects an employee against Murphy's Law: "If anything can go wrong, it will."

(B) For the public good, government has greater freedom in drug testing then managers in the private sector.

(C) Under the right of privacy, employees may refuse drug testing without fear of losing their jobs.

(D) Under the constitutional right of privacy, we can assume that applicants for a job may withdraw the application if the potential employer requires drug testing as a condition for the job.

(E) Bias rather than economics will figure most prominently when employers reject applicants whose tests are positive.

51. How can nineteenth and twentieth century social issues be compared?

    (A) The author called for a return to policy making made on a value-free basis where economics was of prime importance.

    (B) The author implies that the leaves of absence policy is based on Parkinson's Law: "Work expands so as to fill the time for its completion."

    (C) The author concludes that although specific issues have changed, problems remain for employees and employers which have both social and economic significance.

    (D) Reuben Dagenhart, if he was alive today and still working in a mill, absolutely would not support leaves of absence without pay.

    (E) The author implies that legal and social philosophies should have more weight in policy making than economic theories.

52. How does the author feel about some of the recent personnel management issues?

    (A) The author senses that unpaid leaves for birth of a child or sickness of a relative is not a simple issue.

    (B) The author heavily criticizes married women employees for taking jobs away from males and then for complaining because they cannot take long leaves for personal reasons.

    (C) When released time was discussed above, the author is ambivalent about the role of politics.

    (D) Reading between the lines, it soon becomes evident that the author is pro-labor and anti-management.

    (E) Choice of how management deals with requests for leaves of absence is strictly a business decision, and government should stay out.

READING MEDIUM PASSAGES
DIAGNOSTIC TEST

ANSWER KEY

1.	(B)	14.	(D)	27.	(E)	40.	(B)
2.	(D)	15.	(A)	28.	(A)	41.	(B)
3.	(A)	16.	(D)	29.	(B)	42.	(B)
4.	(E)	17.	(C)	30.	(A)	43.	(C)
5.	(B)	18.	(A)	31.	(C)	44.	(A)
6.	(B)	19.	(C)	32.	(A)	45.	(B)
7.	(C)	20.	(B)	33.	(D)	46.	(B)
8.	(D)	21.	(D)	34.	(D)	47.	(A)
9.	(E)	22.	(A)	35.	(D)	48.	(C)
10.	(E)	23.	(B)	36.	(D)	49.	(A)
11.	(C)	24.	(E)	37.	(D)	50.	(D)
12.	(B)	25.	(D)	38.	(B)	51.	(C)
13.	(E)	26.	(B)	39.	(A)	52.	(A)

DETAILED EXPLANATIONS OF ANSWERS

1.   **(B)**   This should be clear from the first paragraph. The remainder of the passage describes some of the specifics of why people find such joy and pleasure in opera. As part of this description the author mentions Wagner's creative philosophy, but he does not mention any of Wagner's specific works. Thus, (A) is incorrect. Similarly, in the last paragraph the author notes the increased popularity of opera due to increased exposure via the mass media. Here again, however, the author is merely making one point in his overall theme of why opera is so popular. Thus, (C) is also incorrect. (D) is incorrect because in the fourth paragraph the author reports with enthusiasm the comments of Kenneth Clark who suggested that the artificiality of opera is what made it so popular and enduring. The author makes no plea for the support of opera, especially financially. In the last paragraph the author suggests opera is growing in popularity. Thus, (E) is incorrect.

2.   **(D)**   In the fourth paragraph the author favorably reports the comments of Kenneth Clark. Clark notes that it is the irrationality or silliness of opera which allows revelation of one's innermost thoughts and feelings. Thus, the author favorably concurs that opera is artificial, making (A) incorrect. Undoubtedly the author recognizes the importance of *Gesamtkunstwerk* (otherwise he would not have mentioned it in such a positive manner), but by the time the author mentions the artificiality of opera he has moved on to another point in his discussion unrelated to *Gesamtkunstwerk*. Thus, (B) is incorrect. (C) is incorrect because the author does not conclude opera is irrational entertainment—a negative conclusion, but rather, that it is opera's irrationality which makes it entertaining. (E) is incorrect because the author mentions the artificiality of opera in favorable terms, and he also does not criticize Wagner's operas.

3.   **(A)**   This is made clear in the quoted material attributed to Clark in the fourth paragraph. (B) is probably true as an explanation for the longevity of opera, but it is the author's explanation not Clark's, and is thus incorrect. Similarly, (D) is also probably true, but, again, not part of Clark's explanation, and, again, incorrect. The author seems to be making the general point raised by (C), which undoubtedly has contributed to opera's increased popularity. Here again, however, this is not part of Clark's ex-

planation and is incorrect. (E) is incorrect because Clark does not deny opera's irrationality; rather he accepts it as a reason for its longevity.

4. **(E)** In the second paragraph the author describes the manifestations of the passion between opera and its audiences. The conclusion to be reached is that opera triggers a wide range of deeply felt emotions (approval to displeasure).Such outbursts, positive or negative, cannot be said to be the result of audience indifference, making (C) incorrect. The author does not specifically indicate that there is inconsistency in the quality of operatic productions. The symbols of displeasure might be directed toward the action occurring onstage or toward a particularly heinous character. In addition, we can probably assume that if the quality of the production was inconsistent, opera would not be growing in popularity. Thus, (A) is incorrect. (B) is also incorrect because the author does not suggest that outbursts are a sign of lack of sophisication in the audience. (D) is incorrect because the author's comments on audience outbursts and the artificiality of opera are part of two different points: the return of passion for passion and the entertaining nature of opera's irrationality.

5. **(B)** is the correct answer. Opera has adapted to many technological changes; the video screen may be another medium for the opera. The booming video market will probably be another medium for the opera; (A) is incorrect because it states that the video market may put an end to opera attendance. (C) should not be selected; the opera is not an art form of the past. (D) is incorrect; the opera has been very popular in the past and continues to be popular. (D) states that opera has never been popular so it is an incorrect statement. (E) is incorrect because it states that opera was popular at the time it was first performed but it was never popular thereafter. (B) is the best answer.

6. **(B)** The author believes that "profit-oriented business people" are motivated by a desire to "increase their incomes." Technological innovations per se are neither welcomed nor opposed by agribusiness groups but are considered only in terms of profitability. (A) and (D) are incorrect. Anglo-American economists have recognized the influence of profit motives on technological change; (C) is incorrect. The author believes that agribusiness groups will adopt innovations that increase profits even when these innovations harm the poor and reduce food availability; (E) is incorrect.

7. **(C)** The author believes that technological advances may be needed to solve the problem of world food shortages, but that equalizing eco-

nomic power among various segments of the population in developing countries will ultimately be more important in addressing this problem (hence (B) is incorrect). (A), (D), and (E) may be true, but they are less important than economic reform.

8. **(D)** The author believes that technological advances in food production must not only be economically viable and technologically feasible but must also produce food that is culturally acceptable to consumers; cultural acceptability is a problem with protein from algae and fish-protein concentrate. He says producing protein from algae was technologically feasible; (A) is incorrect. The author does not mention whether this technology received governmental support or was understood by local producers; (B) and (C) are incorrect. He believes that profit-motivated producers will alter production systems if doing so results in economic gain; (E) is incorrect.

9. **(E)** The author believes that Anglo-American economists have mistakenly disregarded the "substantial effects of culture" on technical change. They have correctly stressed the importance of profit motives in shaping technological innovations. (A) is incorrect. (B), (C), and (D) may or may not be true; the author offers no evidence to support any of these assertions.

10. **(E)** is the correct answer. Context clues can be used to help the reader. The passage states "...Antarctic krill, and the wheat-rye hybrid triticale seem more promising..." The reader knows that wheat and rye are plants and that the word *hybrid* refers to plants. (E) is the best answer to this comprehension question. Plants are living; (A) refers to a nonliving form. (A) is wrong. Triticale is neither an animal (B) nor a rock (C); neither (B) nor (C) should be chosen. Triticale is not a low form of animal life; (D) is incorrect.

11. **(C)** This question requires the test-taker to pick the primary purpose of the passage. The passage begins by suggesting the courts have not received sufficient scientific scrutiny because they have not been viewed as political bodies. The passage continues by noting the traditional use of case analysis. The author argues that this method has too narrow a focus and does not allow one to see the broader aspects of the workings of courts. The author admits that case studies have some merit, but advocates broader, more scientific, studies. (C) is correct because the first two sentences of the passage suggest that the judiciary is not studied properly. Next the author describes why the judiciary is studied, using the case

analysis method, then continues by pointing out the problems of this method. The author concludes the passage by suggesting greater benefits would occur if the judiciary were studied differently. (A) is incorrect because by stating it is a "myth that judges are nonpolitical arbiters of the law" (fourth paragraph), the author shows a belief that judges are political, and notes most judicial scholars are also aware that judges are political actors. The assertion by the author that judges are political actors is only one piece of evidence in support of his more general thesis. (B) is incorrect because the author clearly states, "[t]his is not to say the judicial branch has lacked all scrutiny, only that it has traditionally been viewed from a perspective different from the other two branches of government" (first paragraph). (D) is incorrect because very little information on the case analysis method is given. It is mentioned only as supporting evidence for the broader proposition that study of the judiciary must be more scientific. (E) is also incorrect. As with response (D), the passage only mentions judicial review in passing. The mention of judicial review is used only to give an example of how the cult of the robe has led people to view judges as being nonpolitical.

12. **(B)**   Marshall's conclusion is that judges should interpret the Constitution because they are nonpolitical. This suggests whether decision makers are political makes a difference in how they interpret the Constitution. Marshall's assumption in choosing the courts for this task is that political actors such as executives and legislatures cannot be impartial. (A) is incorrect because there is no mention in the passage of education levels. The reference to qualifications in the passage concerns whether the decision makers are politically motivated, not how well educated they are. (C) is incorrect because there is no mention that Marshall believed judges to have a greater understanding of the Constitution. Again, Marshall emphasized the *political* differences between judges and other members of government. (D) is incorrect because Marshall's statements do not relate to the study of the judiciary. Marshall was concerned with interpretation of the Constitution. It is the author of the passage who is concerned with the study of the judiciary. The author only uses Marshall's comments as an example of the kind of thinking which led to the emphasis on studying individual cases. (E) is incorrect. As with (D), Marshall's comments do not pertain to the use of precedent. His comments are concerned with the *who* of interpreting the Constitution, not the *how*.

13. **(E)**   The phrase *cult of the robe* is introduced immediately after Marshall's comments on the inability of the politically motivated branches

of government to be nonpolitical arbiters of the Constitution (first paragraph). The author directly links Marshall's comments to the cult of the robe by saying his comments are "a classic example" of these beliefs. (A) is incorrect because the cult of the robe is shown to be a belief in the neutrality of judges, not a particular method of interpreting the Constitution. (B) is incorrect for the same reason as (A). In addition, it is *stare decisis* which is the *use* of past cases, not the cult of the robe. (C) is incorrect. The author argues that the cult of the robe has *influenced* the study of the courts, but it is not itself a method of study. (D) is incorrect. The author makes clear that the use of individual cases in decision making, or the use of precedent, is "known in legal terms as *stare decisis*" (third paragraph).

14. **(D)**   In the third and fourth paragraphs the author argues belief in the cult of the robe has led to a reliance on the case analysis method. In the fourth and fifth paragraphs the author argues this method is inadequate. (A) is incorrect because the author argues that the cult of the robe is a myth. The author also indicates "judicial scholars by and large do not subscribe to the myth" (fourth paragraph). (B) is incorrect because the author is not contrasting the advantages of *stare decisis* and the cult of the robe. In addition, as mentioned in the explanation to question three, the cult is not a method, but the belief that judges are nonpolitical. (C) is incorrect because the author notes that most judicial scholars do not subscribe to the myth of the cult of the robe (fourth paragraph). The author continues by arguing that even though researchers do not believe the myth, they still focus on judicial biographies and case studies. Thus, according to the author, researchers are not being misled, but are also not properly studying the courts. (E) is incorrect because just the opposite has occurred. The author is suggesting there is too much study of individual cases, which follows from the belief that judges are nonpolitical arbiters of the law (second paragraph).

15. **(A)**   The paraphrase of Wieland suggests that by concentrating on the details of individual cases, researchers lose sight of the broader workings of courts. This fits the author's overall theme that broader studies of the courts must be undertaken. (B) is incorrect. The author is not suggesting courts are organic entities, or that they are trees. The reference to Wieland's statement about trees is intended as a metaphor for the consequences of examining something in minute detail. (C) is incorrect. Other parts of the passage do argue that judges are political, but the reference to Wieland does not. At this stage in the passage the author has already

provided evidence of the cult of the robe, and how it has led to the traditional study of individual cases. In referring to Wieland, the author is suggesting that one loses sight of the greater whole when concentrating on individual cases. (D) is incorrect. Precedent, *per se*, is not a problem. The author says so in the reference to Joyce Kilmer by saying, metaphorically, that there is value in examining individual cases. According to the author, the problem is the *exclusive* reliance on precedent. It is for this reason the author advocates broader studies of courts (A). (E) is incorrect. The case analysis method relies on the study of individual cases. In referring to Wieland, the author is suggesting that something is lost or missing by only concentrating on the details (individual cases).

16. **(D)**   In the preceding reference to Wieland, the author suggests something is lost or missing by concentrating only on individual cases. Nevertheless, in referring to Kilmer, the author suggests that the study of individual cases does have some merit. (A) is incorrect because the passage does not address the question of the beauty of studying courts. It can be assumed that the author feels the study of courts has merit. The reference to beauty, however, metaphorically suggests that there is value in studying individual cases. (B) is incorrect. The author is concerned about too much emphasis on individual *cases,* but the author does not mention individual *courts*. (C) is incorrect. As noted above, the reference to Kilmer is intended to recognize there is some merit in studying individual cases, but this does not mean researchers should *rely* on them. Attaching such a meaning to the Kilmer reference would make the author's arguments contradictory. (E) is incorrect. The author recognizes "judicial scholars by and large do not subscribe to the myth that judges are nonpolitical arbiters of the law" (fourth paragraph), so it is unnecessary to discourage belief in the cult. In addition, as with (C), if (E) were true it would lead to a contradictory argument by the author.

17. **(C)**   This is the point of the Wieland reference. The author is arguing for broader studies of courts rather than narrowly focused biographies and case studies. (A) is incorrect. Although it may be true that every case is different in some regard, this is not the problem the author is addressing. The author is concerned with the method of studying cases, not the cases themselves. (B) is incorrect. The author's concern is not with recognition of the political aspects of courts. The author recognizes that most judicial scholars do not believe judges are nonpolitical actors (fourth paragraph). Nevertheless, the author believes there to be undue reliance on case studies in judicial research, so the problem is not with recognition of the political aspects of courts. (D) is incorrect for the same reasons as (B). The

cult of the robe is mentioned merely to show what led to the current reliance on case studies and judicial biographies. The author does not believe the cult of the robe to be a current problem (fourth paragraph). (E) is incorrect. The author specifically rejects any suggestion that the details should be ignored by stating: "One must remain cognizant of the details" (third paragraph).

18. **(A)** The author recognizes some value in the study of individual cases (fourth paragraph), but argues that such studies cannot grasp the broader aspects of how courts work. Thus, the author is skeptical as to the value of relying solely on individual case studies. (B) is incorrect. Although the author does recognize there is some value in case studies (fourth paragraph), the author's argument centers on the belief they are used too often. The author is unsupportive of continued *reliance* on case studies for judicial analysis. (C) is incorrect. The point of the passage is to argue for more broad-based studies and less reliance on case studies. It cannot, therefore, be said the author's attitude toward case studies is neutral. (D) is incorrect. The author recognizes there is some value in case studies and judicial biographies (fourth paragraph). The author is not disdainful of such studies, only concerned that they dominate judicial research and fail to capture the broader aspects of courts. (E) is incorrect. Indifference suggests not caring about case studies and judicial biographies. The author does care about them. The value of such studies is specifically noted (fourth paragraph). In addition, the author's argument centers on the belief that such studies are used too much in judicial research. Thus, it cannot be said the author is indifferent to case studies and judicial biographies.

19. **(C)** The author specifically mentions strong leadership four times in the passage: 1) the death of Harold left no one able to successfully organize a resistance, 2) the election of Edgar to provide a symbol of unity, 3) the submission of the English lords to William because he was a strong leader, and 4) England's increased resistance to foreign rule when William left the country. The passage certainly describes some of William's exploits, but not in sufficient quantity or depth to be considered a chronicle. Thus, (A) is incorrect. (B) is also incorrect. Although the passage does suggest the importance of London, it does so only as one point in a broader theme. The author uses the fall of London to show how English lords were impressed with strong leadership. (D) is incorrect because the author seems to recognize William's presence was needed there as well (perhaps a fifth reference to strong leadership). The author merely notes William's absence from England caused additional resistance without making a judgment about the decision to leave. (E) is incorrect because the

author *emphasizes* the importance of Harold's death. Without Harold, there was no one of sufficient ability left to organize and lead England's defense.

20. **(B)**   The author specifically notes the English lords rallied their surviving forces in London to resist William's advance. Thus, (E) is incorrect. We are told that William's assault on London bridge failed and he realized he did not have the equipment to storm London. This shows (A) to be incorrect. William did not give up on London and turn to other parts of England, as (D) suggests. Instead he laid waste to the area surrounding London, cutting it off from supplies and reinforcements (B). Although the Anglo-Saxon lords did meet with William and surrendered to him, these were peace talks and cannot be considered treachery, making (C) incorrect.

21. **(D)**   The author emphasizes the importance of strong leadership throughout the passage. The implication is that William should have realized this as well. By killing England's only strong leader and being a strong leader himself, he was able to conquer England and become its king. It is thus ironic that William's strong leadership gained him two kingdoms, *both* of which required his presence. The author does not suggest William's return to Normandy was based on a whim or otherwise unnecessary (A), nor does he suggest it was for administrative purposes (E). The fact a resistance was organized in William's absence means it *was* of consequence (C). The author certainly feels the decision to return to Normandy was not unimportant. Nevertheless, it was not a key element in England's resistance effort. The length of time William spent putting down resistance efforts (eight years) does not suggest if he had stayed there would have been no attempt to resist foreign rule.

22. **(A)**   The last sentence of the passage makes (A) the clear answer by suggesting resistance to foreign rule was more important than the poor leadership skills of William's lieutenants. It is true that William needed to delegate administrative duties, but the more important consideration is English resistance to foreign rule. The degree of resistance William faced suggests even benevolent and diplomatic lieutenants would have met resistance eventually. (C) and (D) are both clearly wrong. In the last paragraph we are told that William did leave England to return to his duchy. In addition, there would be no point in noting English resistance to foreign rule if William was from England. The harsh rule of William's lieutenants probably forced him to return to England much sooner than he expected or preferred, so it was important. The remaining portion of (E) is pure speculation not supported by the passage.

23. **(B)** As (B) suggests, the author says, "They immediately elected as king Edgar...to provide a symbol of resistance and unity." Although Edgar was a Saxon, as was Harold, there is no suggestion in the passage that Edgar was a descendant of Harold's (D), nor that Edgar's heritage was of significance apart from serving as a rallying point. Thus, (A) is also incorrect. The purpose of electing Edgar king was to rally English forces to defeat William. There is no suggestion in the passage electing Edgar king would in any way prevent William's ascension to the throne other than his possible military defeat—which did not occur (C). There is also no mention of constitutional requirements which makes (E) irrelevant.

24. **(E)** The author notes that after the death of Harold there was a willingness to resist, but "no leadership to call it forth." Recognizing this lack of leadership and the strong leadership of William makes it clear the death of Harold signals the fall of England. This makes (A) wrong, and (B) wrong simply because there was no strong English leader. There is no suggestion in the passage that the English planned to mount a counteroffensive in Normandy or had allies there who would. The entire passage is concerned with events in England, thus making (D) incorrect. Although the author notes Stigand, the Archbishop of Canterbury, was the first to submit to William, the implication seems to be that this was merely the first of what would eventually be many. There is no indication the archbishop was a determining factor in the fate of England (C).

25. **(D)** The author notes after his victory in London and ascension to the throne, "William strengthened his hold upon the new land." (A) is incorrect because William returned to Normandy three months after being crowned, and only after he felt he was in sufficient control. The passage begins with the battle of Hastings where Harold was defeated, and then William advanced on London. Thus, (B) is incorrect. (C) is wrong because we are told it was the resistance of Kentishmen which forced William to return to England from Normandy. (E) is wrong because Edgar was defeated at London, and also because Saxony is not part of England.

26. **(B)** The author begins the passage by suggesting absolute moral rules are implausible. He then provides evidence and examples leading to the conclusion that they are also impossible to maintain. (A) is incorrect because the discussion of Dutch fishermen is only mentioned as an example of how two absolute moral rules can come into conflict, forcing the actors (the Dutch fishermen in the example) to violate at least one of two absolute rules. The author does point out a difference between Kant and Geach, but this difference is not central to the passage (C). The author

mentions the difference to show how each philosopher deals with the possibility of conflicting absolute moral rules and then refutes each position. The author is not arguing against moral rules in general, nor is their inconsistency of paramount concern (D). The problem, according to the author, is the *absoluteness* of the rules. This is emphasized in the last sentence of the passage. The consideration of hypothetical philosophical problems (E) is used to show how absolute moral rules can come into conflict. The hypotheticals are used as examples only and are not the central focus of the passage.

27. **(E)** The author notes Geach's position at the end of the second paragraph: "God will not permit such circumstances to exist in the real world." One may invent fictitious conflicts, but, according to Geach, since absolute moral rules are divine commands, God would not allow a conflict to arise in the real world. The passage makes no mention of how Geach would explain the case of the Dutch fishermen (A), or the Inquiring Murderer (D). (B) is clearly the opposite of Geach's position. The author makes it clear in the second paragraph that although both Kant and Geach believe in absolute moral rules, their reasons are very different (C).

28. **(A)** The passage mentions The Case of the Inquiring Murderer, but does not tell us what it is about. Nevertheless, the author does indicate in the first sentence that it serves as an argument against absolute moral rules. In the third paragraph the author indicates the example of the Dutch fishermen provides a real example which makes the same point as that of the Inquiring Murderer; more than one absolute moral rule raises the possibility of conflict. We can deduce that The Case of the Inquiring Murderer also illustrates the possibility of conflict. Given the author's description of the two cases in the third paragraph (B) cannot be correct. The Case of the Inquiring Murderer is used to argue *against* absolute moral rules. Thus, (D) is incorrect, as is (C), since Geach supports the existence of absolute moral rules. (E) is incorrect because the author specifically states The Case of the Inquiring Murderer is fictitious.

29. **(B)** The author's purpose is to argue against absolute moral rules. He cannot, therefore, believe Kant's position which supports their existence. This makes (A) incorrect, as well as (D). Given the effort the author spends refuting Kant's position, it cannot be said that he is indifferent to it (C). Nevertheless, the author gives no indication that he thinks Kant's position is stupid, trivial, or otherwise deserving of disdain (E). He merely disagrees with Kant's position and attempts to prove it wrong.

30. **(A)** As noted in the explanation to question 27, Geach believes absolute moral rules to be of divine origin, and God will not permit conflict to actually arise. Geach may find hypotheticals interesting, but nevertheless irrelevant to the real world. By arguing God will not permit conflict to occur in the real world, Geach must recognize that examples of hypothetical conflict do exist, making (B) incorrect. Geach's position is not that examples of hypothetical conflict are unlikely to occur (C). It is that God will not allow them to occur. (D) is incorrect because it is clear from the passage that although Geach recognizes the existence of examples of hypothetical conflict between absolute moral rules, he still believes they exist. (E) is incorrect because Kant's position supports absolute moral rules and the hypotheticals argue against them, and because there is no mention in the passage of Geach commenting on Kant's position.

31. **(C)** The author states this directly in the last paragraph to explain why Kant's defense is untenable. It is also in this last paragraph where the author rejects the possibility that if two absolute moral rules exist they will not come into conflict (A). The author feels Kant's defense, which is (E), is weak and cannot explain every possibility. (B) is more in line with Geach's position. The author provides a real world example of conflict by discussing the Dutch fishermen. (D) is incorrect because Geach's position raises a different defense, that of divine intervention.

32. **(A)** The passage begins by indicating the implausibility of absolute moral rules. It continues by presenting arguments, and eventually concluding, that they are also impossible to maintain. (B) is incorrect because the author is not denouncing Kant, merely trying to show why he is wrong with regard to absolute moral rules. Other writings by Kant are neither mentioned nor relevant. Geach's position may raise questions of free will versus determinism (C), but the author does not raise the issue in his arguments. The author's example of the Dutch fishermen (D) is just that, an example. It is used in support of the basic argument, but it is not the argument itself, i.e., the author is not trying to prove something about Dutch fishermen. The author's position against absolute moral rules makes (E) clearly wrong.

33. **(D)** (D) nicely summarizes how management practices have had to change in order to take into consideration laws, agency rules, and court decisions. (A) is incorrect. As the author explains, courts often struck laws designed to eradicate unhealthy and unfair practices. (B) fails to take into account major changes, especially after the Supreme Court changed its interpretation of the Constitution. (C) has missed the point of the author

who pointed out that profit motives often led to harsh working conditions for children and women. (E) is not totally correct. While the executive branch played a role, the judicial branch played the greatest role in protecting workers through upholding laws designed to protect health and safety.

34. **(D)**   (D) certainly reflects how management which did not want interference from government was most delighted with Supreme Court decisions that struck laws. (A) has misinterpreted the author's intent as he provides information about the history and philosophy that lay behind court decisions. (B) has confused the role of the court in the early 1900s and the fact that its decisions which protected contracts actually failed to protect women and children. Although there is room for improvement, (C) did not take into consideration how poor working conditions in earlier years would depress workers much more than present-day work environments. (E) cannot be supported by the description of management/labor conditions in the early years.

35. **(D)**   The author has apparently chosen a topic that shows how profit motives can lead to poor personnel practices. (A) is a narrow assessment of the author's values because morality is not confined to persons of the cloth. (B) is wrong. One of the great freedoms in America is the ability to observe and express freely opinions about the way government operated over the years. Critics are not necessarily socialites or socialists. (C) offers the reader an opportunity to make a personal judgment on fairness. Actually, the author finds no problems when dissenting opinions are adopted by later courts in an effort to protect workers from poor working conditions. (E) has gone far beyond the intent of the author. In fact in earlier years, children were indeed off the streets, but suffering from terrible working conditions in factories, a system rejected by the author.

36. **(D)**   (D) correctly identifies how women were under repressive working conditions. While some mothers may have been happy to get away from children and/or happy to agree to work long hours in unsanitary and unsafe conditions, most women were most likely miserable under the early policies of the private sector. (A) and (B), therefore, are incorrect. With women caught in the lowest positions without power under court decisions and laws to change the poor conditions, it is reasonable to conclude that they offered no competition to male bosses.

37. **(D)**   (D) discusses the 1923 case described in the passages. It should be recalled that the court justified its decision to strike the minimum wage

law by stating: "adult women...are legally as capable of contracting for themselves as men." (A) incorrectly reports early court decisions that struck laws governing wages of workers. (B) is only partially true. However, enough male legislators voted approval of laws protecting female workers to discount the conclusion that all males were insensitive to needs of female employees. (C) is wrong. The author offered no evidence that presidents played an active role in influencing private sector owners to increase wages through such agencies as an industrial board. (E) contradicts the facts about the judicial role compared to the legislative role in protecting workers.

38. **(B)** (B) is correct. After the young man married, Dagenhart expressed regret about the Supreme Court decision that "protected" him as a child laborer from governmental regulations. (A), as the author shows, is incorrect in that Supreme Court decisions on laws governing working conditions were not unanimous opinions. (C) may have correctly described the Supreme Court judges as being conscientious men, but most of the judges' dedication was aimed at protecting free enterprise, not the workers. (D) expresses a wrong opinion. Press exposure of Dagenhart's negative remarks about how his health made both industry and the court appear callous. (E) has ignored the fact that dissenters voted to uphold laws that protected social welfare.

39. **(A)** (A) reaches the correct conclusion about how disagreement among judges on the high bench indicated that the persuasive abilities of the minority judges were ineffective during those years. (B) has incorrectly assessed the role of legislative leaders required to secure passage of controversial laws in years when industrial and business elite were economically and politically powerful. (C) has erroneously concluded without evidence in the paragraphs above that blue collar workers exercised political power at the polls. In (D), the dates are incorrect. (E) misinterprets the decision of the Supreme Court which staunchly opposed standardization of ages.

40. **(B)** Although President Roosevelt was powerless when the Supreme Court made void several new laws, he persisted. Under other presidents Congress had earlier passed laws to protect the safety and health of children. It is the proper conclusion that Roosevelt's record showed that he was indeed more social welfare oriented while in the Oval Office than earlier presidents. (A) tries to figure out the author's preferences. His analysis of the judicial process does not indicate that he favored the judicial over the executive. (C) is wrong. The pre-1950 laws initiated tremen-

dous change in governmental regulation of management practices previously left to the private sector. (D) deals with chronology. Reviewing the text above, the reader will find that the judicial branch resisted change wanted by both Congress and the President. (E) deals with sociological inferences. Consider the fate of young Dagenhart who as a young uneducated man was penalized by personnel practices of his boss when he was a child laborer.

41. **(B)** (B) correctly assumes that such benefits as higher wages and fewer working hours would increase expenditures of manufacturing and business. (A) requires review of how federal legislation attempted to change management/labor relations and improve the lot of the workers. Executive-sponsored bills described by the author were challenged in courts of law by business and industry. (C) does not consider new justices whose legal philosophy would radically increase the amount of government regulation, much to the detriment of freedom to make decisions in the private sector. (D) is wrong. Check the paragraphs again, and note that the author correctly gave no credit to Roosevelt for aggressive leadership in civil rights. There is no such act. (E) is chronologically and factually incorrect. Note that the author discusses how the Supreme Court voided social legislation supported by Roosevelt. Later, he nominated justices to the Supreme Court. Nowhere does the author suggest that the Supreme Court acted in an advisory capacity before Congress passed social legislation.

42. **(B)** (B) correctly concludes that although Congress had tried in earlier years to make great differences in labor policies, it was not until the Supreme Court interpretation changed during Roosevelt's term of office that new labor laws were rapidly passed and enforced. (A) is wrong. The author does not imply that the term New Deal originated from such bizarre circumstances. (C) is wrong. The Great Depression dealt with the economic situation, the author did not suggest any other definition. Rather he writes of economic problems. (D) has misinterpreted the author's analysis. Since the welfare state seeks to assure minimum standards of all people, both workers and their representatives agreed that labor conditions and wages should be improved. (E) is incorrect. Note the dates cited by the author. Roosevelt was President during the 1930s and early 1940s. The Civil Rights Act was passed in 1964.

43. **(C)** (C) correctly illustrates how governmental intrusion expands when leaders in the private sector fail to make fair policies. (A) does not consider how the act works to the detriment of illegal aliens trying to find jobs rather than protecting them against discrimination. (B) improperly

assessed the status of illegal aliens. Their political weakness lies in the fact that they have very few links with those who are in power. (D) is erroneous, as proved by the author as he traces tensions between the two sectors. (E) misconstrues the statement, for he affirms that laws have provided ways to grieve unfair policies and behavior.

44. **(A)**   (A) is certainly well illustrated in the author's passage. As nine million people of foreign birth enter the United States when jobs are at a premium, friction will most likely develop. (B) is incorrect in defining "melting pot" and introducing the term "direct representation" which was not suggested by the author. (C) is wrong. In fact the author carefully outlines how government has addressed several issues that affect political socialization of immigrants. (D) is in error. The author examined the problem of inequities that blacks experienced and how laws should help overcome inequality in the workplace—an important factor in income distribution. (E) has misread the description of Johnson's role in fostering civil rights.

45. **(B)**   (B) is the correct answer. Note how the NAACP successfully filed action in the federal court. Finally, President Johnson worked with Congress in fashioning civil rights laws. (A) is incorrect. The record shows, as the author relates, that Congress was insensitive to the needs of black citizens during the years immediately following Roosevelt's administration. (C) is wrong. Both the legislative and executive branches took little action in erasing inequality. (D) wrongly assigns aggressive executive leadership in the civil rights movement to President Roosevelt. President Johnson's civil rights activities far exceeded Roosevelt's influence in passing laws, such as Title VII. (E) is only partially correct. President Johnson was a Texan. Although Title VII was a giant step in enforcing equality, the author pointed out that pockets of prejudice remain.

46. **(B)**   Many Americans are oriented toward a capitalistic system that promotes free enterprise, as opposed to health coverage for all people. (A) is incorrect. Voters who leave choices in the hands of a few legislators do not reflect the meaning of representation of citizens in a democracy. (C) is wrong. As government assumes more and more authority in areas where enterprise provides service to individuals, some observers feel that their country moves toward socialism. (D) does not take into consideration the meaning of the term "universal" which would cover all medical expenses. (E) cannot be justified according to the text above. Certainly, Congress has not degenerated to inert uniformity as the debate continues to polarize the legislators and their constituents.

47. **(A)**   (A) is correct. Congress has not mustered enough votes to pass a universal health care plan which, if it did, would alienate business. Yet Congress has on a piecemeal fashion passed such laws as the Health Maintenance Organization Act to satisfy supporters of increased government action. (B) is wrong. Unfortunately, many employees in the private sector lack any kind of health coverage. (C) overstates the situation. As the author portrays, rarely do workers, especially in non-union factories, have any bargaining power with regard to the kind of insurance coverage. (D) is not correct. As the author shows, pro-health care people certainly are not mumbling about what they want. (E) is unfair for many industries. The author points out that employees in the private sector very well may be covered by virtue of business policies.

48. **(C)**   Business's stance is to reject the leave of absence law because from where they sit, such leaves will have costs of hiring and training temporaries who as beginners will be less productive. (A) is wrong. Job protection during times of stress or emergencies when employees must be away from work would be supported by most workers. (E) is incorrect. Actually the policy on leaves would add to labor costs when production slows down due to absent employees or temporary employees. Training expenditures and expensive mistakes on the part of temporaries are examples of other costs. (D) misunderstands the policy. The leaves are optional on the part of the employees. (E) is wrong. The author would agree that people who support the leave policy would not use a slogan that raises suspicion.

49. **(A)**   (A) has made an assumption that is correct, based on the author's description of the policy. Under present circumstances, many mothers may not have an opportunity to stay home with the new baby or the sick child. Under the leaves policy, the family becomes a more cohesive unit. (B) misquotes Senator Dodd's statistics. (C) is a unfavorable judgment that is not based on the facts presented by the author. Women who must earn income will not become drop-in employees. (D) has erroneously included Senator Dodd as politically allied with business. (E) is wrong. The Chamber's compassion does not go so far as to work against the economic interests of business.

50. **(D)**   (D) is a correct assumption. Employees are under no obligation to undergo required drug tests when applying for a job, but employers, according to the author, may make the test one of the conditions during the hiring stage. (A) is wrong. Unfortunately, no constitutional

protection gives absolute protection against all misfortunes. (B) has incorrectly interpreted the passage where the author warns public administrators to be very cautious in justifying why the tests are administered. (C) may be incorrect at times. Personnel managers must know under what legal terms tests may be administered or a union employee may waste time and money grieving the tests. While prejudice may play a role, employers must think in terms of what a drug user will cost the company when he misses work, has accidents, etc. (E) is not correct.

51. **(C)** The author compares the problems of earlier years with problems today and finds that emotional, physical, and economic needs have similar impact on employees, their families, and their employers for whom they work. (A) is not correct. The author, especially in the last paragraph, implies that values should play a strong role making policies. (B) is humorous but wrong. When employees are absent, the amount of work exceeds the usual amount of time required to perform the tasks, and therein lies the problem. (D) is most likely the wrong conclusion. Reuben was denied a normal family relationship due to economic interests of the mill. He would probably welcome the advantage that leaves would offer his children. (E) is wrong. The author recognizes that legal, social, and economic philosophies play an important role in determining policy that protect public and private interests.

52. **(A)** The author notes a few of the problems associated with unpaid leaves of absence. His question implies that management must find someone who is trained to perform the task and who is willing to work on a temporary, short-term basis. He also notes that implementing the policy will be expensive. (B) is wrong. The author does not make a value judgment, but rather reports the large influx of female employees and the special needs that they have identified. (C) is incorrect. The author notes several political activities that range from the role of lobbyists to the reaction of members of Congress. (D) does not reflect the fact that the author is an analyst and as such how he must consider personnel problems from labor's vantage point and then how he must consider the responses of managers from their own point of view. (E) is incorrect. Although many people may share this opinion, the author does not imply that governmental regulation is inappropriate or unwarranted.

READING MEDIUM PASSAGES REVIEW

Reading comprehension questions with medium-length passages (between 200 and 700 words) are designed to test your ability to read complex passages similar to high school or college assignments. The questions that follow each passage indicate to some degree your ability to understand and comprehend the passage, and to reason. These type of passages are to the point, usually do not have titles to guide you, and are based on a variety of topics.

THE DIRECTIONS

You should study the directions now, as this will prevent your having to take precious seconds to study them on the day of the test. Instead, you should quickly skim the directions during the exam to refresh your memory.

Take a few minutes NOW to study the directions below:

DIRECTIONS: Each passage in this section is followed by a group of questions to be answered on the basis of what is stated or implied in the passage. For some questions, more than one of the choices could conceivably answer the question. However, you are to choose the best answer; that is, the response that most accurately and completely answers the question, and blacken the corresponding space on your answer sheet.

Below are tips on following directions:

1. **Notice that you are instructed to choose the *best* answer, based only on what is *stated* or *implied* in the passage.** This means that all test takers will start out on equal footing in regard to knowledge of the topics since no one will have previously read the passages. Knowing this should increase your confidence. You are not to base your answer choice on information you already know *if it is not in the passage!*

2. **Be sure that the answer you choose answers the question.** For instance, you should not select an answer simply because it is a true statement; the answer must be the one which best answers the question.

READING PRACTICE

Reading many types of materials in the weeks before you take the test can help you "shape up" for this important test. As you read a newspaper, magazine, or book, you can also prepare. After you read a passage, practice answering these questions:

> What was the main idea of the article?

> Why did the author write the article? What was the purpose?

> What was the structure of the passage?

> How did the author make the main points?

> Were there specific details? If so, what were they?

> Were there implied ideas? If so, what were they?

> Can the information be applied?

> What was the tone of the passage or the attitude of the author?

The reading comprehension questions on the test will require you to find these items.

CONTENT OF THE PASSAGES

Questions on a test with medium-length passages usually contain one, but can contain more than one, passage for a series of questions. Each passage can include subjects from virtually anywhere; law, humanities, natural sciences, social sciences, even ethics.

The category of humanities can include theater, literature, architecture, art, music, and philosophy. Passages may cover topics like the film making of Alfred Hitchcock, the writing of Sherwood Anderson, the design of Gothic architecture, the use of collage as an art medium, jazz as a means of musical expression, and the comparisons and contrasts of deductive and inductive thinking.

The category of natural sciences can include chemistry, geology, physics, and astronomy. A natural science reading passage might include information on consumer chemistry, photosynthesis, sedimentary rocks, friction, and galaxies.

The social sciences typically include anthropology, psychology, history, sociology, and archaeology. Reading passages may cover such topics as CroMagnon man, behaviorism, the causes of the American Revolutionary War, the caste system, and Pompeii.

Since so many disciplines may be represented on the test, it is likely that at least some of the material will be unfamiliar to you. Remind yourself again that the questions which follow the passage will not require prior or additional knowledge of the material; the passages alone will be adequate for answering the comprehension questions. No one will have an advantage because of prior knowledge or experience with all the material, but you will have an advantage because of your preparation with this book.

ORDER OF READING THE PASSAGES

Many students find it helpful to read first the passages which appear easier, more familiar, and more interesting to them; these students save the longer, more difficult passages for last. Other students consider the searching for the easier passages to be a waste of valuable time and they simply plow ahead. When you begin to work through the sample tests, you might wish to try both methods to see which works better for you.

READING SPEED

There is no *best* rate of reading. "Good" readers adjust their rate to the purpose for which they are reading. Successful readers, however, are aware of the strategies they use in reading. You can improve your reading skills and your performance on the reading comprehension sections of tests by becoming aware of these successful strategies and practicing them.

The average person reads at the rate of about 250 words per minute. Since the average medium-length reading passage is about 400 words, this means that it takes less than two minutes to read one of the passages.

What speed should you use? Reading very slowly is not the best approach to use. Reading too slowly may give your mind time to wander and reduce your comprehension. Reading as fast as you can comfortably read will help you to comprehend better. YOU DO NOT HAVE TO BE A SPEED READER TO DO WELL. In fact, reading too fast may cause reduced comprehension.

As you prepare for a test, however, you should determine your reading speed. To do this, use the following passage. Get out your watch and prepare to time yourself! Read this passage now.

Passage

"From *Fort Apache* on," writes Andrew Sarris, "Ford's films seemed to have abandoned the Tradition of Quality for a Cult of Personality." As the critical mainstream veered increasingly toward astringent social relevance, the ex-poet laureate looked increasingly irrelevant, as he holed up in Monument Valley churning out matinee Westerns. In fact, the bitterness of social comment in Ford's movies was more acerbic than before. The '30s revolutionary had not embraced the establishment. But what Ford had to say, Americans did not wish to hear. To his credit, he no longer sought prestige by couching his thought within trendy styles. Instead his pictures became intensely private, formulated within well-worn commercial genres, fraught with myth, irony, and double-leveled narratives. Still today, many a casual critic, underestimating Ford, not only misses the subtlety, but also misconstrues denunciations as celebrations.

This period is distinguished by the vitality of its invention, at every level of cinema, but with particular intensity in montage, motion, and music. Ford at his most energetic intellectually is also Ford at his most optimistic. The defeatism of the preceding period has been largely rejected—or at least recontextualized. Although virtually all the pictures take place in the past (or in Africa or Korea), it is evident that Ford felt some hope in America.

In this period the community theme in Ford is in ascendance, a period of social analysis, akin to the early '30s pictures. Military or military-like societies are chosen because they provide clear sets of the customs, ideologies, and structures relevant to America. Although 10 prior pictures dealt with such groups, only two had attempted quasi-documentary approaches to such communities. But of the 33 films made after 1948, 18 are directly concerned with studying the problems of military communities, while nine others treat, in much the same terms, quasi-military communities (wagon trains, missionaries, political parties, police), while two others have military life as a background. In all 33 films the specific question is, "What makes people tick? Why do they do what they do?" or, 29 times, "What makes people fight?"

There is less determinism and more free will than elsewhere in Ford in this period. Duty, previously regarded by the hero as divinely appointed, henceforth resides in the group and is socially assigned.

But the films grow progressively darker. A few old men sustain the viability of society, only faith can find an ontological distinction between man and ape, the parade is a substitute for the insufficiency of reason. The films dwell on the coercive tendencies of society, of instruments becoming malevolent institutions. The period concludes with *The Searchers,* a farewell to youth and the entry of Ford's work of acute ambivalence, of a dialectic equivalent to pessimism and uncertainty about Good and Evil. Yet even so, these eight years constitute a period of glory, of stability and sureness, more blessed with masterpieces than any other period.

The number of words in the passage above is 480; divide this number by the number of minutes it took you to read the passage. Compare your reading rate with the average of 250 words per minute.

If you need to improve your reading speed, you can do this easily. For practice purposes choose an article from a magazine or newspaper; you may even use one of the many passages from the tests. (Remember, however, that reading a passage ahead of time may make your using it later in a timed test less valid.) Time yourself as you read and try to read faster on each paragraph until you read about 250 words per minute.

Some people read slowly because of a habit called regression, or reading the same section more than once. If you have this habit of regression, you can break yourself from rereading by a simple device. Simply take a piece of paper and place it above the line you are reading. Move the paper down the page line by line as you read. If you try to reread above the line you are now reading, the piece of paper will prevent you from doing so. You will be encouraged to read carefully since regressing will be difficult for you; your comprehension should be improved.

To practice improving your reading speed, you might find it helpful to move your finger or the tip of a pencil down the center of the page. The pencil tip should move slightly faster than your normal reading speed; move the finger or pencil down the page at a slow, steady pace. Do your best to keep up with the pencil or finger tip. The moving object will encourage you to read smoothly and help prevent you from starting or stopping frequently. This will help you to read more quickly and to make steady progress as you read. MOST IMPORTANTLY increasing your reading speed (up to a point) will increase comprehension and result in fewer regressions which harm comprehension. Improved comprehension is the reason for trying to increase reading speed. One does not have to be a speed reader to perform well on the reading comprehension section of any test.

Now test your reading speed on the passage below. Try using 1) the finger/pencil tip device to speed up your reading or 2) the piece of paper placed just above the line you are now reading.

Passage

The First Amendment to the Constitution of the United States guarantees that Congress shall not make a law prohibiting the free exercise of religion or respecting an establishment of religion. Many voices in the country offer conflicting ideas. A Chief Justice of the Supreme Court of the United States described the separation of church and state as a wall based on bad history, a guide which is useless to judging, and a metaphor which should be discarded. A contemporary, prominent church pastor viewed this enforced separation of civil and religious authority as the result of the work of an infidel. A religious leader of the colonial period reaffirmed this amendment by asking that government continue to let people speak as they please and worship freely whether it be none, one, or 20 gods. In the modern context, then, it seems that threats to religious freedom still exist. Separation of church and state is not universally accepted.

The number of words in the passage above is 157; divide this number by the number of minutes it took you to read the passage. Compare your rate with your reading rate on the longer passage. Did you improve? Now compare your reading rate with the average of 250 words per minute. Do you need to practice even more?

Tips on Reading Speed

1. Try to compete with **yourself** as you prepare for a test. For example, if the national average reading speed is 250 words per minute but you are only reading at 120 words per minute, try to improve on the 120 words per minute (**without** decreasing your understanding).

2. Set possible goals for yourself. The earlier you begin to study, the more time you will have to sharpen your skills. By allowing ample time to prepare, you will be able to answer more questions than the person who began studying only the week before the test.

3. Remember that improving reading speed is not a means in itself. Improved comprehension with fewer regressions **must** accompany this speed increase.

THE QUESTIONS

Following each passage are usually five to eight questions based on the information in the passage. These questions might be taken from several categories (or types) of comprehension, which can be identified or tested.

Most medium-length passages present three types of questions:

    1. Knowledge-based questions,

    2. Application-type questions, and

    3. Analysis questions.

Question Type 1: Knowledge-Based Questions

Knowledge-based questions are formed at the literal level and come directly from the reading material. Only a surface reading is required for knowledge-based questions. You are expected to know only what the author presents; you are to receive the literal message of the writer. You must not only look for a direct statement from the passage, but you must also make sure the statement has the specific details to answer the question.

You must **read the lines** to answer the questions. Consider the following passage:

Passage

The First Amendment to the Constitution of the United States guarantees that Congress shall not make a law prohibiting the free exercise of religion or respecting an establishment of religion. Many voices in the country offer conflicting ideas. A Chief Justice of the Supreme Court of
5 the United States described the separation of church and state as a wall based on bad history, a guide which is useless to judging, and a metaphor which should be discarded. A contemporary, prominent church pastor viewed this enforced separation of civil and religious authority as the result of the work of an infidel. A religious leader of the colonial period
10 reaffirmed this amendment by asking that government continue to let people speak as they please and worship freely whether it be none, one, or 20 gods. In the modern context, then, it seems that threats to religious freedom still exist. Separation of church and state is not universally accepted.

Drill 1: Knowledge-Based Questions

The following question is based on the passage from the previous page.

1. Colonial religious leaders

   (A) were unanimously opposed to the First Amendment because it was the result of the work of an infidel.

   (B) were not faced with the threat to religious freedom as their modern counterparts are.

   (C) sometimes reaffirmed this amendment and asked government to continue to allow people to speak and worship freely as they volunteered to do.

   (D) and Supreme Court Justices consistently opposed the separation of church and state.

   (E) ensured that never again would there be opposition to religious freedom in American society.

Question Type 2: Application-Type Questions

The application question requires you to use or apply the information given in the passage to a new or different situation. Be sure you can justify your reasoning! Consider the following passage and the application question which follows.

Passage

The First Amendment to the Constitution of the United States guarantees that Congress shall not make a law prohibiting the free exercise of religion or respecting an establishment of religion. Many voices in the country offer conflicting ideas. A Chief Justice of the Supreme Court of
5 the United States described the separation of church and state as a wall based on bad history, a guide which is useless to judging, and a metaphor which should be discarded. A contemporary, prominent church pastor viewed this enforced separation of civil and religious authority as the result of the work of an infidel. A religious leader of the colonial period
10 reaffirmed this amendment by asking that government continue to let people speak as they please and worship freely whether it be none, one, or 20 gods. In the modern context, then, it seems that threats to religious freedom still exist. Separation of church and state is not universally accepted.

375

Drill 2: Application-Type Questions

The following question is based on the passage given on the previous page.

1. The colonial religious leader quoted above would, if given the following choices, probably advocate

   (A) an opening prayer in the school each day.

   (B) a period of silent prayer which all the students in a school would observe.

   (C) a prayer time conducted by a different religious group during each school day.

   (D) for the schools a structured devotional period with a formal program which does not recognize any particular group yet gives attention to religion.

   (E) no structured devotional time during the school day.

Question Type 3: Analysis Questions

An analysis question may require you to break the passage into parts, to determine the main idea or the primary purpose of the passage, to describe how the author makes his or her points, to identify the tone of the passage or to describe the attitude of the author as revealed by the language of the passage. Be sure any answer you choose for the main idea question

   1. covers the main points of the article and

   2. is material that is contained only in the passage.

An example of such a question is given after the passage below.

Passage

The First Amendment to the Constitution of the United States guarantees that Congress shall not make a law prohibiting the free exercise of religion or respecting an establishment of religion. Many voices in the country offer conflicting ideas. A Chief Justice of the Supreme Court of
5 the United States described the separation of church and state as a wall based on bad history, a guide which is useless to judging, and a metaphor which should be discarded. A contemporary, prominent church pastor

viewed this enforced separation of civil and religious authority as the result of the work of an infidel. A religious leader of the colonial period
10 reaffirmed this amendment by asking that government continue to let people speak as they please and worship freely whether it be none, one, or 20 gods. In the modern context, then, it seems that threats to religious freedom still exist. Separation of church and state is not universally accepted.

Drill 3: Analysis Questions

The following question is based on the passage given above.

1. The main idea of the author is that

    (A) separation of church and state is a decision which is not likely to change.

    (B) separation of church and state is inevitable.

    (C) separation of church and state is desirable.

    (D) separation of church and state has never existed.

    (E) separation of church and state was prohibited by the First Amendment to the Constitution.

A FOUR-STEP APPROACH (SEE CHAPTER 3)

When you take the reading comprehension section you will have two tasks:

1. to read the passage and

2. to answer the questions.

Of the two, carefully reading the passage is the most important; answering the questions is based on an understanding of the passage. Here is a four-step approach to reading:

Step 1: preview,

Step 2: read actively,

Step 3: review the passage, and

Step 4: answer the questions.

Additional Tips for Answering Questions

Consider these tips:

1. You will find that some answers are predictable. The answer to "a main idea question" is usually found in the first sentence or the last sentence of the first paragraph or the last paragraph.

2. Try not to spend too much time deciphering the meaning of words and statements upon first reading the passage. It will be helpful to go back over specific parts of the passage for in-depth understanding after reading each question.

3. Watch out for questions with line numbers! The answer might not be found on the line which is indicated.

4. While reading the passages, look particularly for the tone, the main idea, the topic sentences, the theme, and the purpose—especially if the stem of the question seems to be asking for these.

5. Use caution with direct quotations from the passage.

6. Paraphrasing is more likely to be the best answer—not direct quotations. Choices which are word for word repeats of materials from a passage are usually trap answers.

7. The reading comprehension section usually contains some opinion passages. Very often the authors will distinguish their beliefs from "conventional wisdom."

8. Enter the reading comprehension section with a positive attitude. Say to yourself, "I knew how to prepare for the test. I know the types of questions I will encounter. I know what the directions will be like. There will be no surprises for me. We will all enter the reading comprehension section on equal footing since answers will be based on information in the passage and not on prior knowledge." A positive attitude will help your score since you will feel more self-confident and will not become easily rattled.

Drill 4: A Four-Step Approach

1   Dr. Robert H. Goddard, at one time a physics professor at Clark University, Worcester, Massachusetts, was largely responsible for the sudden interest in rockets back in the 1920s. When Dr. Goddard first started his experiments with rockets, no related technical information was avail-
5 able. He started a new science, industry, and field of engineering. Through his scientific experiments, he pointed the way to the development of rockets as we know them today. The Smithsonian Institute agreed to finance his experiments in 1920. From these experiments he wrote a paper titled "A Method of Reaching Extreme Altitudes," in which he outlined a space
10 rocket of the step (multistage) principle, theoretically capable of reaching the moon.

      Goddard discovered that with a properly shaped, smooth, tapered nozzle he could increase the ejection velocity eight times with the same weight of fuel. This would not only drive a rocket eight times faster, but
15 64 times farther, according to his theory. Early in his experiments he found that solid-fuel rockets would not give him the high power or the duration of power needed for a dependable supersonic motor capable of extreme altitudes. On March 16, 1926, after many trials, Dr. Goddard successfully fired, for the first time in history, a liquid-fuel rocket into the
20 air. It attained an altitude of 184 feet and a speed of 60 mph. This seems small as compared to present-day speeds and heights of missile flights, but instead of trying to achieve speed or altitude at this time, Dr. Goddard was trying to develop a dependable rocket motor.

      Dr. Goddard later was the first to fire a rocket that reached a speed
25 faster than the speed of sound. He was first to develop a gyroscopic steering apparatus for rockets. He was the first to use vanes in the jet stream for rocket stabilization during the initial phase of a rocket flight. And he was first to patent the idea of step rockets. After proving on paper and in actual tests that a rocket can travel in a vacuum, he developed the
30 mathematical theory of rocket propulsion and rocket flight, including basic designs for long-range rockets. All of this information was available to our military men before World War II, but evidently its immediate use did not seem applicable. Near the end of World War II we started intense work on rocket-powered guided missiles, using the experiments and developments
35 of Dr. Goddard and the American Rocket Society.

1. The passage implies that Dr. Goddard, a physics professor,

    (A) was the father of the science of rocketry.

    (B) started a new science, industry, and field of engineering.

    (C) pointed the way to the development of rockets.

    (D) outlined the principle of multistage space rockets.

    (E) was responsible for interest in rockets in the 1920s.

2. One can assume from the article that

    (A) , all factors being equal, a proper shape of the rocket nozzle would increase the ejection velocity and travel distance.

    (B) solid-fuel rockets would give higher power and duration.

    (C) blunt nozzle would negatively affect speed and distance.

    (D) supersonic motors are needed for extreme altitudes.

    (E) the first successfully fired liquid fueled rocket was for developing a dependable rocket motor.

3. Among Dr. Goddard's many achievements, the most far-reaching was

    (A) the development of a rocket stabilizing steering mechanism.

    (B) the development of liquid rocket fuel.

    (C) the development of use of vanes for rocket stabilizing.

    (D) the development of the gyroscope.

    (E) his thesis for multistage rocket design.

4. It can be inferred from the selection that Goddard's mathematical theory and design

    (A) are applicable to other types of rocket-powered vehicles.

    (B) included basic designs for long-range rockets.

    (C) utilized vanes in jet streams for rocket stabilization.

    (D) tested rocket travel in a vacuum.

    (E) produced gyroscopic steering apparatus.

5. Dr. Goddard made which of the following assumptions about rockets?

   (A) The amount of fuel had to be in direct proportion to the ejection
   velocity desired.

   (B) All other factors being equal, the shape of the rocket nozzle
   increases the ejection velocity and distance to the desired effect.

   (C) A medium of air was not a required component for rocket flight.

   (D) Dependability was more important than speed and distance.

   (E) Solid rocket fuel failed to deliver high power for an extended
   duration.

READING MEDIUM PASSAGES DRILLS

ANSWER KEY

Drill 1 — Knowledge-Based Questions

1. (C)

Drill 2 — Application-Type Questions

1. (E)

Drill 3 — Analysis Questions

1. (C)

Drill 4 — A Four-Step Approach

1. (A)
2. (C)
3. (E)
4. (A)
5. (C)

VOCABULARY LIST

amical
    adj.- harmonious

anathema
    n.- a person or thing accursed; anything greatly detested

beguile
    v.- to deceive or mislead

braggadocian
    adj.- boastful

cacophonous
    adj.-inharmonious; harsh, jarring, discord

carom
    v.- to glance, to look

daedalian
    adj.- complex

disquietude
    n.- anxiety, restlessness

ecclesiastical
    adj.- spiritual, of the church

effrontery
    n.- impudence, presumption

facundity
    n.- eloquence

fastigium
    n.- height

gentility
    n.- the position of a person in the upper classes of society; politeness,
    refinement

glissade
  v.- to glide

hauteur
  n.- arrogance, disdainful pride

hebetude
  n.- lethargy

idiosyncratic
  adj.- eccentric or peculiar

ignoble
  adj.- lowly, sordid

incorporeal
  adj.- immaterial

indigenous
  adj.- existing, born or produced naturally in a land or region

lineal
  adj.- in the direct line of descent from an ancestor; hereditary, linear

locution
  n.- expression, a particular style of speech

lucubrate
  v.- to study or work laboriously, esp. late at night

machinate
  v.- to plot or plan artfully, esp. to do evil

medial
  adj.- central, middle, average

mendacious
  adj.- dishonest, lying

minutiae
  n.- trivia

mollify
  v.- to pacify or soothe; to appease

mordant
 adj.- biting, sarcastic

mucronate
 adj.- pointed

muliebral
 adj.- feminine

narcissistic
 adj.- egotistical, vain

nescient
 adj.- ignorant

nicitate
 v.- to blink

nonchalance
 n.- the state or quality of being casual or indifferent

noncommittal
 adj.- not committing one to a definite stand; reserved

nonfeasance
 n.- failure

nonpartisan
 adj.- fair, neutral; not connected to any political party

nostrum
 n.- a cure; a patent medicine

oblation
 n.- benevolence, offering

obsolesce
 v.- to make or become obsolete or outdated

obstinate
 adj.- tenaciously unwilling to yield

onus
 n.- blame, burden, task

opprobrium

> n.- anything bringing shame; disgrace

opus

> n.- composition, publication

oratorical

> adj.- of or relating to the art of public speaking

ostracize

> v.- to banish or blackball

parlous

> adj.- dangerous; perilous

patrimonial

> adj.- ancestral; inheritance

patronage

> n.- aid or support given by a patron: sponsorship, backing

paucity

> n.- shortage, scarcity

pensile

> adj.- hanging

perambulate

> v.- to stroll or walk

CHAPTER 8

Reading Long Passages

➤ Diagnostic Test
➤ Reading Long Passages
  Review & Drills
➤ Vocabulary List

READING LONG PASSAGES DIAGNOSTIC TEST

1. Ⓐ Ⓑ Ⓒ Ⓓ Ⓔ
2. Ⓐ Ⓑ Ⓒ Ⓓ Ⓔ
3. Ⓐ Ⓑ Ⓒ Ⓓ Ⓔ
4. Ⓐ Ⓑ Ⓒ Ⓓ Ⓔ
5. Ⓐ Ⓑ Ⓒ Ⓓ Ⓔ
6. Ⓐ Ⓑ Ⓒ Ⓓ Ⓔ
7. Ⓐ Ⓑ Ⓒ Ⓓ Ⓔ
8. Ⓐ Ⓑ Ⓒ Ⓓ Ⓔ
9. Ⓐ Ⓑ Ⓒ Ⓓ Ⓔ
10. Ⓐ Ⓑ Ⓒ Ⓓ Ⓔ
11. Ⓐ Ⓑ Ⓒ Ⓓ Ⓔ
12. Ⓐ Ⓑ Ⓒ Ⓓ Ⓔ
13. Ⓐ Ⓑ Ⓒ Ⓓ Ⓔ
14. Ⓐ Ⓑ Ⓒ Ⓓ Ⓔ
15. Ⓐ Ⓑ Ⓒ Ⓓ Ⓔ
16. Ⓐ Ⓑ Ⓒ Ⓓ Ⓔ
17. Ⓐ Ⓑ Ⓒ Ⓓ Ⓔ
18. Ⓐ Ⓑ Ⓒ Ⓓ Ⓔ
19. Ⓐ Ⓑ Ⓒ Ⓓ Ⓔ
20. Ⓐ Ⓑ Ⓒ Ⓓ Ⓔ
21. Ⓐ Ⓑ Ⓒ Ⓓ Ⓔ
22. Ⓐ Ⓑ Ⓒ Ⓓ Ⓔ
23. Ⓐ Ⓑ Ⓒ Ⓓ Ⓔ
24. Ⓐ Ⓑ Ⓒ Ⓓ Ⓔ
25. Ⓐ Ⓑ Ⓒ Ⓓ Ⓔ

26. Ⓐ Ⓑ Ⓒ Ⓓ Ⓔ
27. Ⓐ Ⓑ Ⓒ Ⓓ Ⓔ
28. Ⓐ Ⓑ Ⓒ Ⓓ Ⓔ
29. Ⓐ Ⓑ Ⓒ Ⓓ Ⓔ
30. Ⓐ Ⓑ Ⓒ Ⓓ Ⓔ
31. Ⓐ Ⓑ Ⓒ Ⓓ Ⓔ
32. Ⓐ Ⓑ Ⓒ Ⓓ Ⓔ
33. Ⓐ Ⓑ Ⓒ Ⓓ Ⓔ
34. Ⓐ Ⓑ Ⓒ Ⓓ Ⓔ
35. Ⓐ Ⓑ Ⓒ Ⓓ Ⓔ
36. Ⓐ Ⓑ Ⓒ Ⓓ Ⓔ
37. Ⓐ Ⓑ Ⓒ Ⓓ Ⓔ
38. Ⓐ Ⓑ Ⓒ Ⓓ Ⓔ
39. Ⓐ Ⓑ Ⓒ Ⓓ Ⓔ
40. Ⓐ Ⓑ Ⓒ Ⓓ Ⓔ
41. Ⓐ Ⓑ Ⓒ Ⓓ Ⓔ
42. Ⓐ Ⓑ Ⓒ Ⓓ Ⓔ
43. Ⓐ Ⓑ Ⓒ Ⓓ Ⓔ
44. Ⓐ Ⓑ Ⓒ Ⓓ Ⓔ
45. Ⓐ Ⓑ Ⓒ Ⓓ Ⓔ
46. Ⓐ Ⓑ Ⓒ Ⓓ Ⓔ
47. Ⓐ Ⓑ Ⓒ Ⓓ Ⓔ
48. Ⓐ Ⓑ Ⓒ Ⓓ Ⓔ
49. Ⓐ Ⓑ Ⓒ Ⓓ Ⓔ
50. Ⓐ Ⓑ Ⓒ Ⓓ Ⓔ

READING LONG PASSAGES DIAGNOSTIC TEST

This diagnostic test is designed to help you determine your strengths and your weaknesses in reading long passages. Follow the directions for each part and check your answers.

These types of questions are found in the following tests: SAT, ACT, and LSAT

---

50 Questions

DIRECTIONS: Each passage is followed by questions based on its content. After reading the passage, choose the best answer to each question. Answer all questions based on what is indicated or implied in that passage.

Questions 1–12 are based on the following passage.

In the following passage, Thomas Henry Huxley argues that science is an integral part of culture, and should be studied along with traditional courses, which include the classics and other liberal arts.

1   How often have we not been told that the study of physical science is incompetent to confer culture; that it touches none of the higher problems of life; and, what is worse, that the continual devotion to scientific studies tends to generate a narrow and bigoted belief in the applicability of scien-
5   tific methods to the search after truth of all kinds? How frequently one has reason to observe that no reply to a troublesome argument tells so well as calling its author a "mere scientific specialist." And, as I am afraid it is not permissible to speak of this form of opposition to scientific education in the past tense; may we not expect to be told that this, not only omission,
10   but prohibition, of "mere literary instruction and education" is a patent example of scientific narrow-mindedness?

I am not acquainted with Sir Josiah Mason's reasons for the action which he has taken; but if, as I apprehend is the case, he refers to the ordinary classical course of our schools and universities by the name of
15   "mere literary instruction and education," I venture to offer sundry reasons of my own in support of that action.

For I hold very strongly by two convictions: The first is, that neither the discipline nor the subject-matter of classical education is of such direct value to the student of physical science as to justify the expenditure of
20 valuable time upon either; and the second is, that for the purpose of attaining real culture, an exclusively scientific education is at least as effectual as an exclusively literary education.

I need hardly point out to you that these opinions, especially the latter, are diametrically opposed to those of the great majority of educated
25 Englishmen, influenced as they are by school and university traditions. In their belief, culture is obtainable only by a liberal education; and a liberal education is synonymous, not merely with education and instruction in literature, but in one particular form of literature, namely, that of Greek and Roman antiquity. They hold that the man who has learned Latin and
30 Greek, however little, is educated; while he who is versed in other branches of knowledge, however deeply, is a more or less respectable specialist, not admissible into the cultured caste. The stamp of the educated man, the University degree, is not for him.

I am too well acquainted with the generous catholicity of spirit, the
35 true sympathy with scientific thought, which pervades the writings of our chief apostle of culture to identify him with these opinions; and yet one may cull from one and another of those epistles to the Philistines, which so much delight all who do not answer to that name, sentences which lend them some support.

40 Mr. Arnold tells us that the meaning of culture is "to know the best that has been thought and said in the world." It is the criticism of life contained in literature. That criticism regards "Europe as being, for intellectual and spiritual purposes, one great confederation, bound to a joint action and working to a common result; and whose members have, for
45 their common outfit, a knowledge of Greek, Roman, and Eastern antiquity, and of one another. Special, local, and temporary advantages being put out of account, that modern nation will in the intellectual and spiritual sphere make most progress, which most thoroughly carries out this programme. And what is that but saying that we too, all of us, as individuals, the more
50 thoroughly we carry it out, shall make the more progress?"

We have here to deal with two distinct propositions. The first, that a criticism of life is the essence of culture; the second, that literature contains the materials which suffice for the construction of such criticism.

I think that we must all assent to the first proposition. For culture
55 certainly means something quite different from learning or technical skill.

It implies the possession of an ideal and the habit of critically estimating the value of things by comparison with a theoretic standard. Perfect culture should supply a complete theory of life, based upon a clear knowledge alike of its possibilities and of its limitations.

60   But we may agree to all this, and yet strongly dissent from the assumption that literature alone is competent to supply this knowledge. After having learnt all that Greek, Roman, and Eastern antiquity have thought and said, and all that modern literatures have to tell us, it is not self-evident that we have laid a sufficiently broad and deep foundation for that
65 criticism of life, which constitutes culture.

Indeed, to any one acquainted with the scope of physical science, it is not at all evident. Considering progress only in the "intellectual and spiritual sphere," I find myself wholly unable to admit that either nations or individuals will really advance, if their common outfit draws nothing from
70 the stores of physical science. I should say that an army, without weapons of precision and with no particular base of operations, might more hopefully enter upon a campaign on the Rhine, than a man, devoid of a knowledge of what physical science has done in the last century, upon a criticism of life.

1. Which best describes what the author is doing in the sentence "And as I am afraid...narrow-mindedness" (lines 7–11)?

    (A) Stating the terms of his argument

    (B) Arguing for scientific training

    (C) Stating common beliefs of his opponents

    (D) Redefining the term "culture"

    (E) Establishing the central analogy of the passage

2. From the first four paragraphs, we can infer that the college has decided to

    (A) include classical studies in its curriculum.

    (B) exclude classical studies from its curriculum.

    (C) establish Latin and Greek as required subjects.

    (D) define university education as exclusively scientific.

    (E) incorporate scientific studies within the curriculum.

3.   In line 15, the term "sundry" most nearly means

    (A) significant.   (D) related.

    (B) various.   (E) dependent.

    (C) convincing.

4.   The author's use of the term "cultured caste" (line 32) suggests

    (A) distinctive merit.   (D) superiority of the wealthy.

    (B) exclusion of merit.   (E) inclusion of the poor.

    (C) social inequality.

5.   In the sentence "I am too well acquainted...some support" (lines 34–39), the author argues that "our chief apostle"

    (A) unintentionally reinforces prejudices.

    (B) has contributed valuable insights.

    (C) holds views contrary to those of the author.

    (D) does not deserve his current reputation.

    (E) is a valuable supporter of the author.

6.   The word "outfit" in line 45 most nearly means

    (A) company.   (D) tools.

    (B) uniform.   (E) beliefs.

    (C) gathering.

7.   In lines 51–60, the author agrees with Arnold that culture should

    (A) be based upon literature.

    (B) be a theory of human life.

    (C) encompass science.

    (D) provide moral codes.

    (E) be distinct from education.

8.   The tone of this passage is

    (A) sarcastic.   (B) argumentative.

(C) elation.

(D) facetious.

(E) cynical.

9. According to the author, a perfect culture should provide

    (A) critical literature.

    (B) a liberal, classical education.

    (C) a scientific education.

    (D) a complete theory of life.

    (E) an intellectual and spiritual sphere.

10. The main idea of the passage is

    (A) that a scientific education is as culturally valuable as a classical education.

    (B) to denigrate classical education.

    (C) to provide an historical outline of the educational system.

    (D) to argue that scientific education is not comparable to a liberal education and should be left out of the college curriculum.

    (E) to give a philosophical view on what should be taught by a culture.

11. According to lines 34–39, the "Philistines" are people who

    (A) have true sympathy with scientific thought.

    (B) spend much time in the pursuit of art and knowledge.

    (C) have a cultural bias against Greek and Latin literature.

    (D) all guided by material rather than intellectual values, such as the study of science.

    (E) have dedicated themselves exclusively to the liberal and classical educational movements.

12. According to the passage, the majority of Englishmen believe a knowledgeable person is

    (A) one who is schooled in the sciences.

    (B) one who contributes to a perfect culture.

(C)   one who has a classical education.

(D)   one who is aware of the limitations of education.

(E)   someone with an education in science and the liberal arts.

Questions 13–25 are based on the following passages.

In the following passages, the two authors discuss the changes in man and animals throughout their evolution. Both specifically focus on the loss of hair and the reasons why this came about.

Passage 1

1   Why have most of our domestic animals lost their original colouring? Clearly because colour became of little or no importance to them as soon as they were sheltered under the protection of man, while in a wild state it was a great safeguard against detection by their enemies.

5   Similarly the hairy covering has ceased to be of importance to certain of the Mammalia—and has disappeared. Thus whales and dolphins have a naked skin for the most part entirely devoid of hair, although they are unquestionably descended from hairy ancestors, and even now rudimentary hairs may be detected in certain parts of the body by the aid of the 10 microscope. Obviously, the disappearance of the hairy covering cannot be a direct consequence of disuse, for hair will grow as well, whether its protective warmth be useful or of no importance to the animal. But its disappearance as an indirect consequence of disuse is plain; for as soon as an immense thickness of blubber was developed beneath the skin of the 15 whale, the warmth of an additional covering was unnecessary: the hair becoming superfluous, natural selection ceased to affect it, and degeneration at once set in. If anyone is inclined to doubt whether the direct action of seawater may not have caused the disappearance of the hair, it is only necessary to point to the group of seals, in which all the smaller species 20 possess a thick coat of fur, while, among the larger kinds, the walrus has but a scanty covering of bristles, because, like the whale, it has developed a layer of blubber, which is amply sufficient to protect its huge body from cold.

Examples of an entirely different kind are afforded by those animals 25 which hide themselves in cases or houses. The hermit-crab partly conceals itself in empty shells, the aquatic larvae of caddis-flies build cases within which their cylindrical bodies are enclosed, and the larvae of certain small moths do the same. Whenever the body of any such animal is thus partially enclosed in a case, the protected parts are soft and whitish, i.e., more

30 or less colourless, while the exposed parts retain the ordinary hard integument of the Arthropoda and are variously and strongly coloured. Now we
may maintain that, in a certain sense, the hard integument of crabs and
insects fulfils the "function" of protecting the soft parts of the animal from
injury, but, correctly speaking, this defence is not a real function at all,
35 because the exercise of function implies activity, while the use of the hard
integument can only be of a passive kind.

Passage 2

In man the hairy covering of the body has almost totally disappeared,
and, what is very remarkable, it has disappeared more completely from the
back than from any other part of the body. Bearded and beardless races
40 alike have the back smooth, and even when a considerable quantity of hair
appears on the limbs and breast, the back, and especially the spinal region,
is absolutely free, thus completely reversing the characteristics of all other
mammalia.

We find, then, that so far from there being any reason to believe that
45 a hairy covering to the back could have been hurtful or even useless to
prehistoric man, the habits of modern savages indicate exactly the opposite view, as they evidently feel the want of it and are obliged to provide
substitutes of various kinds. The perfectly erect posture of man may be
supposed to have something to do with the disappearance of the hair from
50 his body while it remains on his head; but when walking, exposed to rain
and wind, a man naturally stoops forwards and thus exposes his back; and
the undoubted fact that most savages feel the effects of cold and wet most
severely in that part of the body, sufficiently demonstrates that the hair
could not have ceased to grow there merely because it was useless, even if
55 it were likely that a character so long persistent in the entire order of
mammalia could have so completely disappeared under the influence of so
weak a selective power as a diminished usefulness.

It seems to me, then, to be absolutely certain that natural selection
could not have produced man's hairless body by the accumulation of
60 variations from a hairy ancestor. The evidence all goes to show that such
variations could not have been useful, but must, on the contrary, have been
to some extent hurtful. If even, owing to an unknown correlation with
other hurtful qualities, it had been abolished in the ancestral tropical man,
we cannot conceive that, as man spread into colder climates, it should not
65 have returned under the powerful influence of reversion to such long persistent ancestral type. But the very foundation of such a supposition as this
is untenable, for we cannot suppose that a character which, like hairiness,
exists throughout the whole of the mammalia, can have become, in one

form only, so constantly correlated with an injurious character as to lead to
70 its permanent suppression—a suppression so complete and effectual that it
never, or scarcely ever, reappears in mongrels of the most widely different
races of man.

Two characters could hardly be wider apart than the size and development of man's brain and the distribution of hair upon the surface of his
75 body, yet they both lead us to the same conclusion—that some other
power than natural selection has been engaged in his production.

13. According to the author of Passage 1, why do animals at times lose
certain characteristics or features?

(A) It becomes necessary for survival.

(B) They lose the part so animals of a different class may survive.

(C) Because they mate with other animals of a different class.

(D) The part becomes unimportant to them.

(E) Such losses do not occur in the wild.

14. The writer of Passage 2 seems to believe that hair on the back of
people disappeared

(A) when it became unimportant to them.

(B) for people in warm climates but not for people in cold climates.

(C) when it became injurious to them.

(D) when people began to walk upright and it was no longer of use.

(E) by some power other than natural selection.

15. The writer of Passage 1 and the writer of Passage 2

(A) both upheld natural selection as a cause.

(B) both disagree with natural selection as a cause of the disappearance of certain natural features like the hair on the back.

(C) differ in their beliefs; the writer of Passage 1 seems to uphold
natural selection as a cause of hairlessness but the writer of
Passage 2 would not uphold natural selection.

(D) differ in their beliefs; the writer of Passage 1 seems to disagree
with natural selection as a cause of hairlessness but the writer of
Passage 2 would uphold natural selection as a cause of hairlessness.

(E) are unconcerned with the subject of natural selection in these passages.

16. The writer of Passage 2 believes hair on the back of people

(A) is useful.

(B) is useless.

(C) is an unimportant topic to consider.

(D) is there because of natural selection.

(E) has always been a vital feature.

17. In Passage 1 (line 29) the writer states that soft and whitish body parts

(A) occur when the animal part is exposed to the bleaching rays of the sun.

(B) result from soaking in sea water.

(C) occur when the part is enclosed in a case.

(D) come about when blubber is eliminated.

(E) result from a scanty cover of bristles.

18. The author of Passage 1

(A) contends that domestic animals lost their protective coloration when it became of little use to them.

(B) states that protective coloration was not needed in the wild.

(C) believes the hairy covering of whales was added when the water and climate became cooler.

(D) believes the disappearance of the hairy covering was a direct consequence of disuse.

(E) refers to degeneration as an outmoded theory.

19. The author of Passage 2

(A) considers diminished usefulness to be a strong influence on animals.

(B) emphasizes that when people began to walk the hair on the back was no longer needed.

     (C) believes that natural selection produced the hairless body.

     (D) believes the hairless body is hurtful.

     (E) states that the absence of back hair in people corresponds to the characteristics in other mammals.

20. The author of Passage 1

     (A) sees the function of the integument of an arthropod as an active kind of use.

     (B) sees the function of the integument of an arthropod as a passive kind of use.

     (C) attributes the growth of body hair to degeneration.

     (D) believes the loss of hair is a direct consequence of disuse.

     (E) attributes the blubber of the whale as contributing to the loss of body hair in humans.

21. In line 16 the word "superfluous" means

     (A) more than is needed.

     (B) of a superior grade or quality.

     (C) in an insufficient quantity.

     (D) less than is needed.

     (E) strong.

22. The author of Passage 1

     (A) refers to degeneration as attributing to the loss of body hair.

     (B) believes natural selection was instrumental to the loss of body hair.

     (C) discusses the hair as constantly correlated with an injurious character.

     (D) states that hair on the back ceased to grow because it was useless.

     (E) attributes the loss to diminished usefulness.

23. The reason for hair loss on the back of people

   (A) is clear after reading Passage 2.

   (B) is an indirect consequence of disuse, according to Passage 2.

   (C) is an indirect consequence of disuse, according to Passage 1.

   (D) is an indirect consequence of disuse, according to both Passage 1 and Passage 2.

   (E) is an indirect consequence of disuse, according to neither Passage 1 nor Passage 2.

24. The meaning of "integument" in line 30 of Passage 1 is

   (A) an inner protective device.

   (B) a hard shell or case.

   (C) an inner skeletal make-up.

   (D) a function.

   (E) an activity, either active or passive.

25. The attitude of Passage 1 toward hairlessness is

   (A) disinterest.   (D) sarcasm.

   (B) interest.   (E) animosity.

   (C) repugnance.

Questions 26–38 are based on the following passages.

The following are taken from two of the most famous documents in American history—the Constitution and the Declaration of Independence.

Passage 1

1   A.   The Congress shall have power:

   1.   To lay and collect taxes, duties, imposts, and excises, to pay the debts and provide for the common defence and general welfare of the United States; but all duties, imposts, and excises shall be
5   uniform throughout the United States.

   2.   To borrow money on the credit of the United States.

   3.   To regulate commerce with foreign nations, and among the several States, and with the Indian tribes.

4. To establish a uniform rule of naturalization and uniform laws on the subject of bankruptcies throughout the United States.

5. To coin money, regulate the value thereof, and of foreign coin, and fix the standards of weights and measures.

6. To provide for the punishment of counterfeiting the securities and current coin of the United States.

7. To establish post-offices and post-roads.

8. To promote the progress of science and useful arts by securing for limited times to authors and investors the exclusive rights to their respective writings and discoveries.

9. To constitute tribunals inferior to the Supreme Court.

10. To define and punish piracies and felonies committed on the high seas, and offences against the laws of nations.

11. To declare war, grant letters of marque and reprisal, and make rules concerning captures on land and water.

12. To raise and support armies, but no appropriation of money to that use shall be for a longer term than two years.

13. To provide and maintain a navy.

14. To make rules for the government and regulation of the land and naval forces.

15. To provide for calling forth the militia to execute the laws of the Union, suppress insurrections, and repel invasions.

B. The President shall have power:

1. To make treaties, by and with the advice and consent of the Sentate provided two-thirds of the Senators present concur, and he shall nominate and by and with the advice and consent of the Senate shall appoint ambassadors, other public ministers and consuls, judges of the Supreme Court, and all other officers of the United States whose appointments are not herein otherwise provided for, and which shall be established by law; but the Congress may by law vest the appointment of such inferior officers as they think proper in the President alone, in the courts of law, or in the heads of departments.

2. To fill up all vacancies that may happen during the recess of the Senate by granting commissions, which shall expire at the end of their next session.

Passage 2

He has refused his Assent to Laws, the most wholesome and necessary for the public good.

He has forbidden his Governors to pass Laws of immediate and pressing importance, unless suspended in their operation till his Assent should be obtained; and when so suspended, he has utterly neglected to attend to them.

He has refused to pass other Laws for the accommodation of large districts of people, unless those people would relinquish the right of Representation in the Legislature, a right inestimable to them and formidable to tyrants only.

He has called together legislative bodies at places unusual, uncomfortable, and distant from the depository of their public Records, for the sole purpose of fatiguing them into compliance with his measures.

He has dissolved Representative Houses repeatedly, for opposing with manly firmness his invasions on the rights of the people.

He has refused for a long time, after such dissolutions, to cause others to be elected; whereby the Legislative powers, incapable of Annihilation, have returned to the People at large for their exercise; the State remaining in the mean time exposed to all the dangers of invasion from without, and convulsions within.

He has endeavoured to prevent the population of these States; for that purpose obstructing the Laws of Naturalization of Foreigners; refusing to pass others to encourage their migration hither, and raising the conditions of new Appropriations of Lands.

He has obstructed the Administration of Justice, by refusing his Assent to Laws for establishing Judiciary Powers.

He has made Judges dependent on his Will alone, for the tenure of their offices, and the amount and payment of their salaries.

He has erected a multitude of New Offices, and sent hither swarms of Officers to harass our People, and eat out their substance.

He has kept among us, in times of peace, Standing Armies without the Consent of our legislature.

He has affected to render the Military independent of and superior to the Civil Power.

He has abdicated Government here, by declaring us out of his Protection and waging War against us.

He has plundered our seas, ravaged our Coasts, burnt our towns, and destroyed the lives of our people.

He is at this time transporting large armies of foreign mercenaries to compleat the works of death, desolation and tyranny, already begun with circumstances of Cruelty and perfidy scarcely paralleled in the most barbarous ages, and totally unworthy the Head of a civilized nation.

26. In line 9 "a uniform rule of naturalization" most nearly means

   (A) law as nature intended.

   (B) law which is ordinary or natural.

   (C) human law according to laws of nature.

   (D) orderly laws of commerce.

   (E) law conferring the rights of a natural citizen.

27. The right "to coin money, regulate the value thereof, and of foreign coin, and fix the standards of weights and measures" gives Congress the right, according to lines 11–12

   (A) to assign a value to foreign coins and coins in countries other than the United States.

   (B) to assign a value to a foreign coin and use it as currency within the United States.

   (C) to assign an exchange value to a foreign coin brought to the United States or an exchange value to U.S. money taken abroad.

   (D) to assign an exchange value to a foreign coin brought to the United States.

   (E) to fix the standards of weights and measures for each place of business; these values may, therefore, vary from place to place as Congress so wills.

28. In line 3–4, the "excises shall be uniform throughout the United States"

   (A) refers to the number of people leaving one area of the country not being excessive over that of people leaving another area.

   (B) refers to Congress being able to control all taxes throughout the United States.

(C)   refers to the uniform excise taxes only.

(D)   refers to both uniform excise taxes and local sales taxes.

(E)   refers to local uniform property taxes, as well as excise taxes.

29.   The numbered item of Passage 1, Part A, which indicates best that economic prosperity is no guarantee for all citizens is

(A)   12, which refers to appropriation of money.

(B)   5, which deals with coining money.

(C)   1, which is concerned with paying the debts.

(D)   3, which relates to regulating commerce.

(E)   4, related to bankruptcy.

30.   How did the authors of Passage 1 prevent a future ruler from "making judges dependent on his will alone"?

(A)   They made tribunals inferior to the Supreme Court appointed by Congress.

(B)   The legislature established uniform laws on the subject of bankruptcy.

(C)   The legislature was allowed to call forth the militia to execute the laws of the land.

(D)   The legislature allowed the promotion of the progress of useful arts by securing exclusive rights to authors.

(E)   The legislature can suppress insurrections.

31.   Provisions for patents and copyrights are made in Passage 1, part

(A)   Part A9, with the reference to tribunals.

(B)   Part A11, with the reference to letters of marque and reprisal.

(C)   Part A6, with the reference to counterfeiting.

(D)   Part A8, with the reference to securing of exclusive rights.

(E)   Part A15, with the repelling of invasions.

32. The best meaning of the term "perfidy" in line 84 is

    (A) destruction.   (D) theft.

    (B) violence.   (E) violating of a promise.

    (C) murder.

33. The numbered item of Passage 1 which would allow protection from the conflict from "the foreign mercenaries" referred to in line 82 is

    (A) Part A4, which allows "a uniform rule of naturalization."

    (B) Part A10, which allows punishment of "piracies and felonies."

    (C) Part A11, which refers to "letters of marque and reprisal."

    (D) Part A15, which allows "calling forth the militia."

    (E) Part A1, which allows the laying of "imposts."

34. In Passage 2 what "fact" about the King of Great Britain had most directly affected the laws passed?

    (A) "He has obstructed the Administration of Justice...."

    (B) "He has kept...Standing Armies...."

    (C) "He has made Judges dependent on his Will alone...."

    (D) "He has called together legislative bodies at places unusual...."

    (E) "He has plundered our seas."

35. In what action in Passage 2 is the King of Great Britain presently engaging that is offensive to the colonies?

    (A) Refusing his Assent to Laws

    (B) Forbidding his Governors to pass Laws

    (C) Obstructing the Administration of Justice

    (D) Erecting a multitude of New Offices

    (E) Transporting large armies of foreign mercenaries

36. In Passage 2 the regard the King of Great Britain held for the colonists was most evident by

    (A) abdicating government here.

    (B) raising conditions of new appropriations.

(C) refusing his Assent to Laws.

(D) declaring us out of his protection and waging war against colonists.

(E) sending swarms of Officers to eat out their substance.

37. The statement that the King of Great Britain has "utterly neglected to attend to things" is an example of

(A) hesitation.

(B) procrastination.

(C) indoctrination.

(D) inclination.

(E) disorganization.

38. The only difference between the U.S. having a militia as mentioned in lines 29–30 and the King keeping a Standing Army is that

(A) the people agree to allow the presence of a U.S. militia.

(B) line 27 mentions war time and peace time.

(C) the King's men are there as law enforcement.

(D) the English soldiers have the right to bear arms.

(E) there is no difference.

Questions 39–50 are based on the following passage.

The following passages, written at the turn of the century, present two views of child labor. Passage 1 was written by Jane Addams and the second is by T.M. Young.

Passage 1

1   The first child labor laws were enacted in England through the efforts of those members of parliament whose hearts were wrung by the condition of the little parish apprentices bound out to the early textile manufacturers of the north; and through the long years required to build up the code of
5 child labor legislation which England now possesses, knowledge of the conditions has always preceded effective legislation. The efforts of that small number in every community who believe in legislative control have always been reinforced by the efforts of trades-unionists rather than by the efforts of employers. Partly because the employment of workingmen in
10 the factories brings them in contact with the children who tend to lower wages and demoralize their trades and partly because workingmen have no

money nor time to spend for alleviating philanthropy, and must perforce seize upon agitation and legal enactment as the only channel of redress which is open to them.

15   We may illustrate by imagining a row of people seated in a moving streetcar into which darts a boy of eight, calling out the details of the last murder, in the hope of selling an evening newspaper. A comfortable look-ing man buys a paper from him with no sense of moral shock; he may even be a trifle complacent that he has helped along the little fellow, who
20   is making his way in the world. The philanthropic lady sitting next to him may perhaps reflect that it is a pity that such a bright boy is not in school. She may make up her mind in a moment of compunction to redouble her efforts for various newsboys' schools and homes, that this poor child may have better teaching…Next to her sits a workingman trained in trades-
25   union methods. He knows that the boy's natural development is arrested, and that the abnormal activity of his body and mind uses up the force which should go into growth; moreover, that this premature use of his powers has but a momentary and specious value. He is forced to those conclusions because he has seen many a man, entering the factory at
30   eighteen and twenty, so worn out by premature work that he was "laid on the shelf" within ten or fifteen years. He knows very well that he can do nothing in the way of ameliorating the lot of this particular boy; that his only possible chance is to agitate for proper child-labor laws; to regulate, and if possible prohibit, street-vending by children, in order that the child
35   of the poorest may have his school time secured to him, and may have at least his short chance for growth.

Passage 2

The wages paid to the boys who clean, sweep, and carry weft to the looms are $15 a week. These boys, from twelve to fourteen years of age, are "half-timers," but in the State of Rhode Island a half-timer does not
40   work half the day in school and the other half in the mill; he works full time in the mill for four months and full time at school for the next four months, and so on. In order to convey an absolutely faithful impression of what I saw of the Northrop loom in this mill, I ought to say that a number—perhaps a dozen—of young children were going about amongst
45   the looms helping to keep the magazines full. When I questioned the overseer about this, he told me that these children were not employed by the mill, but came in to help their parents….

The floors of this mill were kept beautifully clean by an army of small boys, who are continually sweeping and scrubbing. These young-
50   sters are paid $2 a day, and as far as I could judge, most of them were

from twelve to fourteen years of age. Upon this point, however, it was rather difficult to get exact information. One boy whom I questioned told me that he was thirteen.

"How long have you been in the mill?" I asked.

55 "Don't know."

"Have you been here a year?" said I.

"Yep," was the prompt response, and I felt that it was hopeless to pursue the investigation further....

Between this magnificent mill and much of the work that was being
60 done in it there was, however, a remarkable contrast. I was told, quite candidly, that the management had found great difficulty in obtaining good "help," and from what I saw, in the spinning room especially, I should say that the difficulty had so far proved insuperable. Some of the machinery was standing idle for want of efficient labour, and some of the
65 machinery that was running was only spoiling cotton. Children seemed to be doing three-fourths of the work, and very young children many of them were. I spoke to one boy who said that he was just ten, to another who gave his age as nine, and to a third little chap who said that he was eight, and that there were plenty of boys in the mill younger than himself—
70 "some only five." I was glad to find no evidence in support of this startling assertion, and I hope that it was not true. Here again the mill superintendent assured me that he would rather not employ young children, but that he was forced to take them in order to get the older and more useful members of the family.

39. Child labor laws, according to Passage 1,

   (A) were enacted to protect management in case of injury to children.

   (B) were first enacted in England by members of parliament at the request of the manufacturers of the North.

   (C) became necessary and were sought by the children themselves.

   (D) were sought by the workers themselves because cheap child labor resulted in lower wages for adults and because the working class had to rely on legislation.

   (E) came about because U.S. lawmakers' hearts were wrung by the condition of the children.

40. According to Passage 1,

    (A) legislation results in knowledge of conditions.

    (B) a knowledge of conditions precedes legislation.

    (C) workers oppose legislation because it demoralizes their values.

    (D) the author seems to advocate less legislative control.

    (E) legislation is not the answer to child labor problems.

41. The word "alleviating" in line 12 of Passage 1

    (A) means eliminating the philanthropy.

    (B) is an adjective describing the philanthropy; it means the philanthropy makes things easier.

    (C) means removing the philanthropy.

    (D) is a term [rare] meaning to lessen the magnitude of the philanthropy.

    (E) is a term [rare] meaning to lessen the criminality of the philanthropy.

42. In line 32 of Passage 1, the word "ameliorating" means

    (A) deteriorating.   (D) improving.

    (B) overseeing.   (E) canceling.

    (C) managing.

43. The illustration in Passage 1 is primarily used to show

    (A) the importance of the workers in improving the plight of children.

    (B) the sadness of the upper class at this situation.

    (C) the upper class does much to agitate for child labor laws.

    (D) that sympathy alone can achieve much to help conditions of the children.

    (E) that no one is complacent with child labor.

44. The attitude of the author of Passage 1 toward child labor is

    (A) supportive.   (B) enthusiastic.

(C) accepting.   (D) violently opposed.

(E) uninterested.

45. Management, in Passage 2, stated it was

    (A) obliged to hire children to keep the schools open for four months.

    (B) hiring children because the children wanted to work.

    (C) not employing children as was evidenced by the non-operating equipment.

    (D) disappointed in the performance of the children.

    (E) obliged to hire children to secure the help of the rest of the family.

46. To give credence to his writings, the author of Passage 2

    (A) calls on history and the laws of the past.

    (B) reports on the results of questionnaires administered.

    (C) gives the results of interviews and on-site visits conducted.

    (D) reports on the three riders in the street-car.

    (E) discusses the laws passed by parliament in the past.

47. The author of Passage 2

    (A) seems to recognize the necessity of employing children and, given the clean working conditions and the schooling provided, seems content with the situation now.

    (B) is adamant about the removal of children from the work environment.

    (C) does not believe children under the age of 16 are actually employed.

    (D) found substantial evidence to support the statement that children under the age of five were employed.

    (E) was dissatisfied with the cleaning the child laborers were doing.

48. The author of Passage 2 assumes

    (A) that the children cleaning the floors were not being paid.

    (B) that the children were not attending school.

(C) that the children filling the magazines were being paid.

(D) that the children filling the magazines were not being paid and that they were attending school four months a year.

(E) that the difficulties in the spinning room would soon be solved.

49. In line 63 of Passage 2 the word "insuperable" means

(A) insufferable, or not able to be endured.

(B) not sufficient.

(C) not able to be overcome.

(D) improbable.

(E) incomplete.

50. The writer of Passage 2 seems to show that the work environment of child laborers

(A) is clean and healthy.

(B) is filthy and unhealthful.

(C) does not provide for education.

(D) is not necessary but is used to keep children off the street.

(E) neglects mind and body.

READING LONG PASSAGES DIAGNOSTIC TEST

ANSWER KEY

1.	(C)	14.	(E)	27.	(D)	40.	(B)
2.	(E)	15.	(B)	28.	(C)	41.	(B)
3.	(B)	16.	(A)	29.	(E)	42.	(D)
4.	(B)	17.	(C)	30.	(A)	43.	(A)
5.	(A)	18.	(A)	31.	(D)	44.	(D)
6.	(B)	19.	(D)	32.	(E)	45.	(E)
7.	(B)	20.	(B)	33.	(D)	46.	(C)
8.	(B)	21.	(A)	34.	(D)	47.	(A)
9.	(D)	22.	(A)	35.	(E)	48.	(D)
10.	(A)	23.	(C)	36.	(D)	49.	(C)
11.	(E)	24.	(B)	37.	(B)	50.	(A)
12.	(C)	25.	(B)	38.	(A)		
13.	(D)	26.	(E)	39.	(D)		

DETAILED EXPLANATIONS OF ANSWERS

1.   **(C)**   He is actually exaggerating his opponents' views through conventional irony. The argument *per se* (A) is not developed here. The section occurs within (B) the broader plea for scientific training. Culture is taken up much later in the passage (D). There is no *central* analogy in this passage (E).

2.   **(E)**   From the displeasure of Huxley's opponents, we can infer that scientific studies have gained some ground. Classical studies have long been within the curriculum (A). There is no suggestion of their abolition (B). Classical studies continue to be (C) required subjects, though Huxley questions their utility in scientific education. Despite his opponents' fears, exclusively scientific education (D) hardly appears possible.

3.   **(B)**   The term has the neutral meaning of number, with a slight connotation of offhandedness. It is devoid of significance (A). Nor are his views *necessarily* sound arguments (C). There is no necessary relationship among them (D). Further, the specific relation of dependence here is irrelevant (E).

4.   **(B)**   Understanding of this term depends upon appreciation of Huxley's subtle irony. Many with distinctive merit but little Greek are excluded (A). The question of social as opposed to educational inequality does not arise here (C). The "caste" includes only those with classical educations, which may include the wealthy to some extent (D). Huxley does not address class considerations in this passage (E).

5.   **(A)**   Arnold, the "chief apostle," cited out of context lends support to those with biases against science. He may well have contributed insights; (B) Huxley makes no explicit comment. Arnold probably holds some views contrary to those of the author; this point is not made explicitly in the paragraph (C). Huxley implies that Arnold certainly deserves his current reputation (D), even if he is not a valuable ally of the author (E).

6.   **(B)**   Here the word means regalia or costuming. Huxley later (line 70) modifies it to suggest weaponry. The company (A) of educated Europeans is itself outfitted. The company again forms a uniformed gathering (C). The idea of "tools" might be conceivable in the later usage (line 70) (D). Beliefs are only one element in the group's common uniform (E).

7. **(B)**   He agrees with only the first of Arnold's propositions. He has rejected the second, which stresses the primacy of literature (C). The theory of life may lead to a moral code, but Huxley nowhere makes this explicit (D). Culture is the direct result of education in the best sense (E).

8. **(B)**   The passage is structured in a way that is designed to convert the reader to the author's opinion. In lines 17–22, Huxley presents his "two convictions," and for the remainder of the passage, supports his thesis with supporting details. While Huxley is upset with the college's actions, his tone is neither sarcastic (A) or cynical (E). Therefore, it is also clear that he does not feel elation (C), which is a state of heightened spirits. A facetious tone (D) which is characterized by a whimsical, joking manner, is not found in the passage.

9. **(D)**   is the correct answer according to line 58. (A) is not the correct response because Huxley mentions that literature contains materials for the construction of criticism but not that it be supplied by a perfect culture. (B) is also not correct because Huxley attributes the classical, liberal education to the opinions of Englishmen. Although he argues for having a scientific education (C), Huxley does not explicitly say that it should be provided in a perfect culture. Huxley discusses the intellectual and spiritual sphere (E) as progressing not as being supplied.

10. **(A)**   The correct response is (A). Huxley's main purpose for writing this passage is to argue that a scientific education is as important as a classical education. In a way he is deflating a classical education (B), but it is not the main idea. The passage is definitely not an outline of education (C). Huxley argues the value of a scientific education not to argue it is inferior to a liberal education (D). (E) is also incorrect because the passage states that classical and scientific education are important but does not spell out what should and should not be taught in these areas.

11. **(E)**   In the context of the passage, the "Philistines" are people who take from the writings of Arnold only those items which fit their own agenda, namely the cause of classical education. There is no mention of spending too much time pursuing art and knowledge (B). Since the "Philistines" support classical education, they certainly would not have a cultural bias against Greek and Latin literature (C). Although the dictionary definition of "Philistine" is a person guided by material rather than intellectual values (D), the context of the passage does not support this choice.

12. **(C)**   The correct answer is (C) because the passage states in lines 26–30 that the English thought true knowledge was obtained only through

a liberal arts education, and a liberal arts education included Greek and Latin literature, or, the classics. (A) is incorrect because the sciences were not considered part of a liberal arts education. (B) is incorrect because they were not of the opinion that a perfect culture should include both scientific and liberal arts knowledge. (D) is wrong because education has no limitations, it is boundless. (E) is incorrect, because, as stated before, the English did not consider science part of a liberal arts, or cultured education.

13. **(D)** According to the author of Passage 1, animals at times lose certain characteristics or features because the part becomes unimportant to them. Usually an animal would not lose a part that is necessary for survival according to the theory espoused here. (A) Neither passage discusses losing the part so animals of a different class may survive. (B) Neither passage discusses mating with other animals of a different class or even if such is done. (C) Both passages discuss changes which occur in the wild; statement (E) states that such losses do not occur in the wild.

14. **(E)** The writer of Passage 2 seems to believe that hair on the back of people disappeared by some power other than natural selection. The writer of Passage 2 believes that hair on the back is still important; (A) which states that it disappeared when it became unimportant is not the best choice. (B) The loss of hair seems to have occurred for all people, not just for people in warm climates. The writer does not see body hair as being injurious; (C), which states that the body hair disappeared when it became injurious to them, is not a good choice. (D) The writer does not hold with the idea that hair on the body disappeared when people began to walk upright and it was no longer necessary.

15. **(B)** The writer of Passage 1 and the writer of Passage 2 both disagree with natural selection as a cause of the disappearance of certain natural features like the hair on the back. Both writers do not uphold natural selection as a cause (A). The writer of Passage 1 does not seem to uphold natural selection as a cause of hairlessness; the writer of Passage 2 would not uphold natural selection as a cause. The two writers do not differ in their beliefs. (D) Both writers are concerned with the subject of body hair; (E) should not be selected since it states that both writers are unconcerned with the subject of natural selection.

16. **(A)** The writer of Passage 2 believes hair on the back of people is useful. (B) The writer discusses the importance of body hair—not its uselessness. (C) The very fact that the writer spent so much time on the

topic seems to indicate that he does not think it is an unimportant topic to consider. (D) Both writers are not sure the loss is a result of natural selection. (E) Body hair is not a vital feature.

17. **(C)** In Passage 1 the writer states that soft and whitish body parts occur when the part is enclosed in a case. (A) The white, soft parts do not occur, according to this passage, when the animal part is exposed to the bleaching rays of the sun. (B) Soaking in sea water does not necessarily result in soft, whitish body parts. (D) The passage does not indicate that the soft, whitish body parts come about when blubber is eliminated. Rather, the passage indicates that the parts come about when there is a hard case over them. (E) is incorrect. The passage does not even hint that the soft parts result from a scanty cover of bristles.

18. **(A)** The author of Passage 1 contends that domestic animals lost their protective coloration when it became of little use to them. Since protective coloration was needed in the wild, (B)—which states that protective coloration was not needed in the wild—should not be chosen. The passage states that the hairy covering of whales was not necessary when the layers of blubber were added; (C) states just the opposite and should not be chosen. (D) is incorrect because it uses the term "direct" rather than "indirect." (E) The writer does not refer to degeneration as an outmoded theory.

19. **(D)** The author of Passage 2 believes the hairless body is hurtful. (A) The writer considers diminished usefulness to be a weak, not a strong, influence on animals. The author believes that hair on the back is important to people. (B) states it was no longer needed and should be eliminated and not used as an answer choice. The author states that "some other power than natural selection has been engaged in his production," so (C) should not be selected. Since most mammals do have back hair, the absence of back hair in people does not correspond to the characteristics in other mammals (E).

20. **(B)** The author of Passage 1 sees the function of the integument of an arthropod as a passive kind of use. (B) is the best answer. (A) is an incorrect choice since it describes the function of the integument as active, rather than passive. The writer of Passage 1 uses degeneration in reference to the loss, not the growth, of body hair; (C) should not be chosen. The writer thinks the loss is an indirect—not direct—consequence of disuse. (D) should not be chosen. The writer does not attribute the blubber of the whale as contributing to the loss of body hair in humans—in whales perhaps (E).

21. **(A)** In line 16 the word "superfluous" means "more than is needed." "Superfluous" comes from the word "superfluere," to overflow. "Superfluous" does not mean of a superior grade or quality (B), in an insufficient quantity (C), less than is needed (D), or strong (E).

22. **(A)** The author of Passage 1 refers to degeneration as attributing to the loss of body hair. (B) The author does not believe natural selection was instrumental to the loss of body hair. The author does not discuss the hair as constantly correlated with an injurious character, so (C) should not be chosen. (D) The author does not believe that hair on the back ceased to grow because it was useless. (E) The writer does not attribute the loss to diminished usefulness.

23. **(C)** The reason for hair loss on the back of people is an indirect consequence of disuse, according to writer 1. The writer of Passage 2 is unclear as to the direct cause of hair loss, so (A) is not the best answer. (B) Passage 1—not Passage 2—says that hair loss is an indirect consequence of disuse. Since both writers do not claim the hair loss is an indirect consequence of disuse; (D) should not be selected. Since one writer does claim hair loss is an indirect consequence of disuse, (E)—which states neither writer makes the claim—should not be chosen.

24. **(B)** The meaning of "integument" in line 36 of Passage 1 is a hard shell or case. The integument is not necessarily an inner protective device so (A) is not an appropriate device. (C) The integument is not necessarily an inner skeletal make-up. (D) "Integument" does not necessarily mean function. An integument is not necessarily an activity; (E) should not be selected.

25. **(B)** The attitude of Passage 1 toward hairlessness is interest. The very fact that the writer has written on the topic eliminates "disinterest" (A) as a choice. Since the writer is not repelled by the topic, "repugnance" (C) is not a good choice. The writer is not sarcastic toward the topic; (D) should not be chosen. There is no animosity or hard feelings apparent from the writer so (E) should not be chosen.

26. **(E)** "...the uniform rule of naturalization" most nearly means law conferring the rights of a natural citizen. (E) is the best answer. "...the uniform rule of naturalization" has nothing to do with the law of nature. (A) is not the best choice. In answer (B), "naturalization" again has nothing to do with natural or ordinary law; (B) is not the correct answer. "...the uniform rule of naturalization" has to do with conferring the rights

of a natural citizen on a person; it does not relate to the laws of nature. (C) is not the correct choice. Since the uniform rule of naturalization has to do with the rights of a natural citizen and not with the laws of commerce, (D) is not the right choice.

27. **(D)** The right to assign an exchange value to a foreign coin brought to the United States is in the Constitution (Passage I); (D) is, therefore, the correct answer. The Congress has no right to assign a value to foreign coins and coins in countries other than in the United States; (A) is not the correct choice. The Constitution does not grant the right to assign a value to a foreign coin and use it as currency within the United States; (B) is not the correct answer. The Congress is not able to assign an exchange value to U.S. money taken abroad; (C) is an incorrect choice. The Congress must fix the standards of weights and measures; these values must be uniform and must not vary from place to place. (E) is an incorrect choice.

28. **(C)** The excise taxes established by the Congress must be uniform; (C) is correct. The passage referring to the number of people leaving one area of the country has nothing to do with the excise tax; (B) is not correct. Congress is not able to control all taxes throughout the United States; for example, local sales taxes are not controlled by the Congress. Because (D) includes local sales taxes, (D) is incorrect. Local uniform property taxes are not a part of the excise tax power given to Congress; (E) is incorrect and should not be chosen.

29. **(E)** Since numbered item 4 relates to bankruptcy, it is implied that financial prosperity may not be in store for all people. (E) is the best answer. The appropriation of money for the armies is not the best answer; (A) should not be chosen. Coining money (B) does not relate directly to prosperity for all citizens; (B) should not be chosen. Paying debts (C) is not directly related to prosperity of individuals; (C) is not the best answer. Since regulating commerce (D) is not directly related to the economic prosperity of individuals, (D) should not be chosen.

30. **(A)** By making the tribunals inferior to the Supreme Court appointed by Congress, a future ruler would not be able to make judges dependent on his will alone. (A) is the best answer. Uniform laws on the subject of bankruptcy have little to do with making judges dependent on his will alone; (B) is not a good answer. Calling forth the militia to execute the laws of the land is not the best way to make the judges dependent on a future ruler's will alone; (C) is not the best choice. Copyright protection has little to do with making judges dependent on the will of a

future ruler; (D) should not be chosen. Suppressing insurrections through the legislature (E) might possibly help to prevent a future ruler from making judges dependent on his will alone, but (A) is still the best answer.

31. **(D)**   Answer (D) provides for the securing of exclusive rights; it is the best choice. Tribunals (seats of justice) does not refer to copyright; (A) is not the best answer. Letters of marque (reprisal) do not pertain to copyright; (B) is not the selection of choice. Counterfeiting (C) is not the best choice for copyrighting. (C) should not be chosen. Copyright has nothing to do with rebelling invasions; (E) is evidently not the correct choice.

32. **(E)**   "Perfidy" means the violating of a promise; (E) is the correct answer. "Perfidy" does not mean destruction; (A) should not be chosen. Violence (B) is not the correct meaning of perfidy. "Perfidy" does not mean murder, so (C) should not be chosen. Since "perfidy" does not mean theft, (D) is not the best choice.

33. **(D)**   Number 15 provides "for calling forth the militia to execute the laws of the Union, suppress insurrections, and repel invasions." (D) is the best answer. Naturalization (A) refers to conferring upon an alien the privileges of a citizen. One usually thinks of piracies as being on the seas; mercenaries of foreign armies are more likely to occur on the lands. (B) is not the best answer. "Letters of marque" or seizures of goods do not relate directly to mercenaries; (C) is not the best answer. "Imposts" or duty on goods do not relate directly to foreign mercenaries; (E) is not the best choice.

34. **(D)**   Passage 2 states that the King of Great Britain has "called together legislative bodies at places unusual, uncomfortable, and distant from the depository of their public Records, for the sole purpose of fatiguing them into compliance with his measures." (D) suggests these facts; (D) is the best answer. "...the Administration of Justice" refers to the courts and not to the legislative process. (A) is not the best answer. The Standing Armies did not directly affect the laws passed; (B) is not the best answer. Since judges do not directly make the laws, (C) is not the best choice. Plundering the seas does not directly relate to the laws; (E) is a poor choice.

35. **(E)**   At the present time the King of Great Britain was transporting large armies of foreign mercenaries; (E) is the best answer. Refusing his assent to laws was done in the past; (A) is not the best choice. In the past he did forbid his governors to pass laws, but that is not listed as a present

problem; (B) is not the best choice. Obstructing justice (C) and erecting new offices (D) are not the best choices. (C) and (D) should not be chosen.

36. **(D)**   "Waging war against us" was certainly an evidence of the contempt of the King of Great Britain. (D) is the best answer. Abdicating (abandoning) government would not be evidence of contempt; (A) would not be a satisfactory choice. Besides, this action was one of the past. Raising conditions of new appropriations might show low regard for the colonists, but not as much so as (D). (B) was a past occurrence and not a present occurrence called for by the question. (B) is not the best choice. Although refusing his assent to laws initiated by the colonists might indicate contempt (C), true contempt is more evident by war; (C) is not the best choice also because it occurred in the past. New offices (D) was a past action and is, therefore, not the best choice.

37. **(B)**   Passage 2 suggests that the King of Great Britain has "neglected" to attend to the laws which have been suspended. (B) which refers to procrastination (putting things off) seems to be the best answer. Hesitation implies a momentary waiting; (A) is not the best choice. Indoctrination (instruction, teaching) does not seem to fit here; (C) is not the best choice. Inclination (a leaning to) does not seem to fit the question; (D) is not the best choice. Disorganization of the King of Great Britain does not seem to be the reason for the neglect of the King of Great Britain. (E) is not the best selection.

38. **(A)**   (A) is correct because it is stated that the Congress, representatives of the people, has the power to call forth the militia. The people must therefore, by majority, agree to the presence of this army. No mention of war or peace time is given (B). (C) is incorrect because it is the Constitution that states the militia can execute laws of the Union. No right to bear arms is mentioned in the passages (D). If (A) is correct, then (E) is automatically wrong.

39. **(D)**   Child labor laws, according to Passage 1, were sought by the workers themselves because cheap child labor resulted in lower wages for adults and because the working class had to rely on legislation. (D) is the best answer; it points out that the motivation for child labor laws was not necessarily unselfishly motivated. The child labor laws were not enacted to protect management in case of injury to children. (A) is not the best choice. Passage 1 does not state that the laws were first enacted in England by members of parliament at the request of the manufacturers of the North. The author states that they were enacted because "their hearts were wrung."

It was not the children who pushed for the laws; choice (C), which states that the laws became necessary and were sought by the children themselves, should not be chosen. The passage states that it was parliament (not the U.S. lawmakers) who had their hearts "wrung"; (E) should not be chosen.

40. **(B)** According to Passage 1, the order is 1) knowledge and 2) legislation; (B) is the best choice. Since knowledge comes before legislation, the order of (A) is wrong; (A) should not be selected. Workers do not oppose legislation because it demoralizes their values; they oppose children working alongside them. (C) is not the best choice. The author does not seem to indicate his view of legislative control; neither (D) nor (E) should be chosen.

41. **(B)** The word "alleviating" in line 12 of Passage 1 is an adjective describing the philanthropy; it means the philanthropy makes things easier. (B) is the best answer. The word does not refer to eliminating the philanthropy. (A) should not be chosen. Neither does "alleviating" refer to removing the philanthropy. (C) should not be selected. The statement does not mean that the magnitude of the philanthropy will be lessened. (D) must be omitted as a correct choice. The passage has nothing to do with lessening the criminality of the philanthropy. Thus, (E) should not be chosen.

42. **(D)** In line 32 in Passage 1, the word "ameliorating" means improving or making better. (D) is the best choice. "Ameliorating" does not mean worsening or deteriorating. (A) should not be chosen. The word has nothing to do with overseeing (B), managing (C), or canceling (E). (B), (C), and (E) should not be selected.

43. **(A)** The illustration in Passage 1 is primarily used to show the importance of the workers in improving the plight of children. (A) is the best choice. The writer would not have gone into so much detail just to show the sadness of the upper class at this situation. Their sadness does not bring results. (B) should not be selected. The illustration actually shows that the upper class does little to agitate for child labor laws. (C) should not be chosen. The illustration shows that sympathy alone can do little to help conditions of the children. The illustration shows the complacency of many to child labor; (E) should not be chosen since it says that no one is complacent with child labor.

44. **(D)** The attitude of the author of Passage 1 toward child labor is

violently opposed; (D) is the best answer. The writer is certainly not supportive (A), enthusiastic (B), accepting (C), or uninterested (E). (D) is the best—and only—choice.

45. **(E)**   Management, in Passage 2, stated it was obliged to hire children to secure the help of the rest of the family. (E) is the best answer. The schools in many places were open four months and closed four months, but this did not mean that management was obliged to hire children to keep the schools open for the four months. (A) is not the best choice. Management was not necessarily hiring children because the children wanted to work, according to Young; (B) should not be chosen. Children were being used so choice (C) which stated that the mills were not employing children as was evidenced by the non-operating equipment is not the best answer. The passage did not state that management was disappointed in the performance of the children. (D) should not be chosen.

46. **(C)**   To give credence to his writings, the author of Passage 2 gives the results of interviews and on-site visits conducted. (C) is the best answer. Passage 1—not Passage 2—calls on history and the laws of the past. (A) is incorrect. Since no questionnaires were administered, choice (B) which states that reports on the results of questionnaires administered is not to be chosen. It was Passage 1—not Passage 2—which reports on the three riders in the street-car. (D) should not be chosen. Again, Passage 1—not Passage 2—discusses the laws passed by parliament in the past. (E) should not be selected.

47. **(A)**   The author of Passage 2 seems to recognize the necessity of employing children and, given the clean working conditions and the schooling provided, seems content with the situation now. (A) is the best choice. The author does not seem at all adamant about the removal of children from the work environment. (B) should not be chosen. Since the writer talked with children under the age of 16, (C) does not seem acceptable. The writer did not seem to find substantial evidence to support the statement that children under the age of five were employed. (D) should not be selected. The writer seemed pleased with the cleaning the children were doing; (E) should not be chosen.

48. **(D)**   The author of Passage 2 assumes that the children filling the magazines were not being paid AND that they were attending school four months a year. (D) is the best answer. The writer gives the salary of the children cleaning the floors; (A) should not be used. The writer assumes that the children are attending school four months as per the law. (B) states

that he assumes they were NOT attending school. (B) should not be chosen. The person who answers with (C) is giving only part of the answer. The writer does not see the difficulties in the spinning room as being easily overcome. (E) should not be chosen.

49. **(C)**   The word "insuperable" means (C), not able to be overcome. (C) is the best answer. The word looks somewhat like "insufferable," but they are not related. (A) should not be chosen. The word does not mean just not sufficient; (B) should not be selected. Neither "improbable" (D) nor "incomplete" (E) should be selected.

50. **(A)**   The writer of Passage 2 seems to show that the work environment of child laborers is clean and healthy. (A) is the best choice. The writer does not suggest the environment is filthy and unhealthful. (B) should not be chosen. The writer seems content with the provisions for education. (C) is not a good choice. (D) is not a point in Passage 2. (D) should not be selected. The author does not suggest that the environment neglects mind and body. (E) should not be chosen.

READING LONG PASSAGES REVIEW

STRATEGIES FOR READING LONG PASSAGES

Long reading passages average about 700 words and often prove to be a challenge to the already anxious test taker. These burdensome sections tax the reader's ability to cut straight to the core of the content and to extract intended or implied meaning. They can also diminish the student's self-confidence and adversely affect test endurance. When approached with correct strategies, these challenging passages may be conquered efficiently. To be most productive in the shortest time, these strategies for reading long passages must not only be learned but also put into practice.

Students sometimes wonder if reading the questions before the passage is more efficient. Especially true with longer passages, reading the questions first will more than likely be more time consuming and confusing. Reading all of the questions first, usually four incorrect answers and one correct answer, puts an added burden on the reader's concentration. Tips to tackle the questions with confidence are presented later in this chapter.

Reading is a skill that can be improved with correct and consistent drill. Study the suggested strategies for reading and conquering long passages presented on the following pages and put them into operation—not just once or twice, but as often as you can before test time. You will discover that in conquering those long passages, you will improve your reading comprehension as well as your reading efficiency.

READING STRATEGY 1: Read Quickly While Keeping in Mind That Questions Will Follow.

Reading long passages quickly is important, but it should not be confused with speed reading. *Quickly* in this context means efficiently, and to be efficient, you must first know what kind of reader you are. Reading experts have identified three kinds of readers:

(1) The Motor Reader or the Vocalizer—reads about 150 words per minute

(2) The Auditory Reader—reads about 300 words per minute

(3) The Visual Reader—reads about 800 or more words per minute

The Motor Reader slows himself down by vocalizing the words, obviously or subvocally. The consequence is an inefficient level of performance. If you find yourself vocalizing to any degree, immediately put your finger or your pencil to your lips as a reminder and stop. Continue this until this habit is either extinguished or controlled to a manageable degree.

The Auditory Reader slows himself down by overdoing the amount of detailed thinking that he projects into each word of print. His silent reading is not silent at all, but replete with the sound of each word he uses. An auditory reader can correct this habit by deemphasizing unnecessary detail and concentrating on concepts or the whole picture.

The Visual Reader is the most efficient and often the most accurate kind of reader. There is a direct transmission from the printed word to meaning without interfering habits or other obstacles which hamper comprehension. Once you have identified which kind of reader you are, you will no doubt wish to improve your efficiency. The following background information concerning the reading process will help you identify three common hindrances to efficient reading—lack of concentration, regression, and fixation.

This active and engaged activity with the author's meaning is called **concentration**. Reading is a skill, as previously noted, and it is also a thinking activity. The eyes assist in transmitting information to the brain, but it is the reader actively engaged in the process who brings meaning to the print. Readers who do not actively pursue the author's intended or implied meaning will not be efficient readers. Since you have established the kind of reader you are, you must determine your purpose for reading the passage. Introductory statements which precede the passages generally help to establish a purpose. As you read aggressively, keep focused on the author's message. You may want to underline a word or a phrase or use a circle or an asterisk to highlight important points. Remember to be conservative with these marks since they later may confuse you if used too often. More about marking key words will be presented in Strategy 4. The more purposefully you read, the more you will increase your powers of concentration.

Regression is a habit of inefficient readers whose eyes revert back to prior text frequently enough to slow them down. Train yourself to move along at a pace that allows you to comprehend without difficulty. You will resist the urge to backtrack once you have established a steady pace. Your finger or pencil can be used as a pacing device. This not only keeps you actively on task but productively pushing ahead.

Pacing is one way to overcome the habit of regression as well as fixation which will be discussed below. The reader establishes control over his reading progress by causing his eyes to move steadily along in the direction of the pacer. The pacer can be any artificial device as common as a pencil or the reader's hand. The pacer is kept moving slightly ahead of the eyes' path, more or less directing their steady progression ahead. It is important to note that any machine or mechanical device cannot replace the efforts of the reader actively engaged with the text.

Fixation is a common habit of slow readers who allow their eyes to stop too long on a word, a group of words, or on a line. Although the eye must stop on the line in order to process the actual reading, the more words grouped in a single fixation, the faster the reading process. Extremely slow readers are word by word or syllable by syllable readers. Moderately slow readers fixate or stop too often on the line. Efficient readers group their words and stop as little as three or four times per line of print. When confronted with long passages which average about 700 words, you can see where lack of concentration, regression, and fixation can hinder your reading efficiency as well as adversely affect your verbal scores.

Drill 1: Reading Strategy 1

DIRECTIONS: Choose several informative passages from newspapers, magazines, journals, or texts between 600 to 800 words long each. Establish a purpose for your reading similar to the following: I will be able to read this selection within five minutes or less and be able to identify the author's intended or implied meaning. Then, set a timer for five minutes and pace yourself efficiently. As you progress, be aware of any hindrances such as regressions, prolonged fixations, and distractions. Adjust your goal for the second reading to meet your needs.

An Informal Word Per Minute Formula: If you are curious about the approximate number of words you are reading, the following formula is an informal method for estimating your reading rate. Be sure that you understand that this is only a rough estimate of reading rate since you cannot equate speed with efficiency. Faster does not necessarily mean better.

To calculate your approximate word per minute reading rate, select about 10 pages of challenging text (not too difficult, yet not too easy) from an instructional book or journal. Choose a typical page. Typical means that it is a full page of print with no dialogue to reduce the line length. Find five full sentences which cross the page and count every word except **the** or **a**. Divide that number by five. You now have an average word per line count.

From a full page, count the number of lines that go down, vertically, from top to bottom. Do not count any short lines which fail to cross midway across the page. you now have a typical line per page count for your reading selection. Next, multiply the average word per line count by the average line per page count. Keep that sum handy. This is your word per page (wpp) count. Now set your timer for five minutes. Any timing device will do; you do not need special equipment for this. When you are ready, read for the full duration of time. Multiply the number of pages you have read times your wpp count, rounding off to the nearest whole figure when you have read half of a page or more. That is, if you have read four pages and a few lines on the next, you will multiply your wpp count times four. However if you have read at least half the page, use the figure five. Divide the number of minutes you have read into that sum. You now have an estimate of your reading rate per minute.

READING STRATEGY 2: Uncover the main idea of the passage. Many times it is contained in the first or last few lines of the passage.

Long test passages have the same basic structure as shorter or medium length passages since they all have a main or a basic idea which is their foundation. The job of an efficient reader is to discover this key element in as little time as possible. The main idea of the passage is the unifying device and should not be mistaken for topic sentences within each separate paragraph. They, too, are important to find since they contribute to the author's underlying message. Once the passage's main idea is identified, the structure, writing style, tone, and mood can also be established.

Where do you look to uncover the main idea? Instead of searching throughout each paragraph, efficient readers cut to the chase and look in the most predictable places—the first or last few lines.

Drill 2: Reading Strategy 2

DIRECTIONS: A passage from an actual test is reproduced below. Read actively the first few sentences, then move directly to the last lines to grasp the main idea in the shortest time.

Is This Artist "America's First Modernist Painter?"

The atmosphere is one of sunlit charm. Children ride merry-go-rounds. Tourists festively promenade up the Spanish steps in Rome. Parasol-toting weekenders buy balloons on the South Boston Pier. This is the turn-of-the-century world brought to life in Maurice Prendergast's paintings and watercolors. This world view is also, unfortunately, the main reason that Prendergast has remained a neglected artist. Ostensibly, such vibrant images were the product of an artist who has taken all the work out and left only the joy. Little wonder, then, that the modernist movement found Prendergast's work too easy and tranquil and shouldered him to the sidelines. Now, it is startling to learn that some historians consider him America's first modernist painter: the first to journey to Paris, to become familiar with the new trends in art, and to spread the word back in America

Boston was Prendergast's home for all but twelve years of his life, although his five trips to Europe and his many sojourns to New York City—where he became a member of the group known as "The Eight" and exhibited in the famous 1913 Armory Show— were the greatest influences on his work. His art, as with any true pathfinder, resists easy classification. From the Impressionists he took his improvisational brushwork; from the Postimpressionists, his subjective, stylized view of reality; from the Nabis— Pierre Bonnard in particular—his decorative expression of color. This rich stew was then flavored with a gentle simplicity to create a uniquely American mix.

Above all, his color—or rather, the amount he used—was new. He would have none of the "brown sauce" with which many Bostonian artists of the day served up their paintings. In fact, he used so many colors, one critic called his work "an explosion in a color factory." To this spectrum, he added a sparklingly animated line that blocked out forms as fluidly as an abstractionist—forms he also used in more than two hundred masterful monotypes.

As this show reveals, Prendergast (1859–1924) was an important link between the masters of the nineteenth century and the new ones of the twentieth....

This passage illustrates how quickly the strategy of search the first and last few lines of a passage can uncover the main idea of a passage. Long passages can also be attacked as efficiently and effectively.

READING STRATEGY 3: Uncover the main idea of each paragraph. Usually it is contained in either the first or last sentence of the passage.

Just as entire passages of short, medium, or long length, have main or central ideas, so do each of the paragraphs contained within the super-structure. It is essential when reading long passages to budget your time. Efficient readers are flexible in their approach to different passages since there are varying levels of difficulty which are dictated by the content and by the reader's familiarity with the subject matter. This strategy of first identifying the main idea of each paragraph will help you immeasureably to cut to the core of the message, thus cutting your time on task significantly.

What is a flexible reader? A flexible reader is wisely strategic in his approach to different passages because he varies his speed and intensity according to the difficulty of the textual contents facing him. For instance, highly technical or unfamiliar material demands slower reading with more intensity. Standardized tests routinely advise students that technical material outside of what is in the passage is not needed to answer the questions which follow. Experience as well as logic tells us that familiarity with the topic will allow the reader to progress more confidently and comprehend more efficiently. Do not confuse this with relying on prior information acquired outside of the text. Flexible readers exercise control by determining how rapidly or slowly, how intensely, or how casually they need to read.

Drill 3: Reading Strategy 3

DIRECTIONS: Review Strategies 1, 2, and 3 as presented on the preceding pages, and put them into operation while reading the following passage concerning speed and comprehension in reading. As you practice, be alerted to any hindrances such as fixation, regression, or lack of concentration, and correct them. Pace yourself; be sure your flexibility in speed and intensiveness is based on your knowledge of the subject matter. Before you read, set a timer for five minutes.

Fact and Fiction About Reading Improvement

With the mounting interest in better reading there have grown up certain misconceptions. One of these concerns speed. There is widespread belief that reading courses regularly train people to read at 1,500 words per minute or better, and that some people can read a full length book in an hour. Despite frequent refutations in the literature on reading, the myth still circulates that some people read a paragraph or even a page at a glance.

In one carefully-executed investigation of 62 adults ranging in age from 17 to 50 years, the initial rates per minute ranged from 111 words to 333 words. At the end of twenty hour-long periods of corrective exercises the average rates ranged from 311 to 469 words. In an experiment with business executives, 18 hours of directed practice resulted in increases in the average rate from 198 words to 358 words per minute. A third program—for Air Force officers—reported that the average rate per minute increased from 240 to 600 words.

Since academic work probably leans more heavily on reading than any other profession, it may be assumed that college professors are among the most competent readers anywhere. Yet a recent study of professors at the University of Michigan showed that few could read faster than 500 words per minute, even in their own fields of specialization.

Over a course of years every reading specialist occasionally finds people who reach or exceed 1,000 words per minute with adequate comprehension, but these people are rare exceptions rather than the rule. A rate of 500 to 600 words per minute is good; and rates above that are excellent, provided, of course, the material is understood.

The idea that people may learn to read at 1,500 or 2,000 words per minute probably traces back to the fact that with timed-exposure techniques they can be trained to recognize digits or words at a rate of 1/100 second. But this does not mean that such units could be grasped in the same second. Reading is a sequential, connected process, with each unit of thought fusing in turn with the others to constitute the substance of the whole; and the movements of the eyes and the intergration of the material in comprehension cannot be left out of the time calculations.

It is impossible to read a page or even a paragraph at a glance. The eye movement camera has shown that the eye moves along each line of print in a series of moves and pauses, with clear vision taking place only when the eye is at rest. The person who has never really learned to read and who reads little more than the daily paper, may pause 20 times or more to the line. Experts have been known to pause only 3 or 4 times, when the material was simple and the line short. Usually good adult readers pause 5, 6, or 7 times to the line. The mature reader surpasses the poor reader in several ways; he pauses more briefly and less frequently and he regresses less often.

Since no one reads an ordinary line of print with less than 3 or 4 fixations, the page-at-a glance myth has no defense. People who are credited with such feats are actually engaging in a highly proficient type of scanning or skimming. Unquestionably, masterful skimming is an extremely valuable skill, but it is not to be confused with reading.

A second misconception is related to the use of the term "speed reading." With the growth in interest in adult reading, certain investigators were curious about a particular question; they wanted to know whether it was possible to increase speed without loss of comprehension. In order to find the answer, they selected individuals with adequate comprehension, trained them with speed techniques, and measured the results. They found that speed can be increased without loss of comprehension; they also found that speed training alone does not improve comprehension.

It is important to note that in these experiments the scientists were not concerned with building total effectiveness in reading, nor with the diversified problems of adult readers. They were interested in just one question, and they carefully selected for their experiments only those people with adequate initial comprehension.

The time factor is important in current living, and the term "speed reading" caught the popular fancy and became as familiar as some of the advertising slogans. It has been applied indiscriminately to reading improvement courses of all types.

The development of maximum speed is a major objective of reading instruction but it is not the only objective. Speed does not function in isolation, and not all adult readers are alike in comprehension.

A few examples from the writer's classes illustrate the diversity of adult reading classes. A graduate student majoring in city administration had to devote excessive amounts of time to study and attributed his slowness to poor reading. Standardized tests confirmed his diagnosis and showed that a major cause of difficulty was a weak vocabulary. He had never had any need for extended knowledge of words during his childhood. He had grown up on a ranch where each member of the family had heavy responsibilities and long hours of physical labor. After work there was little interest in reading or conversation.

A woman who found constant pleasure in novel reading developed a speed of 750 words per minute and a good grasp of details which were necessary to the plot of the story. After her husband's death it was necessary to seek employment, and, since she had a little knowledge of chemistry, she accepted a position as a reader with a chemical firm. It was her work to read trade and professional journals and make abstracts of the articles. She found herself unable to cope with the job because she had never learned to read meticulously for the kinds of details which are important in science.

A physician who had been an excellent reader during his undergraduate days formed the habit of regressing in his professional reading to make sure of each fine point. When he was tired, he vocalized to keep his attention on his task. In time these habits transferred to all his reading and slowed down his rate. He was interested in literature, politics, and biography, but was finally forced to forego all but his medical reading.

An undergraduate was dropped from his university because of poor grades. He was interested in sports, college activities, and social affairs. On standardized reading tests he ranked at the 85th percentile for his academic level, yet he avoided reading. He stated that when he sat down to study his mind wandered to more interesting subjects. He felt that he comprehended while he was reading, but he didn't remember the material and couldn't organize the facts he read to answer examination questions.

Those four examples illustrate the futility of limiting reading improvement programs to "speed reading" alone. Speed training could not have improved the word knowledge of the graduate student in city administration. It could (and did) help the physician. It was not the basic requirement of the woman whose rate was extremely good at the start, nor of the college student who needed to improve his concentration, his study techniques, and his retention.

From Power and Speed in Reading *by Doris Wilcox Gilbert*

The author's main purpose in this section is stated quite clearly rather than implied. She presents and illustrates some popular misconceptions about speed reading. In paragraph one, lines one and two contain these revealing terms—**mounting interest, misconception, speed**. The second paragraph presents a significant difference in reading rate gains between civilian and military adults. Paragraphs three through six share a common theme by disclaiming a correlation between speed gains and gains in comprehension. The one key to paragraph eight stands out in the last sentence: *speed can be increased without loss of comprehension* and *speed training alone does not improve comprehension*. This theme is repeated throughout paragraphs nine through 14.

This rather simplified review of strategies 1, 2, and 3 can be applied to more challenging long reading passages with relative ease, especially with the addition of Strategy 4, key words, which will round off your regimen for reading long passages.

READING STRATEGY 4: Skim over the detailed points of the passage while circling key words or phrases. These are words or phrases such as but, on the other hand, however, yet, and except.

Everyone who reads regularly skims to a certain extent. Skimming is the ability to get the gist or the heart of the message without reading every word. For challenging material that requires attention to detail and concentration, very few readers can get along by skimming alone. Efficient readers are, however, flexible and know when it is possible to rev up and skim, or when they must downshift and slow down for more intense reading. Using partial skimming is a hallmark of an efficient reader, one who is in command and can adjust his speed according to purpose. Be careful, though, since there is a right way and a wrong way to skim.

Skimming, if done properly, is an intensive search by an engaged and purposeful reader who is seeking information. While skimming, the reader must conduct an ongoing inner direction and decision about what is important, irrelevant, introductory, or transitional. Finally, the skimmer needs to determine if he has secured the author's message and adequate information. If not, a closer reading must then be conducted.

Especially for long passages in a timed situation, implementing strategy 4 is an excellent tool for the burdened reader. When you are skimming, circle words such as those listed above which indicate a change in the meaning of the passage. These buzz words are your signal that a significant difference or oppositional view is presented. With the use of this criteria, consider this sentence from the preceding passage—

> Unquestionably, masterful skimming is an extremely valuable skill, (but) it is not to be confused with reading.

This circled key word will signal you when answering specific questions that the author is injecting a relevant, however different, meaning. Consider another example from the same passage which presents a longer, more complicated sentence, reinforcing nevertheless the value of noting key words.

> Over a course of years every reading specialist finds occasional people who reach or exceed 1,000 words per minute, (but) these people are the rare exceptions rather than the rule.

Here, once again, if the reader is not actively engaged in reading and skimming purposefully cued to key words, an erroneous concept of attainable reading rates could be derived. Over-using circles, symbols, and underlining is self-defeating, however, since too many signals will confuse you and defeat your purpose. In this instance, the purpose of signal words is to help you remember and locate needed details quickly.

STRATEGIES FOR ANSWERING QUESTIONS FROM LONG PASSAGES

Your passport to successful verbal scores is determined by how strategically you attack the questions. Your confidence should be bolstered now by the knowledge that you have read actively, skimmed, circled, and literally sliced through to the core of the author's message, intended or implied. A wise tactic would be to summarize, or paraphrase, that underlying idea and prepare yourself to attack the questions.

QUESTION ANSWERING STRATEGY 1: Attack one question at a time. Read the question carefully.

The order of questions which follow long passages follow the text in organization. For instance, what occurs in the first paragraph will precede what occurs in the second, and the questions are also presented in that order. This saves needless searching and needed time. Double passages also follow that order, and they will be considered separately a little further along. When considering the question, zero in on the question stem, that kernel of information which introduces the answer choices. Question stems appear in a number of forms, such as:

According to the author, photojournalism, unlike painting, is
The author is least concerned with
The author's attitude toward Van Gogh is
In this narrative, to be "intolerant of ignorance but understanding of literacy" most closely means

A close look at the stems above point out that not every one is very informative. The second one is the least informative since it provides no clues to the passage meaning. The others contain kernels of clues in the direction of the correct answer. Next, the efficient reader should consider the entire question. Basically, there are only two kinds of questions: general and specific.

General questions ask about that which involves the whole rather than anything in particular. General questions appear in the following forms:

What is the significance of this passage?
The author's main purpose or intent is
The best title for this selection would be
The narrator's attitude can be compared with
An accurate description of the author's tone
The style of writing exhibited in this passage

Reject immediately any answers which go beyond the scope of the message when answering general questions. As you eliminate them mentally, cross out those rejected with an air of finality, and do not consider them again. It is efficient to answer general questions first since they do not require going back into the text. If you have proceeded efficiently, there is no need to wait.

Passages selected for the verbal sections of standardized tests are written by informed or famous and talented individuals. If you perceive overly aggressive or derogatory comments, or any pervasively negative tone, it is wise to be wary of such answers and exercise good taste and judgment when considering them. It is likely that they are not correct choices. The following excerpt from a longer narrative passage illustrates how tone and attitude as well as character relationship can be perceived quickly by looking at the author's language and style.

Drill 4: Question Answering Strategies

DIRECTIONS: Choose the *one best answer* to each item.

Items 1 to 3 refer to the following excerpt from a story.

How Do You Let Go of Something You Love?

1   I had decided to let my raccoon make his own decision. But I took off his collar and his leash and put them in a pocket of my corduroy jacket as something to remember him by if he should choose to leave me. We sat together in the canoe, listening to the night sounds all around us, but for
5 one sound in particular.

It came at last, the sound I had been waiting for, almost exactly like the crooning tremolo we had heard where the romantic female raccoon had tried to reach him through the chicken wire. Rascal became increasingly excited. Soon he answered with a slightly deeper crooning of his
10 own. The female was now approaching along the edge of the stream, trilling a plaintive call, infinitely tender and questing. Rascal raced to the prow of the canoe, straining to see through the moonlight and shadow, sniffing the air, and asking questions.

Do as you please, my little raccoon. It's your life, I told him.

15   He hesitated for a full minute, turned once to look back at me, then took the plunge and swam to the other shore. He had chosen to join that entrancing female somewhere in the shadows. I caught only one glimpse of them in a moonlit glade before they disappeared to begin their new life together.

From Rascal *by Sterling North*

After having read this abbreviated passage aggressively you are prepared to attack each question at a time. A quick look at each places them all in the category of general questions which are answered immediately. Remember to judiciously narrow down your answers, eliminating those which are overly negative or derogatory. Then compare your answers with the detailed explanations which follow the questions.

1.   What is the overall tone of this passage?

   (A) Uplifting

   (B) Melancholy

   (C) Forlorn

   (D) Cynical

   (E) Sarcastic

2.   Which of the following best describes the narrator's attitude toward his pet's departure?

(A) Sentimental   (D) Angry

(B) Bitter yet resigned   (E) Tolerant but disappointed

(C) Relieved

3.   The reader can infer that the narrator and his pet

(A) would soon forget about one another.

(B) would never meet again.

(C) were companions who understood each other.

(D) would soon be united

(E) were never suited for one another.

QUESTION ANSWERING STRATEGY 2: If the question is asking for an answer that can only be found in a specific place in the passage, save it for last since this type of question requires you to go back to the passage, and therefore, takes more of your time.

Within the superstructure of general and specific questions, a substructure exists which further classifies specific questions into separate types, most commonly called precise, inferential, application, and line dependent questions.

Precise questions are easy to detect since they require you to locate information within the passage. Some examples of stems to precise questions are:

An analysis of this passage reveals
According to the author
The passage clearly informs us

Inferential questions call upon the reader to use information which is implied, not stated. Some examples are:

No doubt, the author wants us to
The opening paragraph suggests
Which of the following adages could be inferred

To answer inferential questions, try to paraphrase what you have decided is the explicit answer. Often it can be a helpful strategy in narrowing down your answer choices.

Application questions are those which ask you to apply specific information from the text to other situations. These are some examples:

You can apply this theory to the twentieth century by
Which of the following situations would not be included in the author's plan
In what way could medical science benefit from

Line dependent questions are popularly used and easy to detect since they point us squarely in the direction of words, phrases, statistic, or other specifics. Vocabulary as used in context is one favorite type of line dependent question and used frequently on standardized tests. Very often, the word is used in a technical or unusual sense which necessitates a study of the lines which precede and follow it. For example, refer back to the shortened passage on the preceding pages entitled **How Do You Let Go of Something You Love?** How would you answer this line dependent question:

Questing as used in line 11 most nearly means

(A) howling.

(B) screeching.

(C) seeking.

(D) calling.

(E) bleating.

If you choose (C) **seeking,** you are correct since it is used in a special sense, and the context before and after it assist the reader in his selection. (A), (B), (D), and (E) are incorrect choices since the author has used provocative language elsewhere in the passage such as **plaintive**, **trilling**, and **tender** which negate those choices. Consider the words **tremelo** in line seven and **prow** in line twelve, these too could be line dependent vocabulary words unless the reader is familiar with musical or sailing terminology.

QUESTION ANSWERING STRATEGY 3: For the detail-oriented questions, try to eliminate or narrow down your choices before looking for the answer in the passage.

We have already reviewed some answer choices that could be eliminated or viewed cautiously. They are overly negative or exaggerated words that describe the author's tone, attitude, or point of view; words in context that are defined in their literal sense; and explicit answers to implied or inferential questions. Here are some other strategies to help you eliminate or narrow down choices.

Be wary of the use of **always, never,** and **must** since they often signal incorrect answers and defy the laws of logic. When they are modified with **nearly, seldom, may,** or **might** they are often the correct choice. Choices which contain **sometimes** are very often correct.

QUESTION ANSWERING STRATEGY 4: Go back to the passage, utilizing the key words you circled to find answers.

Once you have narrowed down or eliminated certain choices, you are prepared to attack those sticklers which require that you dig deeply into the passage and root out the answers. To save valuable time, it is important to use those key words, symbols, or phrases that you signaled. They will serve you well now as a time saving review of key points.

Four important points need to be considered about answering specific questions: First, you cannot afford to search randomly since it is futile and promotes anxiety. Secondly, you should not attempt to rely on memory alone because passages which average about 700 words contain too much information for instant recall. Thirdly, you must not rely on knowledge outside of the passage's content since everything you need to know is contained within and anything over and beyond its scope is usually an incorrect answer. Finally, it is helpful to remember that test questions usually follow the organizational pattern of the passage. For example, this means that if you have answered questions one, two and four, but not three, key words for question three should come after those you have already used for one and two, preceding those used for question four. What you are actually using are location skills, and like an efficient map reader, you are saving time and possible errors. All the question strategies we have reviewed thus far are also applicable to double passages which will be considered in the following section.

QUESTION ANSWERING STRATEGY 5: Reading Double Passage Efficiently and Accurately

The common inclusion of double or paired passages in standardized testing is relatively new. As forbidding as they appear to the anxious test taker, they, too, can be conquered with background information and strategy. The general focus of these doubles is to evaluate the reader's ability to use higher order, or critical, thinking skills which are discussed extensively in Chapter 9.

Paired passages have a relationship to one another in some way. The relationship may be one in agreement, opposition, or simply in similarity of the subject matter. In a couple of the questions, you will be asked to recognize that a relationship exists and those are usually the last questions. The reason is that questions for double passages also follow the organizational pattern of the sections themselves. Specifically, the first four or five questions relate to passage one while the next four or five relate to passage two; and the last two or three questions require that you consider them both.

QUESTION ANSWERING NUMBER 6: Anytime you cannot find the answer, use the process of elimination to the greatest extent possible and guess.

Eliminating and narrowing down your answer choices for specific questions has already been discussed in detail in Question Answering Strategy 4. A quick review will bring to mind that the reader should be cautious of overly negative or exaggerated language as well as absolutes such as **never** or **always**. For general questions, any that go beyond the scope of the passage, stated or implied, should be eliminated. When you have exhausted your plan of attack to the fullest, you should guess. The reason for guessing at this point is that you will have nothing to lose in most cases since it is usually (practically always) the correct answers that score for you. That means, of course, that those which you could not answer as well as those that you answer incorrectly are equally of no value. With that in mind, as a last resort—guess.

Drill 5: Reading Double Passages

DIRECTIONS: The following paired passages were selected from an actual test to give you an opportunity to put your question answering strategies to use. Before you begin, rapidly review your entire plan of strategies for reading and answering long passages. Detailed explanations and answers follow the passages. You may wish to set a timer when you are ready to read.

What do painting and photo journalism reveal authentically about life? Both of the reviews below are concerned either explicitly or implicitly with that question.

Passage 1

Van Gogh Was A Genius, But Was He Really Mad?

1   It has been almost exactly 100 years since Vincent van Gogh propped his easel against a haystack near the Château d'Auvers in France and fired a bullet into his chest. He managed to crawl back to the house of a family named Ravoux, with whom he was living. Doctors were summoned and
5 the artist's younger brother, Theo, rushed by train from Paris as soon as he heard the news.

      "I wish I could pass away like this," Vincent said as he lay beside his brother, shortly before dying in the early morning of July 29, 1890, leaving behind hundreds of paintings and drawings no one wanted. Theo had
10 tried for years to sell them, not least in the hope of recouping a fraction of the money he had shelled out to support his hapless brother over the course of more than a decade. He had no luck, and neither did the Paris dealer, Julien François (Pére) Tanguy, who had agreed to keep some of Vincent's paintings in the attic of his shop.

15   Was Vincent addicted to absinthe? Did he really chase Paul Gauguin with a razor, or was that a story embroidered by Gauguin to justify abandoning van Gogh in Arles? Did Theo die—six months after his brother, at the age of 33, in an asylum near Utrecht—from grief over Vincent's suicide? Was the artist epileptic or manic depressive or did he suffer, as a
20 recent article in the *Journal of the American Medical Association* suggests, from an inner-ear disorder that finally drove him in the winter of 1888 to lop off part of his left ear in a desperate attempt to alleviate the pain?

      An earlier generation of van Gogh biographers wove such fanciful
25 tales of the pathetic starving painter driven to drink and lunacy that the latest crop of historians and writers has found it necessary to undo, at least in part, the myth that has obscured the man. As David Sweetman, author of the engaging new "Van Gogh: His Life and His Art," says of the old biographies: "The one significant conclusion that can be reached from
30 them is that whatever he was suffering from cannot be directly 'read' into his art...the image of Vincent as an isolated Holy Fool, artist-sage or whatever, has finally been exposed as the nonsense it always was...."

From "Vincent Obsessed" by Michael Kimmelman

Passage 2

How Can Time Be Imprisoned in a Rectangle?

Balzac had a "vague dread" of being photographed. Like some primitive peoples, he thought the camera stole something of the soul that, as he
35 told a friend, "every body in its natural state is made up of a series of ghostly images superimposed in layers to infinity, wrapped in infinitesimal films." Each time a photograph was made, he believed, another thin layer of the subject's being would be stripped off to become not life as before but a membrane of memory in a sort of translucent anti-world.

40 If that is what photography is up to, then the onion of the world is being peeled away, layer by layer—lenses like black holes gobbling up life's emanations. Mere images proliferate, while history pares down to a phosphorescence of itself.

The pictures made by photojournalists have the legitimacy of being
45 news, fresh information. They slice along the hard edge of the present. Photojournalism is not self-conscious, since it first enters the room (the brain) as a battle report from the far-flung Now. It is only later that the artifacts of photojournalism sink into the textures of the civilization and tincture its memory.

50 If journalism—the kind done with words—is the first draft of history, what is photojournalism? Is it the first impression of history, the first graphic flash? Yes, but it is also (and this is the disturbing thing) history's lasting visual impression. The service that the pictures perform is splendid, and so powerful as to seem preternatural. But sometimes the power they
55 possess is more than they deserve.

All great photographs have lives of their own, but they can be as false as dreams. Somehow the mind knows that and sorts out the matter, and permits itself to enjoy the pictures without getting sunk in the really mysterious business that they involve.

From "Imprisoning Time in a Rectangle" by Lance Morrow

1. According to this review, the notion of Vincent van Gogh being a "mad genius" is best explained as

   (A) substantiated by incidents in his life.

   (B) just a myth.

   (C) created by his brother.

   (D) proven by his suicide.

   (E) challenged by recent historians and writers.

2.   The series of questions posed in lines 15–23 is used by the reviewer
     as a literary device to

   (A) prove his point that van Gogh was mad.

   (B) give the reader insight into the controversial stories about van
        Gogh's life.

   (C) baffle the reader.

   (D) amuse the reader.

   (E) prove that van Gogh was not mad, but physically ill.

3.   In lines 24–32 one new biographer

   (A) questions old theories about van Gogh.

   (B) accepts the "old" biographers' and writers' statements.

   (C) rejects past and present theories.

   (D) is uncertain about "old" and "new" reviews.

   (E) None of the above.

4.   The tone of this review is generally

   (A) serious and informative.   (D) derogatory and inflammatory.

   (B) humorous and entertaining.   (E) None of the above.

   (C) slanted and one sided.

5.   You can readily determine in lines 27–32 that van Gogh as the genius
     and madman

   (A) has no basis in truth.

   (B) has finally been exposed as the truth.

   (C) is still debatable.

   (D) has yet to be resolved.

   (E) is best left for future biographers.

6. In line 30, the word "read" as used in the sentence means

   (A) summarized.   (D) interpreted.

   (B) questioned.   (E) removed from.

   (C) painted.

7. The author believes that, at times, photojournalism

   (A) is not powerful enough.

   (B) is not "good" journalism.

   (C) can be more powerful than it is thought to be.

   (D) is simply entertainment.

   (E) is underestimated as a news media.

8. A literary device used effectively in this essay is

   (A) repetition   (D) rhyme.

   (B) alliteration.   (E) cacophony.

   (C) personification.

9. The writer implies that we should regard photojournalism

   (A) casually.   (D) tolerantly.

   (B) cautiously.   (E) disrespectfully.

   (C) suspiciously.

10. According to the essayist, time can be imprisoned in a rectangle by

    (A) revealing criminal misuse of photojournalism.

    (B) capturing historic moments in photographs.

    (C) accepting Balzac's dread of photographs.

    (D) discontinuing the use of photojournalism.

    (E) None of the above.

11. Both passages suggest that painting and photojournalism

    (A) are accurate replicas of life.

    (B) cannot portray an artist's life.

(C) can be read into and misunderstood.

(D) are ancient art forms.

(E) grossly exaggerate the real world.

12. You can compare Balzac's dread of being photographed to Van Gogh's

(A) addiction to absinthe.

(B) lack of material success as a painter.

(C) estranged relationship with his brother.

(D) medical problems.

(E) life as the old biographies relate.

READING LONG PASSAGES DRILLS

ANSWER KEY

Drill 1 — Reading Strategy 1
Objective Response

Drill 2 — Reading Strategy 2
Objective Response

Drill 3 — Reading Strategy 3
Objective Response

Drill 4 — Question Answering Strategies

1. (B)   2. (A)   3. (C)

Drill 5 — Reading Double Passages

1. (E)   2. (B)   3. (A)
4. (A)   5. (A)   6. (D)
7. (C)   8. (C)   9. (B)
10. (B)   11. (C)   12. (E)

VOCABULARY LIST

perspicuity

> n.- clarity, something easily understood

pertinacious

> adj.- obstinate, stubborn

pestilent

> adj.- virulent; likely to cause death

phlegm

> n.- apathy

picayune

> adj.- petty, trivial

pious

> adj.- holy; having or showing religious devotion

plaintiff

> n.- complainant; one who brings a suit into a court of law

plethora

> n,- excess; the state of being too full

poignant

> adj.- affecting, pungent

poltroon

> n.- a thorough coward

ponderous

> adj.- lacking fluency or gracefulness

portent

> n.- omen; something that portends an event, usually evil

praetorian

  adj.-corrupt

praxis

  n.- custom

precedent

  n.- a closely similar case in existence or in the past

predilection

  n.- bent; a preconceived liking, partiality

prepotency

  n.- dominance

prescience

  n.- vision; foresight

prevaricate

  v.- equivocate, lie; to evade the truth

primordial

  adj.- early, primitive, fundamental

princely

  adj.- grand; of a prince; generous; magnificent

requite

  v.- avenge, compensate, reciprocate

retrogress

  v.- back, recede, relapse

rigor

  n.- difficulty, severity

risible

  adj.- amusing, laughable

rogue

  n.- mischief; a scoundrel; a fun loving mischievous person

ruse

n.- deception, trick

sacrosanct

adj.- holy, sacred

sanctioned

adj.- accepted, authoritative, orthodox

sapient

adj.- sane, wise

savior-faire

n.- tact; ready knowledge of what to do or say

scathe

v.- to slam or blast with remarks

scourge

n.- curse; to punish severely

scrupulousness

n.- thoroughness; conscientiousness

secede

v.- to break away or withdraw from membership in an association or federation

semblance

n.- facade, shade

sequester

v.- to isolate or seclude

shard

n.-a fragment or broken piece

shoal

n.- a shallow part of a body of water

sinuous

adj.- winding in and out; bending

solemnity

    n.- gravity; seriousness

solitary

    adj.- set away from all others

sovereignty

    n.- freedom

speculative

    adj.- theoretical, thoughtful

staunch

    adj.- faithful, sure

stigmatize

    v.- to mark with disgrace or infamy

stipulate

    v.- to make specific

stratagem

    n.- deception, trick

suppress

    v.- to bring to an end forcibly

supervenient

    adj.- accidental; unexpected

CHAPTER 9

Attacking Critical Reading Questions

➤ Diagnostic Test
➤ Attacking Critical Reading
  Questions Review & Drills
➤ Vocabulary List

CRITICAL READING QUESTIONS DIAGNOSTIC TEST

1. (A) (B) (C) (D) (E)
2. (A) (B) (C) (D) (E)
3. (A) (B) (C) (D) (E)
4. (A) (B) (C) (D) (E)
5. (A) (B) (C) (D) (E)
6. (A) (B) (C) (D) (E)
7. (A) (B) (C) (D) (E)
8. (A) (B) (C) (D) (E)
9. (A) (B) (C) (D) (E)
10. (A) (B) (C) (D) (E)
11. (A) (B) (C) (D) (E)
12. (A) (B) (C) (D) (E)
13. (A) (B) (C) (D) (E)
14. (A) (B) (C) (D) (E)
15. (A) (B) (C) (D) (E)
16. (A) (B) (C) (D) (E)
17. (A) (B) (C) (D) (E)
18. (A) (B) (C) (D) (E)
19. (A) (B) (C) (D) (E)
20. (A) (B) (C) (D) (E)
21. (A) (B) (C) (D) (E)
22. (A) (B) (C) (D) (E)
23. (A) (B) (C) (D) (E)
24. (A) (B) (C) (D) (E)
25. (A) (B) (C) (D) (E)

26. (A) (B) (C) (D) (E)
27. (A) (B) (C) (D) (E)
28. (A) (B) (C) (D) (E)
29. (A) (B) (C) (D) (E)
30. (A) (B) (C) (D) (E)
31. (A) (B) (C) (D) (E)
32. (A) (B) (C) (D) (E)
33. (A) (B) (C) (D) (E)
34. (A) (B) (C) (D) (E)
35. (A) (B) (C) (D) (E)
36. (A) (B) (C) (D) (E)
37. (A) (B) (C) (D) (E)
38. (A) (B) (C) (D) (E)
39. (A) (B) (C) (D) (E)
40. (A) (B) (C) (D) (E)
41. (A) (B) (C) (D) (E)
42. (A) (B) (C) (D) (E)
43. (A) (B) (C) (D) (E)
44. (A) (B) (C) (D) (E)
45. (A) (B) (C) (D) (E)
46. (A) (B) (C) (D) (E)
47. (A) (B) (C) (D) (E)
48. (A) (B) (C) (D) (E)
49. (A) (B) (C) (D) (E)
50. (A) (B) (C) (D) (E)

CRITICAL READING QUESTIONS DIAGNOSTIC TEST

This diagnostic test is designed to help you determine your strengths and your weaknesses in critical reading. Follow the directions for each part and check your answers.

**Study this chapter for the following tests:
PSAT and SAT**

---

50 Questions

DIRECTIONS: Each passage is followed by questions based on its content. After reading the passage, choose the best answer to each question. Answer all questions based on what is indicated or implied in that passage.

Questions 1–6 are based on the following passage.

The following passage is adapted from: "A letter to Martin Van Buren, President of the United States," by Ralph Waldo Emerson.

1   Sir, my communication concerns the evil rumors that fill this part of the country concerning the Cherokee people. The interests always felt in the Indian population has been heightened in regard to this tribe. Even in our distant state some good rumor of their worth and civility has arrived.
5   We have learned with joy their improvements in the *social arts*. We have read their newspapers. We have seen some of them in our schools and colleges. Along with the great body of the American people, we have witnessed with sympathy the painful labors of these red men to rescue
10   their own race from the threat of feelings of eternal inferiority and to include in their tribe the arts and customs of the white race.

The newspapers now inform us that, in December 1835, a treaty calling for the sale of all the Cherokee territory was pretended to be made by an agent on the part of the United States with some persons appearing on the part of the Cherokees; afterwards the fact surfaced that these depu-
15   ties did not by any means represent the will of the nation. Out of 18,000

souls composing the Cherokee nation, 15,668 have protested against the so-called treaty. It now appears the government of the United States chooses to hold the Cherokees to this sham treaty. Almost the entire Cherokee nation stands up and says, "This is not our act. Behold us. Here are we. Do 20 not mistake that handful of deserters for us."

The principle that is left in the United States—if only in its roughest form—forbids us to entertain this rumor as a fact. Such a failure of all faith and virtue, such a denial of justice, and such deafness to screams for mercy were never heard of in times of peace and in the dealing of a nation 25 with its own allies since the Earth was made. Sir, does this government think that the people of the United States have become savage and mad? From our minds are the feelings of love and a good nature wiped out? The soul of man, the justice, the mercy that is the hearts of all men, from Maine to Georgia, abhors this business.

30 You will not do us the injustice of connecting this plea with the feelings and convictions of any political party. It is the simplest command-ment of brotherly love. We will not have this great claim upon human justice brushed aside under the flimsy plea of being the act of a political party. Sir, the questions which have aggravated both the government and 35 the people during the past year—those of the economy—are mild issues compared to this one. Times are hard indeed, but above these hard times rings an important question: Will a civilized people such as those in these United States do injustice to a race of savage men? Will the American people put aside reason, civility, justice, and mercy in their dealings with 40 the Cherokee?

1. Emerson testifies to the *accommodation* by the Cherokee tribe of "outside" values in his

   (A) reference to the Treaty of 1835.

   (B) claims that he is acting for a political party.

   (C) calling the Cherokee "a race of savage men" (line 38).

   (D) assessment that their social arts include "white" elements.

   (E) estimate of the number of Cherokee in their nation.

2. Above the laws and treaties of the United States, Emerson pays hom-age to

   (A) "the simplest commandment of brotherly love" (lines 31–32).

   (B) "the threat of feelings of eternal inferiority" (line 9).

   (C) the President, Martin van Buren, himself.

   (D) "their newspapers" (line 6).

   (E) "an agent on the part of the United States" (lines 12–13).

3.   The "rumor" (line 22) Emerson reacts to is

   (A) related to the idea that whites and Indians are equal.

   (B) based on a business venture between Maine and Georgia.

   (C) the immoral treaty that the Cherokees are forced to recognize.

   (D) a result of the party system that concocted the 1835 treaty.

   (E) less concerned with "savages" than with the economy.

4.   According to Emerson, the American people would be both "savage and mad" (line 26) if they were to

   (A) continue to assimilate Cherokee ideals into their government.

   (B) succumb to the inferred greed motivating the sale of Cherokee lands.

   (C) abandon their loyalties to the dominant political parties.

   (D) ignore the 2,000 deputies representing the Cherokee nation.

   (E) be sidetracked away from the economic issues aggravating the country.

5.   Emerson suggests that the "principle that is left in the United States" (line 21)

   (A) violates the original principles upon which the country was founded.

   (B) is a humanitarian plea that transcends the races involved in the conflict.

   (C) issues from a directive based in either the Republican or Democratic party.

   (D) is a product of the hard times (line 36) plaguing the country.

   (E) is based on a faulty estimate as to the value of the Cherokee lands.

6. The "deserters" (line 20) to which Emerson refers

    (A) are political candidates who abandon their original party.

    (B) are those Cherokee refusing to obey the treaty of 1835.

    (C) are judges and political appointees who misinterpret the treaty.

    (D) are those Cherokee who seek their own gain above the will of the nation.

    (E) are those who abandon the merciful values that created the United States.

Questions 7–15 are based on the following passage.

In this excerpt from Jules Vernes's Twenty Thousand Leagues Under the Sea, *we are presented with a danger on board the* Nautilus, *Captain Nemo's legendary submarine.*

1   The next day, the 22nd of March, at six in the morning, preparations for departure were begun. The last gleams of twilight were melting into night. The cold was great, the constellations shone with wonderful intensity. In the zenith glittered that wondrous Southern Cross—the polar bear
5   of Antarctic regions. The thermometer showed 12° below zero, and when the wind freshened it, it was most biting. Flakes of ice increased on the open water. The sea seemed everywhere alike. Numerous blackish patches spread on the surface, showing the formation of fresh ice. Evidently the southern basin, frozen during the six winter months, was absolutely inac-
10   cessible. What became of the whales in that time? Doubtless they went beneath the icebergs, seeking more practicable seas. As to the seals and morses, accustomed to live in a hard climate, they remained on these icy shores. The creatures have the instinct to break holes in the ice-fields and to keep them open. To these holes they come for breath; when the birds,
15   driven away by the cold, have emigrated to the north, these sea mammals remain sole masters of the polar continent. But the reservoirs were filling with water, and the *Nautilus* was slowly descending. At 1,000 feet deep it stopped; its screw beat the waves, and it advanced straight towards the north at a speed of fifteen miles an hour. Towards night it was already
20   floating under the immense body of the iceberg. At three in the morning I was awakened by a violent shock. I sat up in my bed and listened in the darkness, when I was thrown into the middle of the room. The *Nautilus,* after having struck, had rebounded violently. I groped along the partition, and by the staircase to the saloon, which was lit by the luminous ceiling.
25   The furniture was upset. Fortunately the windows were firmly set, and had held fast. The pictures on the starboard side, from being no longer vertical,

were clinging to the paper, whilst those of the port side were hanging at least a foot from the wall. The *Nautilus* was lying on its starboard side perfectly motionless. I heard footsteps, and a confusion of voices; but
30 Captain Nemo did not appear. As I was leaving the saloon, Ned Land and Conseil entered....

We left the saloon. There was no one in the library. At the centre staircase, by the berths of the ship's crew, there was no one. I thought that Captain Nemo must be in the pilot's cage. It was best to wait. We all
35 returned to the saloon. For twenty minutes we remained thus, trying to hear the slightest noise which might be made on board the *Nautilus,* when Captain Nemo entered. He seemed not to see us; his face, generally so impassive, showed signs of uneasiness. He watched the compass silently, then the manometer; and, going to the planisphere, placed his finger on a
40 spot representing the southern seas. I would not interrupt him; but, some minutes later, when he turned towards me, I said, using one of his own expressions in the Torres Straits:

"An incident, Captain?"

"No, sir; an accident this time."

45 "Serious?"

"Perhaps."

"Is the danger immediate?"

"No."

"The *Nautilus* has stranded?"

50 "Yes."

"And this has happened—how?"

"From a caprice of nature, not from the ignorance of man. Not a mistake has been made in the working. But we cannot prevent equilibrium from producing its effects. We may brave human laws, but we cannot
55 resist natural ones."

Captain Nemo had chosen a strange moment for uttering this philosophical reflection. On the whole, his answer helped me little.

7.   Why do the birds fly to the north in lines 14–16?

(A) The only type of cold that they may endure is in the North Pole.

(B) Extreme cold allows them to hibernate until the summer months.

(C) The seals and morses, seeking supremacy in the land, drive the birds away.

(D) The birds flee to the warmer climates of the north.

(E) The cold drives the birds into a panic, and they fly in the wrong direction.

8. What is meant when the narrator informs us that the *Nautilus* has "stopped" in line 18?

(A) The *Nautilus* has completely ceased to move.

(B) The *Nautilus* has paused only briefly before descending further.

(C) The *Nautilus* no longer descends, but continues to move.

(D) The *Nautilus* halts only long enough to fill its reservoirs with much-needed water.

(E) The *Nautilus* never ended its descent completely; it only slowed down its continuing descent.

9. In line 24, "luminous" most nearly means

(A) extravagant.

(B) glowing.

(C) enormous.

(D) artificial.

(E) damaged.

10. Why is the furniture "upset" in line 25?

(A) The furniture is inundated with flooding water; and is, therefore, completely ruined.

(B) The furniture was broken to pieces during the shock of collision.

(C) The furniture's expensive luster has faded over the years.

(D) The furniture is in disarray after a shady gathering took place in the saloon.

(E) The furniture now rests on the walls instead of the floor.

11. What is the most likely reason that the narrator seeks Captain Nemo after he leaves the saloon?

(A) He is angry, and wishes to chastise Nemo for his ineptitude.

(B) He wants to do a favor for Ned Land and Conseil, who were looking for Nemo.

(C) He wants Nemo to repair the furniture in the saloon.

(D) He knows that Nemo is the only person capable of rectifying the situation.

(E) He is afraid that Nemo may have been injured in the collision.

12. The narrator notes that Nemo's face is normally "so impassive" (lines 37–38) in order to

(A) show how Nemo's current visage emphasizes the gravity of their situation.

(B) stress Nemo's arrogance to others whom he feels are beneath his station.

(C) explain why Nemo's expression is so uneasy.

(D) show why others are never able to approach Nemo intimately.

(E) reiterate Nemo's inability to deal with a crisis situation.

13. Why does Nemo feel the need to qualify the narrator's suggestion that the *Nautilus's* situation be considered an "incident" (lines 43–44)?

(A) Nemo always corrects the narrator, no matter what the latter suggests.

(B) Nemo believes their current situation is of a significantly different character than what they experienced in the Torres Straits.

(C) Nemo considers "accidents" to be far more important than "incidents."

(D) Nemo fears that they will never survive their current situation, and therefore changes the narrator's choice of definition.

(E) Nemo blames himself for his folly in bringing them into dangerous, uncharted territory.

14. What is the message of Nemo's "philosophical reflection" in lines 52–55?

(A) Nature despises the artificial creations of mankind.

(B) Were it not for man's fallibility, nothing would be impossible.

(C) Despite man's perfection of the sciences, he may still succumb to the whims of Nature.

(D) Human beings are unable to complete a great project without including some terrible, fatal flaw.

(E) Man is ignorant only because Nature makes him so.

15. What is the narrator's overall attitude toward Captain Nemo?

(A) Contempt   (D) Confusion

(B) Respect   (E) Condescension

(C) Anger

Questions 16–28 are based on the following passage.

The following selections discuss the technological advances and negative implications of both the Industrial Revolution and the Atomic Age.

Passage 1

1   It is clear to political historians that the Industrial Revolution did not occur overnight. The formation of the mechanical age was a comparatively slow process, punctuated by fits and starts and affected only certain manufacturers and specific means of production. For the most part it spread
5 region by region throughout Great Britain and later, the whole of Europe and America, until by 1780 its impact could not be ignored. By this time, the changing of European economies from agrarian-based to industrial was, in the words of one noted expert, as significant as the transformation from Paleolithic hunter-gatherer to Neolithic farmer.

10   At the forefront of the "Revolution" was the introduction of mill-driven machinery and the way in which running water was converted into mechanical power. In this way was born the era of precise, tireless machines. The benefits of this type of technology were nothing short of stupendous. Weavers alone, by the 1820s, increased their output to 20 times that of a
15 hand worker, with power-driven spinning machines making clothing a marketable commodity to the general masses for the first time. Similarly, the introduction of the steam-driven locomotive allowed the transportation of goods over long distances to improve dramatically, so much so that political shifts of power within the newly industrialized European commu-
20 nities redefined world-wide alliances.

    But the Industrial Revolution, for all its lofty aspirations, far too often engendered neglect and abuse of the individual, the dehumanization of factory workers and the blatant, heartless abuse of children in the labor force being the most notable examples. The introduction of manifold mov-

25 ing parts, gears, logs, coils, etc. necessitated frequent and often costly repairs. Since these mammoth machines required unusually long "startup" times, manufacturers were reluctant to stop production to fix minor problems in fully functioning machines. As a result, loss of limbs were common and deaths were not infrequent, often with the machines continuing to

30 operate as the brutally mangled "messes" were cleaned-up. In the same way, children, paid just a fraction of adult wages, were introduced to the factory labor force. Working as long as 16 hours per day with scant breaks, children often met fates similar to their adult counterparts, some succumbing to the dangers of mechanized production, others from illness brought

35 on by unsanitary working conditions and extreme exhaustion.

Governments basking in the heady glow of revitalized economies ignored the gross atrocities being committed against these laborers, placing the onus instead upon the employers, who remained impassive. In the end, the workers were forced to fight for more palatable working condi-

40 tions, proper renumerative compensation, and acceptable safety standards. Though it changed the course of geo-political relations and vaulted the world into a new age of technology, the dichotomy of the Industrial Revolution prevents it from being a completely benign force.

Passage 2

On July 16, 1945, in a desert in New Mexico, the first atomic explo-

45 sion forever altered the face of global politics. Atomic capabilities, the heralds of an entirely new age, came not through a gradual awakening, but with a blinding flash. Like a world of Rip Van Winkles, the global population went to sleep in the industrial era and awoke on Aug. 6, 1945 firmly ensconced in the atomic age, when the United States dropped a single

50 atomic bomb on the Japanese industrial city of Hiroshima. Four days later, a second bomb, dropped on Japan's Nagasaki, effectively ended the Second World War. Conservative estimates put the death toll for the detonation of these two bombs at over 110,000 people. To some, the act was seen as a remorseless imperative, to others, a heinous disregard of humanity.

55 Yet, regardless of one's opinion, Nagasaki and Hiroshima are the only cities to have ever borne the brunt of an atomic attack.

Instead, mankind has endeavored to harness the power of this herculean force. The world, divided at the end of World War II into a bipolar arena headed on the one side by the United States and on the other by the Soviet

60 Union, sought to transform destruction into production and influence. It is quite clear that neither the United States nor the Soviet Union were motivated in these matters by benevolent interest; each nation, engaged in its

own realpolitik, saw a window of influence being offered to the country
able to provide its neighbors with nuclear power and protection. Thus was
65   the Cold War born.

With the raising of the Iron Curtain and the formation of the North
Atlantic Treaty Organization (NATO) and the Warsaw Pact, the results of
each country's drive for hegemony became clear. Alliances and economic
interdependencies were formed on the basis of contiguity rather than need,
70   and the results were often strained. Only through rigorous arms control
treaties and many failed attempts at detente were both countries able to
end overt hostilities. By the latter half of the 1980s, the notion of mutual
assured destruction (MAD), upon which the nominally peaceful coexist-
ence of the bipolar world existed, had become an anathema, as economic
75   concerns forced the peoples of the Soviet Union and the United States
together. What began as a last ditch effort to end World War II ultimately
helped prevent the possibility of a third world war. The bombings of
Nagasaki and Hiroshima, for all their immediate destructive force, served
as a sufficient reminder to the rest of the world of the atom's potential for
80   destruction.

16. In Passage 1, the statement "as significant as the transformation from
Paleolithic hunter-gatherer to Neolithic farmer" (lines 8–9) conveys a
sense of

    (A) how long ago the Industrial Revolution took place.

    (B) the types of developments the Industrial Revolution produced.

    (C) the profound change the Industrial Revolution had on mankind.

    (D) the dietary predilections of the world's population during the
Industrial Revolution.

    (E) the class struggle that took place during the Industrial Revolu-
tion.

17. In lines 10–12 and 17–18, the steam engine and mill-driven machinery are presented as primary examples of

    (A) mechanical advances that fueled the Industrial Revolution.

    (B) profitable things to own.

    (C) daring applications of the use of water.

    (D) machines done away with at the beginning of the Industrial Revo-
lution.

    (E) failed attempts by companies to develop new products.

18. In line 22, "engendered" most nearly means

    (A) prevented.   (D) defeated.

    (B) brought about.   (E) ruled out.

    (C) forestalled.

19. In lines 21–24, the author most likely describes a particular experi-
    ence in order to

    (A) engage the interest of the reader.

    (B) horrify the reader.

    (C) explain how important children were to the Industrial Revolu-
        tion.

    (D) impress upon the reader the revolutionary nature of the ma-
        chines.

    (E) make the reader sympathetic to the abuse of children.

20. In line 42 "dichotomy" most nearly means

    (A) hugeness.   (D) contradiction.

    (B) quickness   (E) success.

    (C) changing nature.

21. The author of Passage 1 most likely views the development of the
    Industrial Revolution as

    (A) a comparatively fruitless event in world history.

    (B) an heroic advance that ended the problems of the common man.

    (C) an important advance that created its own distinctive problems.

    (D) a major technological advance that led to the Cold War.

    (E) a predominantly agrarian advance.

22. The author of Passage 2 most likely considers the use of atomic
    weapons

    (A) necessary in most instances.

    (B) the best way to achieve peace.

    (C) unnecessary following the bombings of Nagasaki and Hiroshima.

(D) the worst atrocity every committed by mankind.

(E) justifiable only if used against Japan.

23. In lines 53–56, the author most likely describes a specific event in order to

(A) show how it deterred others from using atomic weapons.

(B) explain the principles of nuclear physics.

(C) show the power of an atomic device.

(D) explain the true benefits of atomic capabilities.

(E) place the end of World War II in historical context.

24. In lines 58–60, the author's description of the bipolar arena

(A) shows the direct result of dropping an atomic bomb.

(B) explains the global political situation after 1945.

(C) describes the site of U.S. and U.S.S.R. peace talks.

(D) recognizes the influence of Arctic temperature.

(E) shows a heinous disregard for human life.

25. The word "realpolitik" used in line 63 of Passage 2 can also be used to describe

(A) the increased output of weavers using power-driven spinning machines.

(B) the change from hunter gatherer to farmer.

(C) the birth of the Industrial Revolution and its effects on global economics.

(D) the way in which Great Britain used the Industrial Revolution to become a world power.

(E) the problems faced by the workers of the Industrial Revolution.

26. According to the authors, which of the following is believed to be integral to the development of a revolution?

(A) Gross atrocities committed against the working class.

(B) The development of a drastically new idea or technology.

(C) The realignment of world-wide alliances.

(D) A single country's drive for hegemony.

(E) Economic interdependencies formed on the basis of contiguity.

27. What additional information would reduce the apparent similarity between these two events?

(A) The Industrial Revolution changed the class structure of Europe.

(B) Many people became rich during the Industrial Revolution.

(C) The Industrial Revolution made Great Britain the most powerful nation in the world.

(D) Atomic energy created thousands of jobs.

(E) Most nations of the world do not have atomic or nuclear weapons capabilities.

28. The author of Passage 2 believes the birth of the atomic age

(A) spelled the end of a Soviet dominated political arena.

(B) caused massive political and technological changes.

(C) allowed for man to produce clean and safe power.

(D) prevented world dominance by Japan.

(E) set the stage for World War III.

Questions 29–40 are based on the following passage.

In this passage, John Donne discusses the philosophical similarities between Earth and Man.

1   It is too little to call man a little world; except God, man is dimunitive to nothing. Man consists of more pieces, more parts, than the world; than the world doth, nay, than the world is. And if these pieces were extended and stretched out in man as they are in the world, man would be the giant
5 and the world the dwarf; the world but the map, and the man the world. If all the veins in our bodies were extended to rivers, and all the sinews to veins of mines, and all the muscles that lie upon one another to hills, and all the bones to quarries of stones, and all the other pieces to the proportion of those which correspond to them in the world, the air would be too
10 little for this orb of man to move in, the firmament would be but enough for this star. For as the whole world hath nothing to which something in man doth not answer, so hath man many pieces of which the whole world

hath no representation. Enlarge this meditation upon this great world, man, so far as to consider the immensity of the creatures this world produces.

15 Our creatures are our thoughts, creatures that are born giants, that reach from east to west, from earth to heaven, that do not only bestride all the sea and land, but span the sun and firmament at once: my thoughts reach all, comprehend all.

Inexplicable mystery! I their creator am in a close prison, in a sick bed,
20 anywhere, and any one of my creatures, my thoughts, is with the sun, and beyond the sun, overtakes the sun, and overgoes the sun in one pace, one step, everywhere. And then as the other world produces serpents and vipers, malignant and venomous creatures, and worms and caterpillars, that endeavor to devour that world which produces them, and monsters compiled and compli-
25 cated of divers parents and kinds, so this world, our selves, produces all these in us, producing diseases and sicknesses of all those sorts; venomous and infectious diseases, feeding and consuming diseases, and manifold and entangles diseases made up of many several ones. And can the other world name so many venomous, so many consuming, so many monstrous creatures, as we
30 can diseases, of all these kinds? O miserable abundance, O beggarly riches! How much do we lack of having remedies for every disease when as yet we have not names for them?

But we have a Hercules against these giants, these monsters: that is the physician. He musters up all the resources of the other world to succor
35 this, all nature to relieve man. We have the physician but we are not the physician. Here we shrink in our proportion, sink in our dignity in respect of very mean creatures who are physicians to themselves. The hart that is pursued and wounded, they say, knows an herb which, being eaten, throws off the arrow: a strange kind of vomit. The dog that pursues it, though he
40 is subject to sickness, even proverbially knows his grass that recovers him. And it may be true that the drugger is as near to man as to other creatures; it may be that obvious and present simples, easy to be had, would cure him; but the apothecary is not so near him, nor the physician so near him, as they two are to other creatures. Man hath not that innate instinct to
45 apply these nature medicines to his present danger, as those inferior creatures have. He is not his own apothecary, his own physician, as they are. Call back therefore thy meditation again, and bring it down. What's become of man's great extent and proportion, when himself shrinks himself and consumes himself to a handful of dust? What's become of his soaring
50 thoughts, his compassing thoughts, when himself brings himself to the ignorance, to the thoughtlessness of the grave? His diseases are his own, but the physician is not, he hath them at home, but he must send for the physician.

29. Donne finds an ironic contrast

    (A) among the venomous creatures of this world.

    (B) between Hercules and the physician.

    (C) between the hart and the dog.

    (D) between man's confinements and man's thoughts.

    (E) between apothecaries and physicians.

30. The word "simples" (line 43) means

    (A) uncomplicated possessions.

    (B) foolish people.

    (C) direct procedures.

    (D) remedies.

    (E) mathematical formulas.

31. In his opening discussion, Donne inverts

    (A) microscopic organisms with cosmic giants.

    (B) the relation between maps and geographic locations.

    (C) the magnitude of men with that of Earth.

    (D) the proportions of sinews and muscles.

    (E) the relationship of hills to stones.

32. Phrases like "O miserable abundance, O beggarly riches!" (line 31) reveal

    (A) Donne's contradictory style.

    (B) Donne's inability to see the positive aspects of life.

    (C) the effects of venom on the human constitution.

    (D) the poet's use of oxymoron in describing a union of opposites.

    (E) how much happier beasts are than men.

33. Donne employs the word "answer" (line 12) to mean

    (A) correspond.

    (B) verbally reply.

(C) justify itself.

(D) intuitively respond.

(E) anticipate.

34. Donne's reference to "the other world" (line 35) signifies

(A) the world of supernatural beings.

(B) the physician relies on his imagination.

(C) the world of books.

(D) the religious order.

(E) remedies made from natural sources.

35. The nature of the "very mean creatures" (line 38)

(A) tends to raise man's estimate of himself.

(B) provides the proper study for science.

(C) prohibits their adapting to change or struggle.

(D) shows man to be comparatively inept at healing himself.

(E) raises the dignity of the physician's skill.

36. For Donne, the ultimate negation of the power of thought is

(A) sleep.

(B) unscientific speculation.

(C) death.

(D) simple nature.

(E) imaginary concern with "monsters."

37. When Donne says that "he hath them at home" (line 53), the "them" refers to

(A) man's imaginings.

(B) man's illnesses.

(C) the physicians.

(D) creatures.

(E) medicines.

38. The "diseases and sicknesses" (line 26) of men

    (A) are sent as a punishment for human pride.

    (B) are produced by men themselves.

    (C) are no worse than the venomous beasts in nature.

    (D) baffle the physicians who try to cure them.

    (E) are merely metaphors for Donne's troubled times.

39. When Donne says, "my thoughts reach all, comprehend all" (lines 17–18), he confirms

    (A) his earlier estimation of the power of poetry.

    (B) his prior comparison of man with God.

    (C) the pride and conceit that he says lead to downfall.

    (D) his contrasting ideas on the creatures of this world.

    (E) his claim that the world is literally populated by giants.

40. Donne's command to "bring it down" (line 48)

    (A) means he wishes to simplify the language.

    (B) forces us to reassess the position of man in the universe.

    (C) symbolizes the lack of morals and compassion in the world.

    (D) suggests that the sphere of heaven be made available on Earth.

    (E) warns us that we are too materialistic in our values.

Questions 41–50 are based on the following passage.

The following passage discusses the earliest scientific research in sleep and dreams.

1   Before 1952, most people thought that dreams were rare events, perhaps caused by bodily discomfort or aching conscience, by trauma, sensory stimulation, or the insurgence of an unruly subconscious. The discovery that all people dream every night came as a surprise to many although
5   a large number of classical studies had already heralded the finding. Like many developments in science, a long progression of researchers composed the prelude to the work of this decade although the earlier work attracted less public attention.

The germinal studies, from which much of modern sleep research has burgeoned, began innocuously enough at the University of Chicago where Dr. Nathaniel Kleitman devoted himself single-mindedly to the study of sleep. Dr. Eugene Aserinsky, then a graduate student working with Kleitman, turned attention toward phenomena that had been spotted before and never thoroughly studied. Aserinsky, studying the movements of sleeping infants, was arrested by the fact that the slow rolling movements of the eyes would stop periodically, for intervals. He began to watch adults and saw that there were recurrent intervals of body quiescence when the eyes began making rapid jerky movements beneath the closed lids. At the time it was a curious and startling observation, and it took some doing on the part of a graduate student to demonstrate that this periodic activity did indeed occur in sleep. When Aserinsky and Kleitman watched sleeping volunteers, they saw that the rapid eye movements (REMs) occurred periodically, at a time when there were sharp increases in respiration and heart rate and the electroencephalogram (EEG) showed a low-voltage, desynchronized pattern very different from the rolling waves of deep sleep.

Back in the 1930s, shrewd observers indicated that this EEG pattern meant dreaming qualitatively different from dreaming in other stages of sleep but the time was not then ripe for a surge of corroborating research on this phase of sleep. When Aserinsky and Kleitman awakened volunteers during this REM and EEG pattern, subjects almost always narrated a dream, while awakenings at other periods of sleep rarely evoked such reports. Dr. William C. Dement, then also a graduate student at Chicago, pursued the finding, affirming the coincidence of dreaming with the REM and low-voltage EEG pattern. Subsequently he noted the same pattern in the sleep of cats, a finding confirmed by Dr. Michel Jouvet of the Faculty of Medicine in Lyon. At this point two major paths of dream exploration had begun in the animal laboratory of neurophysiology and in the EEG laboratory where human volunteers came to sleep out the night.

Nobody could have predicted how rapidly sleep research would capture the scientific imagination. Where a few men with solitary persistence had concentrated on the overlooked third of life, in 10 years there followed a new generation of scientists, many of whom elected sleep as their province of research. From the start, the arresting differences between the REM intervals and the rest of sleep suggested that REM was a unique physiological and psychological state.

Back in the olden days of dream research, little more than a decade ago, two very remarkable facts were discovered. Today they are taken for granted, but at that time masses of data and many confirmations were

required to persuade the scientists that they really had found what they
50 thought they had found. Everybody dreamt every night, and moreover,
they dreamt in regular cycles, each for roughly the same amount of time.
Subjectively it is easier to think of dreaming as infrequent, because, in
part, memory for dreams is so brief. Yet the assortment of students and
housewives who were paid to sleep in Abbot Hall at the University of
55 Chicago gave richly detailed dream narratives when awakened during REM
periods. As Dement and other investigators repeatedly awakened volunteers it became clear that young adults had a similar pattern of vivid dream
episodes. About 90 minutes after falling asleep they would rise into a
REM state, usually for a short period, about 10 minutes, then sink down
60 into deep sleep for about an hour before rising again for a longer dream
period. Hundreds and hundreds of people have now been recorded, and the
average young adult seems to dream about 20–25 percent of his or her
sleeping time, in five or so REM periods, at roughly hourly intervals.
Individuals appear to have somewhat distinctive patterns, and some inves-
65 tigators can look at a person's EEG record of several nights' sleep and
predict when he will start dreaming, and for how long.

41. In line 17 the best meaning of the word "quiescence" is

   (A) movement.   (D) upheaval.

   (B) agitation.   (E) intervention.

   (C) peace.

42. Aserinsky and Kleitman noted

   (A) that REMs occur when respiration decreased.

   (B) that REMs occur when heart rate decreased.

   (C) that REMs were accompanied by sharp increases in respiration
       and a decrease in heart rate.

   (D) that REMs were accompanied by sharp increases in respiration
       and heart rate and a high voltage, desynchronized pattern differ-
       ent from that of deep sleep.

   (E) that REMs were accompanied by sharp increases in respiration
       and heart rate and a low voltage, desynchronized pattern differ-
       ent from that of deep sleep.

43. It is true that

    (A) all people dream every night.

    (B) the eyes of an infant, unlike those of an adult, remain still during sleep.

    (C) rapid eye movement patterns occur generally only in people and not in animals like the cat; this was confirmed by Dement.

    (D) dreams are rare events, caused by bodily discomfort, aching conscience, and trauma.

    (E) the discovery that people dream every night was not made until after 1956.

44. Two strong evidences of nightly dreaming are

    (A) the findings of both neurophysiology laboratories and the veterinary laboratories.

    (B) the findings in the EEG laboratories and the neurophysiology laboratories.

    (C) the findings in the EEG laboratories and the veterinary laboratories.

    (D) the age of the studies and the age of the volunteers.

    (E) the fact that the researchers were not merely observers but full professors.

45. An advantage of the study was that the subjects were

    (A) forced to participate.

    (B) human subjects only and no mammals were involved.

    (C) animal subjects only.

    (D) willing subjects.

    (E) chosen during the 1930s, the depression era when money was in short supply.

46. Aserinsky studied

    (A) the movement of waking infants.

    (B) the movement of sleeping cats.

(C) the movement of both sleeping infants and sleeping cats.

(D) the movement of both waking infants and waking cats.

(E) the movements of sleeping infants.

47. Aserinsky found that in adults during sleep

(A) body movements were accompanied by rapid eye movements.

(B) periods of body stillness were accompanied by rapid eye movements.

(C) body movements were accompanied by no eye movements.

(D) body movements were accompanied by sporadic eye movements.

(E) body stillness was accompanied by stillness in eye movements.

48. The writer's purpose in this passage is

(A) to contrast sleep research in 1952 with 1992.

(B) to show the lack of thought given to dreams in 1952 and before.

(C) to show the importance of sleep research on animals.

(D) to discuss major findings in dream research before 1952.

(E) to discuss the beginning studies of dream research.

49. In line 9, the word "germinal" most nearly means

(A) definitive.   (D) contaminated.

(B) exhaustive.   (E) refuted.

(C) early.

50. The scientific study of sleep and dreams

(A) came about almost overnight.

(B) was immediately accepted by the scientific community.

(C) was first performed on animals.

(D) took years of research to become accepted.

(E) was initiated by a group of scientists.

CRITICAL READING QUESTIONS
DIAGNOSTIC TEST

ANSWER KEY

1.	(D)	14.	(C)	27.	(E)	40.	(B)
2.	(A)	15.	(B)	28.	(B)	41.	(C)
3.	(C)	16.	(C)	29.	(D)	42.	(E)
4.	(B)	17.	(A)	30.	(D)	43.	(A)
5.	(B)	18.	(B)	31.	(C)	44.	(B)
6.	(D)	19.	(E)	32.	(D)	45.	(D)
7.	(D)	20.	(D)	33.	(A)	46.	(E)
8.	(C)	21.	(C)	34.	(E)	47.	(B)
9.	(B)	22.	(C)	35.	(D)	48.	(E)
10.	(E)	23.	(A)	36.	(C)	49.	(C)
11.	(D)	24.	(B)	37.	(B)	50.	(D)
12.	(A)	25.	(D)	38.	(B)		
13.	(B)	26.	(B)	39.	(B)		

DETAILED EXPLANATIONS OF ANSWERS

1.   **(D)**   Emerson acknowledges the Cherokee incorporation of the arts and customs of the white race in line 10. (C) only aggravates a racist position; (B) is dismissed in lines 30–33. (A) and (E) are incorrect.

2.   **(A)**   Emerson's "transcendentalism" places humanity over contracts; there is no reference to the power of the President, so (C) is incorrect. The "pretended" agent (E) has no authority for Emerson. (B) is exactly what the Cherokee are trying to overcome, not venerate; and (D) is simply the source for the facts of the Treaty of 1835.

3.   **(C)**   Emerson considers the treaty a "sham" (line 18). (D) is dismissed in lines 31–33. While (A) is a democratic ideal, it is nowhere expressed in the letter. (E) is incorrect because Emerson is concerned only with the moral issues, not the business/economic pact.

4.   **(B)**   The principle of brotherhood transcends the "treaty" that permits the seizure of Cherokee lands. (C) is denied by lines 31–33. (A) is a reversal of current, cultural practice. The so-called "deputies" (D) deserve to be ignored; (E) is incorrect based on a misreading of lines 34–36.

5.   **(B)**   The humanitarian approach to the Cherokee arises from that "commandment" which transcends partisanship (C). (A) is not directly addressed, but it is likely that Emerson would say that humanitarianism supports the Founding Fathers. Both (D) and (E) stress economic factors dismissed by Emerson.

6.   **(D)**   The "deserters" are Cherokee, seeking to profit over the majority of the tribe; (B) represents a reversal of the correct reading. The problem of party affiliation (A) does not arise until line 31. (E) is a misreading of the general tenor of the passage, not applicable to the context. No reference is made to judges (C).

7.   **(D)**   The passage states that the *Nautilus* was in the "Antarctic regions," and that the birds who flew to the north were "driven away by the cold." It becomes clear from this that the birds fly north from the

freezing South Pole to reach warmer climates. The scene takes place on the opposite end of the world from the North Pole (A), so going north will not bring the birds to a place of extreme cold in order to "hibernate" (B). Although the seals and morses remain behind, they do not seek to drive the birds away (C). The passage does not imply that the birds were flying about in a blind panic (E).

8. **(C)** The passage states that "the reservoirs were filling with water, and the *Nautilus* was slowly descending. At 1,000 feet deep it stopped; its screw beat the waves, and it advanced straight towards the north at a speed of fifteen miles an hour." Therefore, even though the *Nautilus* stopped descending, it continued to run straight towards the north. Because of this, it did not completely cease to move (A), nor did it descend any further (B). Its reservoirs were filled to allow the *Nautilus* to descend; there was no reason for them to be filled after the vessel had finished its descent (D). We have already shown that the *Nautilus* did indeed halt its descent (E).

9. **(B)** "Luminous" means brilliant, shining, or glowing. This is exemplified by the fact that the saloon "was lit by the luminous ceiling." While the other selection may or may not have applied to the saloon's ceiling, these qualities were not included in the use of the word "luminous."

10. **(E)** The passage states that "the *Nautilus* was lying on its starboard side perfectly motionless." The narrator describes how the pictures were either hanging or clinging to the walls, depending upon which walls they were hung (starboard or port). The furniture would have had nowhere to go but the starboard wall, which in effect had become the new floor. There is no indication in the passage that there was flooding aboard the *Nautilus;* the narrator himself notes that the "windows were firmly set" (A). Nor is there any indication that the furniture was splintered by the collision (B). There is no mention at all about the furniture's luster (C), nor is there any indication that some form of secret gathering took place in the saloon prior to the collision (D).

11. **(D)** It is apparent from his later questioning of Nemo that the narrator has absolutely no idea what has happened to the *Nautilus,* no less how to go about rectifying the situation; he clearly believes Nemo has the ability to right the matter. There is no indication in the passage that the narrator is angry at Nemo (A), nor that he has any interest at the present in repairing the saloon furniture (C). The narrator was curious about Nemo's locale before he met Ned Land and Conseil; he is obviously seeking the

captain for his own reasons (B). Because the narrator decided to wait for Nemo's arrival in the saloon, he probably did not imagine that the captain was injured (E).

12. **(A)** The narrator is concerned that Nemo's apparent uneasiness bodes a serious problem merely because Nemo's countenance does not normally reflect his internal emotions. The narrator does not imply that this is a measure of Nemo's arrogance (B), nor that the captain is unable to communicate with others intimately (D). Nemo's normally stoic expression does not in itself explain his present uneasiness (C). There is no indication in the passage that Nemo is unable to deal with a crisis situation (E).

13. **(B)** Nemo feels the need to correct the narrator in his assumption that the current situation is similar to the captain's "own expression in Torres Straits": an "incident." There is no indication in the passage that Nemo constantly corrects the narrator (A), nor that "accidents" are normally of a graver nature than "incidents"; even though such may coincidentally be the case (C). Nemo never suggests that an "accident" is irreparable (D), nor does he reprimand himself for their current crisis (E).

14. **(C)** The key word here is the "caprice," or whim, of Nature, to which all of Nemo's excellent planning falls victim. Nemo does not mention that Nature has any particular vendetta against man's accomplishments; it is a mere whim that the tides have turned against them (A). Nemo is sure to note that it is not the "ignorance of man" or a "mistake" that has endangered them; therefore, human fallibility of any sort (B) and (D) is not an issue here. Once again, Nemo does not feel that man's ignorance is important here, nor does he suggest that Nature would cause a state of ignorance (E).

15. **(B)** It is clear from several factors that the narrator has a great deal of respect for Captain Nemo. Not only does he wait anxiously for Nemo's arrival to fix matters, but when the captain does arrive, he "would not interrupt him," but held his tongue until Nemo turned specifically to him. The narrator never considers Nemo in a tone of contempt (A), anger (C), or condescension (E). Although the narrator is sometimes unsure of Nemo's motives, he does not express a state of overall confusion when regarding the captain (D).

16. **(C)** The author uses the simile of man's leap from the earliest stage of mankind to the next to show how the Industrial Revolution pro-

foundly changed the fate of the human race. (A) is incorrect since the statement compares significance, not periods of time. (B) is wrong. There is no mention of the types of developments made during the Industrial Revolution. The comparison between the two ages is used solely as a way to show the development of mankind, not the development of tools. (D) is incorrect. Though the simile does show a shift in hunting to farming, the meaning of the comparison is rooted in man's social and intellectual advances. Therefore, (E) is wrong, as it addresses class issues that are never mentioned in the simile.

17. **(A)**   (A) correctly identifies the steam engine and mill-driven machinery as mechanical advances which played a big part in the Industrial Revolution's development. While both (B) and (C) may be true statements, the article is not primarily concerned with profitability or the daring uses of water. (D) and (E) are wrong. The machines were created, not abandoned, during the Industrial Revolution and were very successful.

18. **(B)**   The Industrial Revolution did in fact bring about the neglect and abuse of individuals. This abuse was a direct result of the advances during that era. Therefore (A) and (D) are incorrect. Those in power during the Industrial Revolution made little or no effort to avoid or negate the abuse of workers. In fact, in many instances gross abuses were ignored. (C) is incorrect. The Industrial Revolution, while it boosted economies and the power of nations, did not stave off or rule out neglect and abuse of workers, Though an impersonal force, the Industrial Revolution in many ways treated men like the precise, tireless machines they operated.

19. **(E)**   (E) is correct since the author's purpose, to show the inhumane treatment of children, is best explained by recounting actual abuses. The graphic nature of the description impresses the seriousness of the situation upon the reader. (A) is incorrect. Though the passage may engage the reader's interest, its purpose is to inform rather than entertain. (C) is wrong. Children were an important part of the Industrial Revolution's labor force, but the incident shows their vulnerability, not their importance. (D) is incorrect. Though the passage itself explains the advantages of the machines, this particular section focuses on the dangers faced by children working them.

20. **(D)**   (D) is correct since dichotomy is defined as "a division into two usually contradictory parts" and the benefits of increased production were contradicted by the damage done to the labor force and children. (A) or (B) are wrong. Neither the Industrial Revolution's size nor the quick-

ness with which it developed affected its contradictory nature. (C) is incorrect since the changing nature of the Industrial Revolution would not prevent it from being a benign force. (E) is also incorrect. The fact that the Industrial Revolution was a success cannot change the nature of the benefits and drawbacks it created.

21. **(C)** The author shows how the Industrial Revolution both benefited and damaged European life. (A) and (B) both go well beyond the author's scope. (A) underplays the Industrial Revolution's importance while (B) completely ignores the many drawbacks of the "machine age." (D) is wrong. The Industrial Revolution occurred almost 100 years before the Cold War, though the birth of the atomic age was a factor in the development of the Cold War. (E) is incorrect since the Industrial Revolution moved European economies away from an agrarian base toward an industrial one.

22. **(C)** The author sites a number of statistics explaining the devastating effects the atomic bombs had on Japan, yet he notes that the bombs "served as sufficient reminder(s) to the rest of the world of the atom's potential for destruction." He implies that the fear of comparable destruction prevents its use. (A) and (B) are wrong. The author believes the opposite of both these answers and provides evidence of Soviet and American efforts to avoid the use of atomic and nuclear weapons at all cost. (D) and (E) are also incorrect since the author provides no concrete evidence to support those statements.

23. **(A)** (A) best describes the purpose of the description and explains the purpose of the passage. The author builds a case that justifies the use of the atom bomb, but then explains the reasons why it was never used again. By focusing on the destruction, the author impresses upon the reader the event's power as a deterrent. (B) is incorrect since the author never discusses the theoretic/scientific aspect of atomic weapons, (C) and (E) are incorrect. Even though the description might show the power of an atomic device and show how World War II ended, neither are the reasons the description was included. (D) is obviously wrong since the statement deals with destruction, not benefits.

24. **(B)** (B) discusses the way in which world politics was divided between two factions, following the end of World War II, headed on one side by the United States and on the other by the former Soviet Union. This two-sided breakdown of nations led to the Cold War. (A) is incorrect. The author does not directly link the bombing of Japan to the bipolar

global arena, rather he shows how the two combined to influence history. (C) is wrong. Though the U.S. and the U.S.S.R. peace talks are mentioned, the author's description does not address that issue. (D) and (E) are both incorrect since neither relates to the way in which the bipolar arena impacted upon world politics.

25. **(D)**   Great Britain, concerned only with expanding its base of power, used the Industrial Revolution to become the dominant global force in the same way that both the U.S. and the U.S.S.R. used the threat of nuclear weapons. Since realpolitik is concerned with national developments and goals, (A) and (E) are incorrect. Though the increase of power-driven machines did increase output and the author of Passage 1 did address the problems faced by industrial workers, realpolitik does not apply. (B) is wrong, because the change from hunter to gatherer precludes all such advanced political systems. (C) is also incorrect since the Industrial Revolution's effects on global economics does not in and of itself describe any specific political tactic.

26. **(B)**   (B) is correct since the development of both the Industrial Revolution's massive factories and the atomic bomb provided new intellectual and technological advances that outstripped all other technologies of their time. Only through the introduction of these types of radically new advances could a revolution occur. (A) and (C) are wrong. Though gross atrocities and realignment of world-wide alliances are sometimes a cause or effect of a revolution, the author does not cite either as being integral to a revolution. Likewise, (D) is incorrect since a country's need for control is not in and of itself necessary for a revolution to occur. (E) is wrong. Economic interdependencies are not mentioned in the second passage as having any influence on the development of the atomic age.

27. **(E)**   By stating that very few nations have access to nuclear or atomic weapons, the similarities between the two passages are reduced. Where the Industrial Revolution spread its technology throughout the world, atomic weapons have been strictly guarded. With less widespread development, atomic weapons did not alter day-to-day living to the degree the Industrial Revolution did. Neither (A) nor (B) is correct since the shift in class structure and the accumulation of wealth do little to change the two passages' theme of trade-off inherent in the development of new technologies. (C) and (D) while true, do not lessen the similarities between the two passages. Just as the atomic age created new jobs, so too did the Industrial Revolution. Great Britain's rise to power is similar to the rise of both the U.S. and the U.S.S.R. during the dawn of the atomic age.

28. **(B)** The atomic age did cause massive political and social change in the form of a bipolar world order and the harnessing of nuclear power. (A) is wrong. Atomic technologies played little or no role in the downfall of the Soviet Union. Though (C) may be a true statement, the author never overtly states that it is true. (D) is incorrect. The author does not state that without the atomic bomb Japan would have achieved world dominance, (E) is incorrect. The author provides an argument stating that the notion of Mutual Assured Destruction (MAD) prevented a third world war.

29. **(D)** Lines 19–22 demonstrate how a confined man may enjoy imaginative freedom and dominance of the universe. Apothecaries and physicians (line 47) are not contrasted, but admired as benefactors of man, denying (E) and by extension (B), since physicians are directly compared to the Greek hero (lines 34–35).

30. **(D)** "Simples" are remedies in context, prescriptions from a drug-gist.

31. **(C)** The breadth of men and Earth are given inverse proportions in Donne's conceit (lines 2–3); (A) is a strong distractor only if the reader superimposes "microcosmic" onto the image of man where Donne has not. World and map are inverted (line 5), not geography and map, choice (B). Both (D) and (E) are incorrect based on misreading analogies.

32. **(D)** Even if the student does not know "oxymoron" as a term, he should see choice (A) as insufficient to explain the reversals Donne posits throughout the passage as an explanation of his mystical humanism. Not style, but the world is his intention. All of paragraph one is grandly positive and assertive, denying choices (B) and (C). The disposition of beasts (E) does not arise until the final paragraph (lines 39–41).

33. **(A)** Donne's metaphysical style searches for analogies and correspondences in nature.

34. **(E)** Physicians rely on nature, not the supernatural (A), pure imagination (B), or religion (D). "Books" (C) in fact never appear in the text.

35. **(D)** Ironically, the mean creatures prove more able to heal themselves than man, so we "shrink in proportion," negating (A) and (E), as well as contradicting (C) (see lines 45–46). (B) is never discussed.

36. **(C)** Death is explicit in "the thoughtlessness of the grave" (line 52). (D) is incorrect since nature provokes thought (lines 37–48). (E) is a

distractor simply because imaginings preclude a continuance of thought. (B) is never addressed as a subject.

37. **(B)**   Man nurtures his diseases, his own destruction, at home. Grammatical (and logical) scrutiny should dismiss (C) and (E) quickly; (A) and (D) are almost synonymous—and wrong.

38. **(B)**   According to line 50, man "consumes himself" and so poses no mystery for the physician, choice (D). Man's diseases are quite real, since that "other world" is the natural one, denying (E). Both (A) and (C) are distractors.

39. **(B)**   Donne's metaphysics elevate man to godlike proportions; only later does he qualify his meditation and find man inferior to the simple beasts, (D). "If these pieces were extended" (line 3) is a concession to metaphor, not a literal belief in giants, choice (E). (C) might be inferred by the Biblical or literary reader of Donne; it is not stated. (A) is not addressed in the passage.

40. **(B)**   The admonition is to "bring down" or realistically assess the level of the conceit, the meditation itself. Grammatical and logical analysis should dismiss all other choices as misreadings.

41. **(C)**   The word "quiescence" means still, peaceful. (C) is the best choice. Since movement (A) is not implied, (A) should not be chosen. Agitation (B) is not implied by the word "quiescence"; (B) should be avoided. An upheaval (D) is not implied by a word meaning quiet, calm. (D) should be avoided. "Quiescence" in no way implied intervention; (E) should not be chosen.

42. **(E)**   REMs were accompanied by sharp increases in respiration and heart rate and a low voltage, desynchronized pattern different from that of deep sleep. (E) is the best choice. REMs occurred periodically when there was a sharp increase in respiration heart rate; the EEG showed a low-voltage, desynchronized pattern different from deep sleep. When REMs occur, respiration increases; (A) could not be chosen. When REMs occur, the heart rate increase; (B) should be omitted. Both an increase in respiration and in heart rate accompany REMs, (C), therefore, should be omitted. A low-voltage (not a high-voltage) desynchronized pattern accompanies the sharp increase in respiration and heart rate with REMs; (D) is not a correct response.

43. **(A)**   It is true that all people dream every night (A); this is the

correct choice. It should be remembered, however, that not everyone remembers all these dreams. An infant's eyes move in sleep like an adults; (B) is false. Animals like cats have eye movements just as people do; (C) is false and should not be chosen. Dreams, as already established, are not rare occurrences; (D) is not a correct answer. The discovery that people dream every night was made before 1956; (E)is a poor choice.

44. **(B)**   Neurophysiology and EEG laboratory studies gave us much information about dream research. (B) is the best choice. The correct choice is not veterinary laboratories (A) with neurophysiology; (A) should not be chosen. EEG laboratories and veterinary laboratories should not be selected. (C) is not the correct choice. The age of the studies and the age of the volunteers are not necessarily the strong evidence we need; (D) is incorrect. Observers, and not just full professors, have contributed much to sleep studies; (E) should not be selected.

45. **(D)**   Volunteers were used in the study; (D) seems to be the best choice. The subjects were not coerced into participating; (A) is not the best choice. Since mammals were involved, (B) cannot be an accurate choice. Both human and animal subjects were used; (C) is not the best choice. All subjects were not chosen during the 1930s; (E)is not the best choice.

46. **(E)**   Aserinsky began his studies by studying sleeping infants. (E) seems to be the best choice. His studies were not focused on waking infants. Dement is noted for his studies on sleeping cats; (B) is not the choice to be chosen. Since Aserinsky did not study sleeping cats and infants, choice (C) should not be selected. This article does not deal with waking infants and waking cats, so (D) should not be indicated as the correct choice.

47. **(B)**   Aserinsky found that body movements were still when the eyes began making rapid jerky movements beneath the closed lids. (B) is the best choice. Body movements were not accompanied by rapid eye movements, so (A) could not be chosen. References are not made in the reading to body movements and no eye movements. (C) is not the best choice. Sporadic eye movements are not referred to in the passage, so (D) does not seem to be the best choice. Body stillness seems to be accompanied by eye movements; (E) should not be the choice.

48. **(E)**   The writer has deliberately given us a beginning study of dream study since 1952. (E) is the best choice. The article does not bring us all the way through 1992 so choice (A) cannot be correct. People did

actually think of dreams before 1952, but no scientific studies were done in great detail; (B) is not the best choice. The article does not focus just on animals (people, too, were studied). (C) is not the best choice. The article does not really research dream research before 1952; (D) should not be selected.

49. **(C)**   In this context, "germinal" is most nearly defined as "early." The context clue is "from which much of modern sleep research has burgeoned." There is nothing to indicate the author feels the studies were "definitive" (A) or "exhaustive" (B). Although "germinal" suggests "contaminated" (D), it is not correct in this context. "Refuted" (E) is incorrect because nowhere in the passage is it suggested that the studies are invalid.

50. **(D)**   It is stated in the passage that it took the work of a selected few in order for studying sleep to be accepted by the scientific community. These select few are discussed by the author and he tells of the large amount of research they had to do in order to prove their beliefs. (A) is incorrect because the passage states the study of sleep caught on slowly and was really only performed by one or two researchers at first. (B) is not correct because it took several researchers to make advancements in order to prove sleep study was important to understand people and dreams. (C) is false, because we are told early research was done on infants and people. The second paragraph states that dream study was first done by one or two men, not a group (E).

ATTACKING CRITICAL READING QUESTIONS REVIEW

ABOUT CRITICAL READING PASSAGES

Not all standardized tests have critical reading sections, however, when they do they are indeed critical. For tests like the SAT, the critical reading section counts for 50 percent of the entire verbal section content and 75 percent of its allotted time. In all, you can expect to encounter as many as 40 critical reading questions. "Why," you must wonder, "would this much importance be attached to reading?" The reason is simple. Your ability to read at a strong pace while grasping solid understanding of the material is a key factor in your high school and college performance. But "critical" can be taken in another sense, for some critical reading sections will also ask you to be a reading critic. Not only will you need to be able to summarize the material you read, but also analyze it, make judgements about it, and make educated guesses about what the writer implies and what you can infer from the writing. Even your ability to understand vocabulary in context will come under scrutiny. The only way to master all of these skills is preparation, and this review is your key to that preparation.

Within a given critical reading section you will be given a series of reading passages of various lengths, and in some tests a set of double passages. These double passages will be composed of two separate works which you will be asked to compare and contrast. Usually these reading passages, both regular and double passages, will cover:

- the humanities (philosophy, the fine arts)

- the social sciences (psychology, archaeology, anthropology, economics, political science, sociology, history)

- the natural sciences (biology, geology, astronomy, chemistry, physics)

- narration (fiction, nonfiction)

Following each passage are about 5–13 questions, depending on the length of the passage. These questions are of four types:

1. Synthesis/Analysis

2. Evaluation

3. Vocabulary-in-context

4. Interpretation

Through this review, you'll learn not only how to identify these types of questions, but how to successfully attack each one. Familiarity with the test format, combined with solid reading strategies, will prove invaluable in answering the questions quickly and accurately.

ABOUT THE DIRECTIONS

Make sure to study and learn the directions to save yourself time during the actual test. You should, however, skim them when beginning the section. The directions will read similar to the following.

DIRECTIONS: Read each passage and answer the questions that follow. Each question will be based on the information stated or implied in the passage or its introduction.

A variation of these directions may be presented as follows for the double passage.

DIRECTIONS: Read the passages and answer the questions that follow. Each question will be based on the information stated or implied in the selections or their introductions and may be based on the relationship between the passages.

ABOUT THE PASSAGES

You may encounter any of a number of passage types in the critical reading sections. These passages may consist of straight text, dialogue and text, or narration. A passage may appear by itself or as part of a pair in a double passage. A brief introduction will be provided for each passage to set the scene for the text being presented.

To familiarize yourself with the types of passages you will encounter, review the examples which follow.

The content of the passages will include the humanities, social sciences, natural sciences, and also narrative text.

A **humanities passage** may discuss such topics as philosophy, the fine arts, and language. The following is an example of such a passage.

Throughout his pursuit of knowledge and enlightenment, the philosopher Socrates made many enemies among the Greek citizens. The following passage is an account of the trial resulting from their accusations.

The great philosopher Socrates was put on trial in Athens in 400 B.C. on charges of corrupting the youth and of impiety. As recorded in Plato's dialogue *The Apology,* Socrates began his defense by saying he was going to "speak plainly and honestly," unlike the eloquent sophists the Athenian jury was accustomed to hearing. His appeal to unadorned language offended the jurors, who were expecting to be entertained.

Socrates identified the two sets of accusers that he had to face: the past and the present. The former had filled the jurors' heads with lies about him when they were young and was considered by Socrates to be the most dangerous. The accusers from the past could not be cross-examined, and they had already influenced the jurors when they were both naive and impressionable. This offended the jury because it called into question their ability to be objective and render a fair judgment.

The philosopher addressed the charges himself and dismissed them as mere covers for the deeper attack on his philosophical activity. That activity, which involved questioning others until they revealed contradictions in their beliefs, had given rise to Socrates' motto, "The unexamined life is not worth living," and the "Socratic Method," which is still employed in many law schools today. This critical questioning of leading Athenians had made Socrates very unpopular with those in power and, he insisted, was what led to his trial. This challenge to the legitimacy of the legal system itself further alienated his judges.

Socrates tried to explain that his philosophical life came about by accident. He had been content to be a humble stone mason until the day that a friend informed him that the Oracle of Delphi had said that "Socrates is the wisest man in Greece." Socrates had been so surprised by this statement, and so sure of its inaccuracy, that he set about disproving it by talking to the reputed wise men of Athens and showing how much more knowledge they possessed. Unfortunately, as he told the jury, those citizens reputed to be wise (politicians, businessmen, artists) turned out to be ignorant, either by knowing absolutely nothing, or by having limited knowledge in their fields of expertise and assuming knowledge of everything else. Of these, Socrates had to admit, "I am wiser, because although all of us have little knowledge, I am aware of my ignorance, while they are not." But this practice of revealing prominent citizens' ignorance and arrogance did not earn Socrates their affection, especially when the bright young men of Athens began following him around and delighting in the disgracing of their elders. Hence, in his view, the formal charges of "corrupting the youth" and "impiety" were a pretext to retaliate for the deeper offense of challenging the pretensions of the establishment.

Although Socrates viewed the whole trial as a sham, he cleverly refuted the charges by using the same method of questioning that got him in trouble in the first place. Against the charges of corrupting the youth, Socrates asked his chief accuser, Meletus, if any wanted to arm himself, to which Meletus answered, "no." Then, Socrates asked if one's associates had an effect on one: Good people for good, and evil people for evil, to which Meletus answered, "yes." Next, Socrates asked if corrupting one's companions makes them better or worse, to which Meletus responded, "worse." Finally Socrates set the trap by asking Meletus if Socrates had corrupted the youth intentionally or unintentionally. Meletus, wanting to make the charges as bad as possible, answered, "intentionally." Socrates showed the contradictory nature of the charge, since by intentionally corrupting his companions he made them worse, thereby bringing harm on himself. He also refuted the second charge of impiety in the same manner, by showing that its two components (teaching about strange gods and atheism) were inconsistent.

Although Socrates had logically refuted the charges against him, the Athenian jury found him guilty, and Meletus proposed the death penalty. The defendant, Socrates, was allowed to propose an alternative penalty and Socrates proposed a state pension, so he could continue his philosophical activity to the benefit of Athens. He stated that this is what he deserved. The Athenian jury, furious over his presumption, voted the death penalty and, thus, one of the great philosophers of the Western heritage was executed.

The **social science** passage may discuss such topics as psychology, archaeology, anthropology, economics, political science, sociology, and history. The following is an example of such a passage.

Not only does music have the ability to entertain and enthrall, but it also has the capacity to heal. The following passage illustrates the recent indoctrination of music therapy.

Music's power to affect moods and stir emotions has been well known for as long as music has existed. Stories about the music of ancient Greece tell of the healing powers of Greek music. Leopold Mozart, the father of Wolfgang, wrote that if the Greeks' music could heal the sick, then our music should be able to bring the dead back to life. Unfortunately, today's music cannot do quite that much.

The healing power of music, taken for granted by ancient man and by many primitive societies, is only recently becoming accepted by medical professionals as a new way of healing the emotionally ill.

Using musical activities involving patients, the music therapist seeks to restore mental and physical health. Music therapists usually work with emotionally disturbed patients as part of a team of therapists and doctors. Music therapists work together with physicians, psychiatrists, psychologists, physical therapists, nurses, teachers, recreation leaders, and families of patients.

The rehabilitation that a music therapist gives to patients can be in the form of listening, performing, lessons on an instrument, or even composing. A therapist may help a patient regain lost coordination by teaching the patient how to play an instrument. Speech defects can sometimes be helped by singing activities. Some patients need the social awareness of group activities, but others may need individual attention to build self-confidence. The music therapist must learn what kinds of activities are best for each patient.

In addition to working with patients, the music therapist has to attend meetings with other therapists and doctors that work with the same patients to discuss progress and plan new activities. Written reports to doctors about patients' responses to treatment are another facet of the music therapist's work.

Hospitals, schools, retirement homes, and community agencies and clinics are some of the sites where music therapists work. Some music therapists work in private studies with patients that are sent to them by medical doctors, psychologists, and psychiatrists. Music therapy can be done in studios, recreation rooms, hospital wards, or classrooms depending on the type of activity and needs of the patients.

Qualified music therapists have followed a four-year course with a major emphasis in music plus courses in biological science, anthropology, sociology, psychology, and music therapy. General studies in English, history, speech, and government complete the requirements for a Bachelor of Music Therapy. After college training, a music therapist must participate in a six-month training internship under the guidance of a registered music therapist.

Students who have completed college courses and have demonstrated their ability during the six-month internship can become registered music therapists by applying to the National Association for Music Therapy, Inc. New methods and techniques of music therapy are always being developed, so the trained therapist must continue to study new articles, books, and reports throughout his/her career.

The **natural science passage** may discuss such topics as biology, geology, astronomy, chemistry, and physics. The following is an example of such a passage.

The following article was written by a physical chemist and recounts the conflict between volcanic matter in the atmosphere and airplane windows. It was published in a scientific periodical in 1989.

Several years ago the airlines discovered a new kind of problem—a window problem. The acrylic windows on some of their 747s were getting hazy and dirty-looking. Suspicious travelers thought the airlines might have stopped cleaning them, but the windows were not dirty; they were inexplicably deteriorating within as little as 390 hours of flight time, even though they were supposed to last for five to ten years. Boeing looked into it.

At first the company thought the culprit might be one well known in modern technology, the component supplier who changes materials without telling the customer. Boeing quickly learned this was not the case, so there followed an extensive investigation that eventually brought in the Air Transport Association, geologists, and specialists in upper-atmosphere chemistry, and the explanation turned out to be not nearly so mundane. Indeed, it began to look like a grand reenactment of an ancient Aztec myth: the struggle between the eagle and the serpent, which is depicted on the Mexican flag.

The serpent in this case is an angry Mexican volcano, El Chichon. Like its reptilian counterpart, it knows how to spit venom at the eyes of its adversary. In March and April of 1982 the volcano, in an unusual eruption pattern, ejected millions of tons of sulfur-rich material directly into the stratosphere. In less than a year, a stratospheric cloud had blanketed the entire Northern Hemisphere. Soon the photochemistry of the upper atmosphere converted much of the sulfur into tiny droplets of concentrated sulfuric acid.

The eagle in the story is the 747, poking occasionally into the lower part of the stratosphere in hundreds of passenger flights daily. Its two hundred windows are made from an acrylic polymer, which makes beautifully clear, strong windows but was never intended to withstand attack by strong acids.

The stratosphere is very different from our familiar troposphere environment. Down here the air is humid, with a lot of vertical convection to carry things up and down; the stratosphere is bone-dry, home to the continent-striding jet stream, with unceasing horizontal winds at an average of 120 miles per hour. A mist of acid droplets, accumulating gradually near the lower edge of the stratosphere and settling there at a thickness of about a mile a year, was able to wait for planes to come along.

As for sulfuric acid, most people know only the relatively benign liquid in a car battery: 80 percent water and 20 percent acid. The stratosphere dehydrated the sulfuric acid into a persistent, corrosive mist 75 percent pure acid, an extremely aggressive liquid. Every time the 747 poked into the stratosphere—on almost every long flight—acid droplets struck the windows and began to react with their outer surface, causing it to swell. This built up stresses between the softened outer layer and the underlying material. Finally, parallel hairline cracks developed, creating the hazy appearance. The hazing was sped up by the mechanical stresses always present in the windows of a pressurized cabin.

The airlines suffered through more than a year of window replacements before the acid cloud finally dissipated. Ultimately the drops reached the lower edge of the stratosphere, were carried away into the lower atmosphere, and finally came down in the rain. In the meantime, more resistant window materials and coatings were developed. (As for the man-made sulfur dioxide that causes acid rain, it never gets concentrated enough to attack the window material. El Chichon was unusual in its ejection of sulfur directly into the stratosphere, and the 747 is unusual in its frequent entrance into the stratosphere.)

As for the designers of those windows, it is hard to avoid the conclusion that a perfectly adequate engineering design was defeated by bad luck. After all, this was the only time since the invention of the airplane that there were acid droplets of this concentration in the upper atmosphere. But reliability engineers, an eminently rational breed, are very uncomfortable when asked to talk about luck. In principle it should be possible to anticipate events, and the failure to do so somehow seems like a professional failure. The cosmos of the engineer has no room for poltergeists, demons, or other mystic elements. But might it accommodate the inexorable scenario of an ancient Aztec myth?

A **narrative passage dealing with fictional material** may be in the form of dialogue between characters, or one character speaking to the reader. The following is an example of the latter.

In this passage, the narrator discovers that he has been transported to King Arthur's court in the year 528 A.D.

The moment I got a chance I slipped aside privately and touched an ancient common-looking man on the shoulder and said, in an insinuating, confidential way—

"Friend, do me a kindness. Do you belong to the asylum, or are you just here on a visit or something like that?"

He looked me over stupidly, and said—

"Marry, fair sir, me seemeth—"

"That will do," I said; "I reckon you are a patient."

I moved away, cogitating, and at the same time keeping an eye out for any chance passenger in his right mind that might come along and give me some light. I judged I had found one, presently; so I drew him aside and said in his ear—

"If I could see the head keeper a minute—only just a minute—"

"Prithee do not let me."

"Let you *what?*"

"*Hinder* me, then, if the word please thee better." Then he went on to say he was an under-cook and could not stop to gossip, though he would like it another time; for it would comfort his very liver to know where I got my clothes. As he started away he pointed and said yonder was one who was idle enough for my purpose, and was seeking me besides, no doubt. This was an airy slim boy in shrimp-colored tights that made him look like a forked carrot; the rest of his gear was blue silk and dainty laces and ruffles; and he had long yellow curls, and wore a plumed pink satin cap tilted complacently over his ear. By his look, he was good-natured; by his gait, he was satisfied with himself. He was pretty enough to frame. He arrived, looked me over with a smiling and impudent curiosity; said he had come for me, and informed me that he was a page.

"Go 'long," I said; "you ain't more than a paragraph."

It was pretty severe, but I was nettled. However, it never phazed him; he didn't appear to know he was hurt. He began to talk and laugh, in happy, thoughtless, boyish fashion, as we walked along, and made himself old friends with me at once; asked me all sorts of questions about myself and about my clothes, but never waited for an answer—always chattered straight ahead, as if he didn't know he had asked a question and wasn't expecting any reply, until at last he happened to mention that he was born in the beginning of the year 513.

It made the cold chills creep over me! I stopped, and said, a little faintly:

"Maybe I didn't hear you just right. Say it again—and say it slow. What year was it?"

"513."

"513! You don't look it! Come, my boy, I am a stranger and friend-less: be honest and honorable with me. Are you in your right mind?"

He said he was.

"Are these other people in their right minds?"

He said they were.

"And this isn't an asylum? I mean, it isn't a place where they cure crazy people?"

He said it wasn't.

"Well, then," I said, "either I am a lunatic, or something just as awful has happened. Now tell me, honest and true, where am I?"

"In King Arthur's Court."

I waited a minute, to let that idea shudder its way home, and then said:

"And according to your notions, what year is it now?"

"528—nineteenth of June."

I felt a mournful sinking at the heart, and muttered: "I shall never see my friends again—never, never again. They will not be born for more than thirteen hundred years yet."

I seemed to believe the boy, I didn't know why. *Something* in me seemed to believe him—my consciousness, as you may say; but my reason didn't. My reason straightway began to clamor; that was natural. I didn't know how to go about satisfying it, because I knew that the testimony of men wouldn't serve— my reason would say they were lunatics, and throw out their evidence. But all of a sudden I stumbled on the very thing, just by luck. I knew that the only total eclipse of the sun in the first half of the sixth century occurred on the 21st of June, A. D. 528, o. s., and began at 3 minutes after 12 noon. I also knew that no total eclipse of the sun was due in what to *me* was the present year—*i.e.*, 1879. So, if I could keep my anxiety and curiosity from eating the heart out of me for forty-eight hours, I should then find out for certain whether this boy was telling me the truth or not.

A **narrative passage** dealing with nonfiction material may appear in the form of a speech or any such discourse in which one person speaks to a group of people or to the reader. The following two selections are examples of nonfiction narratives. Together, they are also an example of a double passage, in which the subject matter in the selections can be either compared or contrasted.

The following passages are excerpts from two different Presidential Inaugural Addresses. Passage 1 was given by President Franklin D. Roosevelt on March 4, 1933. Passage 2 comes from President John F. Kennedy's Inaugural Address, given on January 20, 1961.

Passage 1

Let every nation know, whether it wishes us well or ill, that we shall pay any price, bear any burden, meet any hardship, support any friend, oppose any foe to assure the survival and the success of liberty.

This much we pledge—and more.

To those old allies whose cultural and spiritual origins we share, we pledge the loyalty of faithful friends. United, there is little we cannot do in a host of co-operative ventures. Divided, there is little we can do, for we dare not meet a powerful challenge at odds and split asunder.

To those new states whom we welcome to the ranks of the free, we pledge our word that one form of colonial control shall not have passed away merely to be replaced by a far more iron tyranny. We shall not always expect to find them supporting our view. But we shall always hope to find them strongly supporting their own freedom, and to remember that, in the past, those who foolishly sought power by riding the back of the tiger ended up inside.

To those peoples in the huts and villages of half the globe struggling to break the bonds of mass misery, we pledge our best efforts to help them help themselves, for whatever period is required, not because the Communists may be doing it, not because we seek their votes, but because it is right. If a free society cannot help the many who are poor, it cannot save the few who are rich.

Passage 2

This is pre-eminently the time to speak the truth, the whole truth, frankly and boldly. Nor need we shrink from honestly facing conditions in our country today. This great nation will endure as it has endured, will revive, and will prosper.

So first of all let me assert my firm belief that the only thing we have to fear is fear itself—nameless, unreasoning, unjustified terror, which paralyzes needed efforts to convert retreat into advance.

In every dark hour of our national life, a leadership of frankness and vigor has met with that understanding and support of the people themselves, which is essential to victory. I am convinced that you will again give that support to leadership in these critical days.

In such a spirit on my part and yours we face our common difficulties. They concern, thank God, only material things. Values have shrunken to fantastic levels; taxes have risen; our ability to pay has fallen; government of all kinds is faced by serious curtailment of income; the means of exchange are frozen in the currents of trade; the withered leaves of industrial enterprise lie on every side; farmers find no markets for their produce; the savings of many years in thousands of families are gone.

More important, a host of unemployed citizens face the grim problem of existence, and an equally great number toil with little return. Only a foolish optimist can deny the dark realities of the moment.

Yet our distress comes from no failure of substance. We are stricken by no plague of locusts. Compared with the perils which our forefathers conquered because they believed and were not afraid, we have still much to be thankful for. Nature still offers her bounty, and human efforts have multiplied it. Plenty is at our doorstep, but a generous use of it languishes in the very sight of the supply.

Primarily, this is because the rulers of the exchange of mankind's goods have failed through their own stubbornness and their own incompetence, have admitted their failure and abdicated. Practices of the unscrupulous money-changers stand indicted in the court of public opinion, rejected by the hearts and minds of men.

ABOUT THE QUESTIONS

As previously mentioned, there may be four major question types which appear in the critical reading section. The following explains what these questions will cover.

Question Type 1: Synthesis/Analysis

Synthesis/analysis questions deal with the structure of the passage and how one part relates to another part or to the text as a whole. These questions may ask you to look at passage details and from them, point out general themes or concepts. They might ask you to trace problems, causes, effects, and solutions or to understand the points of an argument or persuasive passage. They might ask you to compare or contrast different aspects of the passage. *Synthesis/analysis* questions may also involve inferences, asking you to decide what the details of the passage imply about the author's general tone or attitude. Key terms in *synthesis/analysis* questions are example, difference, general, compare, contrast, cause, effect, and result.

Question Type 2: Evaluation

Evaluation questions involve judgments about the worth of the essay as a whole. You may be asked to consider concepts the author assumes rather than factually proves and to judge whether or not the author presents a logically consistent case. Does he/she prove the points through generalization, citing an authority, use of example, implication, personal experience, or factual data? You'll need to be able to distinguish the supportive bases for the argumentative theme. Almost as a book reviewer, you'll also be asked to pinpoint the author's writing techniques. What is the style, the tone? Who is the intended audience? How might the author's points relate to information outside the essay itself? Key terms you'll often see in *evaluation* questions and answer choices are generalization, implication, and support.

Question Type 3: Vocabulary-in-Context

Vocabulary-in-context questions occur in several formats. You'll be given easy words with challenging choices or the reverse. You'll need to know multiple meanings of words. You'll encounter difficult words and difficult choices. In some cases, your knowledge of prefixes-roots-suffixes will gain you clear advantage. In addition, connotations will be the means of deciding, in some cases, which answer is the best. Of course, how the term works in the textual context is the key to the issue.

Question Type 4: Interpretation

Interpretation questions ask you to decide on a valid explanation or clarification of the author's points. Based on the text, you'll be asked to distinguish probable motivations and effects or actions not stated outright in the essay. Furthermore, you'll need to be familiar with cliches, euphemisms, catch phrases, colloquialisms, metaphors, and similes, and be able to explain them in straightforward language. *Interpretation* question stems usually have a word or phrase enclosed in quotation marks.

Keep in mind that being able to categorize accurately is not of prime importance. What is important, however, is that you are familiar with all the types of information you will be asked and that you have a set of basic strategies to use when answering questions. The remainder of this review will give you these skills.

Points to Remember

- Do not spend too much time answering any one question.

- Vocabulary plays a large part in successful critical reading. As a long-term approach to improving your ability and therefore your test scores, read as much as you can of any type of material. Your speed, comprehension, and vocabulary will grow.

- Be an engaged reader. Don't let your mind wander. Focus through annotation and key terms.

- Time is an important factor. Therefore, the rate at which you are reading is very important. If you are concerned that you may be reading too slow, try to compete with yourself. For example, if you are reading at 120 words per minute, try to improve your speed to 250 words per minute (without decreasing your understanding). Remember that improving reading speed is not a means in itself. Improved comprehension with fewer regressions must accompany this speed increase. Make sure to read, read, read. The more you read, the more you will sharpen your skills.

ANSWERING CRITICAL READING QUESTIONS

You should follow these steps as you begin each critical reading passage. They will act as a guide when answering the questions.

STEP 1 | Before you address the critical reading, answer all analogies and sentence completions within the given verbal section. You can answer more questions per minute in these short sections than in the reading, and since all answers are credited equally, you'll get the most for your time here.

Now, find the critical reading passage(s). If more than one passage appears, give each a brief overview. Attack the easiest and most interesting passages first. Critical reading passages are not automatically presented in the order of least-to-most difficult. The difficulty or ease of a reading selection is an individual matter, determined by the reader's own specific interests and past experience, so what you might consider easy, someone else might consider hard, and *vice-versa*. Again, time is an issue, so you need to begin with something you can quickly understand in order to get to the questions, where the pay-off lies.

STEP 2   First, read the question stems (the part of the question that "asks" the question, not the answer choices) following the passage, making sure to block out the answer choices with your free hand. (You don't want to be misled by incorrect choices.)

In question stems, underline key words, phrases, and dates. For example:

1. In line 27, "*stand*" means:

2. From *1776 to 1812 King George* did:

3. *Lincoln* was *similar* to *Pericles* in that:

The act of underlining takes little time and will force you to focus first on the main ideas in the questions, then in the essays.

You will notice that questions often note a line number for reference. Place a small mark by the appropriate lines in the essay itself to remind yourself to read those parts very carefully. You'll still have to refer to these lines upon answering the questions, but you'll be able to find them quickly.

STEP 3   If the passage is not divided into paragraphs, read the first 10 lines. If the passage is divided into manageable paragraphs, read the first paragraph. Make sure to read at a moderate pace, as fast skimming will not be sufficient for comprehension, while slow, forced reading will take too much time and yield too little understanding of the overall passage.

In the margin of your test booklet, using two or three words, note the main point of the paragraph/section. Don't labor long over the exact wording. Underline key terms, phrases, or ideas when you notice them. If a sentence is particularly difficult, don't spend too much time trying to figure it out. Bracket it, though, for easy reference in the remote instance that it might serve as the basis for a question.

You should proceed through each paragraph/section in a similar manner. Don't read the whole passage with the intention of going back and filling in the main points. Read carefully and consistently, annotating and underlining to keep your mind on the context.

Upon finishing the entire passage, quickly review your notes in the margin. They should give you main ideas and passage structure (chronological, cause and effect, process, comparison-contrast). Ask yourself what the author's attitude is toward his/her subject. What might you infer from the selection? What might the author say next? Some of these questions may appear, and you'll be immediately prepared to answer.

> **STEP 4** Start with the first question and work through to the last question. The order in which the questions are presented follows the order of the passage, so going for the "easy" questions first rather than answering the questions consecutively will cost you valuable time in searching and backtracking.

Be sure to block the answer choices for each question before you read the question, itself. Again, you don't want to be misled.

If a line number is mentioned, quickly re-read that section. In addition, circle your own answer to the question *before* viewing the choices. Then, carefully examine each answer choice, eliminating those which are obviously incorrect. If you find a close match to your own answer, don't assume that it is the best answer, as an even better one may be among the last choices. Remember, only one answer is correct, and it is the *best* one, not simply one that will work.

Once you've proceeded through all the choices, eliminating incorrect answers as you go, choose from among those remaining. If the choice is not clear, reread the question stem and the referenced passage lines to seek tone or content you might have missed. If the answer now is not readily obvious and you have reduced your choices by eliminating at least one, then simply choose one of the remaining and proceed to the next question. Place a small mark in your test booklet to remind you, should you have time at the end of this test section, to review the question and seek a more accurate answer.

Now, let's go back to our natural sciences passage. Read the passage, and then answer the questions which follow using the skills gained through this review.

The following article was written by a physical chemist and recounts the conflict between volcanic matter in the atmosphere and airplane windows. It was published in a scientific periodical in 1989.

1   Several years ago the airlines discovered a new kind of problem—a window problem. The acrylic windows on some of their 747s were getting hazy and dirty-looking. Suspicious travelers thought the airlines might have stopped cleaning them, but the windows were not dirty; they were
5   inexplicably deteriorating within as little as 390 hours of flight time, even though they were supposed to last for five to ten years. Boeing looked into it.

At first the company thought the culprit might be one well known in modern technology, the component supplier who changes materials with-
10   out telling the customer. Boeing quickly learned this was not the case, so there followed an extensive investigation that eventually brought in the Air Transport Association, geologists, and specialists in upper-atmosphere chemistry, and the explanation turned out to be not nearly so mundane. Indeed, it began to look like a grand reenactment of an ancient Aztec
15   myth: the struggle between the eagle and the serpent, which is depicted on the Mexican flag.

The serpent in this case is an angry Mexican volcano, El Chichon. Like its reptilian counterpart, it knows how to spit venom at the eyes of its adversary. In March and April of 1982 the volcano, in an unusual eruption
20   pattern, ejected millions of tons of sulfur-rich material directly into the stratosphere. In less than a year, a stratospheric cloud had blanketed the entire Northern Hemisphere. Soon the photochemistry of the upper atmosphere converted much of the sulfur into tiny droplets of concentrated sulfuric acid.

25   The eagle in the story is the 747, poking occasionally into the lower part of the stratosphere in hundreds of passenger flights daily. Its two hundred windows are made from an acrylic polymer, which makes beautifully clear, strong windows but was never intended to withstand attack by strong acids.

30   The stratosphere is very different from our familiar troposphere environment. Down here the air is humid, with a lot of vertical convection to carry things up and down; the stratosphere is bone-dry, home to the continent-striding jet stream, with unceasing horizontal winds at an average of 120 miles per hour. A mist of acid droplets accumulated gradually
35   near the lower edge of the stratosphere, settling there at a thickness of about a mile a year, was able to wait for planes to come along.

As for sulfuric acid, most people know only the relatively benign liquid in a car battery: 80 percent water and 20 percent acid. The strato-sphere dehydrated the sulfuric acid into a persistent, corrosive mist 75
40 percent pure acid, an extremely aggressive liquid. Every time the 747 poked into the stratosphere—on almost every long flight—acid droplets struck the windows and began to react with their outer surface, causing it to swell. This built up stresses between the softened outer layer and the underlying material. Finally, parallel hairline cracks developed, creating
45 the hazy appearance. The hazing was sped up by the mechanical stresses always present in the windows of a pressurized cabin.

The airlines suffered through more than a year of window replace-ments before the acid cloud finally dissipated. Ultimately the drops reached the lower edge of the stratosphere, were carried away into the lower atmo-
50 sphere, and finally came down in the rain. In the meantime, more resistant window materials and coatings were developed. (As for the man-made sulfur dioxide that causes acid rain, it never gets concentrated enough to attack the window material. El Chichon was unusual in its ejection of sulfur directly into the stratosphere, and the 747 is unusual in its frequent
55 entrance into the stratosphere.)

As for the designers of those windows, it is hard to avoid the conclu-sion that a perfectly adequate engineering design was defeated by bad luck. After all, this was the only time since the invention of the airplane that there were acid droplets of this concentration in the upper atmosphere.
60 But reliability engineers, an eminently rational breed, are very uncomfort-able when asked to talk about luck. In principle it should be possible to anticipate events, and the failure to do so somehow seems like a profes-sional failure. The cosmos of the engineer has no room for poltergeists, demons, or other mystic elements. But might it accommodate the inexo-
65 rable scenario of an ancient Aztec myth?

1. Initially the hazy windows were thought by the company to be a result of

    (A) small particles of volcanic glass abrading their surfaces.

    (B) substandard window material substituted by the parts supplier.

    (C) ineffectual cleaning products used by the maintenance crew.

    (D) a build-up of the man-made sulfur dioxide that also causes acid rain.

    (E) the humidity.

2. When first seeking a reason for the abraded windows, both the passengers and Boeing management exhibited attitudes of

    (A) disbelief.   (D) pacifism.

    (B) optimism.   (E) disregard.

    (C) cynicism.

3. In line 13, "mundane" means

    (A) simple.   (D) ordinary.

    (B) complicated.   (E) important.

    (C) far-reaching.

4. In what ways is El Chichon like the serpent on the Mexican flag, knowing how to "spit venom at the eyes of its adversary" (lines 18–19)?

    (A) It seeks to poison its adversary with its bite.

    (B) It carefully plans its attack on an awaited intruder.

    (C) It ejects tons of destructive sulfuric acid to damage jet windows.

    (D) It angrily blankets the Northern Hemisphere with sulfuric acid.

    (E) It protects itself with the acid rain it produces.

5. The term "photochemistry" in line 22 refers to a chemical change caused by

    (A) the proximity of the sun.

    (B) the drop in temperature at stratospheric altitudes.

    (C) the jet stream's "unceasing horizontal winds."

    (D) the vertical convection of the troposphere.

    (E) the amount of sulfur present in the atmosphere.

6. Unlike the troposphere, the stratosphere

    (A) is extremely humid as it is home to the jet stream.

    (B) contains primarily vertical convections to cause air particles to rise and fall rapidly.

    (C) is approximately one mile thick.

(D) contains powerful horizontal winds resulting in an excessively dry atmosphere.

(E) contains very little wind activity.

7. In line 40, "aggressive" means

(A) exasperating.

(B) enterprising.

(C) prone to attack.

(D) assertive.

(E) surprising.

8. As the eagle triumphed over the serpent in the Mexican flag,

(A) El Chichon triumphed over the plane as the 747s had to change their flight altitudes.

(B) the newly designed window material deflected the damaging acid droplets.

(C) the 747 was able to fly unchallenged by acid droplets a year later as they drifted away to the lower atmosphere.

(D) the reliability engineers are now prepared for any run of "bad luck" which may approach their aircraft.

(E) the component supplier of the windows changed materials without telling the customers.

9. The reliability engineers are typified as people who

(A) are uncomfortable considering natural disasters.

(B) believe that all events are predictable through scientific methodology.

(C) accept luck as an inevitable and unpredictable part of life.

(D) easily accept their failure to predict and protect against nature's surprises.

(E) are extremely irrational and are comfortable speaking about luck.

The questions following the passage which you just read are typical of those in the Critical Reading section. After carefully reading the passage, you can begin to answer these questions. Let's look again at the questions.

1.   Initially the hazy windows were thought by the company to be a result of

(A) small particles of volcanic glass abrading their surfaces.

(B) substandard window material substituted by the parts supplier.

(C) ineffectual cleaning products used by the maintenance crew.

(D) a build-up of the man-made sulfur dioxide that also causes acid rain.

(E) the humidity.

As you read the question stem, blocking the answer choices, you'll note the key term "result" which should alert you to the question category *synthesis/analysis*. Argument structure is the focus here. Ask yourself what part of the argument is being questioned: cause, problem, result, or solution. Careful reading of the stem and perhaps mental rewording to "_____caused hazy windows" reveals cause is the issue. Once you're clear on the stem, proceed to the choices.

The word "initially" clues you in to the fact that the correct choice should be the first cause considered. Choice (B) is the correct response, as "substandard window material" was the *company's* first (initial) culprit, as explained in the first sentence of the second paragraph. They had no hint of (A) a volcanic eruption's ability to cause such damage. In addition, they were not concerned, as were the *passengers,* that (C) the windows were not properly cleaned. (D) is not correct since scientists had yet to consider testing the atmosphere. Along the same lines, choice (E) is incorrect.

2.   When first seeking a reason for the abraded windows, both the passengers and Boeing management exhibited attitudes of

(A) disbelief.   (D) pacifism.

(B) optimism.   (E) disregard.

(C) cynicism.

As you read the stem before viewing the choices, you'll know you're being asked to judge or *evaluate* the tone of a passage. The tone is not stated outright, so you'll need to rely on your perception as you re-read that section, if necessary. Remember, questions follow the order of the passage, so you know to look after the initial company reaction to the windows, but not far after, as many more questions are to follow. Now, formulate your own word for the attitude of the passengers and employees. "Skepticism" or "criticism" work well. If you can't come up with a term, at least note if the tone is negative or positive. In this case, negative is clearly indicated as the passengers are distrustful of the maintenance crew and the company mistrusts the window supplier. Proceed to each choice, seeking the closest match to your term and/or eliminating words with positive connotations.

Choice (C) is correct because "cynicism" best describes the skepticism and distrust with which the passengers view the cleaning company and the parts suppliers. Choice (A) is not correct because both Boeing and the passengers believed the windows were hazy, they just didn't know why. Choice (B) is not correct because people were somewhat agitated that the windows were hazy—certainly not "optimistic." Choice (D), "pacifism," has a rather positive connotation, which the tone of the section does not. Choice (E) is incorrect because the people involved took notice of the situation and did not disregard it. In addition to the ability to discern tone, of course, your vocabulary knowledge is being tested. "Cynicism," should you be unsure of the term, can be viewed in its root, "cynic," which may trigger you to remember that it is negative, and therefore, appropriate in tone.

3. In line 13, "mundane" means

    (A) simple.   (D) ordinary.

    (B) complicated.   (E) important.

    (C) far-reaching.

This question obviously tests *vocabulary-in-context*. Your strategy here should be quickly to view line 13 to confirm usage, block answer choices while devising your own synonym for "mundane," perhaps "common," and then viewing each choice separately, looking for the closest match. Although you might not be familiar with "mundane," the choices are all relatively simple terms. Look for contextual clues in the passage if you can't define the term outright. While the "component supplies" explanation is "mundane," the Aztec myth is not. Perhaps, you could then look for an opposite of mythical; "real" or "down-to-earth" comes to mind.

Choice (D), "ordinary," fits best as it is clearly the opposite of the extraordinary Aztec myth of the serpent and the eagle, which is not as common as a supplier switching materials. Choice (A), "simple," works contextually, but not as an accurate synonym for the word "mundane"; it does not deal with "mundane's" "down-to-earth" definition. Choice (B), "complicated," is inaccurate because the parts switch is anything but complicated. Choice (C), "far-reaching," is not better as it would apply to the myth rather than the common, everyday action of switching parts. Choice (E), "important," does not work either, because the explanation was an integral part of solving the problem. Had you eliminated (B), (C), and (E) due to contextual inappropriateness, you were left with "ordinary" and "simple." A quick re-reading of the section, then, should clarify the better choice. But, if the re-reading did not clarify the better choice, your strategy would be to choose one answer, place a small mark in the booklet, and proceed to the next question. If time is left at the end of the test, you can then review your answer choice.

4.   In what ways is El Chichon like the serpent on the Mexican flag, knowing how to "spit venom at the eyes of its adversary" (lines 1819)?

   (A) It seeks to poison its adversary with its bite.

   (B) It carefully plans its attack on an awaited intruder.

   (C) It ejects tons of destructive sulfuric acid to damage jet windows.

   (D) It angrily blankets the Northern Hemisphere with sulfuric acid.

   (E) It protects itself with the acid rain it produces.

As you view the question, note the word "like" indicates a comparison is being made. The quoted simile forms the comparative basis of the question, and you must *interpret* that phrase with respect to the actual process. You must carefully seek to duplicate the tenor of the terms, coming close to the spitting action in which a harmful substance is expelled in the direction of an object similar to the eyes of an opponent. Look for key words when comparing images. "Spit," "venom," "eyes," and "adversary" are these keys.

In choice (C), the verb that is most similar to the serpent's "spitting" venom is the sulfuric acid "ejected" from the Mexican volcano, El Chichon. Also, the jet windows most closely resemble the "eyes of the adversary" that are struck by El Chichon. Being a volcano, El Chichon is certainly incapable of injecting poison into an adversary, as in choice (A), or planning an attack on an intruder, as in choice (B). In choice (D), although the volcano does indeed "blanket the Northern Hemisphere" with sulfuric acid, this image does not coincide with the "spitting" image of the serpent. Finally, in choice (E), although a volcano can indirectly cause acid rain, it cannot produce acid rain on its own and then spew it out into the atmosphere.

5. The term "photochemistry" in line 22 refers to a chemical change caused by

    (A) the proximity of the sun.

    (B) the drop in temperature at stratospheric altitudes.

    (C) the jet stream's "unceasing horizontal winds."

    (D) the vertical convection of the troposphere.

    (E) the amount of sulfur present in the atmosphere.

Even if you are unfamiliar with the term "photochemistry," you probably know its root or its prefix. Clearly, this question fits in the *vocabulary-in-context* mode. Your first step may be a quick reference to line 22. If you don't know the term, context may provide you a clue. The conversion of sulfur-rich *upper* atmosphere into droplets may help. If context does not yield information, look at the term "photochemistry," itself. "Photo" has to do with light or sun, as in photosynthesis. Chemistry deals with substance composition and change. Knowing these two parts can take you a long way toward a correct answer.

Choice (A) is the correct response, as the light of the sun closely compares with the prefix "photo." Although choice (B), "the drop in temperature," might lead you to associate the droplet formation with condensation, light is not a factor here, nor is it in choice (C), "the jet stream's winds"; choice (D), "the vertical convection"; or choice (E), "the amount of sulfur present."

6. Unlike the troposphere, the stratosphere

    (A) is extremely humid as it is home to the jet stream.

    (B) contains primarily vertical convections to cause air particles to rise and fall rapidly.

    (C) is approximately one mile thick.

    (D) contains powerful horizontal winds resulting in an excessively dry atmosphere.

    (E) contains very little wind activity.

"Unlike" should immediately alert you to a *synthesis/analysis* question asking you to contrast specific parts of the text. Your margin notes should take you right to the section contrasting the atmospheres. Quickly scan it before considering the answers. Usually you won't remember this broad type of comparison from your first passage reading. Don't spend much time, though, on the scan before beginning to answer, as time is still a factor.

This question is tricky because all the answer choices contain key elements/ phrases in the passage, but again, a quick, careful scan will yield results. Answer (D) proves best as the "horizontal winds" dry the air of the stratosphere. Choices (A), (B), (C), and (E) are all characteristic of the troposphere, while only the acid droplets accumulate at the rate of one mile per year within the much larger stratosphere. As you answer such questions, remember to eliminate incorrect choices as you go; don't be misled by what seems familiar, yet isn't accurate—read all the answer choices.

7. In line 40, "aggressive" means

    (A) exasperating.   (D) assertive.

    (B) enterprising.   (E) surprising.

    (C) prone to attack.

Another *vocabulary-in-context* surfaces here; yet, this time, the word is probably familiar to you. Again, before forming a synonym, quickly refer to the line number, aware that perhaps a secondary meaning is appropriate as the term already is a familiar one. Upon reading the line, you'll note "persistent" and "corrosive," both strong terms, the latter being quite negative in its destruction. Now, form an appropriate synonym for aggressive, one that has a negative connotation. "Hostile" might come to mind. You are ready at this point to view all choices for a match.

Using your vocabulary knowledge, you can answer this question. "Hostile" most closely resembles choice (C), "prone to attack," and is therefore the correct response. Choice (A), "exasperating," or irritating, is too weak a term, while choice (B), "enterprising," and (D), "assertive," are too positive. Choice (E), "surprising," is not a synonym for "aggressive."

8. As the eagle triumphed over the serpent in the Mexican flag,

    (A) El Chichon triumphed over the plane as the 747s had to change their flight altitudes.

    (B) the newly designed window material deflected the damaging acid droplets.

    (C) the 747 was able to fly unchallenged by acid droplets a year later as they drifted away to the lower atmosphere.

(D) the reliability engineers are now prepared for any run of "bad luck" which may approach their aircraft.

(E) the component supplier of the windows changed materials without telling the customer.

This question asks you to compare the eagle's triumph over the serpent to another part of the text. "As" often signals comparative relationships, so you are forewarned of the *synthesis/analysis* question. You are also dealing again with a simile, so, of course, the question can also be categorized as *interpretation*. The eagle-serpent issue is a major theme in the text. You are being asked, as you will soon discover in the answer choices, what this general theme is. Look at the stem keys: eagle, triumphed, and serpent. Ask yourself to what each corresponds. You'll arrive at the eagle and the 747, some sort of victory, and the volcano or its sulfur. Now that you've formed that corresponding image in your own mind, you're ready to view the choices.

Choice (C) is the correct choice because we know the statement "the 747 was able to fly unchallenged..." to be true. Not only do the remaining choices fail to reflect the eagle-triumphs-over-serpent image, but choice (A) is inaccurate because the 747 did not "change its flight altitudes." In choice (B), the windows did not deflect "the damaging acid droplets." Furthermore, in choice (D), "the reliability engineers" cannot be correct because they cannot possibly predict the future, and therefore, cannot anticipate what could go wrong in the future. Finally, we know that in (E) the window materials were never changed.

9. The reliability engineers are typified as people who

   (A) are uncomfortable considering natural disasters.

   (B) believe that all events are predictable through scientific methodology.

   (C) accept luck as an inevitable and unpredictable part of life.

   (D) easily accept their failure to predict and protect against nature's surprises.

   (E) are extremely irrational and are comfortable speaking about luck.

When the question involves such terms as type, kind, example, or typified, be aware of possible *synthesis/analysis* or *interpretation* issues. Here the question deals with implications: what the author means but doesn't state outright. Types can also lead you to situations which ask you to make an unstated generalization based on specifically stated details. In fact, this question could even be categorized as *evaluation* because specific detail to generalization is a type of argument/essay structure. In any case, before viewing the answer choices, ask yourself what general traits the reliability engineers portray. You may need to check back in the text for typical characteristics. You'll find the engineers to be rational unbelievers in luck. These key characteristics will help you to make a step toward a correct answer.

Choice (B) is the correct answer because the passage specifically states that the reliability engineers "are very uncomfortable when asked to talk about luck" and believe "it should be possible to anticipate events" scientifically. The engineers might be uncomfortable, as in choice (A), but this is not a main concern in the passage. Choice (C) is obviously incorrect, because the engineers do not believe in luck at all, and choice (D) is not correct because "professional failure" is certainly unacceptable to these scientists. There is no indication in the passage that (E) the scientists are "irrational and are comfortable speaking about luck."

The following drill should be used to test what you have just learned. Read the passages and answer the questions. If you are unsure of an answer, refer back to the review for help.

Drill 1: Answering Critical Reading Questions

DIRECTIONS: Read each passage and answer the questions that follow. Each question will be based on the information stated or implied in the passage or its introduction.

In this excerpt from Dickens's Oliver Twist, *we read the early account of Oliver's birth and the beginning of his impoverished life.*

1   Although I am not disposed to maintain that the being born in a workhouse, is in itself the most fortunate and enviable circumstance that can possibly befall a human being, I do mean to say that in this particular instance, it was the best thing for Oliver Twist that could by possibility

5 have occurred. The fact is, that there was considerable difficulty in inducing Oliver to take upon himself the office of respiration,—a troublesome practice, but one which custom has rendered necessary to our easy existence; and for some time he lay gasping on a little flock mattress, rather unequally poised between this world and the next: the balance being de-

10 cidedly in favour of the latter. Now, if, during this brief period, Oliver had been surrounded by careful grandmothers, anxious aunts, experienced

nurses, and doctors of profound wisdom, he would most inevitably and indubitably have been killed in no time. There being nobody by, however, but a pauper old woman, who was rendered rather misty by an unwonted
15 allowance of beer; and a parish surgeon who did such matters by contract; Oliver and Nature fought out the point between them. The result was, that, after a few struggles, Oliver breathed, sneezed, and proceeded to advertise to the inmates of the workhouse the fact of a new burden having been imposed upon the parish, by setting up as loud a cry as could reasonably
20 have been expected from a male infant who had not been possessed of that very useful appendage, a voice, for a much longer space of time than three minutes and a quarter....

For the next eight or ten months, Oliver was the victim of a systematic course of treachery and deception. He was brought up by hand. The
25 hungry and destitute situation of the infant orphan was duly reported by the workhouse authorities to the parish authorities. The parish authorities inquired with dignity of the workhouse authorities, whether there was no female then domiciled in 'the house' who was in a situation to impart to Oliver Twist, the consolation and nourishment of which he stood in need.
30 The workhouse authorities replied with humility, that there was not. Upon this, the parish authorities magnanimously and humanely resolved, that Oliver should be 'farmed,' or, in other words, that he should be despatched to a branchworkhouse some three miles off, where twenty or thirty other juvenile offenders against the poor-laws, rolled about the floor
35 all day, without the inconvenience of too much food or too much clothing, under the parental superintendence of an elderly female, who received the culprits at and for the consideration of sevenpence-halfpenny per small head per week. Sevenpence-halfpenny's worth per week is a good round diet for a child; a great deal may be got for sevenpence-halfpenny: quite
40 enough to overload its stomach, and make it uncomfortable. The elderly female was a woman of wisdom and experience; she knew what was good for children; and she had a very accurate perception of what was good for herself. So, she appropriated the greater part of the weekly stipend to her own use, and consigned the rising parochial generation to even a shorter
45 allowance than was originally provided for them. Thereby finding in the lowest depth a deeper still; and proving herself a very great experimental philosopher.

Everybody knows the story of another experimental philosopher, who had a great theory about a horse being able to live without eating, and who
50 demonstrated it so well, that he got his own horse down to a straw a day, and would most unquestionably have rendered him a very spirited and rampacious animal on nothing at all, if he had not died, just four-and-

twenty hours before he was to have had his first comfortable bait of air. Unfortunately for the experimental philosophy of the female to whose 55 protecting care Oliver Twist was delivered over, a similar result usually attended the operation of *her* system...

It cannot be expected that this system of farming would produce any very extraordinary or luxuriant crop. Oliver Twist's ninth birthday found him a pale thin child, somewhat diminutive in stature, and decidedly small 60 in circumference. But nature or inheritance had implanted a good sturdy spirit in Oliver's breast. It had had plenty of room to expand, thanks to the spare diet of the establishment; and perhaps to this circumstance may be attributed his having any ninth birth-day at all.

1. After Oliver was born, he had an immediate problem with his

(A) heart rate.   (D) hearing.

(B) breathing.   (E) memory.

(C) vision.

2. What are the two worlds that Oliver stands "unequally poised between" in lines 8–10?

(A) Poverty and riches

(B) Infancy and childhood

(C) Childhood and adolescence

(D) Love and hatred

(E) Life and death

3. What does the author imply about "careful grandmothers, anxious aunts, experienced nurses, and doctors of profound wisdom" in lines 11–12?

(A) They can help nurse sick children back to health.

(B) They are necessary for every being's survival.

(C) They are the pride of the human race.

(D) They tend to adversely affect the early years of children.

(E) Their involvement in Oliver's birth would have had no outcome on his survival.

4.   What is the outcome of Oliver's bout with Nature?

   (A) He is unable to overcome Nature's fierceness.

   (B) He loses, but gains some dignity from his will to fight.

   (C) It initially appears that Oliver has won, but moments later he cries out in crushing defeat.

   (D) Oliver cries out with the breath of life in his lungs.

   (E) There is no way of knowing who won the struggle.

5.   What is the "systematic course of treachery and deception" that Oliver falls victim to in the early months of his life?

   (A) He is thrown out into the streets.

   (B) His inheritance is stolen by caretakers of the workhouse.

   (C) He is relocated by the uncaring authorities of the workhouse and the parish.

   (D) The records of his birth are either lost or destroyed.

   (E) He is publicly humiliated by the parish authorities.

6.   What is meant when the residents of the branch-workhouse are referred to by the phrase "juvenile offenders against the poor-laws" (line 34)?

   (A) They are children who have learned to steal early in life.

   (B) They are adolescents who work on probation.

   (C) They are infants who have no money to support them.

   (D) They are infants whose parents were law offenders.

   (E) They are adults who have continuously broken the law.

7.   What is the author's tone when he writes that the elderly caretaker "knew what was good for children" (lines 41–42)?

   (A) Sarcastic   (D) Astonished

   (B) Complimentary   (E) Outraged

   (C) Impressed

8. What does the author imply when he further writes that the elderly caretaker "had a very accurate perception of what was good for herself" (lines 42–43)?

    (A) She knew how to keep herself groomed and clean.

    (B) She knew how to revenge herself on her enemies.

    (C) She had a sense of confidence that inspired others.

    (D) She really had no idea how to take care of herself.

    (E) She knew how to selfishly benefit herself despite the cost to others.

9. Why is the elderly caretaker considered "a very great experimental philosopher" (lines 46–47)?

    (A) She was scientifically weaning the children off of food trying to create stronger humans.

    (B) She experimented with the survival of the children in her care.

    (C) She thought children were the key to a meaningful life.

    (D) She made sure that the children received adequate training in philosophy.

    (E) She often engaged in parochial and philosophical discussions.

10. In line 53, "bait" most nearly means

    (A) worms.

    (B) a hook.

    (C) a breeze.

    (D) a trap.

    (E) a meal.

11. To what does the author attribute Oliver's survival to his ninth year?

    (A) A strong, healthy diet

    (B) Money from an anonymous donor

    (C) Sheer luck

    (D) His diminutive stature

    (E) His sturdy spirit

12. Based upon the passage, what is the author's overall attitude concerning the city where Oliver lives?

(A) It is the best of all possible worlds.

(B) It should be the prototype for future cities.

(C) It is a dark place filled with greedy, selfish people.

(D) Although impoverished, most of its citizens are kind.

(E) It is a flawed place, but many good things often happen there.

The following passage analyzes the legal and political philosophy of John Marshall, a chief justice of the Supreme Court in the nineteenth century.

1   As chief justice of the Supreme Court from 1801 until his death in 1835, John Marshall was a staunch nationalist and upholder of property rights. He was not, however, as the folklore of American politics would have it, the lonely and embattled Federalist defending these values against
5 the hostile forces of Jeffersonian democracy. On the contrary, Marshall's opinions dealing with federalism, property rights, and national economic development were consistent with the policies of the Republican Party in its mercantilist phase from 1815 to 1828. Never an extreme Federalist, Marshall opposed his party's reactionary wing in the crisis of 1798–1800.
10 Like almost all Americans of his day, Marshall was a Lockean republican who valued property not as an economic end in itself, but rather as the foundation of civil liberty and a free society. Property was the source both of individual happiness and social stability and progress.

   Marshall evinced strong centralizing tendencies in his theory of fed-
15 eralism and completely rejected the compact theory of the Union expressed in the Virginia and Kentucky Resolutions. Yet his outlook was compatible with the Unionism that formed the basis of the post-1815 American System of the Republican Party. Not that Marshall shared the democratic sensibilities of the Republicans; like his fellow Federalists, he tended to
20 distrust the common people and saw in legislative majoritarianism a force that was potentially hostile to constitutionalism and the rule of law. But aversion to democracy was not the hallmark of Marshall's constitutional jurisprudence. Its central features rather were a commitment to federal authority versus states' rights and a socially productive and economically
25 dynamic conception of property rights. Marshall's support of these principles placed him near the mainstream of American politics in the years between the War of 1812 and the conquest of Jacksonian Democracy.

In the long run, the most important decisions of the Marshall Court were those upholding the authority of the federal government against the
30 states. *Marbury vs. Madison* provided a jurisprudential basis for this undertaking, but the practical significance of judicial review in the Marshall era concerned the state legislatures rather than Congress. The most serious challenge to national authority resulted from state attempts to administer their judicial systems independent of the Supreme Court's appellate super-
35 visions as directed by the Judiciary Act of 1789. In successfully resisting this challenge, the Marshall Court not only averted a practical disruption of the federal system, but it also evolved doctrines of national supremacy which helped preserve the Union during the Civil War.

13. The primary purpose of this passage is to

    (A) describe Marshall's political jurisprudence.

    (B) discuss the importance of centralization to the preservation of the Union.

    (C) criticize Marshall for being disloyal to his party.

    (D) examine the role of the Supreme Court in national politics.

    (E) chronicle Marshall's tenure on the Supreme Court.

14. According to the author, Marshall viewed property as

    (A) an investment.

    (B) irrelevant to constitutional liberties.

    (C) the basis of a stable society.

    (D) inherent to the upper class.

    (E) an important centralizing incentive.

15. In line 15, the "compact theory" was most likely a theory

    (A) supporting states' rights.

    (B) of the extreme Federalists.

    (C) of the Marshall Court's approach to the Civil War.

    (D) supporting centralization.

    (E) advocating jurisprudential activism.

16. According to the author, Marshall's attitude toward mass democratic politics can best be described as

    (A) hostile.

    (B) supportive.

    (C) indifferent.

    (D) nurturing.

    (E) distrustful.

17. In line 22, the word "aversion" means

    (A) loathing.

    (B) acceptance.

    (C) fondness.

    (D) forbidding.

    (E) misdirection.

18. The author argues the Marshall Court

    (A) failed to achieve its centralizing policies.

    (B) failed to achieve its decentralizing policies.

    (C) helped to bring on the Civil War.

    (D) supported federalism via judicial review.

    (E) had its greatest impact on Congress.

19. According to the author, Marshall's politics were

    (A) extremist.

    (B) right-wing.

    (C) democratic.

    (D) moderate.

    (E) majoritarian.

In this passage, the author discusses the properties and uses of selenium cells, which convert sunlight to energy, creating solar power.

1   The physical phenomenon responsible for converting light to electricity—the photovoltaic effect—was first observed in 1839 by the renowned French physicist, Edmund Becquerel. Becquerel noted that a voltage appeared when one of two identical electrodes in a weak conducting solution
5   was illuminated. The PV effect was first studied in solids, such as selenium, in the 1870s. In the 1880s, selenium photovoltaic cells were built that exhibited 1%–2% efficiency in converting light to electricity. Selenium converts light in the visible part of the sun's spectrum; for this reason, it was quickly adopted by the then merging field of photography

10 for photometric (light-measuring) devices. Even today, the light-sensitive cells on cameras used for adjusting shutter speed to match illumination are made of selenium.

Selenium cells have never become practical as energy converters because their cost is too high relative to the tiny amount of power they
15 produce (at 1% efficiency). Meanwhile, work on the physics of PV phenomena has expanded. In the 1920s and 1930s, quantum mechanics laid the theoretical foundation for our present understanding of PV. A major step forward in solar-cell technology came in the 1940s and early 1950s when a new method (called the Czochralski method) was developed for
20 producing highly pure crystalline silicon. In 1954, work at Bell Telephone Laboratories resulted in a silicon photovoltaic cell with a 4% efficiency. Bell Labs soon bettered this to a 6% and then 11% efficiency, heralding an entirely new era of power-producing cells.

A few schemes were tried in the 1950s to use silicon PV cells com-
25 mercially. Most were for cells in regions geographically isolated from electric utility lines. But an unexpected boom in PV technology came from a different quarter. In 1958, the U.S. Vanguard space satellite used a small (less than one-watt) array of cells to power its radio. The cells worked so well that space scientists soon realized the PV could be an effective power
30 source for many space missions. Technology development of the solar cell has been a part of the space program ever since.

Today, photovoltaic systems are capable of transforming one kilowatt of solar energy falling on one square meter into about a hundred watts of electricity. One hundred watts can power most household appliances: a
35 television, a stereo, an electric typewriter, or a lamp. In fact, standard solar cells covering the sun-facing roof space of a typical home can provide about 8,500-kilowatt-hours of electricity annually, which is about the average household's yearly electric consumption. By comparison, a modern, 200-ton electric-arc steel furnace, demanding 50,000 kilowatts of electric-
40 ity, would require about a square kilometer of land for a PV power supply.

Certain factors make capturing solar energy difficult. Besides the sun's low illuminating power per square meter, sunlight is intermittent, affected by time of day, climate, pollution, and season. Power sources based on photovoltaics require either back-up from other sources or stor-
45 age for times when the sun is obscured.

In addition, the cost of a photovoltaic system is far from negligible (electricity from PV systems in 1980 cost about 20 times more than that from conventional fossil-fuel-powered systems).

Thus, solar energy for photovoltaic conversion into electricity is abun-
50 dant, inexhaustible, and clean; yet, it also requires special techniques to
gather enough of it effectively.

20. To the author, Edmund Becquerel's research was

  (A) unimportant.

  (B) of some significance.

  (C) not recognized in its time.

  (D) weak.

  (E) an important breakthrough.

21. In the first paragraph, it can be concluded that the photovoltaic effect
is the result of

  (A) two identical negative electrodes.

  (B) one weak solution and two negative electrodes.

  (C) two positive electrodes of different qualities.

  (D) positive electrodes interacting in a weak environment.

  (E) one negative electrode and one weak solution.

22. The author establishes that selenium was used for photometric devices because

  (A) selenium was the first solid to be observed to have the PV effect.

  (B) selenium is inexpensive.

  (C) selenium converts the visible part of the sun's spectrum.

  (D) selenium can adjust shutter speeds on cameras.

  (E) selenium is abundant.

23. Which of the following can be concluded from the passage?

  (A) Solar energy is still limited by problems of technological efficiency.

  (B) Solar energy is the most efficient source of heat for most families.

  (C) Solar energy represents the PV effect in its most complicated
form.

(D) Solar energy is 20 percent cheaper than fossil-fuel-powered systems.

(E) Solar energy is 40 percent more expensive than fossil-fuel-powered systems.

24. In line 22, the word "heralding" most nearly means

(A) celebrating.   (D) anticipating.

(B) observing.   (E) introducing.

(C) commemorating.

25. According to the passage, commercially used PV cells have powered

(A) car radios.   (D) electric utility lines.

(B) space satellite radios.   (E) space stations.

(C) telephones.

26. Through the information in lines 32–34, it can be inferred that two kilowatts of solar energy transformed by a PV system equal

(A) 200 watts of electricity.

(B) 100 watts of electricity.

(C) no electricity.

(D) two square meters.

(E) 2,000 watts of electricity.

27. Sunlight is difficult to procure for transformation into solar energy. Which of the following statements most accurately supports this belief derived from the passage?

(A) Sunlight is erratic and subject to variables.

(B) Sunlight is steady but never available.

(C) Sunlight is not visible because of pollution.

(D) Sunlight would have to be artificially produced.

(E) Sunlight is never erratic.

28. The author's concluding paragraph would be best supported with additional information regarding

   (A) specific benefits of solar energy for photovoltaic conversion into electricity.

   (B) the negative effects of solar energy for photovoltaic conversion into electricity.

   (C) the negative effects of photovoltaic conversion.

   (D) why solar energy is clean.

   (E) why solar energy is abundant.

DIRECTIONS: Read the passages and answer the questions that follow. Each question will be based on the information stated or implied in the selections or their introductions, and may be based on the relationship between the passages.

In Passage 1, the author writes a general summary about the nature of comedy. In Passage 2, the author sums up the essentials of tragedy.

Passage 1

1   The primary aim of comedy is to amuse us with a happy ending, although comedies can vary according to the attitudes they project, which can be broadly identified as either high or low, terms having nothing to do with an evaluation of the play's merit. Generally, the amusement found in
5   comedy comes from an eventual victory over threats or ill fortune. Much of the dialogue and plot development might be laughable, yet a play need not be funny to be comic. In fact, some critics in the Renaissance era thought that the highest form of comedy should elicit no laughter at all from its audience. A comedy that forced its audience into laughter failed
10   in the highest comic endeavor, whose purpose was to amuse as subtly as possible. Note that Shakespeare's comedies themselves were often under attack for their appeal to laughter.

     Farce is low comedy intended to make us laugh by means of a series of exaggerated, unlikely situations that depend less on plot and character
15   than on gross absurdities, sight gags, and coarse dialogue. The "higher" a comedy goes, the more natural the characters seem and the less boisterous their behavior. The plots become more sustained, and the dialogue shows more weighty thought. As with all dramas, comedies are about things that

go wrong. Accordingly, comedies create deviations from accepted nor-
20 malcy, presenting problems which we might or might not see as harmless.
If these problems make us judgmental about the involved characters and
events, the play takes on the features of satire, a rather high comic form
implying that humanity and human institutions are in need of reform. If
the action triggers our sympathy for the characters, we feel even less
25 protected from the incongruities as the play tilts more in the direction of
tragicomedy. In other words, the action determines a figurative distance
between the audience and the play. Such factors as characters' personalities and the plot's predictability influence this distance. The farther away
we sit, the more protected we feel and usually the funnier the play be-
30 comes. Closer proximity to believability in the script draws us nearer to
the conflict, making us feel more involved in the action and less safe in its
presence.

Passage 2

The term "tragedy" when used to define a play has historically meant
something very precise, not simply a drama which ends with unfortunate
35 consequences. This definition originated with Aristotle, who insisted that
the play be an imitation of complex actions which should arouse an emotional response combining fear and pity. Aristotle believed that only a
certain kind of plot could generate such a powerful reaction. Comedy
shows us a progression from adversity to prosperity. Tragedy must show
40 the reverse; moreover, this progression must be experienced by a certain
kind of character, says Aristotle, someone whom we can designate as the
tragic hero. This central figure must be basically good and noble: "good"
because we will not be aroused to fear and pity over the misfortunes of a
villain, and "noble" both by social position and moral stature because the
45 fall to misfortune would not otherwise be great enough for tragic impact.
These virtues do not make the tragic hero perfect, however, for he must
also possess hamartia—a tragic flaw—the weakness which leads him to
make an error in judgment which initiates the reversal in his fortunes,
causing his death or the death of others or both. These dire consequences
50 become the hero's catastrophe. The most common tragic flaw is hubris; an
excessive pride that adversely influences the protagonist's judgment.

Often the catastrophic consequences involve an entire nation because
the tragic hero's social rank carries great responsibilities. Witnessing these
events produces the emotional reaction Aristotle believed the audience
55 should experience, the catharsis. Although tragedy must arouse our pity
for the tragic hero as he endures his catastrophe and must frighten us as we
witness the consequences of a flawed behavior which anyone could exhibit, there must also be a purgation, "a cleansing," of these emotions

60 which should leave the audience feeling not depressed but relieved and almost elated. The assumption is that while the tragic hero endures a crushing reversal, somehow he is not thoroughly defeated as he gains new stature through suffering and the knowledge that comes with suffering. Classical tragedy insists that the universe is ordered. If truth or universal law is ignored, the results are devastating, causing the audience to react 65 emotionally; simultaneously, the tragic results prove the existence of truth, thereby reassuring our faith that existence is sensible.

29. In Passage 1, the term "laughable" (line 6) suggests that on occasion comic dialogue and plot development can be

    (A) senselessly ridiculous.

    (B) foolishly stupid.

    (C) amusingly droll.

    (D) theoretically depressing.

    (E) critically unsavory.

30. The author of Passage 1 makes an example of Shakespeare (lines 11–12) in order to

    (A) make the playwright look much poorer in our eyes.

    (B) emphasize that he wrote the highest form of comedy.

    (C) degrade higher forms of comedy.

    (D) suggest the foolishness of Renaissance critics.

    (E) show that even great authors do not always use high comedy.

31. The protagonist in a play discovers he has won the lottery, only to misplace the winning ticket. According to the author's definition, this situation would be an example of which type of comedy?

    (A) Satire   (D) Sarcasm

    (B) Farce   (E) Slapstick

    (C) Tragicomedy

32. In line 26, the phrase "figurative distance" suggests

    (A) the distance between the seats in the theater and the stage.

    (B) the lengths the comedy will go to elicit laughter.

(C) the years separating the composition of the play and the time of its performance.

(D) the degree to which an audience relates with the play's action.

(E) that the play's matter is too high for the audience to grasp.

33. What is the author trying to espouse in lines 28–32?

(A) He warns us not to get too involved with the action of the drama.

(B) He wants the audience to immerse itself in the world of the drama.

(C) He wants us to feel safe in the presence of the drama.

(D) He wants us to be critical of the drama's integrity.

(E) He feels that we should not enjoy the drama overly much.

34. In Passage 2, the author introduces Aristotle as a leading source for the definition of tragedy. He does this

(A) to emphasize how outdated the tragedy is for the modern audience.

(B) because Greek philosophy is the only way to truly understand the world of the theater.

(C) because Aristotle was one of Greece's greatest actors.

(D) because Aristotle instituted the definition of tragedy still used widely today.

(E) in order to prove that Aristotle's sense of tragedy was based on false conclusions.

35. In line 42, "noble" most nearly means

(A) of high degree and superior virtue.

(B) of great wealth and self-esteem.

(C) of quick wit and high intelligence.

(D) of manly courage and great strength.

(E) of handsome features and social charm.

36. Which of the following is an example of *harmartia* (line 47)?

    (A) Courtesy to the lower class

    (B) The ability to communicate freely with others

    (C) A refusal to acknowledge the power of the gods

    (D) A weak, miserly peasant

    (E) A desire to do penance for one's crimes

37. Which of the following best summarizes the idea of *catharsis* explained in lines 52–55?

    (A) All of the tragic consequences are reversed at the last moment; the hero is rescued from certain doom and is allowed to live happily for the rest of his life.

    (B) The audience gains a perverse pleasure from watching another's suffering.

    (C) The play's action ends immediately, unresolved, and the audience is left in a state of blissful confusion.

    (D) When the play ends, the audience is happy to escape the drudgery of the tragedy's depressing conclusion.

    (E) The audience lifts itself from a state of fear and pity for the tragic hero to a sense of renewal and absolution for the hero's endurance of great suffering.

38. The authors of both passages make an attempt to

    (A) ridicule their subject matter.

    (B) outline the general terms and guidelines of a particular aspect of drama.

    (C) thrill their readers with sensational information.

    (D) draw upon Shakespeare as an authority to back up their work.

    (E) persuade their readers to study only one or the other type of drama (i.e., comedy or tragedy).

39. Which of the following best describes the differences between the structure of both passages?

    (A) Passage 1 is concerned primarily with the Renaissance era. Passage 2 is concerned primarily with Classical Greece.

    (B) Passage 1 is concerned with dividing its subject into subcategories. Passage 2 is concerned with extracting its subject's individual elements.

    (C) Passage 1 makes fun of its subject matter. Passage 2 treats its subject matter very solemnly.

    (D) Passage 1 draws upon a series of plays that serve as examples. Passage 2 draws upon no outside sources.

    (E) Passage 1 introduces special vocabulary to illuminate the subject matter; Passage 2 fails to do this.

40. What assumption do both passages seem to draw upon?

    (A) Tragedy is a higher form of drama than comedy.

    (B) Tragedy is on the decline in modern society; comedy, however, is on the rise.

    (C) *Catharsis* is an integral part of both comedy and tragedy.

    (D) An audience's role in the performance of either comedy or tragedy is a vital one.

    (E) The tragicomedy is a form that is considered greater than drama that is merely comic or tragic.

CRITICAL READING QUESTIONS DRILLS

ANSWER KEY

Drill 1 — Answering Critical Reading Questions

1.	(B)	11.	(E)	21.	(D)	31.	(C)
2.	(E)	12.	(C)	22.	(C)	32.	(D)
3.	(D)	13.	(A)	23.	(A)	33.	(B)
4.	(D)	14.	(C)	24.	(E)	34.	(D)
5.	(C)	15.	(A)	25.	(B)	35.	(A)
6.	(C)	16.	(E)	26.	(A)	36.	(C)
7	(A)	17.	(A)	27.	(A)	37.	(E)
8.	(E)	18.	(D)	28.	(A)	38.	(B)
9.	(B)	19.	(D)	29.	(C)	39.	(B)
10.	(E)	20.	(E)	30.	(E)	40.	(D)

VOCABULARY LIST

bathetic
   adj.- sentimental, trite

benefaction
   n.- benevolence, donation

bequeath
   v.- to hand down or to leave to someone

collusion
   n.- plot; a secret agreement for fraudulent or illegal purposes

comburent
   adj.- blazing

contentious
   adj.- aggressive, argumentative, belligerent

contumelious
   adj.- abusive, impudent

denunciate
   v.- to accuse or blame

deplorable
   adj.- worthy of severe disapproval

enucleate
   v.- to explain

ephemeral
   adj.- transitory; lasting one day; short-lived

erratic
   adj.- without a fixed or regular course

evade
   v.- to avoid fulfilling or answering completely

exegetic
adj.- explanatory

fetter
v.- to hamper or hinder

fictive
adj.- fictitious

flagrant
adj.- conspicuously bad or offensive

forbearance
n.- patience, tolerance

forebode
v.- to threaten

furbish
v.- to renew or gloss

galvanize
v.- to activate or provoke

gelastic
adj.- laughable

gossamer
adj.- filmy and light

harmonize
v.- to bring into accord

havoc
n.- great destruction and devastation

idiom
n.- language; the dialect of a people, region, etc.

imponderable
adj.- imperceptible

incommodious
adj.- embarrassing, inconvenient

indefatigable
　　adj.- tireless

juvenescence
　　n.- youth

lachrymose
　　adj.- tearful

lassitude
　　n.- apathy, exhaustion, lethargy

loquacious
　　adj.- very talkative

metanoia
　　n.- conversion

mimicry
　　n.- the act, practice or art of copying the manner or expression of another

nexus
　　n.- bond; a link or connection

tangible
　　adj.- discernible by touch

telluric
　　adj.- earthly

temperate
　　adj.- exercising moderation and self-restraint in appetites and behavior

tergiversate
　　v.- to defect or equivocate

tirade
　　n.- a long, violent or blustering speech usually of censure or denunciation

transfuse
　　v.- to instill, imbue

transmogrify
> v.- to convert

turbid
> adj.- having sediment or foreign particles stirred up or suspended

turgid
> adj.- inflated; pompous, bombastic

tyro
> n.- amateur; a beginner in learning something

unadulterated
> adj.- natural, pure

unparalleled
> adj.- that has no parallel, equal or counterpart; unique

upsurge
> adj.- increase

verisimilitude
> n.- appearance of truth or authenticity

CHAPTER 10

Mini Tests

➤ Mini Test 1
➤ Mini Test 2
➤ Mini Test 3

MINI TEST 1

1. Ⓐ Ⓑ Ⓒ Ⓓ Ⓔ
2. Ⓐ Ⓑ Ⓒ Ⓓ Ⓔ
3. Ⓐ Ⓑ Ⓒ Ⓓ Ⓔ
4. Ⓐ Ⓑ Ⓒ Ⓓ Ⓔ
5. Ⓐ Ⓑ Ⓒ Ⓓ Ⓔ
6. Ⓐ Ⓑ Ⓒ Ⓓ Ⓔ
7. Ⓐ Ⓑ Ⓒ Ⓓ Ⓔ
8. Ⓐ Ⓑ Ⓒ Ⓓ Ⓔ
9. Ⓐ Ⓑ Ⓒ Ⓓ Ⓔ
10. Ⓐ Ⓑ Ⓒ Ⓓ Ⓔ
11. Ⓐ Ⓑ Ⓒ Ⓓ Ⓔ
12. Ⓐ Ⓑ Ⓒ Ⓓ Ⓔ
13. Ⓐ Ⓑ Ⓒ Ⓓ Ⓔ
14. Ⓐ Ⓑ Ⓒ Ⓓ Ⓔ
15. Ⓐ Ⓑ Ⓒ Ⓓ Ⓔ
16. Ⓐ Ⓑ Ⓒ Ⓓ Ⓔ
17. Ⓐ Ⓑ Ⓒ Ⓓ Ⓔ
18. Ⓐ Ⓑ Ⓒ Ⓓ Ⓔ
19. Ⓐ Ⓑ Ⓒ Ⓓ Ⓔ
20. Ⓐ Ⓑ Ⓒ Ⓓ Ⓔ
21. Ⓐ Ⓑ Ⓒ Ⓓ Ⓔ
22. Ⓐ Ⓑ Ⓒ Ⓓ Ⓔ
23. Ⓐ Ⓑ Ⓒ Ⓓ Ⓔ
24. Ⓐ Ⓑ Ⓒ Ⓓ Ⓔ
25. Ⓐ Ⓑ Ⓒ Ⓓ Ⓔ

MINI TEST 1

DIRECTIONS: Each passage is followed by questions based on its content. After reading the passage, choose the best answer to each question. Answer all questions based on what is indicated or implied in that passage.

Questions 1–4 are based on the following passage.

Based on recent research studies conducted by specialists at Rollins Graduate University, in order for teachers to provide effective instruction, they must continuously engage in diagnosis. According to the research findings, (1) students of teachers who follow prescribed diagnostic procedures perform better academically than students of teachers who do not follow prescribed diagnostic procedures; (2) teachers who engage in diagnosis have a better knowledge of their students' strengths and are able to use these strengths to positively impact learning; (3) teachers who engage in diagnosis have a better knowledge of their students' weaknesses and are able to use this knowledge to meet the needs of their students; and (4) teachers who engage in diagnosis are better able to plan instruction because they are endowed with a thorough knowledge of their students' assets and liabilities.

1. Which of the following best describes the organization of the passage?

    (A) A series of events that are chronologically listed.

    (B) An unimportant issue that is presented and defended by a list of ideas.

    (C) A summary of key ideas about a designated subject.

    (D) A step-by-step demonstration of the solution to a problem.

    (E) A listing of related arguments that support an initial concern.

2. What is the author's purpose in writing this passage?

    (A) To report research findings.

    (B) To demonstrate research skills.

    (C) To inform parents about research findings concerning diagnosis.

    (D) To inform teachers and other school personnel about the importance of research.

    (E) To help teachers improve instruction.

3.   What is the main idea of this passage?

    (A) Students perform better when teachers engage in diagnosis.

    (B) Teachers who engage in diagnosis have a better knowledge of their students' strengths.

    (C) In order for teachers to provide effective instruction, they must continuously engage in diagnosis.

    (D) Teachers who engage in diagnosis have a better knowledge of their students' weaknesses.

    (E) Teachers should engage in research.

4.   How much intitial faith should be placed in the author's argument, based on the amount of support he/she provides?

    (A) None—the author's argument was based on a non-representative sample.

    (B) A small amount, because the author knows a bit more than the reader.

    (C) A great deal, because the author seems totally convinced.

    (D) A moderate amount, until more is learned about the subject and the reader can determine whether the cited study is valid, reliable, etc.

    (E) The author's argument should be accepted unconditionally because it is based on research findings from a university.

Questions 5–7 are based on the following passage.

My daughter, Marie, has two cats. The older cat is named Annie. She is white with large black spots. Annie has long hair and sheds constantly in warm weather. Cinnamon is a two-year-old male tabby. He loves to chase squirrels in the backyard, but he probably would be very surprised to catch one. Cinnamon prefers to stay outside all night unless it is extremely cold. In the morning, Cinnamon wants to come into the house and sleep. Annie seldom goes outside. She prefers to sit on the table or a chair where she can look outside through the windows. Marie has cared for both cats since they were kittens. She is very fond of both of them.

5. How old is Annie?

(A) Two years

(D) One year

(B) Five years

(E) Same age as Cinnamon

(C) Not stated

6. According to the passage, which of the following is NOT true?

(A) Annie chases squirrels.

(B) Cinnamon stays outside at night.

(C) Cinnamon is a male tabby.

(D) Annie has long hair.

(E) Annie is a female cat

7. According to the passage, which of the following statements is true?

(A) Marie likes Annie more than Cinnamon.

(B) Marie has cared for both cats since they were kittens.

(C) Annie and Cinnamon often fight with each other.

(D) Annie spends most nights outside.

(E) Annie has had three litters of kittens.

Questions 8–10 are based on the following passage.

The domestic oil industry continues to cut back its production, and the percentage of oil imported into the United States continues to increase. Increased dependence on foreign oil will have two results: first, foreign producers will raise prices, and we can be confident that U. S. importers will pay the higher price because of increased demand; second, more huge oil tankers will be needed to move the oil to the U.S. This increases the risk of oil spills and environmental damage to the U.S . shoreline. Domestic producers will be reluctant to increase production because they will benefit more from foreign oil price increases than from expanding their own capacities. Further, after the disastrous oil spill in Alaska, many domestic oil producers feel the need to "lay low" and let foreign oil producers take the blame for future price increases.

8. What is the author's purpose in this passage?

(A) To explain the reasons for oil spills and environmental damage to the U.S. shoreline.

(B) To explain the reasons for decreased foreign oil production.

(C) To explain why more oil tankers are needed.

(D) To discuss ways to lower oil prices.

(E) To discuss the probable results of increased dependence on foreign oil.

9. According to the passage, what is the main reason domestic producers will not increase production?

(A) They have more to gain by not increasing production.

(B) Huge oil tankers are too expensive.

(C) They are afraid of oil spills.

(D) Foreign oil is falling in price.

(E) All of the above.

10. Which of the following is NOT given as a reason for higher prices?

(A) Foreign producers will raise prices.

(B) Domestic producers will cut production.

(C) Domestic producers want to avoid publicity.

(D) Increased cost of insurance for oil tanker ships after the recent Alaska oil spill.

(E) More oil tankers will be needed.

Questions 11–16 are based on the following passage.

1   Americans who enjoyed the movie "Shogun" would find the role of warriors who were devoted followers of the shogun an interesting period of Japanese history. During the feudal period, warriors were intensely loyal to their leaders. Faithfully fulfilling orders of their lord was an hon-
5 orable duty. The warriors *(samurai)* expected their wives to make similar sacrificial efforts to assure victory. Samurai wore two swords and at times were feared by the commoners. During those feudal years, an insensitive warrior could without hesitation cut down a person who stood in his way. Yet not all samurai were crude fighters. In fact, many of them developed a
10 number of cultural skills. Great interest in writing poetry by samurai was passed from generation to generation. To this day, ordinary Japanese citizens find pleasure in writing poems. After feudal wars ended and lords no longer needed their protective services, the educated warriors were fre-

quently transferred to urban centers and appointed to carry out bureau-
15 cratic duties.

During the Tokugawa Period, many people were educated through a
private tutoring system. Samurai and commoners participated in the educational process. Domain schools for samurai were established. Private
academies enrolled samurai and other members of the community. Bud-
20 dhist temple schools also figured prominently in educating common people,
including a small percentage of women. Toward the latter part of the
nineteenth century during the Meiji Period, the first Ministry of Education
was established. Today Japan's educational standards and policies are widely
debated. Those who admire the educational system point to the high lit-
25 eracy and productivity of the Japanese people. Those who criticize the
system complain about the high stress placed on young people who are
pressured to pass key tests at certain intervals. The tests determine whether
or not students can enroll in top-rate kindergartens, elementary schools,
high schools, and elite universities. Japanese mothers devote their lives to
30 the educational progress of their children. Completion of heavy homework
assignments and class ranking are central concerns of the family. Many
children attend afterschool private schools or cram schools (*juku*) and/or
are taught by private tutors in the afternoons and evenings. Rote learning
is a necessity for preparation for tests. Pressure on the students stems from
35 the fact that only those students who emerge from elite universities have
opportunities to be groomed for top positions in government and business.
Some observers believe that the time and cost of preparing children for the
best positions account for the low birthrate or many abortions in Japan.
Thus with only a child or two, parents can closely guide each one toward
40 "success." Others also feel that the stress and strain placed on young
people to make the highest scores in their classes may explain the high
rate of suicide among teenagers.

Japanese group interaction is a topic often considered by students of
management. Unlike the American bureaucratic style where the boss is
45 prone to make policy and announce policy to personnel on the lower rungs
of the hierarchy, the Japanese system is based on group decision making
and implementation. Upon graduation, new employees enter government
as a group and work as a group during their long tenure. Groups function
quite well in Japan due to a number of reasons. With the exception of a
50 few citizens who have Korean ancestors, the country is composed of a
homogeneous population. A long tradition of good manners and a uniform
education curriculum necessary for students to prepare for key exams are
important elements required for adults to work harmoniously. The style of
communication leads to reduced friction. Japanese feel no compulsion to

55　strike a deal in a hurry. Rather, they talk around a topic without brusque collision of ideas and personalities. Indirect, vague communication which is called "belly talk" frustrates Americans who are accustomed to being direct, targeting key points, and quickly making decisions. Japanese operate on a basis of group consensus. When details are eventually completed,

60　the group transmits the suggested policy to their superior. Unlike Americans who prefer "top down" communication in the organization, Japanese prefer "bottom up" communication. Unlike Americans, who strive to be identified as "the leader" with subsequent promotions, the Japanese group that originated when first hired is rewarded as a group. The group rises

65　intact in the hierarchy until one individual is appointed to a top position. By this time, the other members of the group are eligible for retirement, or they move out of that particular organization. While most American industries have not attempted to copy Japanese management styles, elements of group decision making have been incorporated.

11. How did ideas about the role of warriors change over a period of time?

　(A)　Samurai were at first among the best educated citizens until war broke out. At that point, they turned against their own people. After the war, philosopher kings requested assistance of Buddhist priests in taming young warriors.

　(B)　Theoretically, warriors with their history of cruelty and loyalty could not be retrained.

　(C)　Samurai and their lords experienced mutual dependence until peace no longer required a warrior class. The samurai's educational foundation made them natural candidates for bureaucratic positions.

　(D)　Shoguns and their warriors were defeated in battles and, one by one, left the rough country to explore civilization. Uneducated, the warriors were at first ill-equipped to function in the more sophisticated hierarchy of organized government.

　(E)　The author infers that the teachers in private and religious schools were fearful of the two-sworded warriors who, the reader might envision, were similar to modern-day gangs in the halls of the temple schools. Once graduated, it appears that the warriors' attempt to take over government offices was successful.

12. What seems to be the purpose of the author's presentation on Japanese education?

(A) The author overwhelmingly rejects the Japanese educational system.

(B) The author has attempted to present the merits of the educational system while at the same time exposing serious defects.

(C) The author is trying to convince Americans that more pressure on parents and children should be exerted by educators in public schools, private schools, and juku.

(D) The author's jaded view of the educational system in Japan is at best a paradox because he seems to advocate sacrifices which must be made in order to elevate the rate of literacy and productivity in American schools.

(E) The author is only trying to present an historical analysis of the education system in earlier periods and modern times in an objective manner without subjective imposition of personal views on the reader.

13. What are commonplace experiences of young women in Japan?

(A) As in early years when women were dominated by samurai husbands, wives and mothers today must make personal sacrifices in order to be successful "education moms" who guide their children through the maze of assignments and exams.

(B) As in early years when a few women enrolled in Buddhist temple schools, young females generally have little education because education is mostly for young boys, commonly known as juku.

(C) The author infers that young mothers actually complete some of the heavy homework assignments of their children so that the children will have time to study under a tutor who prepares them for the next test.

(D) Young women have no future and no happiness unless they themselves make top scores on tests, enter an elite university so that they can marry a successful man, and rear a large family of brilliant children.

(E) Only lower class women undergo abortions. Unfortunately, mothers in the lower economic class with children of average or below average mental abilities must deal with a higher rate of teenage abortions and teenage suicides.

14. Which statement best describes the educational philosophy in Japan?

(A) Students must spend a great deal of time learning long lists of facts. Teaching preparations must be geared to teaching reading skills to all students. Extensive written exams are the best method for determining who should later lead the country in business, industry, and government.

(B) Education is of great value, but social contacts with other children in informal after-school classes are more important.

(C) Despite great emphasis on the part of the Minister of Education to incorporate Meiji teaching techniques, mothers dominate school policies in ways that will promote recognition of the most talented children.

(D) The Japanese education philosophy stresses "practical education" in scientific and mathematical subjects.

(E) The author suggested that warriors' domination of the early educational process has influenced educational curricula today with great emphasis on creativity and decreased emphasis on memorization.

15. What is the management philosophy in Japan today?

(A) Given the difficulty of Japanese individuals to get to the heart of the matter and to make fairly quick decisions, it is best to appoint a supervisor of a group who can tie the ends together when the group bogs down. Supervisors often suffer from ulcers (belly talk) during periods of tension.

(B) Management is forced to react to the difficulty of hiring young graduates of elite universities. The situation is further complicated due to inflated egos. Management must spend a great deal of time supervising heterogeneous groups and avoiding friction among leadership-prone men who were stars throughout their educational experience.

(C) Disgusted with the slow pace of group decision making, Japanese will most likely change their management style and look more to the American single-administrator-type system where things are accomplished on a faster pace and where the boss makes all decisions.

(D) The education philosophy and the management philosophy obviously clash. The education philosophy and practice are based on long years of intimidation by mother-student groups while management philosophy is based on "bottom-up" administration.

(E) As a part of their bid for global economic dominance, Japanese managers will continue trying to increase efficiency at all costs.

16. How does the author view modern Japanese society?

(A) Society functions best when highly intelligent young people and their families feel that ultimate success is promotion to a position of responsibility in government, business, or industry by the time a man has passed middle age.

(B) It is obvious that social needs are accommodated when examinations and entry levels to good jobs are structured so that a class of illiterate people will be available to clean and sweep.

(C) Although education stresses eliminate the lazy, faint-hearted, and emotionally insecure, rote learning and striving for the best jobs will automatically produce the best social order.

(D) Although there are many admirable traits of Japanese society, such as high literacy, ability to work long hours, and courteous interaction among people, questions must be raised about several issues: the high rate of suicides and abortions, stress imposed on all members of families, late-bloomers in schools who have shifted to educational tracks that fail to develop their full potential in the marketplace, etc.

(E) There are many admirable traits of Japanese society, such as literacy and work patterns. Detractors who raise such points as suicide and educational pressures on society are most often jealous or critical Americans, such as the author, who are apologists for defects in the American system and who ascribe to America the one and only way of life.

Questions 17–25 are based on the following passage.

The following passage examines the problem of species extinction and discusses the Endangered Species Act of 1973.

Since life began eons ago, thousands of creatures have come and
1 gone like the dinosaur—sometimes rendered extinct by naturally changing ecological conditions but more recently by humans and their activities.

If extinction is part of the natural order, some people ask: "Why save endangered species? What makes a relatively few animals and plants so
5 special that effort and money should be expended to preserve them?"

Congress addressed these questions in the preamble to the Endangered Species Act of 1973, holding that endangered and threatened species of fish, wildlife, and plants "are of aesthetic, ecological, educational, historical, recreational, and scientific value to the nation and its people." In
10   making this statement, Congress was summarizing a number of convincing arguments advanced by thoughtful scientists, conservationists, and others who are greatly concerned by the disappearance of wildlife.

Sadly, we can no longer attribute the increasing decline in our wild animals and plants to "natural" processes. Many are declining because of
15   exploitation, habitat alteration or destruction, pollution, or the introduction of new species of plants and animals to an area. As mandated by Congress, protecting endangered species and restoring them to the point where their existence is no longer jeopardized is the primary objective of the U.S. Fish and Wildlife Service's Endangered Species Program.
20

Passage of the Endangered Species Act of 1973 gave the United States one of the most far-reaching laws ever enacted by any country to prevent the extinction of imperiled animals and plants. The Act created a national program that today involves the federal government, the states, conservation organizations, individual citizens, business and industry, and
25   foreign governments in a cooperative effort to conserve endangered wildlife throughout the world. Under the law, the Secretary of the Interior (acting through the U.S. Fish and Wildlife Service) has broad powers to protect and conserve all forms of wildlife and plants he finds in serious jeopardy. The Secretary of Commerce, acting through the National Marine
30   Fisheries Service, has similar authority for protecting and conserving most marine life.

As of August 1984, more than 300 native mammals, birds, reptiles, crustaceans, plants, and other life forms were officially protected on the U.S. List of Endangered and Threatened Wildlife and Plants. In addition,
35   more than 500 foreign species have been listed.

Habitat destruction is the most serious worldwide threat to wildlife and plants, followed by overexploitation for commercial, sporting, or other purposes. Disease, predation, inadequate conservation laws, and other natural or man-made factors may also contribute to a species' decline—mak-
40   ing it a candidate for listing as endangered or threatened. The Act defines an "endangered" species as one that is in danger of extinction throughout all or a significant portion of its range. A "threatened" species is defined as one that is likely to become endangered within the foreseeable future.

The Fish and Wildlife Service follows a formal "rulemaking" proce-

45 dure in determining which species should be placed on the U.S. List of
Endangered and Threatened Wildlife and Plants.

A "rulemaking" is the process used by Federal agencies (and many
states) to propose and later adopt regulations which have the effect of law
and apply to all U.S. residents. The proposed rulemaking is published in
50 the *Federal Register,* a daily government publication, and after a suitable
period for public comment and possible revision, it is published again as a
final rule. Endangered or threatened species are placed on the list, reclassi-
fied, or deleted through this process.

17. Which of the following combinations best represents the main contributing factors to the possible extinction of plants and animals?

    (A) Habitat destruction, pollution, natural processes.

    (B) Introduction of new species into an area, disease, natural pro-
    cesses.

    (C) Habitat destruction, overexploitation, pollution.

    (D) Uncontrolled hunting quotas, predation, disease.

    (E) Natural processes, adopted regulations, pollution.

18. The passage implies that it is possible for the public to influence the
government's decisions regarding endangered species by

    (A) mentioning that the rulemaking proposals become final rules
    only after a period of public access allowing for commentary.

    (B) indicating the need for popular vote to pass the Endangered
    Species Act of 1973.

    (C) citing statistics which were based on public feedback.

    (D) stating the law which requires public majority to pass the *Fed-
    eral Register.*

    (E) stating the threats to wildlife and plants.

19. All of the following are presented as reasons for saving endangered
species EXCEPT for which one?

    (A) A variety of plants and animals offer educational value to the
    nation.

    (B) The number of diseased animals contaminating the nation's food supply has increased dramatically over the last century.

(C) In general, plants and animals beautify the country.

(D) The study of such diverse plants and animals is of great scientific value.

(E) All of these are reasons that are presented.

20. Which of the following best represents the main idea of the passage?

(A) The Endangered Species Act of 1973 was an important development in the preservation of endangered wildlife.

(B) The federal government's current involvement in conservation of endangered plants and animals was bolstered by public involvement in the late 1960s.

(C) Man-made factors have had negative effects on wildlife, forcing the intervention of the Secretaries of Commerce and Interior to work in conjunction with the public to create legitimate conservation laws for the nation.

(D) Modern human existence has negatively altered natural habitats, prompting the installment of the Endangered Species Act which promotes the conservation of endangered species worldwide.

(E) There is a need for stricter guidelines in determining which species should be placed on the endangered list.

21. What is the author's purpose in mentioning dinosaurs in the beginning of the passage?

(A) To develop similarities between the plight of one animal to another animal described later in the passage.

(B) To contrast ancient and modern attitudes toward wildlife.

(C) To express the need for government control of wildlife.

(D) To present a well-known example in order to later contrast the difference between natural and man-made extinction.

(E) To provide a historical background for the passage.

22. As opposed to "threatened" wildlife, an "endangered" species has which of the following criteria?

I. Overexploitation for commercial purposes.

II.   Danger of extinction throughout most of its life range.

III. The likelihood of extinction in the near future.

(A) II only.

(B) I and II only.

(C) I and III only.

(D) II and III only.

(E) I, II, and III.

23. The U.S. government's support of wildlife conservation can be seen in which of the following examples from the passage?

(A) The passing of federal and state laws for recording wildlife in the nation.

(B) The assertion that the protection and restoration of endangered species is a main objective in wildlife conservation and in the development of the laws and programs surrounding this issue.

(C) The creation of federal programs to interact with national services for the protection of wildlife.

(D) The accounting of public opinion and comment regarding proposals concerning endangered wildlife.

(E) The concrete definitions of "endangered" and "threatened" species.

24. According to the passage, all of the following apply to the "rule-making" procedure EXCEPT

(A) the procedure is used by federal and state agencies to propose and adopt regulations.

(B) public access to and commentary on the documented rulemaking procedure may prompt the reevaluation of the endangered species list and the proposals.

(C) the procedure produces regulations which act as laws and apply to all U.S. citizens.

(D) the proposals are only made into final rules after a period of time during which the Secretaries of Commerce and Interior approve all revisions and pass them to Congress.

(E) citizens vote on the proposed rules before they are written into law.

25. Statistics from 1984 show which of the following results?

(A) Five-thirds more native species survived than foreign species that were endangered.

(B) There are more foreign than native endangered species which indicates that more funding is needed.

(C) The large number of endangered species listed show the need for and continuance of conservation laws.

(D) Native creatures can survive and adapt better than foreign species to the alterations in their environment.

(E) There was a dramatic decrease in the number of species considered in danger of becoming extinct.

MINI TEST 1

ANSWER KEY

1. (E)	6. (A)	11. (C)	16. (D)	21. (D)
2. (E)	7. (B)	12. (B)	17. (C)	22. (B)
3. (C)	8. (A)	13. (A)	18. (A)	23. (B)
4. (D)	9. (C)	14. (A)	19. (B)	24. (C)
5. (C)	10. (E)	15. (E)	20. (D)	25. (C)

DETAILED EXPLANATIONS OF ANSWERS

1.   **(E)**   This question asks you to analyze the way in which the author organizes the passage. Choice (A) is not correct because the listing of findings from the research is not chronological. Choice (B) is incorrect because the issue is important, and the passage consists of a listing of findings, not of ideas. The list of findings are statements based on research data. Choices (C) and (D) are incorrect because no general summary or step-by-step demonstration takes place. Choice (E) explains the organization: A list of related arguments about research findings support an initial concern about the effectiveness of diagnosis.

2.   **(E)**   This question requires you to identify the author's purpose for writing it. The author does not tell you why he/she is writing this passage; but he/she does state that for teachers to be effective in the classroom, they must engage in continuous diagnosis. Therefore, it can be assumed that the author wants to help teachers improve instruction—choice (E). Choices (A) and (B) may be true, but they have no support. Choice (C) is not appropriate because there is no need to inform parents about the diagnosis since they will not be directly involved in diagnosis . Choice (D) may be true, but it is a logical choice . The correct answer is (E).

3.   **(C)**   This question requires you to identify the main idea of the passage. Choices (A), (B) and (D) are supporting details for the main idea—choice (C)—In order for teachers to provide effective instruction, they must continuously engage in diagnosis. Main ideas are usually supported by details. Choices (A), (B), and (D) have no support. Choice (E) is incorrect because there is no suggestion that teachers involve themselves in research activities. The focal point is on the results of research, not an established need to perform research.

4.   **(D)**   The best response to this question is choice (D). The author supported his argument with a research study conducted by "specialists," but did not, at all, delve into the procedures, sample population, or evaluation methods used by the researchers. Nothing is known about the reliability or validity of the study, the expertise of the researchers, the principles upon which the study was based, or the motivation of the people performing the inquiry. More information is needed before an educated evaluation of this argument can be reached. Choice (A) is inappropriate because

researchers, not the author, conducted the study. Also, not enough is known about the sample to determine whether or not it is, indeed, representative. Choices (B), (C) and (E) are inappropriate because they directly conflict with the reasoning behind the correct answer, (D).

5. **(C)** The correct answer is (C) because Annie's age is not included. The passage states that she is older than Cinnamon, so answer (E) is incorrect.

6. **(A)** This question requires the process of elimination. The passage states that Cinnamon stays outside at night and that Cinnamon is a male tabby. The passage also states that Annie has long hair and is a female cat. Cinnamon chases squirrels, but the passage does not state that Annie also chases squirrels. Choice (A) is correct.

7. **(B)** Choice (B) is correct. This information is stated in the next to the last sentence. There is no mention of Marie preferring one cat to the other, so choice (A) is incorrect. Cinnamon, not Annie, spends most nights outside, so choice (C) is incorrect. The passage does not discuss the cats fighting with each other, nor does the passage mention litters of kittens, so choices (D) and (E) are incorrect.

8. **(E)** In this question you are asked to infer a purpose from the author has written. Choice (A) is incorrect because the author only mentions environmental damage; the topic is not discussed at length. Choice (B) is incorrect because the passage clearly states that foreign oil production is increasing, no decreasing. Choice (C) is incorrect because, although this is discussed, it is not the main purpose for writing. Choice (D) is incorrect because the author does not discuss ways to lower oil prices. Choice (E) is correct because it summarizes the author's main idea, which is that the results of increased dependence on foreign oil can be predicted with relative certainty.

9. **(A)** This question asks you to determine why domestic oil producers will not increase production. The correct choice is (A) because this is specifically stated in the sixth sentence. Choice (D) states information that is opposite to what is stated in the paragraph. Although oil takers are expensive and producers are afraid of spills, these are only contributing reasons to the problem. Therefore, choices (B) and (C) are incorrect.

10. **(D)** This question requires you to review the whole passage and eliminate answer. Choice (A) is stated in the third sentence. Choice (B) is stated ion the first sentence. Choice (D) is correct because although the idea may be logical, insurance is never discussed in the passage.

11. **(C)** Choice (C) traces one of the most interesting developments in Japanese government where warriors were able to adapt to new positions of responsibilities.

Choice (A) is incorrect. Samurai were fairly loyal to Japanese lords, although they could be cruel and crude on occasion. "Taming" is too harsh. However, warriors obtained their education in the Buddhist temples. Choice (B) ignores the fact that samurai were educated to become civil servants. Choice (D) overstates the case with regard to lack of education of warriors. Although some warriors were less educated than others, it should be remembered that samurai were quite good poets and many attended school. Choice (E) has not interpreted the text correctly. The author provides no evidence that schools were places of roving gangs of warriors. The author does explain that samurai were assigned to governmental offices.

12. **(B)** Choice (B) illustrates how analysts should consider both weaknesses and strengths of the topic under investigation, such as education. Choice (A) is an exaggeration. Criticism does not necessarily mean that that author "overwhelmingly" rejected the process. Choice (C) misinterprets the analysis. In fact, the author questions the desirability of the kind of pressure exerted on children in Japan. Choice (D) assumes that the author's analysis is prescriptive. Rather, he examines and comments without suggesting that Americans copy the exact system. Choice (E) is partially correct. However, readers can easily detect negative reaction to the high tension routine in school and at home.

13. **(A)** Choice (A) is correct. Japanese wives are caught in a daily schedule that is geared to the needs of their children and the demands of the educational system, as the author vividly portrays. Choice (B) is incorrect. The author does not imply that only males receive formal education. Choice (C) is wrong. The purpose of the heavy assignments is for students to prepare for the tests—not in any way could they be classified as "busy work." Choice (D) has come to the wrong conclusion that the author has not suggested. Although young women experience the same educational pressures to enter elite universities, certainly future happiness does not entirely depend upon that feat. Choice (E) cannot be inferred from the statements above. In fact, abortions and small families cut across social and economic levels.

14. **(A)** Choice (A) is correct because Japan places a great deal of emphasis on factual information that can be tested on a massive scale. A great deal of faith for choice of leadership tracks is placed on the ability to make top score on exams.

Choice (B) is wrong because the classes after school which are designed to improve skills for tests have no time for social activities. Choice (C) is incorrect. The author does not imply mothers have great power over school policies, nor does he provide a clue that there is such a technique as Meiji! Choice (E) improperly gives credit to the power of warriors over the early educational process. Rather the educational process influenced warrior-students. Choice (D) is wrong. The passage makes no mention of Japanese educational policies stressing one subject over another.

15. **(E)**   Choice (E) is correct. The author explains the philosophy that more can be accomplished successfully through the process of hiring student groups who will work together in groups for years. Choice (A) has missed the entire point of the supervisor's role and has not understood "belly talk" which is a term that describes vague, non-decisive communication. Choice (E) is wrong in that the Japanese system seems to eliminate from the ranks people who have not been conditioned to work in teams. Japan, it must be remembered, has few citizens who are of different races and ethnic groups. Choice (C) is a poor choice because the author does not imply that Japanese are impressed with American management style. Choice (D) is partially true. Actually, the education philosophy prepares people to feel comfortable working under the management philosophy. Schools are not intimidated by mothers. (E) When several people of equal status work together over a long period of time, planning and implementation will be more successful.

16. **(D)**   Choice (D) is correct. The author, without prescribing the best educational goals, stimulates readers to further consider the process that may go beyond his own observations about stress and suicide. Choice (A) is incorrect. Although the author traces the method for selection of leaders of the Japanese society, he does not embrace the idea that society functions best if only the most intelligent hold power positions. Choice (B) is incorrect. The text does not support the idea that a conscious effort is made to create a pool of poorly educated people for the worst kinds of jobs. Choice (C) is incorrect. While the author describes what has taken place in Japan over a long period of time, he has not made the subjective statement that Japan has produced the best social order. Choice (D) is correct. The author, without prescribing the best educational goals, stimulates readers to further consider the process that may go beyond his own observations about stress and suicide. Choice (E) is an overstatement which assigns bias where there is no evidence of bias on the part of the author.

17. **(C)**   The passage states that we can "no longer attribute the increasing decline in our wild animals and plants to natural processes";

therefore, choices (A), (E), and (B) which include natural processes are incorrect. The passage does not argue against any quotas, unlimited or otherwise; therefore, (D) is incorrect. By process of elimination, (C) is correct.

18. **(A)** The passage does not mention popular vote (B), and it offers simple statistics which require no public response (C). While the public may have a chance to comment on the *Federal Register,* it is not a document which needs to be "passed," especially by public vote (D). The passage does mention the accessibility of the *Federal Register* to the public for commentary; therefore, (A) is correct. Stating the threats to wildlife and plants would not influence government's decisions (E).

19. **(B)** While disease among animals is a given reason for the possible decline in animal number, there is no mention of disease as it relates to food supply. The educational, aesthetic, and scientific values of wildlife are extolled by Congress' statement which accompanies the passing of the Endangered Species Act of 1973, making (A), (C), and (D) true and therefore not the exception. Because (A), (C), and (D) are true, (E) can not be correct.

20. **(D)** While it is important to acknowledge the impact of the Endangered Species Act of 1973, choice (A) merely names the act and does not include an explanation of its application. (B) is incorrect because it mentions "public involvement," a topic not covered in this passage. (C) is incorrect not only because it presents again this false public interaction, but it focuses on the United States (the "nation") and omits the connection with other countries which also honor conservation laws. (D) embodies the topics of why species are endangered, what has been done about it and by whom, making (D) the most complete choice of the four choices. (E) is incorrect because it is not explicitly stated in the passage.

21. **(D)** The passage states that habitat destruction, a man-made force, is the most serious threat to wildlife and plants. To demonstrate the importance and consequence of environment, the author uses the dinosaur to show what natural extinction is as compared to man-made, habitat altering extinction of today. (A) is incorrect because the passage does not focus solely on one particular animal. (B) is incorrect because ancient attitudes are not actually presented in the passage. (C) is incorrect because the government in no way affected the life of the dinosaur. (E) is wrong because the purpose of mentioning the dinosaurs is not for historical background.

22. **(B)**   Option III is the definition of a "threatened" species; therefore, any choice with that option is incorrect. Option I applies to both "endangered" and "threatened" species. Option II defines an "endangered" species according to the passage. (B) offers both Options I and II.

23. **(B)**   The passage says that Congress made this statement in regard to the U.S. Fish and Wildlife Service's Endangered Species Program which came about as a result of the Endangered Species Act. Merely "recording" wildlife will do nothing for its preservation, so (A) is incorrect. Government programs which work above generating laws for citizens are also not worthwhile; therefore, (C) is incorrect. (D) also only records the public's comments, but no action is taken, rendering the tasks useless; therefore, (D) is incorrect. No concrete definitions of "endangered" and "threatened" are offered (E).

24. **(C)**   The Fish and Wildlife Service works with the *Federal Register;* there is no involvement of either Secretaries or Congress in the placement of a species on the published endangered list.

25. **(C)**   The information the statistics offer is misinterpreted by answers (A), which distorts the numbers, and (B) which assumes too much based on the little information given, much in the same way that (D) does. (C) offers the best interpretation of the number of animals placed on the List of Endangered Species and Threatened Wildlife and Plants. There was not a dramatic decrease (E) according to the statistics.

MINI TEST 2

1. Ⓐ Ⓑ Ⓒ Ⓓ Ⓔ
2. Ⓐ Ⓑ Ⓒ Ⓓ Ⓔ
3. Ⓐ Ⓑ Ⓒ Ⓓ Ⓔ
4. Ⓐ Ⓑ Ⓒ Ⓓ Ⓔ
5. Ⓐ Ⓑ Ⓒ Ⓓ Ⓔ
6. Ⓐ Ⓑ Ⓒ Ⓓ Ⓔ
7. Ⓐ Ⓑ Ⓒ Ⓓ Ⓔ
8. Ⓐ Ⓑ Ⓒ Ⓓ Ⓔ
9. Ⓐ Ⓑ Ⓒ Ⓓ Ⓔ
10. Ⓐ Ⓑ Ⓒ Ⓓ Ⓔ
11. Ⓐ Ⓑ Ⓒ Ⓓ Ⓔ
12. Ⓐ Ⓑ Ⓒ Ⓓ Ⓔ
13. Ⓐ Ⓑ Ⓒ Ⓓ Ⓔ
14. Ⓐ Ⓑ Ⓒ Ⓓ Ⓔ
15. Ⓐ Ⓑ Ⓒ Ⓓ Ⓔ
16. Ⓐ Ⓑ Ⓒ Ⓓ Ⓔ
17. Ⓐ Ⓑ Ⓒ Ⓓ Ⓔ
18. Ⓐ Ⓑ Ⓒ Ⓓ Ⓔ
19. Ⓐ Ⓑ Ⓒ Ⓓ Ⓔ
20. Ⓐ Ⓑ Ⓒ Ⓓ Ⓔ
21. Ⓐ Ⓑ Ⓒ Ⓓ Ⓔ
22. Ⓐ Ⓑ Ⓒ Ⓓ Ⓔ
23. Ⓐ Ⓑ Ⓒ Ⓓ Ⓔ
24. Ⓐ Ⓑ Ⓒ Ⓓ Ⓔ
25. Ⓐ Ⓑ Ⓒ Ⓓ Ⓔ

MINI TEST 2

DIRECTIONS: Each passage is followed by questions based on its content. After reading the passage, choose the best answer to each question. Answer all questions based on what is indicated or implied in that passage.

Questions 1–6 are based on the following passage.

But the Divell as hee affecteth Deitie, and seeketh to have all the complements of Divine honor applied to his service, so hath he among the rest possessed also most Poets with his idle fansies. For in lieu of solemne and devout matter, to which in duety they owe their abilities, they now busy themselves in expressing such passions, as onely serve for testimonies to how unwoorthy affections they have wedded their wils. And because the best course to let them see the errour of their workes, is to weave a new webbe in their owne loom; I have heere layd a few course threds together, to invite some skillfuller wits to goe forward in the same, or to begin some finer peece, wherin it may be seene, how well verse and vertue sute together. Blame me not (good Cosen) though I send you a blame-woorthy present, in which the most that can commend it, is the good will of the writer, neither Arte nor invention, giving it any credite. If in mee this be a fault, you cannot be faultless that did importune mee to committe it, and therefore you must bear part of the penance, when it shall please sharpe censures to impose it. In the meane time with many good wishes I send you these few ditties, add you the Tunes, and let the Meane, I pray you, be still a part in all your Musicke.

From "The Author to his Loving Cosen," by Robert Southwell

1. In the author's view, poets should write about

    (A) the devil putting on Godly attributes.

    (B) the honor and duty due to God.

    (C) fantasies that help the reader to relax.

    (D) love and passion pertaining to women.

    (E) serious matters pertaining to God.

2. The author criticizes poets because

    I.   they waste their abilities on poems that deal with loving women instead of loving God.

    II. they write about love in such a way that shows they disdain marriage.

    III. their love poems show that worldly passion has got the better of them.

    (A) I only   (D) I and II

    (B) I and III   (E) I, II, and III

    (C) II only

3. What best describes the role of the author in the figure of speech used to describe his purpose?

    (A) He personifies the writer struggling to put across his web of ideas.

    (B) He plays the weaver in the extended metaphor about the loom and weaving, trying to encourage better poetry.

    (C) He plays the role of the new poet weaving new ideas for the old poets to copy.

    (D) He plays the role of the weaver trying to put back old techniques such as alliteration into the poetry of his days.

    (E) He personifies the role of the old jaded writer trying to encourage younger poets to write better rhyming poetry.

4. Why does the author send the book to his "cosen"?

    (A) He wants him to share in the praise if it is good.

    (B) He wants him to share in the blame if it is criticized.

    (C) The cousin asked him to write it.

    (D) He wants the cousin to learn from the book of poems.

    (E) The cousin is a patron who will promote the book.

5. The author's voice changes from

    (A) lecturing to praising.   (B) didactic to pedantic.

(C) critical to encouraging.

(D) harsh to gentle.

(E) arrogant to pleasant.

6. What best describes the last sentence?

(A) The author is punning on the idea of music and moderation.

(B) The author is using a pun on the mean in music and the "Golden mean" in life.

(C) The author is encouraging the cousin to set the poems to music, but to do it in moderation.

(D) The author is encouraging the cousin to write his own poems, but in a moderate way, not the passionate way of the contemporary poets.

(E) The author is warning the cousin to lead a moderate life despite loving to read poetry, because poetry could be the devil's way.

Questions 7–9 are based on the following passage.

There is no explanation for personal taste in art. My Aunt Josephine collected expensive china figurines and beautiful antique Tiffany lamps. She also insisted that two brilliantly colored Picasso prints hang in a prominent place in her dining room. She always said she knew what she liked, and she did not need to explain her collection to anyone. I always marveled that Aunt Josephine would consistently pinch pennies in the grocery store, but spend hundreds to add to her collection, without blinking an eye.

7. What best describes the author's attitude toward Aunt Josephine and her art collection?

(A) The author is amused by Aunt Josephine's art collection.

(B) The author is disgusted by Aunt Josephine's art collection.

(C) The author thinks Aunt Josephine is stingy.

(D) The author thinks Aunt Josephine is crazy.

(E) The author is jealous of Aunt Josephine.

8. What best describes Aunt Josephine's art collection, as a whole?

    (A) Eclectic and personal

    (D) Antique junk

    (B) Expensive and breakable

    (E) Answers (A) and (B) above.

    (C) Under-insured

9. According to the passage, which of the following best describes Aunt Josephine?

    (A) Overweight and overbearing

    (B) Dependent on others' opinions

    (C) Independent of others' opinions

    (D) Very wealthy

    (E) Always interested in talking about art to anyone

Questions 10–12 are based on the following passage.

Housefires result in the deaths of dozens of people every year. Smoke inhalation is the cause of death in most cases. Tragically, most housefires could be prevented. Many more housefires occur during the cold winter months than during the summer. This is because many people use unreliable space heaters. Fireplaces are another cause of housefires, especially fireplaces that do not have screens to prevent sparks from igniting objects nearby. The third most common cause of housefires is untended pans cooking on the stove. A pan of food can burn dry in a very short period of time. This situation creates so much heat that the cabinets and surrounding objects can burst into flames.

10. According to the passage, which of the following is NOT a common cause of housefires?

    (A) Fireplaces

    (D) Fires that begin in the kitchen

    (B) Faulty electrical wiring

    (E) Sparks from fireplaces

    (C) Unreliable space heaters

11. According to the passage, which of the following is NOT true?

    (A) Smoke causes many deaths in housefires.

    (B) Housefires cause many deaths each year.

    (C) Space heaters cause some housefires.

(D) More housefires occur during the winter than during the summer.

(E) Sparks from a fireplace seldom ignite carpets.

12. According to the passage, which of the following should be recommended in order to avoid winter housefires?

(A) Use screens on all fireplaces.

(B) Avoid unreliable space heaters.

(C) Keep doors and windows closed to avoid drafts.

(D) Answers (A) and (B) only.

(E) Answers (B) and (C) only.

Questions 13–19 are based on the following passage.

1   Incremental changes in federal government personnel management practices are the result of a long struggle which is chronologically documented. When our constitution was written, the framers focused on such important factors as separation of powers and sovereignty of "we the
5   people." They left to future policymakers the task of deciding manager/ employee relationships. At first our national government, composed of small agencies, attracted social elites who had prior management experience in either a business or farming. Generally speaking, people who worked in government during those first years maintained high ethical
10 standards and were among the best educated group of citizens. Federal government employees in the earliest years felt responsible for providing excellent service with public interest a central theme. The distinct management philosophy was classified the trustee period.

     As political philosophies changed, the characteristics of federal em-
15 ployment changed. Political parties clashed. Bitter feelings toward the other party led to distrust in government employment. Winners felt that they should reward party workers, regardless of educational preparation for the job, with appointment to government positions. By 1820, the patronage system was born. Loyalty to the elected politicians was the gov-
20 erning principle in hiring and firing practices. Unfortunately, some of the party faithful fostered corruption and other abuses.

     By 1883, disenchanted constituents pressured members of Congress to change the federal personnel system. The Civil Service Reform Act readily became law after President Garfield was shot by an office-seeking
25 party worker who failed to acquire a job after the election. The new law,

commonly known as the Pendleton Act, was a cautious step at best, but it did provide a foundation on which to build a more stable civil service cadre. Patronage as a mode for acquiring a job was eliminated in some of the agencies. A three-person Civil Service Commission provided leader-
30 ship in moving recruitment and hiring practices away from politics and toward hiring based on qualifications which matched job descriptions. The jurisdiction of the commission at first was quite small. By the time the second federal law was passed, the authority of the Commission had expanded, and government employees could not be fired unless the employer
35 substantiated that there was good cause to fire the employee. Employees' Fifth Amendment due process guarantees were a crucial barrier to unfair administrative practices.

Among other laws that affected federal government personnel practices, was the Hatch Act. The new law provided additional protections
40 against removal for political purposes. Critics assert that the law invaded First Amendment rights by denying civil service employees the opportunity to work actively in political campaigns or to run for public office or serve as a party officer.

Racial prejudices, common in the private sector, led to discrimination
45 in federal hiring, promotion, and firing practices. The Civil Service Commission was ineffective in monitoring and enforcing equal protection. Power of enforcement was transferred to the Equal Employment Opportunity Commission in 1978. Federal judges also played a prominent role in getting to the root of inequities in such cases as *Griggs vs. Duke Power*
50 *Company* in 1971 where the Supreme Court ruled that test questions must be related to expected job qualifications and performance.

13. Which statement best summarizes the history of personnel management in the United States?

(A) The values of late eighteenth century public administrators are not and cannot be applicable to modern government.

(B) Benefits of patronage practices outweigh problems. The author implies that civil servants who are loyal to the president, his party, and his policies will work harder in order to win the next election.

(C) As science and technology change, the definition of honesty and merit should change accordingly.

(D) The original basic values of public personnel managers under President Washington have remained intact, for the most part,

similar to the values of twentieth century personnel management, although other values have been introduced.

(E) Due to the wide variety of intelligence and skills, it is impossible
to develop fair personnel policies.

14. What becomes apparent under close examination of the author's analysis?

(A) The author illustrated how tension exists between standards of a
professional, non-patronage personnel system and constitutional
rights of free speech and association of governmental employees.

(B) The author has become bitter about political party conflicts and
personnel loyalties.

(C) The author adheres to the theory that government administrators
must never question strict obedience to agency rules.

(D) The author advocates legislative delegation of unlimited discretion to administrators in hiring and firing.

(E) It is apparent that the author sympathizes with industry in the
Griggs case.

15. Which analysis by the author is valid according to passages above?

(A) The analyst is squarely in the camp of modern day philosophers
who adhere to the theory that popular sovereignty can never lead
to good personnel practices in government.

(B) The writer disagrees with the Supreme Court's interpretation of
the equal protection clause and implies that tests are indeed valuable in personnel placement regardless of impact of scores on
racial groups.

(C) The author carefully analyzes problems which developed during
the affirmative action movement when President Garfield meddled
unfairly in hiring practices of the Civil Service Commission.

(D) The author objectively describes an instance when the EEOC
and the Supreme Court justices found common ground in constitutional interpretation that brought about changes in personnel
policy standards.

(E) The author rejects incrementalism as an explanation for what
has happened in personnel management.

16. What details did constitutional framers incorporate into our fundamental law?

    (A) The constitutional provisions are broadly worded and do not provide specific personnel policies for government bureaucracies.

    (B) The framers' legal philosophy "We the people...." was grounded in patronage rewards of government jobs for political campaign workers.

    (C) The Civil Service Provision of the constitution was dormant until President Garfield enforced that section of the constitution.

    (D) The constitutional separation of powers doctrine, important to the personnel management, was struck by the court in the "separate but equal" case.

    (E) The author fails to discuss the spoils system, a once popular method of hiring people based on the wishes of winners of elections who wanted to offer jobs to people who showed the greatest support during the campaign.

17. What was the philosophy behind the Hatch Act discussed in lines 38–43?

    (A) Civil servants appointed on a system of merit are in a strategic position to be pressured to work actively to reelect whoever holds office at the time with threat of job loss if they refuse.

    (B) The Hatch Act was passed to provide affirmative action in protecting black governmental employees after the election.

    (C) Congress, as punishment to those governmental employees who would not work in election campaigns, took revenge by denying civil servants the privilege of active participation in the next election.

    (D) The philosophy behind the Hatch Act was rather vague and puzzles political observers who have not discovered the real reason the law was passed.

    (E) Civil servants are in a position to know secret data in files which could harm an incumbent seeking election. It appears that under the old law, it is illegal to disclose fraud during elections.

18. What kinds of regulations apply to personnel managers who govern equality during the hiring process?

(A) Prior to 1883, personnel managers had a fairly free hand in deciding whom they would hire, but politics did not count.

(B) The author implies that before a person is hired, the *Griggs* case mandates employers perform what is known as "mixed scanning"—a system of evaluating a large amount of data.

(C) In recent years, employment-screening tests may be challenged by applicants as violating the equal protection clause if the questions have no specific application to skills that are required for the position.

(D) The constitutional requirement of fair procedures has yet to protect a civil servant from losing his job due to racial prejudice of his supervisor.

(E) Under the balance of power theory, Congress has no formal power to govern personnel policies of the federal executive branch.

19. How can the previous paragraphs be evaluated?

(A) The author has demonstrated that he does not fully understand the philosophy of separation of powers and the federal system of government.

(B) The author has developed a systematic frame of reference for analyzing how the three branches of government have succeeded and failed in resolving critical issues of personnel management.

(C) It is evident that the author is dismayed with too many new agencies—better known as "big government."

(D) The author's philosophy is apparent in his support for centralization of government with personnel rule making transferred back to Congress.

(E) Formal study of public administration is hampered because our system of government operates under rules of strict confidentiality, similar to the difficulty of studying decision making within big business.

Questions 20–25 are based on the following passage.

The age of Ancient Greece saw many different philosophies come to light. The following passage looks at the ideas and beliefs of Epicurus, Zeno, and Carneades of Cyrene.

1   The Hellenistic Age produced two major and two minor additions to the history of philosophy. Epicureanism and Stoicism represented the period's dominant philosophical movements. Skepticism and Cynicism found limited support among those unwilling to accept the Epicureans'
5   and Stoics' confidence in reason. Hellenistic philosophy marked a turning point in the western intellectual tradition. The classical Greek philosophers linked the individual's happiness to the community's well being. The philosophers of the Hellenistic period focused on the individual. The business of philosophy shifted from the pursuit of knowledge for its own sake. The
10   goal of philosophy became the individual's peace of mind and personal happiness.

        Epicurus (ca. 342–270 B.C.E.) founded a school in Athens and based his metaphysics on Democritus's atomic theory. Epicurus taught that the goal of philosophy should be to help the individual find happiness. Unlike
15   Socrates and Plato, he did not make citizenship in a polis the basis of happiness. Epicurus argued that a wise man eschewed public affairs and sought self-sufficiency. Later critics accused Epicurus and his followers of advocating a life based on pursuing the pleasures of the flesh. To Epicurus, however, the highest pleasure was to be found in contemplation.

20   Zeno (ca. 335–263 B.C.E.) established a rival philosophical school under the *Stoa Poikile* (painted porch) of the Athenian *Agora* (market-place). There are a number of similarities between Stoicism and Epicure-anism. Like Epicurus, Zeno emphasized the importance of the individual. Moreover, both schools were based on a materialistic metaphysics and
25   claimed universal validity for their teachings. There were, however, sig-nificant differences between the two philosophical outlooks. Zeno taught that the cosmos was a unified whole which was based on a universal order (Logos or Fire). Every man carried a spark of this Logos in his reason. At death this spark returned to its origin. The Stoics taught that each person
30   should strive to discover the natural law governing the universe and live in accordance with it.

        The Skeptics attacked the Epicureans and the Stoics. Carneades of Cyrene (ca. 213–129 B.C.E.) argued that all knowledge was relative. The sensory impressions which we receive from the external world are flawed.
35   Individuals should abandon the quest for knowledge because nothing can

be known for certain. The safest course is to doubt everything. Indifference is the only philosophically defensible position.

Diogenes of Sinope (d. 323 B.C.E.) was the most famous cynic. His goal was to prepare the individual for any disaster. He lived as a beggar 40 and was famous for his outspoken condemnation of sham and hypocrisy. One story has it that when he met Alexander the Great and the world-conqueror asked him what he wanted, Diogenes replied that Alexander should get out of his light.

20. Education for citizenship was a goal of

(A) Epicurus.   (D) Diogenes.

(B) Socrates.   (E) Zeno.

(C) Carneades.

21. The saying, "I am trying to find myself and my happiness" might be employed by a follower of

(A) Diogenes.   (D) Stoics.

(B) Zeno.   (E) Epicurus.

(C) Hellen.

22. The word "polis" in line 15 most nearly means

(A) a group.

(B) in a certain way.

(C) a place of one's own; a place of solitude.

(D) a tradition.

(E) a philosophical outlook.

23. The author focused on the classical Greek philosophers in order to

(A) show similarities with the Jurassic Age.

(B) contrast them with Oriental thinkers.

(C) show their relation to the earlier philosophers of the Hellenistic Age.

(D) contrast them with those of the Hellenistic Age.

(E) show his scorn of the past.

24. The most important element of Stoic thought was

    (A) its similarity to Epicureanism.

    (B) the universal validity of its teaching.

    (C) the idea that each person carried a spark of Logos in his reason.

    (D) its establishment under the painted porch of the Athenian marketplace.

    (E) its emphasis on the individual.

25. Carneades taught that

    (A) all knowledge was relative.

    (B) the goal of philosophy should be to help the individual find happiness.

    (C) a wise man eschewed public affairs and sought self-sufficiency.

    (D) the individual should be prepared for any disaster.

    (E) the highest pleasure was to be found in contemplation.

MINI TEST 2

ANSWER KEY

1.	(E)	6.	(B)	11.	(E)	16.	(A)	21.	(C)
2.	(B)	7.	(A)	12.	(D)	17.	(A)	22.	(A)
3.	(B)	8.	(A)	13.	(D)	18.	(C)	23.	(D)
4.	(C)	9.	(C)	14.	(A)	19.	(B)	24.	(E)
5.	(D)	10.	(B)	15.	(D)	20.	(B)	25.	(A)

DETAILED EXPLANATIONS OF ANSWERS

1.   **(E)**   The language is at first off-putting, but reading carefully through the passage's first few lines reveals clearly the author's viewpoint. He blames the devil but does not say poets write about him. He does not want poets to write about passion of loving women, nor fantasies of any kind. In "lieu of" simply means "instead of"; "solemn and devout" can easily translate to serious matters pertaining to God—the answer is (E).

2.   **(B)**   Although the word "wedded" is in the area of criticism, the author does not criticize poets for their views on marriage; he does criticize that poets have wedded their wills to expressing themselves on "unworthy affections." Because he sets these up in direct contrast to the love of God, one translates such affections as passion for women. He suggests also through the association with the "Divell," that such affections are beyond the poets' control. The answer then is a combination of I and III (B).

3.   **(B)**   You need to find the figure of speech (an extended metaphor of the weaver and weaving) and determine what it means in the context of the whole piece. He is not personifying, nor jaded, nor encouraging alliteration. He makes a plea that his poetry "a few coarse threads" will weave "a new webbe in their loom," so that better poets will carry on what he has started or begin an even better strain of poetry, "a finer peece," which will combine verse and goodness together in the implied sense of woven together. The answer is (B).

4.   **(C)**   You need to sort out all the mannered flattery of the concluding lines and understand the word "importune." The cousin in fact asked the author to write the book (C).

5.   **(D)**   The author's tone is lecturing to begin with, but does not change to praise. It is didatic but moves from that. He is not encouraging the cousin at the end but humbly setting out his reasons for writing poetry. Arrogant does not fully capture the tone at the beginning. It is too sincere for arrogance. The best couple is the simplest—harsh to gentle (D).

6.   **(B)**   The mean in music means the middle part. The author puns on

this and the (Golden) Meane in life, i.e., take the middle way, the way of moderation in the "music of life." The answer is (B), the most complete explanation of the lines.

7. **(A)** In this question you are asked to infer the author's attitude toward Aunt Josephine and her art collection. There are two clues in the passage. The first clue is in the third sentence when the author says that Aunt Josephine "insisted" on combining Picasso and Tiffany lamps. The author apparently feels that this is an unusual combination. The second clue is in the last sentence when the author "marveled" at her spending habits. Clearly, the author is amused and feels Aunt Josephine's behavior is quaint and perhaps eccentric. Choice (A) is the best choice. The author does not give any indication that he feels Aunt Josephine is "crazy" or "stingy" even though he admits she "pinches pennies." The author is neither disgusted, nor jealous, so answers (B) and (E) are incorrect.

8. **(A)** This question requires you to step back and view the art collection as an observer. Picasso prints are expensive, but not breakable, so answers (B) and (E) are incorrect. Choice (C) is incorrect because we have no information about insurance. Choice (D) is incorrect because Tiffany lamps and Picasso prints are not "junk." Eclectic means "choosing the best from diverse sources." This is exactly what Aunt Josephine has done, so choice (A) is correct.

9. **(C)** Choice (C) is correct. The passage does not discuss her weight or wealth, so choices (A) and (D) are incorrect. She is definitely not dependent on other people's opinions, so choice (B) is incorrect. She may be interested in talking with other people, but we do not know that this is true. Therefore, choice (E) is incorrect.

10. **(B)** This question asks you to use the process of elimination to determine an choice. The only choice not discussed in the passage is (B). All other answers are discussed. Choice (B) is correct.

11. **(E)** This question also asks you to determine which choice is not discussed in the passage. Choices (A), (B), (C) and (D) are specifically discussed. The correct choice is (E).

12. **(D)** Choice (D) is correct because screens for fireplaces and space heaters are both discussed in the passage. Keeping doors and windows closed is never discussed.

13. **(D)**   The correct choice is (D). The author examines the trustee period when educated, highly ethical people managed government during President Washington's administration. He traces the deterioration of values under presidential administrations between 1820 and 1883 when party affiliation and loyalty were the controlling factors in hiring and firing government personnel. He examines how in recent years Congress and federal agencies have taken positive steps to assure quality management based on education and to eliminate unethical practices based on self-interest and corruption.

Choice (A) is incorrect. The author does not imply or specify that honesty, education, and public interest have gone out of style. He does recognize that while high achievement in education is important, many jobs do not require broad knowledge. For those positions, specific knowledge needed to perform a job well is the basic requirement. Thus, the early values that he identified remain important today. Choice (B) is wrong. If the reader thought that the author implied that civil servants who are loyal to the president, his party, and his policies will work harder in order to win the next election, the author's point of view was missed. The author pointed out that under the patronage system, unqualified people working in government damaged the reputation of public service, especially when fraud and other corruption were reported in many localities. Choice (C) is incorrect. Although the author said that additional values have governed modern governmental processes, he certainly did not prove that as science and technology change, the definition of honesty and merit should change accordingly. In fact, ethical administrators will remain the bulwark of good government. Standards for measuring and rewarding meritorious service may change, but merit itself remains a basic value under the scrutiny of the author. Choice (E) does not reflect the views of the author who recognizes that differences require development of fair procedures.

14. **(A)**   Choice (A) is the correct choice. The author discusses the need to reduce the pressure of politics often exerted on government employees. He noted that Congress passed the Hatch Act which denies federal employees opportunity to participate actively in political party campaign strategies. At that point tension develops when government employees who want to play a prominent role in party politics face loss of jobs. The Bill of Rights protects citizens who wish to participate in the political process. Specifically, First Amendment free speech and association limit governmental power on citizens' political activities. Federal employees are caught between the Hatch Act limitations and First Amendment freedoms.

Choice (B) is incorrect. Bitterness is not an appropriate description of the way the author portrayed his examination of political pressure on employees. Perhaps analytical precision would be the term that better describes the author's style of writing. Research findings showed party battles and jealousies made it desirable for politicians to appoint party faithful to government positions. But under these conditions, governmental purposes were compromised. The author illustrated the case in point by reminding readers that President Garfield lost his life under the patronage system. Choice (C) is incorrect. The author, while respecting rules and lamenting the fact that some agencies failed to follow rules, did not call for blind obedience to agency rules. He reported that the Civil Service Commission and the Office of Legal Counsel failed to carry out policies to protect applicants and employees, but he also left room for agency interpretation of the constitution in application of the rules. The author called for revision of old rules and promulgation of new rules in order to remedy problems which exist in personnel practices. Choice (D) is incorrect. Unlimited discretion of administrators in hiring and firing is a return to the old patronage system and the days before affirmative action. The author does not propose an unconstitutional law. Choice (E) stated an opinion where there is no evidence how the author feels about the case. His statement about the results of the *Griggs* case was neutral.

15. **(D)**   Choice (D) is correct. The Supreme Court provided leadership when in a 1971 landmark case it made illegal tests that measured *general educational achievement* of job applicants rather than *specific knowledge required of the job description*. The discriminatory practice was a clear violation of the equal protection clause. A few years later, the Equal Employment Opportunity Commission (EEOC) acquired power to protect employees against discrimination after the Civil Service Commission defaulted in enforcing equal protection guarantees of the constitution. Thus the authority of the EEOC for providing equity in personnel practices, which would include content of tests and the negative impact on disadvantaged groups, was reinforced in the court's interpretation of equal protection in *Griggs vs. Duke Power Company*. From this example, readers can conclude that court precedents are valuable tools of agencies who enforce equal protection.

Choice (A) is incorrect. Our constitution is based on popular sovereignty or "We the people...." Under popular sovereignty, citizens have power to change the constitution that governs our country. The author has vividly shown how personnel standards have varied over the years according to the ideas and wishes of the people. For example, the patronage system was permitted by the public until it became tired and disillusioned with the whole process. At that point Congress felt compelled to change the system by passing laws and authorizing mechanisms which monitor and punish wrongdoing by employers and employees. Choice (B) is incorrect. The reader may have misread the paragraphs and made the wrong choice. The conclusion stated in (B) is erroneous. In fact, the author calls for alleviation of numerous grievances of employees in instances where the equal protection clause does not govern the process. Choice (C) is incorrect. The statement shows failure to grasp the historical setting provided by the author. For example, President Garfield's death preceded the Civil Service Commission and affirmative action. Choice (E) misinterprets the author who recognized and understood how policies were made in small steps which were governed by how much change was politically possible during various stages of history.

16. **(A)** Choice (A) is correct. The author examined a number of critical issues in federal employment that have challenged policy makers and implementers of personnel management. For example, sex discrimination, racial discrimination, and age discrimination have been well documented. Government policy makers have power to craft guidelines which remove barriers that impede employment of females, minorities, and older applicants. The author points out that as more women enter the workforce, other issues must be addressed. Leaves of absence when a child is born and sexual harassment are not confined to female employees. Therefore, administrators must be empathetic to all employees when they fashion rules that cover a variety of needs. Although management problems are difficult, administrators cannot ignore them. Government has power to rectify problems identified by the author. Choice (B) is incorrect. Although the author recognizes that, at times, administrators defy legislative intent in making rules and applying them in personnel practices, he does not reject Congressional power to make laws that correct past wrongs in public administration. In fact, he calls for adherence to the law and calls for additional laws and rules that will be based on the highest of values. Choice (C) is incorrect. Lack of space prohibited a definitive examination of the roles of state legislatures and state courts in personnel administration. The author does not, however, imply that *federal* personnel problems can be corrected by legislative, executive, or judicial branches in one or more of our state governments. Rather, he examines ways in which federal branches of government have influenced or controlled personnel guidelines. Choice (D) is incorrect. The author does not ignore the important role of constitutional due process guarantees in administering federal policies. In fact, he felt that the Fifth Amendment due process protections were activated when Congress established the Civil Service Commission

and other agencies later on. He implies that the Constitution must continue to play a prime role as government tries to find solutions for present-day problems. Choice (E) is wrong. The reader should review the passages that discuss the patronage system.

17. **(A)** Choice (A) is correct. The law was to protect employees from job losses if they refused to campaign in a political election. Choice (B) is wrong. Although affirmative action has great merit, the author has not implied that the law was designed to protect any one race. Choice (C) is not correct. As the author stated, the law was designed to protect government workers. Choice (D) is incorrect. The author forthrightly states what is a well-known purpose of the Hatch Act. Choice (E) has fabricated the purpose of the law and the way that the law is enforced.

18. **(C)** Choice (C) is correct. The *Griggs* case is an excellent example of how a job applicant successfully challenged unrelated questions on a test administered by a power company that were used to screen him out of a job. Choice (A) is wrong. If government should arbitrarily decide whom to hire, it is an erroneous assumption that political shenanigans led to unfair decisions. In fact, one of the purposes of the Civil Service Commission was to move away from politics. Choice (B) wrongly concludes that the law requires massive red tape before a person is eligible to work in either the private or public sector. Choice (D) is wrong. The author explained the role of the Civil Service Commission was expanded in order to make the Fifth Amendment viable in federal government. Choice (E) ignored a good example of congressional power over personnel policies when it passed the Pendleton Act.

19. **(B)** Choice (B) is correct. In an orderly way, the author considered the values of the framers of the constitution, the quality of early public administrators, and the deterioration of quality until pressure was exerted on Congress to regulate the hiring and firing practices of government managers. He continued his analysis by commenting on Fifth Amendment due process guarantees in personnel management and the effort Congress made to remove government employees from the stress and strain of working for politicians. He explained the creation of important agencies chartered to protect employees, and he identified grave problems which remain. Finally, he showed how values of the first federal government administrators are similar to standards that govern the process today.

Choice (A) is incorrect. Separation of powers does not mean that Congress and the courts have no roles in governing personnel practices in the executive branch of government. Although legislative powers are lodged in Congress and judicial powers are lodged in the judicial branch, authority to carry out executive policy comes from laws passed by the legislature, and conflicts are settled in the courts. The author shows how the three branches have interacted over the past two centuries in the substantive area of personnel management. Choice (C) is incorrect. The statement is a misinterpretation of the author's criticism of flaws in the federal system. He does not call for elimination or reduction of agencies or personnel. Rather, he recommends improvement so that established agencies will function more effectively. Choice (D) is incorrect. While the author does not call for centralization of government for personnel rule making, he does recognize the important role Congress plays in making laws which will prompt governmental agencies to provide equal protection and due process in all phases of administering personnel regulations. Choice (E) is refuted by the tremendous number of facts made from study and observation of students of government which the author reports. Such details could not be examined if government were protected from public scrutiny.

20. **(B)** Education for citizenship was a goal of Socrates (B). Epicurus (A), on the other hand, emphasized individual happiness. Carneades (C) argued that all knowledge was relative; he was not concerned with society, as was Socrates, and should not be chosen. Diogenes (D) was the most famous cynic; his goal was to prepare the individual for disaster. Zeno (E) taught that the cosmos was a unified whole which was based on a universal order. His primary concern was not with citizenship.

21. **(C)** The saying, "I am trying to find myself and my happiness" might be employed by a follower of (C) Hellen. Diogenes (A) was the most famous cynic; his goal was to prepare the individual for disaster. Zeno (B) taught that the cosmos was a unified whole which was based on a universal order. His primary concern was not with citizenship. The Stoics (D) taught that each person should strive to discover the natural law governing the universe and live in accordance with it. (E) Epicurus founded a school and taught that individual happiness was the goal.

22. **(A)** The word "polis" in line 15 most nearly means (A) a group. In a certain way (B) has nothing to do with the meaning of "polis." Polis (C) does not refer to a place of one's own or a place of solitude. A tradition is not the best meaning for "polis." Polis is not a philosophical outlook (E); therefore, (E) should not be selected.

23. **(D)**   The author focused on the classical Greek philosophers in order to (D) contrast them with those of the Hellenistic Age. The purpose of the focus on the Hellenistic Age is not to contrast the age with a much earlier time; (A) is not the correct choice. Little emphasis is given to the Oriental thinkers, so choice (B) is not the correct choice. Since the Hellenistic Age followed the Greek Age, the purpose was not to show their relation to the earlier philosophers of the Hellenistic Period. (C) should not be chosen. The author exhibits no scorn of the past in his writing. (E) is, therefore, not an appropriate choice.

24. **(E)**   The most important element of Stoic thought was its emphasis on the individual—not the group as earlier schools of thought had emphasized. The Stoic taught that each person carried a spark of Logos in his reason, but (C) is not the best choice. (D) is also a true statement, but it is not the most important element. It is true that Zeno's school was established under the painted porch of the Athenian marketplace; however, (D) should not be selected. Stoic thought was similar to Epicurus's thought, but that was not the most important element of Stoic thought. The writing *claims* universal validity, but since this has not been proven (B) is not the best choice. Similarity to Epicureanism (A) is also incorrect.

25. **(A)**   Carneades taught that all knowledge was relative. (A) is the correct choice. It was Epicurus (B) that taught that the goal of philosophy should be to help the individual find happiness and that (C) a wise man eschewed public affairs and sought self-sufficiency. He also stated that the highest pleasure was to be found in contemplation (E). Neither (B) nor (C) nor (E) should be chosen. Diogenes taught that the individual should be prepared for any disaster; (D) is not the correct answer.

MINI TEST 3

1. Ⓐ Ⓑ Ⓒ Ⓓ Ⓔ
2. Ⓐ Ⓑ Ⓒ Ⓓ Ⓔ
3. Ⓐ Ⓑ Ⓒ Ⓓ Ⓔ
4. Ⓐ Ⓑ Ⓒ Ⓓ Ⓔ
5. Ⓐ Ⓑ Ⓒ Ⓓ Ⓔ
6. Ⓐ Ⓑ Ⓒ Ⓓ Ⓔ
7. Ⓐ Ⓑ Ⓒ Ⓓ Ⓔ
8. Ⓐ Ⓑ Ⓒ Ⓓ Ⓔ
9. Ⓐ Ⓑ Ⓒ Ⓓ Ⓔ
10. Ⓐ Ⓑ Ⓒ Ⓓ Ⓔ
11. Ⓐ Ⓑ Ⓒ Ⓓ Ⓔ
12. Ⓐ Ⓑ Ⓒ Ⓓ Ⓔ
13. Ⓐ Ⓑ Ⓒ Ⓓ Ⓔ
14. Ⓐ Ⓑ Ⓒ Ⓓ Ⓔ
15. Ⓐ Ⓑ Ⓒ Ⓓ Ⓔ
16. Ⓐ Ⓑ Ⓒ Ⓓ Ⓔ
17. Ⓐ Ⓑ Ⓒ Ⓓ Ⓔ
18. Ⓐ Ⓑ Ⓒ Ⓓ Ⓔ
19. Ⓐ Ⓑ Ⓒ Ⓓ Ⓔ
20. Ⓐ Ⓑ Ⓒ Ⓓ Ⓔ
21. Ⓐ Ⓑ Ⓒ Ⓓ Ⓔ
22. Ⓐ Ⓑ Ⓒ Ⓓ Ⓔ
23. Ⓐ Ⓑ Ⓒ Ⓓ Ⓔ
24. Ⓐ Ⓑ Ⓒ Ⓓ Ⓔ
25. Ⓐ Ⓑ Ⓒ Ⓓ Ⓔ

MINI TEST 3

Questions 1–6 are based on the following passage.

*The Prussian army under Frederic the Great is
discussed in the following passage.*

1　　The general principles on which this strange government was conducted deserve attention. The policy of Frederic was essentially the same
as his father's; but Frederic, while he carried that policy to lengths to
which his father never thought of carrying it, cleared it at the same time
5　from the absurdities with which his father had encumbered it. The King's
first object was to have a great, efficient, and well-trained army. He had a
kingdom which in extent and population was hardly in the second rank of
European powers; and yet he aspired to a place not inferior to that of the
sovereigns of England, France, and Austria. For that end it was necessary
10　that Prussia should be all sting. Louis XV, with five times as many subjects as Frederic and more than five times as large a revenue, had not a
more formidable army. The proportion which the soldiers in Prussia bore
to the people seems hardly credible. Of the males in the vigour of life, a
seventh part were probably under arms; and this great force had, by drill-
15　ing, by reviewing, and by the unsparing use of cane and scourge, been
taught to perform all evolutions with a rapidity and a precision which
would have astonished Villars or Eugene. The elevated feelings which are
necessary to the best kind of army were then wanting to the Prussian
service. In those ranks were not found the religious and political enthusi-
20　asm which inspired the pikemen of Cromwell, the patriotic ardour, the
thirst of glory, the devotion to a great leader, which inflamed the Old
Guard of Napoleon. But in all the mechanical parts of the military calling,
the Prussians were as superior to the English and French troops of that day
as the English and French troops to a rustic militia.

25　　Though the pay of the Prussian soldier was small, though every
rixdollar of extraordinary charge was scrutinized by Frederic with a vigi-
lance and suspicion such as Mr. Joseph Hume never brought to the examination of any army estimate, the expense of such an establishment was, for

the means of the country, enormous. In order that it might not be utterly
30 ruinous, it was necessary that every other expense should be cut down to
the lowest possible point. Accordingly Frederic, though his dominion bor-
dered on the sea, had no navy. He neither had nor wished to have colonies.
His judges, his fiscal officers, were meanly paid. His ministers at foreign
courts walked on foot, or drove shabby old carriages till the axletrees gave
35 way. Even to his highest diplomatic agents, who resided at London and
Paris, he allowed less than a thousand pounds sterling a year. The royal
household was managed with a frugality unusual in the establishments of
opulent subjects, unexampled in any other palace. The King loved good
eating and drinking, and during great part of his life took pleasure in
40 seeing his table surrounded by guests; yet the whole charge of his kitchen
was brought within the sum of two thousand pounds sterling a year. He
examined every extraordinary item with a care which might be thought to
suit the mistress of a boarding-house better than a great prince. When
more than four rixdollars were asked of him for a hundred oysters, he
45 stormed as if he had heard that one of his generals had sold a fortress to
the Empress Queen. Not a bottle of Champagne was uncorked without his
express order. The game of the royal parks and forests, a serious head of
expenditure in most kingdoms, was to him a source of profit. The whole
was farmed out; and though the farmers were almost ruined by their con-
50 tract, the King would grant them no remission. His wardrobe consisted of
one fine gala dress, which lasted him all his life; of two or three old coats
fit for Monmouth Street, yellow waistcoats soiled with snuff, and of huge
boots embrowned by time. One taste alone sometimes allured him beyond
the limits of parsimony, nay even beyond the limits of prudence, the taste
55 for building. In all other things his economy was such as we might call by
a harsher name, if we did not reflect that his funds were drawn from a
heavily taxed people, and that it was impossible for him without excessive
tyranny to keep up at once a formidable army and a splendid court.

1. The comparison with Louis XV (lines 10–12) emphasizes

    (A) Frederic's genius for organization.

    (B) the burden of taxation in Frederic's kingdom.

    (C) the hugeness of Frederic's army.

    (D) Frederic's political aims in Europe.

    (E) the training undergone by Prussian soldiers.

2. The author argues that Prussian "drilling" (lines 14–15) produced

    (A) great devotion to a national cause.

    (B) mechanical precision in battle.

    (C) willingness to obey orders.

    (D) blind devotion to a great leader.

    (E) a patriotic population.

3. In line 16, the word "evolutions" most nearly means

    (A) changes.   (D) duties.

    (B) movements.   (E) training.

    (C) firing.

4. To pay for the army, the author shows (lines 29–31), Frederic

    (A) raised taxes on the wealthy.

    (B) borrowed from other governments in Europe.

    (C) reduced spending in other departments.

    (D) reduced the number of Prussian colonies.

    (E) expanded the navy.

5. The word "meanly" in line 33 most nearly means

    (A) slowly.   (D) justly.

    (B) generously.   (E) cruelly.

    (C) poorly.

6. The details concerning the royal household (lines 36–38) are evidence of Frederic's

    (A) mastery of financial management.

    (B) enjoyment of wealth.

    (C) ability to control servants.

    (D) use of royal land for profit.

    (E) devotion to religion in later life.

Questions 7–15 are based on the following passage.

In the following passage John Stuart Mill discusses the right of free speech, which he argues should be afforded to all citizens in the name of liberty.

1   I do not pretend that the most unlimited use of the freedom of enunci-
ating all possible opinions would put an end to the evils of religious or
philosophical sectarianism. Every truth, which men of narrow capacity are
in earnest about, is sure to be asserted, inculcated, and in many ways even
5   acted on, as if no other truth existed in the world, or at all events none that
could limit or qualify the first. I acknowledge that the tendency of all
opinions to become sectarian is not cured by the freest discussion, but is
often heightened and exacerbated thereby; the truth which ought to have
been, but was not, seen, being rejected all the more violently because
10 proclaimed by persons regarded as opponents. But it is not on the impassioned partisan, it is on the calmer and more disinterested bystander, that
this collision of opinions works its salutary effect. Not the violent conflict
between parts of the truth, but the quiet suppression of half of it, is the
formidable evil; there is always hope when people are forced to listen to
15 both sides; it is when they attend only to one that errors harden into
prejudices, and truth itself ceases to have the effect of truth, by being
exaggerated into falsehood. And since there are few mental attributes more
rare than that judicial faculty which can sit in intelligent judgement between two sides of a question, of which only one is represented by an
20 advocate before it, truth has no chance but in proportion as every side of it,
every opinion which embodies any fraction of the truth, not only finds
advocates, but is so advocated as to be listened to.

We have now recognized the necessity to the mental well-being of
mankind (on which all their other well-being depends) of freedom of
25 opinion, and freedom of the expression of opinion, on four distinct grounds;
which we will now briefly recapitulate.

First, if any opinion is compelled to silence, that opinion may, for
aught we can certainly know, be true. To deny this is to assume our own
infallibility.

30 Secondly, though the silenced opinion be an error, it may, and very
commonly does, contain a portion of truth; and since the general or prevailing opinion on any subject is rarely or never the whole truth, it is only
by the collision of adverse opinions that the remainder of the truth has any
chance of being supplied.

35   Thirdly, even if the received opinion be not only true, but the whole

truth; unless it is suffered to be, and actually is, vigorously and earnestly contested, it will, by most of those who receive it, be held in the manner of a prejudice, with little comprehension or feeling of its rational grounds. And not only this, but, fourthly, the meaning of the doctrine itself will be
40 in danger of being lost, or enfeebled, and deprived of its vital effect on the character and conduct: the dogma becoming a mere formal profession, inefficacious for good, but cumbering the ground, and preventing the growth of any real and heartfelt conviction, from reason or personal experience.

7. The word "sectarianism" in line 3 most nearly means

   (A) membership in a church.

   (B) attachment to a single cause.

   (C) belief in progress.

   (D) rebellion against established authority.

   (E) inability to formulate ideals.

8. In the sentence "And since there are few mental attributes...to be listened to" (lines 17–22), the author argues the need for

   (A) clear writing and speaking.

   (B) the open expression of divergent opinions.

   (C) public advocates.

   (D) controls upon dangerous speech.

   (E) the inclusion of all segments of society in debates.

9. The author uses the analogy of the impassioned partisan and the disinterested bystander (lines 10–12) to show

   (A) the danger of censorship.

   (B) the primary benefits of political choice.

   (C) the effect of different views upon the individual.

   (D) the possibility of a truly democratic society.

   (E) the need for informed citizens.

10. The author sees the most serious threat to liberty of thought (lines 12–17) in

    (A) the violent clashes of opponents.

    (B) the extinguishing of half the truth.

    (C) the rigorous transmission of prejudice.

    (D) the spreading of false ideas.

    (E) the use of force by government.

11. In line 33, the word "adverse" most nearly means

    (A) negative.   (D) comparable.

    (B) opposing.   (E) juxtaposed.

    (C) lower.

12. The author argues that perceived truths are strengthened by debate (lines 39–44) because

    (A) they cease to be doctrines.

    (B) they become principles.

    (C) they cease to be prejudices.

    (D) they cease to be convictions.

    (E) they become opinions.

13. In his conclusion, the author defends free discussion of popular beliefs because, in his view, such discussion

    (A) stimulates growth of real belief.

    (B) leads to fresh ideas.

    (C) revolutionizes existing institutions.

    (D) exposes faults in existing concepts.

    (E) trains future speakers.

14. In line 42, the word "cumbering" most nearly means

    (A) obscuring.   (D) bordering.

    (B) ruining.   (E) engaging.

    (C) desecrating.

15. The tone of this passage is

   (A) self-righteous indignation.

   (B) honest zeal.

   (C) disapproval.

   (D) assertive.

   (E) uninfluential.

Questions 16–21 are based on the following passage.

The following passage describes the development and use of the submarine as an offensive weapon of war.

1   A submarine was first used as an offensive weapon during the American Revolutionary War. The Turtle, a one-man submersible designed by an American inventor named David Bushnell and hand-operated by a screw propeller, attempted to sink a British man-of-war in New York Harbor.
5 The plan was to attach a charge of gunpowder to the ship's bottom with screws and explode it with a time fuse. After repeated failures to force the screws through the copper sheathing of the hull of *H.M.S. Eagle,* the submarine gave up and withdrew, exploding its powder a short distance from the *Eagle.* Although the attack was unsuccessful, it caused the Brit-
10 ish to move their blockading ships from the harbor to the outer bay.

       On 17 February 1864, a Confederate craft, a hand-propelled submersible, carrying a crew of eight men, sank a federal corvette that was blockading Charleston Harbor. The hit was accomplished by a torpedo suspended ahead of the Confederate Hunley as she rammed the Union frigate
15 *Housatonic* and is the first recorded instance of a submarine sinking a warship.

       The submarine first became a major component in naval warfare during World War I, when Germany demonstrated its full potential. Wholesale sinking of Allied shipping by the German U-boats almost swung the
20 war in favor of the Central Powers. Then, as now, the submarine's greatest advantage was that it could operate beneath the ocean surface where detection was difficult. Sinking a submarine was comparatively easy, once it was found—but finding it before it could attack was another matter.

       During the closing months of World War I, the Allied Submarine
25 Devices Investigation Committee was formed to obtain from science and technology more effective underwater detection equipment. The committee developed a reasonably accurate device for locating a submerged submarine. This device was a trainable hydrophone, which was attached to

the bottom of the ASW ship, and used to detect screw noises and other
30 sounds that came from a submarine. Although the committee disbanded
after World War I, the British made improvements on the locating device
during the interval between then and World War II, and named it ASDIC
after the committee.

American scientists further improved on the device, calling it SO-
35 NAR, a name derived from the underlined initials of the words *so*und
*na*vigation and *r*anging.

At the end of World War II, the United States improved the snorkel
(a device for bringing air to the crew and engines when operating submerged on diesels) and developed the Guppy (short for greater underwater
40 propulsion power), a conversion of the fleet-type submarine of World War
II fame. The superstructure was changed by reducing the surface area,
streamlining every protruding object and enclosing the periscope shears in
a streamlined metal fairing. Performance increased greatly with improved
electronic equipment, additional battery capacity, and the addition of the
45 snorkel.

16. The thematic emphasis of the passage lies in

    (A) the Americans' improvements in the design of the submarine.

    (B) the discussion of the submarine in nonmilitary contexts.

    (C) the technical explanation of the snorkel as a device.

    (D) the history of submarine development as an effective weapon.

    (E) submarine advancements specific to the Second World War.

17. World War I has particular import for the submarine because

    (A) of the antidetection devices that were developed.

    (B) German use of the submarine exploited its offensive power.

    (C) the sinking of the vessel became comparatively simple.

    (D) the obsolescence of land-craft was made increasingly obvious.

    (E) increasing government subsidies of science and technology aided
        the War Department.

18. We can infer from the British removal of their ships from New York Harbor

    (A) that the British interests lay in the outer bay.

    (B) that the British were confident their men-of-war could withstand assault.

    (C) that submarine warfare had proved of some tactical advantage.

    (D) that they indicated their need to overhaul the *H.M.S. Eagle*.

    (E) that they insured that the importation of American gunpowder would be limited.

19. The word "trainable" (line 28) means

    (A) having domestic, not military use.

    (B) relating to transportation.

    (C) capable of being adapted to various sea transports.

    (D) capable of being focused on a specific target.

    (E) easily dismantled and reassembled onboard ship.

20. The function of the final paragraph is

    (A) to review the contributions to warfare the submarine had made until World War II.

    (B) to develop the operational use of SONAR.

    (C) to discuss the function of the snorkel.

    (D) to telescope several developments in the design of submarine offensive capability.

    (E) to compare SONAR with the use of the Guppy.

21. Lines 30–33 attribute improvements in submarine technology to

    (A) the British exclusively, who worked on the location device.

    (B) the Allied Submarine Devices Investigation Committee.

    (C) the desire to end the World War as quickly as possible.

    (D) a desire to develop antidetection devices to protect the submarine crew.

    (E) the British, who advanced work already performed by ASDIC.

Questions 22–25 are based on the following passage.

Communicable illness and disease were often rampant in the ancient world, incapacitating and killing hundreds on a daily basis. The following passage describes the effects of the Athenian plague on history.

1   The oldest recorded epidemic, often regarded as an outbreak of typhus, is the Athenian plague of the Peloponnesian Wars, which is described in the Second Book of the *History* of Thucydides.

      In trying to make the diagnosis of epidemics from ancient descrip-
5 tions, when the differentiation of simultaneously occurring diseases was impossible, it is important to remember that in any great outbreak, while the large majority of cases may represent a single type of infection, there is usually a coincident increase of other forms of contagious diseases; for the circumstances which favor the spread of one infectious agent often
10 create opportunities for the transmission of others. Very rarely is there a pure transmission of a single malady. It is not unlikely that the description of Thucydides is confused by the fact that a number of diseases were epidemic in Athens at the time of the great plague. The conditions were ripe for it. Early in the summer of 430 B.C. large armies were camped in
15 Attica. The country population swarmed into Athens, which became very much overcrowded. The disease seems to have started in Ethiopia…thence traveled through Egypt and Libya, and at length reached the seaport of Piraeus. It spread rapidly. Patients were seized suddenly, out of a clear sky. The first symptoms were severe headache and redness of the eyes.
20 These were followed by inflammation of the tongue and pharynx, accompanied by sneezing, hoarseness, and cough. Soon after this, there was acute intestinal involvement, with vomiting, diarrhea, and excessive thirst. Delirium was common. The patients that perished usually died between the seventh and ninth days. Many of those who survived the acute stage
25 suffered from extreme weakness and a continued diarrhea that yielded to no treatment. At the height of the fever, the body became covered with reddish spots…some of which ulcerated. When one of the severe cases recovered, convalescence was often accompanied by necrosis of the fingers and the toes. Some lost their eyesight. In many there was complete
30 loss of memory. Those who recovered were immune, so that they could nurse the sick without further danger. None of those who, not thoroughly immunized, had it for the second time died of it. Thucydides himself had the disease. After subsiding for a while, when the winter began, the disease reappeared and seriously diminished the strength of the Athenian
35 state.

The plague of Athens, whatever it may have been, had a profound effect upon historical events. It was one of the main reasons why the Athenian armies, on the advice of Pericles, did not attempt to expel the Lacedaemonians, who were ravaging Attica. Athenian life was completely
40 demoralized, and a spirit of extreme lawlessness resulted....There was no fear of the laws of God or man. Piety and impiety came to the same thing, and no one expected that he would live to be called to account. Finally, the Peloponnesians left Attica in a hurry, not for fear of the Athenians, who were locked up in their cities, but because they were afraid of the disease.

22. The point of this passage is to demonstrate

   (A) that "pure" outbreaks of disease were common in the ancient world.

   (B) that treatments of epidemic diseases remain relatively ineffective.

   (C) the relation that exists between infectious disease and historical events.

   (D) the relatively poor health conditions in ancient Athens.

   (E) the wisdom of Pericles in dealing with foreign invaders.

23. One of the results of extended sickness in Athens was

   (A) to put their democratic constitution in danger.

   (B) to produce a moral nihilism, where death negated ethical life.

   (C) to invite the Peloponnesians for a prolonged occupation of the city.

   (D) to increase general belief in supernatural powers.

   (E) to clarify the exact cause of the outbreak.

24. The symptom "necrosis" (line 25) probably indicates

   (A) tissue death.

   (B) that victims suffered more at night.

   (C) that patients could not be moved.

   (D) the incompetence of doctors at that time.

   (E) the incredible speed at which victims died.

25. Two of the factors exacerbating the spread of the plague were

    (A) low standards of medical practice and poor army discipline.

    (B) severe overpopulation and outbreaks of several maladies.

    (C) poor political judgment and failure to enforce housing codes.

    (D) an influx of Ethiopians and the departure of the Lacedaemonians.

    (E) the failure to identify the disease and poor nutrition.

MINI TEST 3

ANSWER KEY

1. (C)	6. (A)	11. (B)	16. (D)	21. (E)
2. (B)	7. (B)	12. (A)	17. (B)	22. (C)
3. (B)	8. (B)	13. (A)	18. (C)	23. (B)
4. (C)	9. (C)	14. (A)	19. (D)	24. (A)
5. (C)	10. (B)	15. (D)	20. (D)	25. (B)

DETAILED EXPLANATIONS OF ANSWERS

1. **(C)** Frederic's army is equal to that of the French, who had five times the population of Prussia. The formation of the army is only one aspect of Frederic's genius (A). The revenue needed for such an army is discussed in the next paragraph (B). The Prussian military campaigns are implied, but not dealt with directly (D). Their training is discussed later in the paragraph, but only the *result is* compared with that of the French (E).

2. **(B)** The Prussian army is described as an efficient machine. It lacks blind nationalism (A). The will in obedience here is only "indirectly" an issue (C). The Prussians lack a Napoleonic figure to enflame them (D). Macaulay says nothing about the Prussian population as a whole (E).

3. **(B)** All the exercises, marching as well as loading, are included. The shifting of bayonets or other pieces (A) is only part of the drill. Firing, if included at all, would be one minor operation (C). The movements involved in drill are parts of the soldier's overall responsibilities (D). Training produces the efficient soldier (E).

4. **(C)** Frederic cut pay in other departments and gave up expansion of Prussia. Taxation could not be further increased, as lines 26–27 indicate (A). There is no indication that foreign loans were possible (B). Frederic had not inherited any colonies, according to the author (D). He chose not to maintain a navy (E).

5. **(C)** Their salaries are key to the term "lowest possible expense." The amount, not the promptitude, of payment is at issue (A). Given his budget, Frederic may well have been as generous as he could be; his attitude toward payment is not discussed (B). The workers were probably not paid according to their merit or performance (D). Macaulay does not suggest that pay was reduced or withheld as punishment for poor service (E).

6. **(A)** Frederic, as the details show, combined frugality with his love of ceremony. He enjoyed food, drink, and an impressive table (B). Controlling the *costs* of servants was his central achievement (C). He profited from the game of royal parks, not the land itself (D). His attitude toward religion is not discussed in this passage (E).

7. **(B)** While secretarianism can in specific instances be applied to religious affiliation (A), the context here indicates a secular application. The belief in progress (C) might be one tenet of a sect. Those engaged in rebellion (D) might also belong to a sect. The inability to formulate ideals (E) is a negative characteristic and generally not a trait that would place one within a sect.

8. **(B)** Mill here argues for the public discussion of all opinions on each question. This may or may not involve the inclusion (E) of all segments of society. Mill says nothing about the need for clear writing and speaking (A). Controls upon dangerous speech would be contrary to Mill's aim (D), since he does not concede that dangerous speech exists. He does not state or imply that advocates or lawyers are needed (C).

9. **(C)** The greatest benefit of free speech is bestowed upon the uncommitted or "disinterested" individual who is thus able to choose among various arguments. This opportunity exists only when there is no censorship, but Mill is not arguing the dangers of censorship here (A). The benefits of political choice may later become apparent, but they are not immediately concerned in the analogy (B). His concern is with the individual at this point, not (D) a democratic society. While free speech will produce informed citizens (E), Mill is not here arguing for the need of such citizens.

10. **(B)** The most serious threat described in this section of the passage is the "quiet suppression" of half the truth. Mill approaches the issue of prejudice later (C). He sees the violent clash of opposing views as beneficial (A). Falsehoods (D) are spread through the suppression of opposing views. Governmental force (E) is not mentioned explicitly in the passage.

11. **(B)** Mill is describing the collision of opposing ideas. These may be "negative" (A) in a specific context only. They are "comparable" (D) in a very broad sense, in that opposition is one means of comparing two objects. "Juxtaposed" suggests a positioning carried out by the speaker (E). "Lower" suggests a valuation which Mill does not undertake in this passage (C).

12. **(A)** The undebated idea may well come to be held as a prejudice. Debate does not undermine doctrine (A), but strengthens it. It cannot transform truths into principles (B). Nor does it transform convictions (D) into opinions (E). The effect is actually to transform dogma into heartfelt

conviction.

13. **(A)**   Mill affirms that debate stimulates the growth of real belief by describing the prevention of such growth involved in the silencing of diverse opinion. It may incidentally (B) lead to fresh ideas, but these are not mentioned explicitly. Similarly, debate may lead eventually to the revolutionary change of institutions (C). The exposing of faults is an implied result (D), but Mill is explicitly concerned with the strengthening of dogma. The quality or training of speakers is not brought up in the essay (E).

14. **(A)**   The correct answer is (A) because "cumbering" means "to hinder by blocking or being in the way." This is also the definition of "obscuring," (A). Choice (B) "ruining" and (C) "desecrating" are similar, they both refer to destruction. (D) "bordering" means "to touch at the edge" and (E) "engaging" means "attracting or interlocking with," and is therefore incorrect.

15. **(D)**   The author is trying to persuade you to agree with his point of view, in a confident, convincing manner, giving the passage an assertive tone. The passage is not preachy, and therefore does not have a self-righteous tone (A). Although the feelings promoted by the author are "honest," "zeal" connotes a fanatic or crazed state of being, which is clearly contradicted by the logic of the passage, making (B) incorrect. (C) is incorrect because, although the author finds fault with many things, the overall tone is not one of disapproval. (E) is incorrect because the passage was written to influence readers.

16. **(D)**   The passage traces the history of the submarine "as an offensive weapon" (line 1); the dates from 1864 negate the specific reference to WW II in (E). Both German and English advances discussed in lines 17–33 negate (A). The opening sentence specifies military contexts, negating (B). Innovations discussed extend beyond the snorkel (C).

17. **(B)**   Germany exploited the full resources of the submarine; while (A) is a strong distractor, detection devices did not become refined until after WW I. (C) is ambiguous as to whether "the vessel" means the sub or its target—it is untrue in any case. (E) is a misreading corollary of British technological work; (D) is not discussed.

18. **(C)**   The very attempt to sink a British man-of-war proved intimidating; (B) is the wrong conclusion based on the British fear of attack. (A)

may be a rationalization of the British, and (E) merely correlates to that misreading. (D) is a distractor.

19. **(D)**   The hydrophone could be "aimed" at a specific target. (B) is the only "reasonable" distractor.

20. **(D)**   While (A) is a reasonable choice, the last paragraph, especially line 37, exceeds the chronology of WW II. (B) and (E) list specific technologies incidental to submarine history; (C) also deals with a specific element in the course of a list of technological innovations.

21. **(E)**   is more correct than (A), since the early work on detection devices was done by a committee cited on lines 24–25. (B) ignores work by the later group; (C) is reasonable speculation. (D) is illogical.

22. **(C)**   The point of this passage is to demonstrate the relation between infectious disease and historical events (C). (A) is incorrect because it is made clear that epidemics were complex affairs in lines 7–10. (B) is not correct because the current level of treatment is not discussed in this passage. The level of medical prevention in Ancient Athens (D) is also incorrect because it is not the main point. (E) is not correct because the specific wisdom of Pericles is not discussed in great detail.

23. **(B)**   Men's morals are neutralized by the continuous presence of death; therefore, (B) is the correct answer. (A) and (D) are both incorrect because they are not justified by the text. (C) is incorrect because the Peloponnesians fled for fear of infection. (E) is also not correct because the author discusses the lack of certainty in the cause of the epidemic.

24. **(A)**   From the context of the sentence, we can infer that necrosis means the death of tissue. All other choices do not fit into the context as well as choice (A).

25. **(B)**   Lines 9–13 identify the two causes of outbreak as overcrowding and coincident epidemics. (A) is incorrect because poor army discipline is not given as a factor in spreading the plague. (C) is also incorrect because housing codes are not mentioned in this passage. An influx of Ethiopians (D) would be a misreading of the author's statement that it seems the disease started in Ethiopia. Poor nutrition is not mentioned as a cause for the outbreak (E).

REA's VERBAL BUILDER for Admission & Standardized Tests

Specifically designed to prepare you for all tests requiring verbal ability, including

GRE • GMAT • SAT • CLAST
LSAT • ACT • MCAT • NTE
PPST • PSAT • CBEST

Research & Education Association

Available at your local bookstore or order directly from us by sending in coupon below.